Early Cemetery Inscriptions and Early Pastors

Fairfield Reformed Church

(Gansegat Reformed Dutch Church)

Fairfield, Essex County, New Jersey

Compiled by
Carol Personette Comfort

HERITAGE BOOKS
2014

HERITAGE BOOKS
AN IMPRINT OF HERITAGE BOOKS, INC.

Books, CDs, and more—Worldwide

For our listing of thousands of titles see our website
at
www.HeritageBooks.com

Published 2014 by
HERITAGE BOOKS, INC.
Publishing Division
5810 Ruatan Street
Berwyn Heights, Md. 20740

Copyright © 2014 Carol Personette Comfort

Other Heritage Books by the author:

Cedar Grove Cemetery, Cedar Grove, Essex County, New Jersey

Early Cemetery Inscriptions and Early Pastors: Fairfield Reformed Church (Gansegat Reformed Dutch Church) Fairfield, Essex County, New Jersey

Old Burying Ground, Cemetery of the First Presbyterian Church: Orange, Essex County, New Jersey

St. Mark's Episcopal Cemetery, Orange, Essex County, New Jersey, (Near the Southwest Corner of Main Street and Scotland Road, Adjacent to the First Presbyterian Church of Orange). History of the Cemetery; Expanded List of Interments; and Early History of St. Mark's Church, Revised Edition

Cover photo: JeffreyGreenberg@aol.com

All rights reserved. No part of this book may be reproduced or transmitted in any form or by any means, electronic or mechanical, including photocopying, recording or by any information storage and retrieval system without written permission from the author, except for the inclusion of brief quotations in a review.

International Standard Book Numbers
Paperbound: 978-0-7884-5572-8
Clothbound: 978-0-7884-6005-0

CONTENTS

History of the Cemetery	1
Inscriptions reported in 1895 and 1905 Fairfield Reformed Church Cemetery	3
Inscriptions reported in 1895 Pearce Burial Ground	323
Inscriptions reported in 1895 Smith Burial Ground	343
Inscriptions reported in 1895 and 1904 Vanderhoof Burial Ground	345
Inscriptions reported in 1895 and 1904 Van Ness Burial Ground (Old Sindle Farm)	349
Pastors 1720-1902	357
Inscriptions in chronological order of death	407
Inscriptions in order as reported in 1895	419
Sources	431

CEMETERY OF THE
FAIRFIELD REFORMED CHURCH

The Fairfield Reformed Church, earlier known as the Gansegat Reformed Dutch Church, is listed in the New Jersey Register of Historic Places and the National Register of Historic Places. (NR Ref. #75001134)

The cemetery is located in the church yard of the Fairfield Reformed Church. This cemetery is active and well maintained. "In 1832, the Kiersted family sold land to the elders and deacons of Fairfield Church, for $100.00, a site to be used solely as burying grounds. It can be assumed from the Kiersted's insistence upon using the land for a cemetery and the fact that some of the tombstones are earlier than the deed, that the site was used years before to bury members of the church." (*National Register of Historic Places Inventory -- Nomination Form* September 1975)

"Fairfield, Essex Co., N.J. (Horseneck, Gansegat) Founded 1720. The records of this church going back to 1750 were in existence in 1884; a few years later (January 1889) the Parsonage (see: Pastor Lockwood) with all its contents was burned, but there is some question as to whether these records were in the building at the time of the fire. In 1870 it was stated that still earlier records had been burned. A complete record of all the inscriptions in the Churchyard to **1895**, with those in five ancient and modern burial places in the vicinity, are in private hands." (*Year Book. The Holland Society. New York 1912*)

Included here are the inscriptions on extant stones at this cemetery as recorded by John R. Neafie in **1895**. (Mr. Neafie was born in 1856 at New York City; son of Stephen Personett Neafie and Sarah Elizabeth Acker; grandson of John R. Neafie and Sarah Doremus of Little Falls, N.J.) These records are in Volume 108 of the Holland Society New York Church Record Collection. (FHL US/CAN Film. 16511 Item 4)

In **1904** inscriptions on stones in this cemetery were reported in *Monumental Inscriptions of Essex County, N.J., Vol. II.* Anonymous. There is a note: "This cemetery is separated by fences into three sections." These records are located at the New Jersey Historical Society, Newark, New Jersey.

The later the inscriptions were copied the fewer the number of older stones remained. Some of the stones appear to be replacements. This report uses information from the 1895 and the 1904 reports named above as well as data gathered from other sources. Burials after 1904, with few exceptions, as for Veterans of the Civil War, are not listed here.

"It is to be regretted that the old settlers did not keep diaries, for that habit, however it may be scorned in these days of the far-searching press, would have preserved to us valuable historical data, of which, through brief and scattering traditions, we now can hope to catch but a fading glimpse.(*Proceedings of the New Jersey Historical Society.* Vol. 6, p.227. Edison, NJ. 1921)

- - - - -

FAIRFIELD REFORMED CHURCH INSCRIPTIONS REPORTED IN 1895 AND 1904

PLEASE NOTE:
--CAPITALIZED letters indicated burial information was reported or the monument was sighted and recorded or family information was supplied
--* indicates some relationship to another interment; this person may or may not be buried here
--The 1895 report of John Neafie says there are "many unmarked graves, and rough stones without any inscription".
--Please check the reports on the smaller burial grounds.

SOURCE KEY:
(Neafie)   Data found in the 1895 Report by John Neafie
(inscriptions)   Data found in the 1904 Report: *Monumental Inscriptions of Essex County, N.J.*
(monument)   Data found in many sources; Ancestry.com; Findagrave.com; Google.com; and Rootsweb.com; etc.

NOTE: This is a collection of data from many sources. Notes for each interment are meant to be research clues. Please confirm and check carefully.

- - - - -

ACKERMAN

Ackerman, John W.*   b.
                            d.

wife, JENNIE (VanNess)   b. (January 13, 1843)
(Neafie, p.11)   d. October 29, 1871

(monument)

> Jennie Van Ness
> Wife of
> John W. Ackerman
> Died Oct. 29, 1871
> Aged 28 years 9 months
> & 16 days
> We will meet again in death

Notes:
--Jane 'Jennie', dau. of Isaac J. Van Ness, q.v., and Ann Roome
--Marriage: "1870 Nov. 22nd. John W. Ackerman, Paterson, N.J. and Jennie Van Ness, Fairfield, Essex Co., N.J.: witnesses: Isaac J. Van Ness and Lucas R. Van Ness." (*Register of First Reformed Church of Little Falls, NJ*)

--1850 Census: Caldwell Twp., Essex Co., NJ: Isaac J. VanNess, age 36, farmer; Ann, age 37; Mary R., age 12; John, age 11; Caroline, age 10; <u>Jane</u>, age 7; Jacob Bush, age 50, laborer; all b. New Jersey
--1860 Census: Caldwell Twp., Essex Co., NJ: Isaac J. VanNess, age 46, farmer; Ann, age 47; Caroline, age 19, seamstress; <u>Jane</u>, age 17, seamstress; Isaac Conklin, age 63, b. NY, laborer
--1870 Census: Caldwell Twp: Isaac J. Van Ness, age 56, farmer; Ann age 56; <u>Jane</u> age 27; William Howard, age 13, farm boy
--??1870 Census: 2Wd, Paterson, Passaic Co., NJ: Peter (I.) Ackerman, age 54, b. NY, shoemaker; Mary (nee Mourison), age 53 b. NJ; <u>John W.</u>*, age 24, b. NJ, laborer; Ann A., age 11; Hannah, age 14; Ella Perdita, age 10;

- - - - -

ASHMAN

Ashman, JAMES (M.) b. December 29, 1827
(Neafie, p. 10) d. September 23, 1876

James M. Ashman
Born Dec. 29, 1827
Died Sept. 23, 1876
Aged 24 years

wife, MARIA M. (Clark) b. March 28, 1828
(Neafie, p.10) d. January 16, 1879

Maria M.
Wife of
James Ashman
Born March 28, 1828
Died Jan. 16, 1879

NOTE:
This interment was reported at Fairfield by John Neafie. The monument inscription below is at the Community Cemetery, Monroe, Orange Co., NY.

James M. Ashman
Dec. 29, 1827 - Sept. 23, 1876
His Wife
Maria M.
March 28, 1828 - Jan. 16, 1879
ASHMAN

Notes:
--- The New Jersey Deaths and Burials Index lists James M. Ashman: "b. abt. 1827, NY State; d. Sept. 23, 1876, Wayne, Passaic Co., NJ; age 49 years; occupation, foreman on R R; married; son of Robert Ashman and Charlot Ashman"

--James M. Ashman, son of Robert Adolphus Ashman and Charlotte McElroy
--1850 Census: Monroe Twp., Orange Co., NY: Jas. Ashman, age 22, farmer; Maria, age 22; Harriet, age 15; all b. New York
--1860 Census: Monroe Twp., Orange Co., NY: James Ashman, age 32, laborer; Maria, age 32; Alice, age 10; Robert E., age 7; Clara, age 6; Genett, age 2; Amelia A., age 1; all b. NY
--1870 Census,:Monroe, Orange Co., NY: James "Oshman", age 42, b. NY, farm labor; Maria, age 41; Clara, age 15; Ada, age 10; Sarah, age 8; James, age 7; Lottie, age 3; all b. NY
--1880 Census: Brooklyn, Kings Co., NY: Robert Ashman, age 28, road master D.L.& W.RR(?); Sarah, age 19, sister; Lottie, age 13, sister; Susan, age 9, sister; James, age 18, brother, flagman r.r.; all single; all b. New York
--1900 Census: 8 Wd., Brooklyn, Kings Co., NY: Wm. W. Van Houten, age 42, b. NJ, foreman, track Dept. BRT.RR ; Ada A. 38; Irving, 18; Chas. H. 17; Flora E. 15; Georgina 14; Lilllian M. 10; Lester A. age 2; Susie Ashman, age 28, b. Aug. 1871, sister-in-law, ticket agent at ferry

-----

ATKINSON

Atkinson, Thomas   See: Van Ness Burial Ground

BALDWIN

Baldwin, JOSEPH CONDIT   b. November 22, 1836
(Neafie, p.19)   d. May 15, 1864
(monument)   bur. January 31, 1866

<u>Original Stone</u>
In Memory of
Joseph Condit Baldwin
Born at Somerville, NJ
Nov. 22nd 1836
Fell in the service of his Country
at Spotsylvania
Sunday. May 15, 1864

<u>Goverment Stone 2003</u>
Joseph C. Baldwin
2D Lieut Co. E
11 NJ Regt.
Nov. 22, 1836
May 15, 1864

Felled In Battle
Spotsylvania, VA
It is Well

wife, MARY (Speer)	b. November 15, 1837
(Neafie, p. 19)	d. November 15, 1863

Mary S.
Wife of
Joseph C. Baldwin
and Daughter of
William and Adaline Speer
Born Nov. 15, 1837
Died Nov. 15, 1863

Notes:
--Served: <u>Civil War</u>; 2nd Lieut.; Co. E. 11 NJ Reg't.
--Joseph, son of Stephen L. B. Baldwin and Abby Eliza Condit

--Joseph m. June 26, 1862, Little Falls: Mary, dau. of William S. Speer, q.v., and Adaline Stiles

--1840 Census: Bridgewater, Somerset Co., NJ: Stephen L. B. Baldwin

--?1850 Census: Caldwell Twp., Essex Co., NJ: Elias Baldwin (grandfather of Joseph C. Baldwin), age 85, b. NJ; Smith Baldwin, age 55, b. NJ; Amanda Shipp, age 51, b. NJ

--1850 Census: Acquackanonk Twp., Passaic Co., NJ: Adaline Speer, age 34; Harriet, age 14; <u>Mary</u>, age 12; Emma M., age 10; Melvina A., age 8; all b. NJ; 1 laborer

--1860 Census: Little Falls, Acquackanonk Twp., Passaic Co., NJ: Peter Speer, age 74; Harriet, age 68; Adeline, age 44; <u>Mary</u>, age 22; Melvina, age 18; Henry Crane, age 34; Harriet Crane, age 24; Ines Crane, age 2; all b. New Jersey

--1860 Census: New Barbadoes Twp., Bergen Co., NJ: <u>Joseph C. Baldwin</u>, age 23, b. 'NY', editor; Bryon S. Witherell, age 26, b. NJ, printer

--Joseph C. Baldwin "was the editor of two newspapers, first the Bergen County Journal and then the Jersey City Courier and Advertiser." (Glen Pierce)

--"Joseph C. Baldwin entered the service as Sergeant of Company K, Eleventh New Jersey Volunteers, August 11th, 1862; Second Lieutenant, Company K, February 18th, 1863; First Lieutenant, Company C, August 26th, 1863. Baldwin was a man of rare intelligence, and his genial and happy disposition made him a host of friends. He was killed at Spottsylvania Court House, Va., May 15th, 1864. A short time previous to his death he was made acting Adjutant of the regiment, and while leaning against one of the traverses in the line of works occupied by our troops, a shell forced its way through between the logs composing the traverse, crushing his head and causing instant death. A career which undoubtedly would have proved brilliant was suddenly cut off, and his death was a great loss to the regiment and deeply felt by his comrades." (*History of the Eleventh New Jersey Volunteers.* Thomas D. Marbaker. Trenton, NJ)

- - - - -

BONE

Bone, BENJAMIN H. b. (abt. 1797)
(Neafie, p. 9) d. July 10, 1855
(monument)
(NJ Will #489P 1855)

*In
Memory Of
Benjamin H. Bone
Died July 10, 1855
In the 59th year of his age*

wife, LYDIA (Riker) b. (August 1, 1802)
(Neafie, p.9) d. April 29, 1860
(NJ Will #678P Inv. 1860)

*Lydia
Wife of
B. H. Bone
Died April 29, 1860
Aged 57 years 6 months
& 26 days*

Notes:
--Benjamin Horton Bone, son of Dr. Christian Bone and Martha "Polly" Crane
--Benjamin 'Norton' Bone bapt. July 2, 1798, First Presb. Church, Caldwell; 'son of Dr. Bone"
--Benjamin Horton Bone m. December 31, 1816, Lydia Riker, dau. of Isaac Riker, q.v., and Catherine Berry
--Benjamin's son, John Emmons Bone m. Emily Corby, dau. of Stephen L. Corby, moved to Broome County, N.Y;

--Benjamin's sister, Julia Bone, m. Israel Corby, moved to Broome County, N.Y.;
--Benjamin's brother, Stephen Lot Bone, m. Catherine Jacobus moved to Broome County, N.Y.

WILL 1835-1865 Vol.A-B Passaic Co. Image 261
Signed: July 7, 1855; Proven July 24, 1855
First: to wife: all real estate known as the tavern stand at Little Falls, household goods and furniture; 3 cows, pigs, poultry; 50 baskets of wheat; 50 bushels of rye; two tons of hay; 2 loads of corn stocks; $100 per year during her life to be paid yearly by my children, Catharine Morrell, John E. Bone and Emeline Bone in equal portions
second: after decease of wife or by her consent the tavern stand may be sold - to be invested for my wife deducting the sum of six hundred dollars hereinafter bequeathed to my grandsons Horace Bone and Benjamin Deeths.
Third: to dau. Emeline, two thousand dollars and one bedstead
Fourth: to dau. Catherine Morrell, five hundred dollars
Fifth: to grandsons Horace Bone and Benjamin Deeths: 6 hundred dollars: To Horace one old bedstead and my silver watch now in use of my son John E. Bone
Sixth: to son John E. Bone: my farm on Peckman's River, Acquackanonk Twp abt. 55 acres; my new spring wagon; my bay racking horse; my gold watch; my double barrelled gun; saddle and bridle
Seventh: my real estate in Wayne Twp and Mancheseter, Passaic to be sold
Executors: Wife, Lydia and Son-in-law, Wm. M. Morrell

--1830 Census: Acquackanonk Twp., Essex Co., NJ: Benjamin H. Bone, 12 persons
--1836, Jan. 21: appointed US Postmaster, Little Falls, NJ
--1840 Census: Acquackanonk Twp. Passaic Co., NJ: Benjamin H. Bone, 24 persons (hotel)

--1850 Census: Acquackanonk Twp., Passaic Co., NJ: Benjamin H. Bone, age 53, hotel keeper; Lydia, age 48; John E., age 15, farm hand; Emeline, age 12; Horace, age 10; Benjamin Deeths, age 8; Susan (Bone) Deeths, q.v., age 26; all b. New Jersey; 1 laborer

--1850, Feb. 20: Benjamin H. Bone, Esq., appointed commissioner for acknowledgment and proofs of deeds in Acquackanonk Twp.

- - - - -

BOWMAN

Bowman, JAMES b. March 23, 1810
(Neafie, p. 15) d. December 23, 1868
(NJ Will #16787G, 1869)

James Bowman
Died Dec. 23, 1868
Aged 58 years 9 mos.
& 28 days

wife, Ellen* b. (abt. 1813)
  d. (February 4, 1899)

Notes:
--James, b. March 23, 1810, son of Andrew Bowman and Jane Van Houten; bapt. Pompton Plains NJ
--NJ Deaths: "Ellen Bowman, b. abt. 1813; d. Feb. 4, 1899, Caldwell, age 86 yrs., widow, res. of Caldwell Twp."
--Will (Vol. P, #229) of James Bowman: signed March 17, 1866; probate issued Jan. 20, 1869. Names: wife, Ellen; daughter, Margaret Jane; son Peter, all real estate; executor, son, Peter

--1850 Census: Caldwell Twp., Essex Co., NJ: James Bowman, age 40, blacksmith; Ellen, age 36; Peter, age 17, farmer; Margaret J., age 9; all b. NJ
--1860 Census: Caldwell Twp., Essex Co., NJ: James Bowman, age 50, blacksmith; Ellen, age 47; Margaret J., age 19 (see Henry Van Duyne); all b. NJ
--1870
--1880 Census: Caldwell Twp., Essex Co., NJ: Peter Bowman, age 47, farmer; Sarah, wife, age 47; Silvanus, son, age 19, b. NJ, works on farm; Webster I., son, age 14, b. NJ, works on farm; Ellen Bowman, mother, widow, age 71, b. NJ, retired lady
--1895 NJ Census: Caldwell Twp., Essex Co., NJ; Peter Bowman; Sarah Bowman; 5 children; Ellen Bowman "over 60"

- - - - -

Bowman, Peter*   b. (abt. 1833)
(?NJ Will #26798G, 1897)   d. (February 17, 1896)

wife, Sarah* (VanDuyne)   b. (March 3, 1833)
                                  d. (aft. 1900)

daughter, EMILY   b. (abt. September 3, 1855)
(Neafie, p.15)   d. May 16, 1862

Emily
Daughter of
Peter and Sarah
Bowman
Died May 16, 1862
Aged 6 years 8 mos.
& 13 days

Notes:
--Peter, son of James Bowman, q.v., and Ellen .....

--Sarah, dau. of James A. VanDuyne and Catharine Doremus

--1850 Census: Caldwell Twp., Essex Co., NJ: James Bowman, age 40, blacksmith; Ellen, age 36; Peter, age 17, farmer; Margaret J., age 9; all b. New Jersey
--1850 Census: Wayne Twp., Passaic Co. NJ: Catharine Vanduyne, age 57; Giles, age 15; Sarah, age 19; Henry, age 18, farmer; all b. New Jersey
--1860 Census: Caldwell Twp., Essex Co., NJ: Peter Bowman, age 26, laborer, b. NJ; Sarah, age 26, b. NJ; Emily, age 4, b. NJ; William Masker, age 53, b. NJ
--1870 Census: Caldwell Twp., Essex Co., NJ: Peter Bowman, age 35, farmer; Sarah, age 35; Sylvanus, age 9; Webster J., age 4; Henry Jacobus, age 35, pauper; all b. NJ
--1880 Census: Caldwell Twp., Essex Co., NJ: Peter Bowman, age 47, farmer; Sarah, wife, age 47; Silvanus, son, age 19, b. NJ, works on farm; Webster I., son, age 14, b. NJ, works on farm; Ellen Bowman, mother, widow, age 71, b. NJ, retired lady
--1895 NJ Census: Caldwell Twp., Essex Co., NJ; Peter Bowman; Sarah Bowman; 5 children; Ellen Bowman "over 60"
--1900 Census: Caldwell Twp., Essex Co., NJ: Sylvanus Bowman, age 39, b. NJ, farmer; Jennie, age 33, b. NJ, parents b. England; 4 children, Sarah 'Bouman' mother, widow, b. March 1833 NJ, 3 born 2 living; 2 servants

- - - - -

Bowman, John*	b. (abt. 1791)
	d. (August 19, 1881?)
wife, "CAROLINE"	b. (abt. April 4, 1796)
(Neafie, p. 1)	d. April 22, 1854

Caroline (sic)
Wife of
John Bowman
Died Apr. 22, 1854
Aged 58 years and 18 days

Notes:
--Mr. Neafie reported the 'Caroline' Bowman stone on Page 1, adj. to Stephen Cole, q.v. and John E. Van Ness; (the Cole family has sometimes used the name Caroline in their families.)
--?John Bowman, possible first son of Andrew Bowman
--?John Bowman, blacksmith, possible brother of James Bowman, q.v., blacksmith
--"John Bowman, member; 'Mrs. Bowman' died April 21, 1854" (Little Falls Ref. Church Record)
--"Female, Bowman, d. Apr. 22, 1854, age 60, West Milford, Passaic Co., NJ; b. 1794, Little Falls, NJ" (NJ Death Record)
--?NJ Deaths: "Jno Bowman 1790-Aug. 19, 1881, Paterson. Age 91; widowed"

--?1830 Census: Caldwell Twp., Passaic Co., NJ: John Bowman; 6 persons; (adj. Abr. G. Smith and Henry R. Van Ness; near John Riker)
--?1840 Census: Acquackanonk Twp., Passaic Co., NJ: John Bowman, 9 persons; adj. to John Riker
--?1850 Census: Acquackanonk Twp., Passaic Co., NJ: John Bowman, age 59, blacksmith; "Catherine" age 54; Catherine, age 26; George, age 19, carpenter; Wm. H., age 16, boatman; Hannah 'C'., age 12; all b. NJ
--?1857, Dec. 31: (NJ Marriages) "Hannah 'D'. Bowman, b. 1837, age 20; m. William McNab, b. 1832, age 25; dau. of John B. Bowman and Catharine."
--?1880 Census: Paterson, Passaic Co., NJ: Steve 'Cornter' (Courter), age 67, currier; Jane D. Cornter (Courter) age 60; Fanny Cornter, age 27; Ella Cornter age 25, warper; Flora

'Cornter', age 23, weaver; Sarah Paxton, age 31, boarder; John 'Baumann' age 88, father-in-law, widower, no occup.; all b. New Jersey

- - - - -

BOYD

Boyd, DAVID　　　　　b. (abt. October 23, 1843)
(Neafie, p. 16)　　　　d. September 23, 1864

David Boyd
Died Sept. 23 1864
Aged 20 years. 11 mos.

wife, JANE (Riker)　　　b. June 26, 1846
(Neafie, p.15)　　　　　d. February 20, 1871

Jane Boyd
Born June 26, 1846
Died Feb. 20, 1871
Age 26

Notes:
--David, son of John Boyd and Alice ...
--David Boyd m. Jane Riker, dau. of Isaac Riker, q.v., and Jane Paxton (see: Obadiah Riker)
--NJ Deaths: David "Boya" b. c.1844, d. Sept. 20 1864, Paterson, age 20, married, engineer; son of John "Boya" and Alice "Boya"
--NJ Births: Charles Boyd, b. April 3, 1864, Paterson, Passaic Co., NJ; son of David Boyd and Jane Boyd
--?NJ Births: Robert Boyd, b. February 1865, Paterson; son of David Boyd and "Cathrine"
--1850 Census: Acquackanonk Twp.,Passaic Co., NJ: Isaac Riker, age 32, carriage maker; Jane, age 28; John, age 11;

Henry, age 10; Obediah, age 8; Samuel, age 5; <u>Jane</u>, age 3; Zachariah, age 1; one laborer; all b. New Jersey
--1860 Census: 5 Wd. Paterson, Passaic Co., NJ: Isaac Riker, age 44, hotel keeper; Jane, age 40; Henry, age 19, bartender; Obediah, age 17; <u>Jane</u>, age 13; Samuel, age 14; Isaac, age 11; Lydia, age 9; Emma, age 7; Thomas, age 6
--1870 Census: 15 Wd. NYC: <u>Jenny</u> Boyd, age 24, b. NJ, corset maker; Charles Boyd, age 6, b. NJ; at res. of Thomas and Elizabeth Moore
--?1900 Census: 3Wd. Lowell, Middlesex Co., MA: Charles F. Boyd, lodger, married 3 years; age 36 b. April 1864 NJ, father b. NY, mother b. NJ, car inspector

- - - - -

BUDD

Budd, AARON   b. (abt. June 29, 1797)
(Neafie, p.20)   d. January 8, 1859
(monument)
(NJ Will #3955N, 1859)

Aaron Budd
Died Jan. 8, 1859
Aged 61 years, 6 mos.
& 10 days

second wife, FANNIE S. (Tuers)
(Neafie, p.20)   b. (abt. 1797)
     d. November 17, 1879

(monument)

Fannie S. Tuers
Widow of
Aaron Budd
Died Nov. 17, 1879
Aged 81 years 11 months

son, AARON W. b. (abt. April 11, 1828)
(Neafie, p.20) d. September 27, 1854
(monument)

In
Memory of
Aaron W. Budd
Died
Sept. 27th, 1854
Aged 26 years
5 months
and 16 days

daughter, MATILDA b. (abt. September 16, 1835)
(Neafie, p. 20) d. July 12, 1855

Matilda Budd
Died July 12, 1855
Aged 19 years 9 months
& 26 days

Notes:
--Aaron m. #1, Mary Zabriskie, she d. 1829; Aaron m. #2, Mrs. Fannie (Tuers) Harris, dau. of John(?) Tuers and Frances (?).

--1850 Census: Pequannock Twp., Morris Co., NJ: Aaron Budd, age 52, farmer; Frances, age 52; Richard, age 18, laborer; Matilda, age 15; all b. New Jersey
--1860 Census: Pequannock Twp., Morris Co., NJ: Richard Budd, age 27, b. NJ, farmer; Sarah E., age 26, b. Passaic Co., Marilla J., age 10 months, b. Morris Co.; Frances Budd, age 62, b. NJ; Crandel Westervelt, age 14, b. NJ

--1870 Census: Pequannock Twp., Morris Co., NJ: Richard T. Budd, age 38, farmer; Sarah E., age 36; Marilla, age 10; Louis, age 5; Irving, age 2 months; Fannie S., age 72;

- - - - -

Budd, BARNEY   b. (abt. January 28, 1794)
(Neafie p. 15)   d. August 3, 1867

Barney Budd
Died Aug. 3, 1867
Aged 73 years 6 months
& 6 days

wife, NANCY (Lockwood)   b. May 7, 1797
(Neafie, p. 15)   d. June 26, 1861

Nancy Lockwood
wife of
Barney Budd
Born May 7, 1797
Died June 26, 1861
Aged 84 years 1 month
& 3 days

Notes:
--Barney, son of William (or Nathaniel) Budd
--Barney m. December 13, 1814, New Barbados Twp., Nancy Lockwood
--?Barney m. April 2, 1864, Leah Maria Van Ness, dau. of Giles Van Ness and Hester Van Ness
--"By Barney Budd's will his executors were directed to convert nearly the whole of his estate into money and divide it equally among his eleven children"

--1850 Census: Pequannock Twp., Morris Co., NJ: Barney "Beed", age 55, farmer; Nancy, age 53; Caroline, age

27; Ellen, age 17; Joseph, age 15, laborer; Nelson, age 13; Josephine, age 11; all b. New Jersey
--1860 Census: Pequannock Twp., Morris Co., NJ: <u>Barney</u> Budd, age 66, b. Morris Co., farmer; <u>Nancy</u>, age 63, b. Essex Co., NJ

- - - - -

Budd, ISRAEL   b. February 22, 1817
(Neafie, p. 12)   d. August 1, 1890
(monument)

Father
In Memory Of
Israel Budd
Born
Feb. 22, 1817
Died
Aug. 1, 1890

first wife, CATHERINE (Onderdonk)
(Neafie, p.12)   b. (abt. 1815)
                d. Feb 28, 1867

Catherine
Wife of
Israel Budd
Died Feb. 28, 1867
Aged 52 years

daughter, RHODA ANN   b. (abt. January 9, 1839)
(Neafie, p.12)   d. September 4, 1863

Rhoda Ann
Died Sep. 4, 1863
Aged 24 yrs. 7 mos.

& 26 days

Children of
Israel and Catherine Budd

daughter, MARY ELIZA   b. (abt. May 7, 1845)
(Neafie, p. 12)   d. December 22, 1865

Mary Eliza
Died Dec. 22, 1865
Aged 20 years 7 months
& 15 days

Children of
Israel and Catherine Budd

Notes:
--Israel m. #2, 1868, Manhattan, NY, Phebe S. Harford

--1850 Census: Wayne Twp., Passaic Co., NJ: Israel Budd, age 33, farmer; Catherine, age 32; Rhoda Ann, age 11; Leah, age 9; Sarah, age 7; Mary, age 5; Fanny, age 2; Eunice, age 0; all b. New Jersey
--1860 Census: Meads Basin, Wayne Twp., Passaic Co., NJ: Israel Budd, age 34, farmer; Catherine, age 35; Rhoda Ann, age 21; Sarah, age 17; Mary, age 14; Fanny, age 12; Eunice age 10; Milton, age 8; all b. New Jersey
--1870 Census: Wayne Twp., Passaic Co., NJ: Israel Budd, age 53, farmer; Phebe, age 42; Earnie J. (Eunice) age 10; Milton, age 18; all b. New Jersey
--?1880 Census: Richwood Twp., Peoria Co., Illinois: Israel Budd, age '52'. b. NJ, farmer; Phebe, age 51 b. NY; Rebecca 'Hawley', age 74, mother, b. NY

- - - - -

Budd, John T.*   b. (abt. 1825)
                        d. (June 7, 1881)

wife, Jane*   b. (abt. 1824)
                        d. (November 1878)

son, NEWTON RAYMOND   b. August 25, 1848
(Neafie, p. 15)   d. January 7, 1852

Newton Raymond
son of
John T. and Jane Budd
Born Aug. 25, 1848
Died Jan. 7, 1852

Notes:
--John, son of Barney Budd, q.v., and Nancy Lockwood
--NJ Deaths: John T. Budd, b. c.1825, d. June 7, 1881, East Orange; mason, age 56, widowed"
--NJ Deaths: Jane Budd, b. c.1811, d. Nov. 1878, Summit, NJ; age 56, married
--1850 Census: 9Wd., NY, NY: John Budd, age 25, b. NJ, machinist; Jane, age 26, b. NJ; "Marton" (Newton), age 2, b. NY
--1855 NY State Census: John T. Budd, b. NJ, range mfr.; Jane, age 32 b. NJ; Bertha L., age 2, b. NY; 'Susan' J., age 1, b. NY
--1870 Census: 16Wd, New York City: John Budd, age 45, b. NJ, furnace dealer; Jane, age 48, b. NJ; Bertha, age 17, b. NY; Laura, age 16 b. NY; John Babock, age 25, b. NY, expressman; Lydia Babock, age 22, b. NY
--1880 Census: Springfield, Union Co., NJ: John T. Budd, age 55, widower, b. NJ, mason; Bertha L., age 25, single, daughter, b. NY; Laura J., age '33', single, daughter, b. NY, dressmaker

- - - - -

Budd, RICHARD T.   b. 1833
(monument)   d. 1913

B
Richard T. Budd
1833 - 1913
-
Sarah E. Van Ness
His Wife
1834 - 1918
BUDD

wife, SARAH E. (VanNess)   b. 1834
(monument)   d. 1918

son, FRANK L.   b. (abt. January 12, 1862)
(Neafie, p.18)   d. March 29, 1864

Frank L.
son of
Richard T. and Sarah E.
Budd
Died March 29, 1864
Aged 2 years, 2 mos.
& 17 days

Notes:
--?Richard, son of Aaron Budd and Frances .....
--Jane, dau. of James VanNess and Catherine VanHouten
--1850 Census: Pequannock Twp., Morris Co., NJ: Aaron Budd, age 52, farmer Frances, age 52; <u>Richard</u>, age 18, labor; Matilda, age 15; all b. NJ
--1850 Census: Acquackanonk Twp., Passaic Co., NJ: James VanNess, age 40, turning and sawing; <u>Sarah E.</u>, age 16; Elizabeth, age 14; Sophia, age 10; John, age 8; James S., age 1; 1 labor; all b. New Jersey

--1860 Census: Pequannock Twp., Morris Co., NJ: Richard Budd, age 27, farmer; Sarah E., age 26; 'Aurilla' age 10 months; all b. NJ; (adj. to Jacob Budd, age 36 and Barney Budd, q.v., age 66)

--1870 Census: Pequannock Twp., Morris Co., NJ: Richard T. Budd, age 38, farmer; Sarah E., age 36; Marilla, age 10; Louis, age 5; Irving, age 2 months; Fannie S., age 72; Abraham Brower, age 12, at home; all b. New Jersey

--1880 Census: Pequannock Twp., Morris Co., NJ: Richard Budd, age 47, farmer; Sarah, age 46 Marrila, age 20

--1900 Census: Pequannock Twp., Morris Co., NJ: Richard Budd, age 67, farmer; Sarah E., age 66; Aurilla, age 40; all b. NJ

--1910 Census: Wayne Twp., Passaic Co., NJ: Sarah E. Budd, age 76, widow, b. NJ, parents b. NJ; 'Rella J.' age 50, single, daughter, b. NJ, seamstress

- - - - -

BUSH

Bush, Ambrose   See: Pearce Burial Ground
wife, Mary Jane

- - - - -

Bush, CORNELIUS V.   b. September 19, 1841
(monument)   d. July 16, 1934

Cornelius V. Bush
Died July 16, 1934
Aged 92 years, 9 mos. 27 days

-

His Wife
Sarah E. Van Ness
Died April 21, 1880
Aged 38 years

wife, SARAH E. (VanNess) b. (abt. 1843)
(Neafie, p.9) d. April 21, 1880
(monument)

Sarah E. Van Ness
wife of
Cornelius V. Bush
Died Apr. 21, 1880
In the 38th year
of her age

Notes:
Served: Civil War: Battery B., 1st Regt. Light Artillery, NJ Volunteers
--"Pension Application #1321441, filed July 26, 1904. Cornelius V. Bush, 2 Indpt. Batty. NJ. L.A."
--Cornelius, son of Nicholas Bush, q.v., and Hannah Van Ness
--Cornelius Van Ness Bush, m. December 31, 1864, Sarah Ellen Van Ness, dau. of Cornelius I. VanNess, q.v., and Corintha .....
--son, Lee V. Bush served Spanish American War; Pvt. Co. K. 2nd Regt. N.J. National Guard Vol. Inf.
--1850 Census: Caldwell Twp., Essex Co., NJ: Nicholas Bush, age 34, farmer; Hannah age 33; Cornelius 9; Ellen 4; all b. NJ
--1860 Census: 2Wd, Newark, Essex Co., NJ: Cornelius Bush, age 19, b. NJ, apprentice mason; boarder
--1860 Census: Caldwell Twp., Essex Co., NJ: Cornelius I. VanNess, age 50, farmer; Corintha, age 46; Sarah E., age 17; James, age 15; John R., age 13; Mary, age 9; Sarah, age 72; all b. New Jersey
--1870 Census: 8Wd, Newark, Essex Co., NJ: Cornelius "Buch" age 29, stone mason; Sarah age 28; Corinthia age 4; Charles, age 2; Charles VanNess, age 33, carpenter; all b. New Jersey

--1880 Census: Montclair, Essex Co., NJ: Cornl. V. Bush, age 39, mason; Corintha, age 14, dau.; Chas. age 13, son; Ernest, age 9, son; "Newport" (Lee V., 1878 - 1931), age 2, son; Corintha VanNess, age 66, mother(step mother-in-law); all b. New Jersey
--1895 NJ State Census: 2nd Ward, Montclair, Essex Co., New Jersey: C. V. Bush; Lee Bush, male; at res. of Ida Paxton
--1910 Census: Montclair, Essex Co., NJ: Harry T. Smith, age 45, b. England, artist pen & ink; Cora, age 44, b. NJ; Olive P., age 16, b. NJ; Margaret M., age 10, b. NJ; Cornelius Bush, age 67, father-in-law, widower, mason
--1920 Census: 1Wd, Montclair, Essex Co., NJ: Harry F. Smith, age 54, b. England; Cora, age 54; Olive, age 25; Cornelius Bush, age 79, father-in-law, widower;
--1920 Census: 1Wd, Montclair, Essex Co., NJ: Harry T. Smith, age 54, b. England, artist at newspaper; Cor, age 54 b. NJ; Alice, age 25, dau., b. NJ, bank clerk; Cornelius Bush, age 79, father-in-law b. 'NY' widower, retired
--1930 Census: Montclair, Essex Co., NJ: Henry T. Smith, age 64, b. England, manager newspaper; Cora, age 64 b. NJ; Olive P., age 36, b. NJ, sec'y at bank; Cornelius 'B' Bush, age 88, b. NJ, father-in-law

- - - - -

Bush, Henry I.   See: Pearce Burial Ground
wife, Jane

- - - - -

Bush, Monas I.   See: Pearce Burial Ground
wife, Jane

- - - - -

Bush, NICHOLAS   b. April 26, 1816
(Neafie, p.14)   d. August 31, 1884
(NJ Will #21950G, 1885)
(monument)

Nicholas Bush
Born Apr. 26, 1816
Died
Aug. 31, 1884

wife, HANNAH (Van Ness)   b. August 27, 1818)
(monument)   d. June 28, 1910

Hannah Bush
Born
Aug. 27, 1817
Died
June 28, 1910

daughter, SARAH ELLEN   b. (October 7, 1831)
(inscriptions, p.138)   d. April 14, 1840

Sarah Ellen
Died April 14, 1840
aged 8 years, 6 months,
and 7 days

daughter, PHEBE ANN   b. (July 11, 1837)
(inscriptions, p.138)   d. February 26, 1843

Phebe Ann
Died February 26, 1843
Aged 5 years, 7 months
& 15 days

daughter, ELEANOR   b. (abt. 1839)
(inscriptions, p.138)   d. January 19, 1841

(Neafie, p.16)　　　　　　　d. (June 19, 1841)

Eleanor
eldest daughter of
Nicholas and Hannah Bush
Died January 19, 1841
aged 2 years

(2 yrs. 1 month, 13 days) (?)

daughter, MARIA E.　　　b. (October 4, 1843)
(Neafie, p.16)　　　　　　d. September 26, 1845
(inscriptions, p.138)

Maria E.
daughter of
Nicholas and Hannah Bush
Died September 26, 1845
aged 1 year, 11 months
& 22 days

daughter, EMMA MARIA　　b. 1851
(Neafie, p.16)　　　　　　　d. 1856

Emma Maria
Born
1851
Died
1856

Notes:
--Nicholas, son of Henry J. Bush, q.v., and Jane W. Low.
--Nicholas m. November 4, 1837, Hannah Van Ness, dau. of of David T. Van Ness, q.v., and Ellen Vanderhoof.

--1850 Census: Caldwell Twp., Essex Co., NJ: Nicholas Bush, age 34, farmer; Hannah age 33; Cornelius 9; Ellen 4; all b. NJ

--1860 Census: Caldwell Twp., Essex Co., NJ: <u>Nicholas</u> Bush, age 44, farmer; <u>Hannah</u>, age 42; Ellen, age 14; all b. New Jersey

--1870 Census: Caldwell Twp., Essex Co., NJ: <u>Nicholas</u> Bush, age 54, farmer; <u>Hannah</u> age 53; George age 9; all b. New Jersey

--1880 Census: Caldwell Twp. Essex Co., NJ: <u>Nicholas</u> Bush, age 64, farmer; <u>Hannah</u> age 62; Ernest N., age 8, grandson; Henry Freeman, age 51, pauper; all b. New Jersey

--1900 Census: Caldwell Twp., Essex Co., NJ: Samuel Dey b. July 1843, m.35 yrs., farmer; Elen Day b. April 1847, 3 born 2 living; <u>Hannah</u> Bush age 82, widow, mother-in-law b. August 1817, 7 born 3 living; all b. New Jersey

--1910 Census: Caldwell Twp. Essex Co., NJ: 'Sanuel' Dey age 67, m.45 yr, farmer; Ellen Dey age 65, 3 born 2 living; "<u>Helimah</u> Dey" age 93, widow, mother-in-law, age 93, 4 born 3 living; all b. NJ; 4 hired men

- - - - -

Bush, Thomas H. See: Pearce Burial Ground
wife, Margaret J.

- - - - -

Bush, WILLIAM b. June 26, 1813
(Neafie, p.14) d. June 22, 1894
(monument)

William Bush
Born June 26, 1813
Died June 22, 1894

-

Charlotte Pearce
His Wife
Died Dec. 19, 1882
In the 67th year
of her age

wife, CHARLOTTE (Pearce)
(Neafie, p.14)   b. (abt. 1815)
(monument)   d. December 19, 1882

daughter, JOSEPHINE   b. (abt. February 8, 1854)
(Neafie, p.14)   d. July 16, 1857

Josephine
Daughter of
Wm. Bush
and Charlotte Pearce
Died July 16, 1857
Aged 3 yrs. 5 mos.
& 8 days

Notes:
--William, son of Henry J. Bush, q.v., and Jane Low
--Charlotte, dau. of Edward Pearce and Hannah Stagg

--1850 Census: Caldwell Twp., Essex Co., NJ: William Bush, age 37, farmer; Charlotte, age 34; Antonette, age 14; Ezra S., age 13; Charles age 8; James age 8; Cynthia, age 3; Sarah, age 1; Jane, age 71; all b. NJ; 1 laborer
--1860 Census: Caldwell, Essex Co., NJ: William Bush, age 46, farmer; Charlotte, age 43; James, age 16; Cyntha, age 12; Sarah L., age 11; Edward, age 8; all b. NJ
--1870 Census: Caldwell Twp., Essex Co., NJ: 'Willeis' Bush, age 56, farmer; Charlotte, age 53; Cynthia E., age 22; Edward, age 17; all b. New Jersey; (adj. to James Bush, age 26, carpenter and Mary, age 21)
--1880 Census: Caldwell, Essex Co., NJ: William Bush, age 66, farmer; Charlotte C., age 63; Cynthia, age 31; all b. New Jersey

- - - - -

Cables, DANIEL C.   b. (May 22, 1840)
(monument)   d. (April 29, 1912)
                       (Age: 71 yrs. 11 mos. 22 days)

*Daniel C.
Cables
1840 - 1912*

first wife, CATHERINE ANN (Vanderhoof)
(monument?)   b. May 1842
                 d. December 20, 1885

second wife, Carrie Louise* (Decker)
                 b. (abt. September 1866)
                 d. (aft. 1910)

Notes:
Served: Civil War: Bat. D., NJ Lt. Artillery
--Daniel, son of John Cables and Millie (Millicent) Hall
--Daniel m. November 6, 1861, Catherine A. Vanderhoof, dau. of Peter A. Vanderhoof, q.v., and Susanna Youry Crum
--Daniel m. #2, August 21, 1889, Carrie Louise Decker, b. Macopin, NJ, dau. of Silas Decker and Jane E. Vreeland

--1850 Census: Monroe Twp., Orange Co., NY: Aaron Rednor, age 24, farmer; Melissa (Millie) Rednor, age 29; Daniel Cabel, age 10; Wm. H. Rednor, age 5; James W. Rednor, age 1 months; all b. NY
--1850 Census: Caldwell Twp., Essex Co., NJ: Peter A. Vanderhoof, age 32; William H., age 10; Catherine A., age 7; Mary E., age 4; Catherine, age 75
--1860 Census: Pequannock Twp., Morris Co., NJ: John H. VanNess, age 25, farmer, b. Morris Co.; Eliza J., age 27, b. Passaic Co.; Charles S., age 3, b. Morris Co.,; Edwin, age 1, b. Morris Co.,; Daniel Cable, age 20, b. NY, parents b. NY, farm labor

--1860 Census: Caldwell Twp., Essex Co., NJ: Peter Vanderhoof, age 42, farmer; Susan "V", age 41; William, age 20; Catherine A., age 18; Mary E., age 14; all b. NJ
--1870 Census: Caldwell, Essex Co., NJ: Daniel Cables, age 29, b. NY, farm labor; Catherine A., age 27, b. NJ; William H., age 7, b. NJ; Eliza J., age 3, b. NJ; Gerardus, age 1, b. NJ
--1880 Census: Caldwell, Essex Co., NJ: Daniel C. Cables, age 40 b. NY, farmer; Cathrine A., age 37, b. NJ; William Henry, age 17, works on farm; Eliza Jane, age 13; Gerardus B., age 11; Millie, age 6; John V., age 4; Meda, age 1; all children b. New Jersey
--1880 Census: West Milford Twp., Passaic Co., NJ: Silas Decker, age 40, farmer; Jane E., age 39; "Carra", dau., age 13; 5 younger children; all b. New Jersey
--1897: Daniel C. Cables, Postmaster at Echo Lake, Passaic Co., New Jersey
--1900 Census: West Milford Twp., Passaic Co., NJ: Daniel C. Cable age 59 b. NY, May 1841, m. 10 yrs. vet. surgeon; Carrie L., b. September 1866 NJ
--1910 Census: West Milford Twp., Passaic Co., NJ: Daniel C. Cables, age 71, m.#2 for 20 yrs., b. NY, parents NY, 'vet'; Carrie L., age 43, m.#1, for 20 yrs. b. NJ, parents b. NJ

- - - - -

CAMPBELL

Campbell, JOHN   b. (abt. 1821)
(Neafie, p.10)   d. October 9, 1889
(monument)
(NJ Will #23065G, 1889)

John Campbell
Died Oct. 9, 1889
In his 68th year

wife, MARGARET   b. (abt. 1824)

(monument)   d. August 11, 1898

Margaret
Wife of
John Campbell
Dies Aug. 11, 1898
Aged 72 years

Notes:
--1850 Census: Caldwell Twp., Essex Co., NJ: John Campbell, age 22, b. Ireland, labor; at res. of William Bush
--1860 Census: Caldwell Twp., Essex Co., NJ: John 'Cambell' age 35, b. Ireland, farmer; Margaret, age 36, b. Ireland; William M., age 8; Mary J., age 6; Robert, age 4; John, age 2; all children b. New Jersey
--1870 Census: Caldwell Twp., Essex Co., NJ: John Campbell, age 47, b. Ireland, farmer; Margaret, age 45, b. Ireland; William, age 18, farm labor; Mary J., age 15; Robert, age 14; John, age 12; George, age 6; Stella G., age 2
--1880 Census: Caldwell Twp., Essex Co., NJ: John Campbell, age 55, b. Ireland, farmer; Margaret, age 53, b. Ireland; Estella age 12, b. NJ; John, age 19, b. NJ

- - - - -

Campbell, William H.   See: Pearce Burial Ground
wife, Ellen

- - - - -

CANFIELD

Canfield, BENJAMIN   b. September 15, 1799
(Neafie, p.8)   d. May 4, 1865
(NJ Will #16081G, 1865)

Benjamin Canfield

Born
Sept. 15, 1799
Died
May 4, 1865

wife, SARAH (Riker)　　b. October 10, 1804
(Neafie, p.8)　　　　　　d. April 8, 1852

Sarah Riker
wife of
Benj. Canfield
Born Oct. 10, 1804
Died Apr. 8, 1852

Notes:
--Benjamin, son of Ebenezer Canfield and Rhoda Baldwin
--Benjamin m. January 2, 1822, Sarah Riker, dau. of Isaac Riker, q.v., and Catalina Berry

--1850 Census: Caldwell Twp., Essex Co., NJ: Benjamin Canfield, age 50, farmer; Sarah R., age 45; Isaac, age 24, farmer; John, age 15, farmer; William, age 9; Halmagh Cisco, age 23, laborer; all b. New Jersey
--1860 Census: Caldwell Twp., Essex Co., NJ: Benjamin Canfield, age 60, farmer; William, age 20, farmer; adj. John Canfield, age 25, farmer; Susan, age 22; Wilbur age 3; Rachel E., age 2 months; all b. NJ; 1 servant;

- - - - -

Canfield, ISAAC　　　　b. October 11, 1825
(Neafie, p.8)　　　　　　d. July 5, 1892
(monument)
(NJ Will #24415G, Inv.1892)

Isaac Canfield
Oct. 11, 1825 - July 5, 1892
-
Caroline Cole
His Wife
Born Sept. 3, 1833 Died Feb. 20, 1907

wife, CAROLINE (Cole)   b. Sep. 3, 1833
(monument)   d. Feb. 20, 1907

Notes:
--Isaac, son of Benjamin Canfield, q.v., and Sarah Riker
--Isaac m. Jan. 22 1857, Caroline, daughter of Stephen Cole, q.v.,
--Marriage record: "Isaac Canfield, b.1828, son of Benjamin; m. Jan 22, 1857, 'Catherine' Cole, b. 1834 dau. of Rachel"

--1850 Census: Caldwell Twp: Benjamin Canfield, age 50, farmer; Sarah R., age 45; Isaac, age 24, farmer; John, age 15, farmer; William, age 9; Halmagh Cisco, age 23, laborer; all b. New Jersey
--1860 Census: Caldwell Twp: Isaac Canfield, age 34, farmer; Caroline, age 26; Rachel A., age 1
--1870 Census: Caldwell Twp: Henry S. Cole, age 34, farmer; Rachel age 62; Isaac Canfield, age 44, farmer; Caroline Canfield, age 36; Rachel Canfield 11; Charles B. Canfield, age 9; all b. NJ
--1880 Census: Caldwell Twp: Isaac Canfield age 55, farmer; Caroline age 46; Rachel A. age 21; Rachel Cole, age 72, mother-in-law; all b. New Jersey
--1900 Census: Caldwell Boro, Essex Co., NJ: Charles B. "Caufield" age 39 b. June 1860, ins. agent; Marabelle C., age 41; Florence H, age 12; Harry C. age 9; Caroline, mother, widow, age 67, b. Feb. 1833; all b. New Jersey

- - - - -

CARMAN

Carman, GEORGE WESSON
(Neafie, p. 16) b. October 20, 1818
(inscriptions, p.138) d. November 28, 1846

George Wesson Carman
Born October 20, 1818
Died November 28, 1846

Notes:
--George Wesson, son of George Carman and Eliza .....
--George Wesson, brother of Levi Carman, q.v.

- - - - -

Carman, Levi* b. (March 5, 1804)
(Bible Records) d. (November 8, 1878)
(WPA Graves Survey) (bur. Oakdale Cemetery
 Davenport, Iowa)

first wife, MARIA L. (Archer)
(Maria Louise Archer)
(Neafie, p.16) b. (abt. Dec. 1 or 31, 1803)
(inscriptions, p.138 d. June 23, 1845

Maria L.
wife of
Levi Carman
Died June 23, 1845
aged 41 years, 6 months
& 22 days

Notes:
--Levi, b. "NYC", son of George Carman and Eliza .....;
--Levi m. Maria L., of Shawangunk, Ulster Co., NY (IGI)

--Levi, 3 children by Maria Archer: Elmira E.; Martha Young; George Lewis
--Maria Louise Archer, dau. of Jacob Archer and Elsie Allison (*History of the Alison or Allison Family in Europe and America.* pp. 261-262. 1893. Boston)
--1840 Census: Amenia, Dutchess Co., NY
--1850 Census: Niles, Cayuga Co., NY: Levi Carman, age 46, b. NY, farmer; Mary J., age 37, b. NY; George, age 11, b. NY; George, age 74, (b. July 12, 1777) b. NY
--1855 NY State Census: Seneca, Ontario Co., NY: Levi Carman, age 50 b. Dutchess Co., butcher; Mary J., age 45, b. NJ; Almira, age 21, dau., b. NY; Geo. L., age 16, son, b. Dutchess; D. M. (Dickerson Miller Carman), age 3, son, b. (Seneca) Ontario Co. NY; Geo., 76, father, b. Westchester; Mary Kelly, age 18, b. Ireland, servant
--1860 Census: Davenport, Scott Co., Iowa: Levi Carman, age 54, b. NY, no. occup. listed; Mary J., age 45, b. NJ; Dickerson, son, age 8, b. (Geneva) NY; Mary Haack, age 18, b. Holstein, servant
--1870 Census: Davenport, Scott Co., Iowa: Levi "Carnen", age 64, b. NY, drover; Mary, age 54, b. NJ; Dickerson, son, age 18, b. NY, gardener & farmer
--1886, March: Mary Carman d. Davenport, IA; bur. Oakdale Cemetery

- - - - -

COLE

Cole, John R.   See: Pearce Burial Ground
wife, Hannah M.

- - - - -

Cole, Richard   See: Pearce Burial Ground
widow, Mary

- - - - -

Cole, STEPHEN b. (abt. October 1805)
(Neafie, p.1   ) d. April 8, 1839
(inscriptions, p. 138)
(NJ Will #12956G, Inventory 1839)

Stephen Cole
Died April 8, 1839
aged 33 years, 6 months

wife, RACHEL ..... b. August 10, 1807
(Neafie, p.12) d. February 20, 1886

Rachel Cole
Born Aug. 10, 1807
Died Feb. 20, 1886

Notes:

"Mr. Stephen Cole, a respectable farmer of Fairfield, NJ perished in an attempt to rescue his horses and cattle from the barn which was on fire. Two horses and eight head of cattle were destroyed." (*Ledger and Transcript*. Philadelphia. April 12, 1839)

--1850 Census: Caldwell Twp., Essex Co., NJ: Rachel Cole age 42; Caroline 17; Henry age 15, farmer; all b. NJ; adj. to Nicholas Bush
--1860 Census: Caldwell Twp., Essex Co., NJ: Rachel Cole 51, b. NJ farmer; Henry S. age 24, b. NJ; John Smith, age 30, b. England, laborer; Orthnul Jacobus, age 18 b. NJ
--1870 Census: Caldwell Twp., Essex Co., NJ. Henry S. Cole, age 34, farmer; Rachel age 62; Isaac Canfield, age 44, farmer; Caroline Canfield, age 36; Rachel Canfield 11; Charles B. Canfield, age 9; all b. NJ

--1880 Census: Caldwell Twp., Essex Co., NJ: Isaac Canfield age 55, farmer; Caroline age 46; Rachel A. age 21; Rachel Cole, age 72, mother-in-law; all b. New Jersey
--1880 Census: Caldwell, Essex Co., NJ: Henry S. Cole, age 45, single, b. NJ, country store
--1900 Census: Montclair, Essex Co., NJ: Edwin N. Harrison, age 41, wholesale milk; Addie R., age 44; Helen C., age 12; Howard R., age 6; Henry S. Cole, age 64, b. Sept. 1835, 'uncle' single, salesman wholesale milk; all b. NJ

- - - - -

COLYER

Colyer, Ezra* b. (1818)
(NJ Will # 23505G, 1890) d. (October 11, 1890)
(monument) (bur. Prospect Hill Cemetery)

first wife, SARAH S. (Cole)
(Neafie, p.3) b. (abt. July 15, 1824)
(inscriptions, p.138) d. September 4, 1849

*Sarah S.
wife of Ezra Colyer
Died September 4, 1849
aged 25 years, 1 month & 23 days*

second wife, Matilda B.* (Bush)
  b. (1830) (February)
  d. (1907)
  (bur. Prospect Hill Cemetery)

daughter, AMARINTHA b. (October 2, 1848)
(Neafie, p. 3) d. August 20, 1849
(inscriptions, p.138)

Amarintha
daughter of
Ezra & Sarah S. Colyer
died August 20. 1849
aged 10 months & 17 days

Notes:
--Ezra, son of Hendrick? Colyer
--Ezra m. #1, Sarah S. (Cole)
--Ezra m. #2, Dec. 1851, Matilda B. Bush, dau. of ?John M. and Hannah Bush.
--Will signed Aug. 9, 1884; probate, Oct. 24, 1890
Ezra Colyer of Newark: real estate in Livingston; lot in Newark: names wife Matilda B.; dau. Sarah M. Williams, wife of Abram P. Williams; dau. Euphemia Crane, wife b. N. N. Crane; dau., Agnes Colyer (under age)

--1850 Census: Caldwell Twp., Essex Co., NJ: Simeon D. Pier, age 35, carpenter; Caroline 31; Richard 12; Abby Ann 8; Harriet 1; <u>Ezra</u> 'Collyer', age 35, farmer; all b. New Jersey
--1850 Census: Caldwell Twp., Essex Co., NJ: Mary Cole, age 52; Harriet Cole, age 17; John R. Cole, age 16; Sarah M. <u>Colyer</u> age 8; Euphemia <u>Colyer</u>, age 5; all b. NJ
--1860 Census: Livingston, Essex Co. NJ: <u>Ezra</u> 'Colier' age '41' farmer; <u>Matilda B.</u> age 28; Sarah M. age 17; Euphemia age 14; John H. age 6; Henry, age 31, school teacher; all b. New Jersey
--1870 Census: Livingston, Essex Co., NJ: <u>Ezra</u> Collier, age 51, farmer; <u>Matilda</u> age 39; Agnes, age 3; all b. New Jersey
--1880 Census: Newark, Essex Co., NJ: <u>Ezra</u> 'Collier' age 60, no occupation; <u>Matilda</u> age 45, wife; Agnes, age 12, daughter; all b. New Jersey
--1895 NJ State Census: 1Wd. Newark, Essex Co., NJ: <u>Mathelda B.</u> Colyer; Agnes H. Cummins; Ethel M. Cummins; Isaac Colyer; Sadie Colyer
--1900 Census: Newark, Essex Co., NJ: <u>Matilda</u> K. Colyer, age 69; Ethel M. Cummings, age 9, granddaughter; all b. NJ

- - - - -

Colyer, HENRY
(Neafie, p.3)
(NJ Will #13932G, 1850)

b. February 17, 1780
d. September 18, 1850(?)

Henry Colyer
Born Feb. 17, 1780
Died Sept. 18, 1850

first wife, MARTHA
(Neafie, p.3)

b. November, 1784
d. March 30, 1844

Martha
wife of
Henry Colyer
Born Sept. ..., 1784
Died March 30, 1844

Notes:
--Henry, son of Isaac? Colyer
--Henry m. #2, April 16, 1845, widow, Mrs. Elizabeth Wood
--?"1796 Aug. 18: Colyer, Collier, Henry of Essex Co. Ward. son of Isaac Collier of said co. dec'd; being upwards of 14 years and out of the wardship of his Guardian...makes choice of William Burnett Jr. Guardian; Fellowbondsmen Aaron 'Caseted' and Timothy Gould." (Lib. 37, p.318 #8590-8591G)
--Will signed Feb. 22, 1850, probate Oct. 8, 1850: names: beloved wife Elizabeth Colyer; son, Thomas G. Colyer; grandson Henry, son of Thomas; dau. Annah Maria Cobb, wife of Elias W. Cobb; dau. Sarah S. Earl, wife of John N. Earl; son, Isaac Colyer: Executors: Caleb D. Harrison; John N. Earl; Isaac Colyer
--1830 Census: Caldwell Twp., Essex Co., NJ: Henry Collier 5 persons; adj. to Thomas Collier and Robert G. Collier

--1840 Census: Caldwell Twp., Essex Co., NJ: Henry 'Colier' 6 persons; adj. to Elias W. Cobb
--1850 Census: (Sept. 16), Caldwell Twp., Essex Co., NJ: Henry Colyer, age 70, b. NJ, farmer; Elizabeth, age 63, b. England

- - - - -

COOK

Cook, Henry Francis* b. (abt. 1782)
 d.

?wife, ESTHER b. (abt. 1786)
(Neafie, p. 6) d. June 30, 1852
(monument)

Erected
To the memory of
Esther Cook
Died June 30, 1852
Aged 66 years

-

Her great grandson
James E.
Infant son of Amos and Julia How(e)
Died Aug. 11, 1852
Aged 4 mos.

great-grandson JAMES E. (Howe)
(Neafie, p.3) b. 1852
 d. August 11, 1852

Notes:
--see Amos Howe
--see John H. VanNess

--?1850 Census: Stamford, Fairfield Co. CT: Henry Cook, age 68 b. NY, cab. mkr.; Hetty, age 52, b. CT (Xed out); Samuel W., age 18, b. CT

- - - - -

CORNISH

Cornish, LAVINIA (monument)
b. January 11, 1799
d. November 1, 1886

Lavinia Cornish
Born Jan. 11, 1799
Died Nov. 1, 1886

Notes:
--See: Ezra Ely

- - - - -

COURTER

Courter, Charles
wife, Mary Elizabeth
See: Pearce Burial Ground

- - - - -

Courter, James
wife, Jane
See: Pearce Burial Ground

- - - - -

DAVENPORT

Davenport, EZRA (monument)
b. September 12, 1803
d. March 24, 1889

Ezra Davenport
Born
Sept. 12, 1803
Died Mar. 24, 1889

-

Mary Beach
His Wife
Born Oct. 12, 1807
Died Mar. 23, 1871

-

Wallace S. Davenport
Born Nov. 11, 1871
Died Jan. 24, 1892

wife, MARY (Beach) (monument)	b. October 12, 1807 d. Mar. 23, 1871
grandson, WALLACE S. (monument)	b. November 11, 1871 d. January 24, 1892

Notes:
--Mary, dau. of Jonathan Beach and Rachel Jacobus?
--1830 Census: Caldwell Twp., (North Caldwell?)Essex Co., NJ: Ezra Davenport, 5 persons (adj. to Joseph P. Gould)
--1840 Census: Caldwell Twp., Essex Co., NJ: Ezra Davenport. 5 persons
--1850 Census: Caldwell Twp., Essex Co., NJ: Ezra Davenport, age 46, farmer; Mary, age 42; Jonathan B., age 19, farmer; Sarah F., age 16; Catharine, age 74
--1860 Census: Caldwell Twp., Essex Co. NJ: Ezra Davenport, age 56, b. NJ, laborer; Mary, age 52, b. NJ; adj. to: Jno B. Davenport, age 29, b. NJ, farmer; Mary E., age 28 b. NJ; John Roberts, age 25, b. NJ, laborer
--1870 Census: Caldwell Twp., Essex Co., NJ: Ezra Davenport, age 66, b. NJ, farmer; Mary, age 63, b. NJ; Jonathan B., age 38, b. NJ, farmer; Mary, age 37, b. NJ; Clara, age 9, b. NJ; Emma, age 7, b. NJ

--1880 Census: (North?) Caldwell, Essex Co., NJ: Jonathan Davenport, age 49 b. NJ, parents b. NJ, farmer; Mary E., age 49 b. 'NY', parents b. NJ; Emma, age 17, daughter b. NJ; Wallace, age 8, son, b. NJ; Ezra, age 77, b. NJ, no occup.

- - - - -

DEBAUN

DeBaun, JESSE E.　　　b. February 14, 1889
(monument)　　　　　　d. January 20, 1894

Jesse E. DeBaun
Born
Feb. 14, 1889
Died
Jan. 20, 1894

Notes:
--Jesse, son of Amos DeBaun and Wilhelmina'Amenia' 'Amenia' Cole

--1900 Census: Belleville Twp., Essex Co., NJ: Amos Debaun, age 35, b. Sept. 1864, m. 14 years, b. NJ, parents b. NY, milkman; Amenia, age 36, b. May 1864, 4 born 2 living, b. NJ, parents b. NJ; Mazie, dau. b. Oct. 1886, NJ; Edna, dau. b. Aug. 1895, NJ

- - - - -

DeBaun, JOHN　　　　　b. 1814 (September 2, 1814)
(monument)　　　　　　d. 1895 (January 24, 1895)
(NJ Will #25855, 1895)

wife, LETTY FOLLY　　　b. 1818 (July 9, 1818)
(Lutetia Folly)　　　　　d. 1897 (Dec. 3, 1897)
(monument)

John De Baun
1814-1895

-

Letty Folly
His Wife
1818-1897

-

DE BAUN

son, JEREMIAH RIKER   b. 1843 (September 26, 1843)
(monument)   d. 1864 (August 19, 1864)
(Served: Civil War)

Jeremiah R. DeBaun
Co. G, 109 NY Inf
1843 - 1864

Notes:
--John, son of Johan DeBaun and Mary Storms?
--Letty, dau. of Abr. Folly and Catherine Suart/Shurte of Saddle River, Bergen Co., New Jersey
--Jeremiah, son: Served: Civil War: Pvt., Co. G, 109 NY Infantry: ? buried: Cypress Hills National Cemetery, Brooklyn, NY

--1850 Census: Newfield, Tompkins Co., NY: John 'DeBaum', age 37 b. NJ, farmer; Letty, age 32, b. NJ; Abram, age 14, b. NY; Maria, age 12, b. NY; Catherine A., age 10 b. NY; Jeremiah, age 8, b. NY; Peter, age 1 month, b. NY
--1860 Census: Catherine Twp., Schuyler Co., NY: John Debaun, age 45, b. NJ, farmer; Lettie, age 43, b. NJ; Jeremiah, age 16, b. NY: Peter, age 11 b. NY; Miranda, age 8, b. NJ; Emma, age 4, b. NY; Ellie, age 4, b. NY; William, age 2, b. NY

--1870 Census: Caldwell Twp., Essex Co., NJ: John Debaun, age 56, b. NJ, farmer; Lettie, age 53, b. NJ; Ella, age 14, b. NY; Emma, age 14, b. NY; William, age 10, b. NY; Amos, age 6, b. NY
--1880 Census: Caldwell Twp., Essex Co., NJ: John Debaun, age 65, b. NJ, farmer; Lutetia, age 61, b. NJ; John W., age 21, b. NY, works on the farm; Amos, age 16, b. NY, works on the farm
--1895 NJ State Census: Caldwell Twp., Essex Co., NJ: Lettie DeBaun; adj. to Amos DeBaun

- - - - -

DeBaun, RAY C.   b. January 5, 1892
                         d. July 12, 1892

Ray C. DeBaun
Born
Jan. 5, 1892
Died
July 12, 1892

Notes:
--Ray, son of Amos and Minnie DeBaun

- - - - -

DEETHS

Deeths, DANIEL   b. (abt. February 1, 1817)
(Neafie, p. 9)   d. October 11, 1844
(inscriptions, p. 139)

Daniel Deeths
Died
October 11, 1844
aged 27 years, 8 months

& *10 days*

wife, SUSAN ELIZA (Bone)
(Neafie, p.9)   b. (abt. 1824)
                             d. July 20, 1850

Susan Eliza
wife of
Daniel Deeths
and daughter of
Benj. H. and Lydia Bone
Died July 20, 1850
Aged 26 years, 10 mos.
and 3 days

son, DANIEL D.   b. (abt. July 7, 1844)
(Neafie, p.9)   d. November 11, 1844

Daniel D.
son of
Daniel and Susan Eliza
Deeths
Died Nov. 11, 1844
Aged 4 mos. & 4 days

Notes:
--See: Benjamin H. Bone
--Daniel, son of John Deeths and Catherine Vreeland(?)
--Daniel m. Susan Eliza Bone, dau. of Benjamin H. Bone, q.v. and Lydia Riker.
--1850 Census: Acquakanonk Twp., Passsaic Co., NJ: Benjamin H. Bone age 53, hotel keeper; Lydia age 48; John E. age 15, farm hand; Emeline age 12; Horace age 10; Benjamin Deeths age 8; <u>Susan</u> Deeths age 26; all b. New Jersey; 1 laborer

- - - - -

DEY

Dey, CORNELIUS   b. (February 23, 1786)
(Neafie, p.13)   d. October 31, 1865
(monument)
(NJ Will #16097G, 1865)

In
Memory of
Cornelius Day
Who Died
October 31st. 1865
Aged 79 years 8 mos.
and 8 days

first wife, MARGARET (Francisco)
(Neafie, p.13)   b. (abt. March 2, 1795
(inscriptions, p.138)   d. August 8, 1835
(monument)

In
Memory of
Margaret
Wife of
Cornelius Dey
Who Died
August 8th, 1835
Aged 40 Years 5 Mo.
and 6 days

second wife, RACHEL (Willis)
(Neafie, p.13)   b. (November 25, 1801)
(monument)   d. November 24, 1870

Rachel
Wife of

Cornelius Day
Died
Nov. 24th, 1870
Aged 69 Years
A Mother in Israel

Notes:
--Cornelius, son of John Dey and Jannetje Doremus
--Cornelius m. #1, April 1815, Margaret Francisco, dau. of Josiah Francisco, q.v., and Sarah Jacobus
--He m.#2, July 15, 1837, Rachel Willis. She was b. November 25, 1801, dau. of John Willis and Margaret Packer; Rachel was widow of Abraham Romaine

--1850 Census: Caldwell Twp., Essex Co., NJ: Henry Dey age 34, inn keeper; Susan 36; John 13; Cornelius 10; Samuel 7; Mary M. 4; Cornelius age 64, farmer; Rachel, age 50; all b. N.J.
--1860 Census: Caldwell Twp., Essex Co., NJ: Cor.s "Dry" age 74 farmer; Rachel age 68; Cor.s, age 19 (grandson); Ralph Bush, age 12, all b. New Jersey
--1870 Census: 4 Wd. Newark, Essex Co., NJ: Nelson Jacobus, age 45, carpenter; Mary J. Jacobus, age 34; Wm. Jacobus, age 11; 'Rachael Dye' age 69 b. NJ; 1 domestic servant

- - - - -

Dey, CORNELIUS H.   b. (August 21, 1840)
(monument)   d. (March 21, 1928)
wife, Nellie M.* (Sigler)   b.
                             d.

Cornelius H. Dey
Co. D
26 NJ Inf.

Notes:
Served: Civil War

- - - - -

Dey, HENRY   b. (abt. 1815)
(Neafie, p.13)   d. January 29, 1885
(monument)
(NJ Will # 21630G, 1885)

Henry Dey
Died January 29, 1885
In his 70th year

wife, SUSAN (Berry)   b. (November 10. 1814)
(Neafie, p.13)   d. (April 15, 1894)
(monument)

Susan Berry
Wife of
Henry Dey
Died April 5, 1894
In her 80th year

Notes:
--Henry Dey, son of Cornelius Dey, q.v., and Margaret Francisco.
--Henry Dey m. November 14, 1835 Susan Berry, daughter of Martin Berry and Sophia Terhune
--daughter, Mary Margaret, b. October 24, 1846; d. October 24, 1846; m. #1, Dec. 30, 1864, Edward Anthony C. Ogilvie, q.v., son of James Glaen Ogilvie, q.v.; m. #2, Nov. 22, 1878, George Herman Winans.

--1850 Census: Caldwell Twp., Essex Co., NJ: Henry Dey age 34, inn keeper; Susan 36; John 13; Cornelius 10; Samuel 7; Mary M. 4; Cornelius age 64, farmer; Rachel, age 50; all b. N.J.

--1860 Census: Caldwell Twp., Essex Co., NJ: Henry 'Dry' age 45 b. NJ, farmer; Susan age 46 b. NJ; Samuel age 17 b. NJ; Mary age 12, b. NJ; Jane Berry, age 42, b. NJ; A. E. Ogilvie, age 42, b. NY, music? teacher; Elizabeth Ogilvie, age 60, b. NY

--1870 Census: Caldwell Twp., Essex Co., NJ: Henry Dey age 55, farmer; Susan age 58;(same house) Samuel age 27, farmer; Ellen age 25; Leslie, age 4; Albert B., age 3; Tunis Bond, age 17, farm labor

--1880 Census: Caldwell Twp., Essex Co., NJ: Henry Dey age 64, farmer; Susan age 65; Cornelius, age 44, widower, works on farm; Harriet Story, age 13, servant; William Morrisey age 26, works on farm, b. Ireland

- - - - -

Dey, JOHN R. b. November 23, 1809
(Neafie, p.7) d. April 6, 1883

John R. Dey
Born Nov. 23, 1809
Died April 6th, 1883

wife, Hannah* b. abt. 1801
  d. (March 30, 1882?)

Notes:
--Hannah Dey: "died March 30, 1882(?), Montville; married, age 84"

--1850 Census: Pequannock Twp., Morris Co., NJ: John Dey, age 41, farmer; Hannah VanDuyne, age 58; James VanDuyne, age 16; Albert VanDuyne, age 14; Martin VanDuyne, age 9; all b. NJ

--1860 Census: Pequannock Twp., Morris Co., NJ: John "J" Day, age 55, b. Passaic Co., mason; Hannah, age 60, b. Morris Co.

--1870 Census: Montville, Morris Co., NJ: John Dey, age 65, b. NJ; Hannah, age 69, b. NJ
--1880 Census: Montville, Morris Co., NJ: John R. Dey, age 74, b. NJ, farmer; Hannah, age 80, b. NJ

- - - - -

Dey, LESLIE G.   b. (January 23, 1866)
(monument)   d. (October 13, 1912)

Leslie C. Dey
Born Jan. 20, 1876
Died Dec. 13, 1932

-

Lenna
Wife of
Leslie C. Dey
Born March 13, 1866
Died June 20, 1895

DEY

first wife, LENNA (Zeek?)   b. March 13, 1866
(monument)   d. June 20, 1895

second wife, Kate* (Gould)
                         b. (abt. February 1863)
                         d.

Notes:
--Leslie m. #1, Lenna .....; m. #2, abt. 1906(?) Kate Gould, daughter of William Gould; widow of ..... Van Ness.

--1870 Census: Caldwell Twp., Essex Co., NJ: Henry Dey age 55, farmer; Susan age 58;(same house) Samuel age 27,

farmer; Ellen age 25; Leslie, age 4; Albert B., age 3; Tunis Bond, age 17, farm labor
--1880 Census: Newark, Essex Co., NJ: John B. 'Dye" age 42, carpenter; Margaret L., age 42, wife; Nurena age 16, daughter, at school; Leslie G., age 14, nephew, at school
--?1880 Census: Newark, Essex Co., NJ: Thomas Zeek, age 37, wks cotton factory; Mary C., age 32; Lenna, age 14; George age 11; all b. NJ
--1895 NJ State Census: 8Wd Newark, Essex Co., NJ: Leslie G. Dey; Lenna; Albert B.
--1900 Census: 8Wd, Newark, Essex Co., NJ: Leslie G. Dey age 34, b. January 1866, widower, produce salesman; Albert B. Dey, son b. March 1891; Kate Van Ness, age 37, b. Feb. 1863; Harry G. Van Ness b. May 1888, son of housekeeper
--1910 Census: 8Wd, Newark, Essex Co., NJ: Leslie G. Dey 44, m. #2 for 4(?) years; grain broker; Kate, age 47, wife; Albert B., age 28, son, grain salesman; Harry Vanness age 21, son, office clerk; 1 domestic servant
--1920 Census: 1Wd, Orange, Essex Co., NJ: Kate Dey age 56, widow, b. NJ, father b. NY, mother b. NJ; William Gould, age 83, father, widower, b. NY, father b. Maine, mother b. NY

- - - - -

Day, MOSES   b. (abt. 1777)
(Neafie, p. 18)   d. May 8, 1837
(inscriptions, p. 139)
(NJ Will #12785G, 1837)

Moses Day
Died
May 8, 1837
in his 61st year

wife, Rebecca* (Berry)   b. (abt. October 1, 1783)
                                     d. (March 22, 1817)

(bur. Presbyterian Cemetery
Parsippany, Morris Co., NJ)

Notes:
--Moses Day, son of David Day and Mary Denman
--Moses m. March 24, 1803, Rebecca Berry

- - - - -

Dey, SAMUEL BERRY   b. (July 31, 1842)
(monument)   d. (June 11, 1921)

Samuel B. Dey
Born July 31, 1842
Died June 11, 1921

-

Ellen Bush
wife of
Samuel Dey
Born Apr. 7, 1846
Died Feb. 1, 1919

wife, ELLEN (Bush)   b. (April 7, 1846)
(monument)   d. (February 1, 1919)

son, ALBERT B.   b. (September 27, 1867)
(Neafie, p.13)   d. March 10, 1885
(monument)

Albert B. Day
Died Mar. 10, 1885
In his 18th year

Notes:
--Samuel, son of Henry Dey, q.v., and Susan Berry
--Samuel m. abt. 1865, Ellen Vanderhoof Bush, dau. of Nicholas Bush, q.v. and Hannah Van Ness.

--1850 Census: Caldwell Twp. Essex Co., NJ: Henry Dey age 34, inn keeper; Susan 36; John 13; Cornelius 10; Samuel 7; Mary M. 4; Cornelius age 64, farmer; Rachel, age 50; all b. N.J.
--1860 Census: Caldwell Twp., Essex Co., NJ: Henry 'Dry' age 45 b. NJ, farmer; Susan age 46 b. NJ; Samuel age 17 b. NJ; Mary age 12, b. NJ; Jane Berry, age 42, b. NJ; A. E. Ogilvie, age 42, b. NY, music? teacher; Elizabeth Ogilvie, age 60, b. NY
--1870 Census: Caldwell Twp., Essex Co., NJ: Henry Dey age 55, farmer; Susan age 58;(same house) Samuel age 27, farmer; Ellen age 25; Leslie, age 4; Albert B., age 3; Tunis Bond, age 17, farm labor
--1880 Census: Caldwell Twp., Essex Co., NJ: Samuel Dey 37, country merchant; Ellen V. age 34; Albert B. age 12; Cornelius 7; Ella M. Howard, age 16; all b. New Jersey
--1900 Census: Caldwell Twp. Essex Co., NJ: Samuel Dey b. July 1843, m.35 yrs., farmer; Ellen Day b. April 1847, 3 born 2 living; Hannah Bush age 82, widow, mother-in-law b. August 1817, 7 born 3 living; all b. New Jersey
--1910 Census: Caldwell Twp., Essex Co., NJ: 'Sanuel' Dey, age 67, m.45 years, farmer; Ellen age 65, 3 born 2 living; 'Halimah' (Hannah), age 93, mother-in-law, widow; 4 hired men
--1920 Census: Caldwell Twp., Essex Co., NJ: Samuel 'Day' age 77, widower, no occupation; at res. of Aaron E. and Laura Stagg

- - - - -

DODD

Dodd, (Dods) Henry*	b. (abt. 1824)
(Baptism Record)	b. (December 18, 1821)
(NJ Death Record)	d. (September 26, 1879)
(NJ Will #5692N, 1879)	(bur. Pompton Plains Cem.)

first wife, RACHEL JANE (Pier)
(Neafie, p.20)   b. (April 23, 1824)
         d. (July 31, 1854)

Rachel J.
Died July 31, 1854
Aged 30 yrs. 3 mos. 7 days

Children of
Francis and Elizabeth Pier

Notes:
--?Henry, son of Jacob Dodd and Lydia Doremus
Ref. Church Baptism Record: "Henry Dods, b. Dec. 18, 1821 of Jacob Dods and Lydia Doremus. Pompton Plains, NJ"
--Henry Dodd m. #1, October 19, 1850, Rachel Jane Pier, daughter of Francis Pier, q.v. and Elizabeth Van Ness
--Henry m. #2, Sept. 11, 1854, Rachel Hopper, dau. of David Hopper and Sarah Doremus
--Henry, d. September 26, 1879 Pequannock, age 59, married, farmer

--1850 Census: Pequannock Twp., Morris Co., NJ: Jacob Dodd, age 69, farmer; Lydia, age 69; Henry, age 26, b. NJ, farmer; all b. NJ
--1860 Census: Pequannock Twp., Morris Co., NJ: Henry Dods age 36; Rachel, age 26; James W., age 5; Hester L., age 1 month; Sarah Hopper, age 57; all b. Morris Co., NJ
--1863 June 30: Civil War Draft Registration, Pequannock Village. Henry Dods, age 41, b. NJ, farmer
--1870 Census: Pequannock Twp., Morris Co., NJ: 'James' Dod, age 45, farmer; Rachel, age 36; James W., age 14; Hester, age 10; Elma A., age 8; Cornelius age 5; Catherine, age 2; all b. NJ

--1880 Census: Pequannock Twp., Morris Co., NJ: Rachel Dodd, age 45, widow; Elma A., age 18; Cornelius A., age 15; Emma C., age 13; Sarah L., age 9; all b. NJ

- - - - -

DOREMUS

Doremus, HENRY S.   b. (abt. 1810)
(Neafie, p.1)   d. May 15, 1873
(monument)
(NJ Will #17840G, 1873)

*In
Memory Of
Henry S. Doremus
who died
May 15th, 1873
Age 63 Years*

wife, Rachel* (Yorks)
(monument)   b. (abt. 1809)
    d. (October 9, 1895)
    (bur. Rolling Prairie Cem.
    La Porte Co., Indiana)

*Rachel Doremus
Died October 9, 1895
Aged 86 Years*

Notes:
--Henry, son of Simeon Doremus, q.v., and Jane Dey
--Henry m. Rachel Yorks, dau. of Cornelius Yorks

--1850 Census: 16Wd, Dist. 1, NY, NY: Henry S. Doremus, age 41, b. NJ, grocer; Rachel, age 40 b. NJ; Peter, age 20,

clerk, b. NJ; James, age 14, b. NY; Theron, age 11, b. NY; Cynthia ....., age 29, b. Ireland, servant; John Roun, age 18, b. NJ, clerk
--1860 Census: Bloomfield, Essex Co., NJ: Henry S. Doremus, age 50, b. NJ, farmer; Rachel, age 50; Theron, age 8, b. NY; Thomas Levey, age 19, b. NJ, farmer
--1870 Census: 6Wd., Newark: Henry S. Doremus, age 60, b. NJ, retired merchant; Rachel, age 60, b. NJ
--1880 Census: Kankakee, LaPorte Co., Indiana: Benjamin F. "Sailsbury", age 58 b. NY, father b. RI, mother b. NH; Mary J., wife, age 47, b. NY, parents b. NJ; Olin, son, age 13, b. MO, parents b. NY; Rollin, age 8, b.IN, parents b. NY; Rachel Doremus, mother-in-law, widow, age 70, b. NJ, parents b. NJ

- - - - -

Doremus, JOB b. February 12, 1811
(Neafie, p.1) d. November 4, 1881

Job Doremus
Died Nov. 4, 1881
Aged 70 years, 8 mos.,
& 25 days

first wife, RACHEL (VanNess)
(Neafie, p.1) b. (abt. November 25)
  d. April 9, 1858

Rachel Van Ness
wife of
Job Doremus
Died Apr. 9, 1858
Aged 42 year, 5 mos.

second wife, Catherine* (Hopper
                        b. (April 13, 1810)
                        d. (October 17, 1896)
                        (marker at Laurel Grove Mem. Park, Totowa, NJ

daughter, ELIZABETH   b. (abt. January 25, 1842)
(Neafie, p.3)   d. November 14, 1843
(inscriptions, p.139)

> *Elizabeth*
> *Died November 14, 1843*
> *aged 1 year, 9 months*
> *& 20 days*
> -
> *Simeon*
> *Died Aug. 11, 1846*
> *Aged 1 yr. 6 mos.*
> *Both children of*
> *Job and Rachel Doremus*

son, SIMEON   b. (abt. February 11, 1845)
(Neafie, p.3)   d. August 11, 1846
(inscriptions, p.139)

Notes:
--Job, son of Simeon Doremus, q.v., and Maregrietye "Peggy" Van Winkle.
--Job m. #1, 1832, Rachel Van Ness, dau. of Henry H. VanNess, q.v., and Margaret Bush
--Job m.#2, May 7, 1859, at Little Falls: Catharine Hopper, widow of William Van Ness, q.v.

--1850 Census: Caldwell Twp. Essex Co., NJ: Henry H. Vanness 66, farmer; Margaret Vanness 64; Job Doremus age 38, mason; Rachel 35; Susan 13; Warren 3; all b. New Jersey

--1860 Census: Little Falls, Passaic Co.NJ: "James" Doremus age 50, farmer; Catherine age '59'; Francis (Van Ness) age 24, farm labor; Elizabeth (Van Ness) age 20; Emily (Van Ness) age 18; Jane (Van Ness) age 16; 'Wanan' (Warren) age 13; William Riese, 13; John Hopper, age 40, carpenter

--1870 Census: Little Falls, Passaic Co. NJ: "John" Doremus, age 59, mason; Catherine, age 61; Francis age 30, clerk at country store; 'Carry', female age 28; Jane, age 21; Frank Schroder age 11; all b. New Jersey

--1880 Census: Little Falls Twp.,Passaic Co. NJ: Job Doremus age 69, brick mason; Catherine age 71, wife; Janie Shaw age 14, servant; all b. New Jersey

--1885 NJ Census: Little Falls, Passaic Co. NJ: Joseph C. Cooke, age 20-60; Jane L. Cooke, age 20-60' Sara L. Cooke, age 0-4; Catherine Doremus, age over 60; Mary E. Hanlon

--1895 NJ Census: Little Falls, Passaic Co., NJ: Joseph C. Cooke; Jennie L. Cooke; Sara Louise Cooke; Katherine Doremus

- - - - -

Doremus, SIMEON b. September 11, 1765
(Neafie, p.1) d. June 14, 1849
(inscriptions, p. 139)
(monument)

Simeon Doremus
Born
September 11, 1765
Died
June 14, 1849
Aged 83 years, 9 months
& 3 days

wife, JANE (Dey) b. (March 27, 1774)
(Neafie, p. 1) d. July 29, 1847

(inscriptions, p.139)

> *Jane*
> *wife of*
> *Simeon Doremus*
> *died July 29, 1847*
> *aged 73 years, 4 months,*
> *& 2 days*

Notes:
--Simeon, son of Hendricus Doremus and Marregrietye "Peggy" Van Winkle.
--Simeon m. October 17, 1789, Jane Dey, daughter of Thomas Dey and Abigail Lewis.

--1830 Census: Pequannock Twp., Morris Co., NJ: Simeon Doremus; 8 persons

- - - - -

DOUGHERTY

Dougherty, Charles A.   See: Pearce Burial Ground
wife, Bertha O.

- - - - -

DULHAGEN

Dulhagen, John*   b. (abt. 1804)
    d. (aft. 1880)

wife, MARY (Keirstead)   b. December 8, 1802
(Neafie, p.7)   d. August 1, 1865

> *Mary Ann Kiersted*
> *wife of*

John Dulhagen
Born
Dec. 8, 1802
Died
Aug. 1, 1865

son, JAMES M. b. March 9, 1836
(Neafie, p.7) d. May 16, 1860

James M.
Son of
John and Mary A. Dulhagen
Born
Mch. 9, 1836
Died May 16, 1860

Notes:
--John, possible son of John Dulhagen and Elizabeth Vanderhoof
--John "Hagen" m. November 17, 1827, Mary "Kearstede"
--?John Dulhagen m. Mrs. Hannah Brown, Stone House Plains, Feb. 3, 1867
--1840 Census: Manchester Twp., Passaic Co., NJ: John "Malhagen". 6 persons
--1850 Census: Caldwell Twp. Essex Co., NJ: John Dulhagen, age 46, farmer; Mary, age 48; Rachel Ann, age 16; James, age 14; Daniel, age 9; all b. New Jersey
--1860 Census: Caldwell Twp., Essex Co., NJ: John "Dulinhagan" age 55; Mary, age 58 (adj. to Thomas H. Sindle)
--1880 Census: Caldwell Twp., Essex Co., NJ: George M. Sindle, age 26, segar maker; Rachel A., age 27; Ida May, dau., age 8; Alfred, age 4; John Dulhagen, age 75, grandfather; all b. New Jersey; (adj. to Thomas H. Sindle, age 49)

- - - - -

ELY

Ely, EZRA STILES   b. May 17, 1797
(Neafie, p.8)   d. October 31, 1863
(monument)
(NJ Will #15913G, Inv. 1864?)

> *In Memory of*
> *Ezra Stiles Ely*
> *Born May 17, 1797*
> *Died Oct. 31, 1863*
> *For many years a Deacon and Elder*
> *in the Reformed*
> *Church of Fairfield, Essex County,*
> *N.J.*
> *He lived and died in the Lord*

wife, Lavinia* (Cornish)   b. January 11, 1799
(Ely monument)   d. November 1, 1886

> *Lavinia Cornish*
> *Born Jan. 11, 1799*
> *Died Nov. 1, 1886*

Notes:
--Ezra, son of Benjamin Ely and Polly Pettibone
--Ezra m. #1, 1835, Rachel Smith, dau. of Peter Smith, Rockaway Neck, NJ; she d. 1836.
--Ezra m. #2, 1837, Lavinia Cornish, dau. of George Cornish and Susannah Mitchelson

--1840 Census: Caldwell Twp., Essex Co., NJ: Ezra S. Ely: 3 persons

--1850 Census: Caldwell Twp., Essex Co., NJ: Ezra S. Ely, age 52, b. CT, farmer; Lavinia, age 48, b. CT; George C., age 11, b. NJ
--1860 Census: Caldwell, Essex Co., NJ: E. S. Ely, age 63, b. CT, farmer; Lavinia, age 58 b. CT; George C., age 21, b. NJ
--1870 Census: Caldwell, Essex Co., NJ: George C. Ely, age 30 b. NJ, farmer; Lavinia, age 60, b. CT
--1880 Census: Dist. 2, Caldwell, Essex Co., NJ: Lavinia C. Ely, widow, age 81, b. CT, parents b. CT; George C., son, married, age 40, b. NJ, parents b. CT, farmer; Elizabeth Garlunn, age 29, b. Ireland, servant; John Ingle, age 64, b. NJ, works on farm

- - - - -

FAIRBANKS

Fairbanks, Jonathan Wilder* b. (August 28, 1808)
　　　　　　　　　　　　　d. (August 2, 1898)

wife, CATHERINE M. (Eisenbrey)
(Neafie, p.9)　　　　　　b. (April 9, 1805)
　　　　　　　　　　　　d. July 9, 1885

Catherine M.
wife of J. W. Fairbanks
and daughter of
Henry and Sophia Eisenbrey
Died July 9, 1885
Aged 80 yrs. 3 mos.

Notes:
--Jonathan Wilder Fairbanks, son of Joseph Fairbanks and Mary White Brooks
--Jonathan m. May 24, 1826, Catherine Margaret Eisenbrey, dau. of Henry Eisenbrey and Sophia Stillwagon

--Jonathan "b. c.1809, d. Aug. 2, 1898, Pequannock, mason, widowed" (NJ Death Record)

--1850 Census: Glens Falls, Warren Co., NY: <u>Jonathan W.</u> Fairbanks, age 42, b. VT, mason; <u>Catharine M.</u>, age 45, b. PA; Joseph H., age 12 b. NY; Philip E., age 10 b. NY; Wilder, age 7, b. NY

--1860 Census: Pequannock Twp., Morris Co., NJ: <u>Jonathan</u> W. Fairbanks, age 52, b. VT, farmer; <u>Catherine M.</u>, age 55, b. PA; Wilder, age 18, b. NY; Joseph H., age 22, b. NY; Harriet Pike, age 24, b. NY

--1870 Census: Pompton Plains P.O., Pequannock Twp., Morris Co., NJ: <u>John</u> Fairbanks, age 62, farmer; <u>Catherine</u>, age 65; Wilder, age 28, works on farm; Mary, age 3; Joseph P., age 9 months; 1 domestic; all b. "New Jersey"

--1880 Census: Pequannock Twp., Morris Co., NJ: <u>J. W.</u> Fairbanks, age 71, b. VT, parents b. MA, farmer; <u>Catherine</u> M., age 75, b. PA, parents b. PA; Rachel Quick, age 26, housekeeper

--1895 Census: Pequannock Twp., Morris Co., NJ: Wilder Fairbanks Jr.; Sarah; Bertha; Wilder, Sr.

- - - - -

Fairbanks, (Jonathan)Wilder* Jr.
                        b. (February 13, 1842)
                        d. (aft. 1900)

first wife, CASSIE J. (Van Ness)
(Catherine Jane Van Ness)
(Neafie, p.9)   b. (abt. 1845)
                        d. May 18, 1870

Cassie J.
Wife of
Wilder Fairbanks
Died May 18, 1870

Aged 24 yrs. 5 mos
27 days

daughter, MAMIE E.   b. February 24, 1867
Neafie, p.9)   d. June 4, 1884

Mamie E.
Daughter of
Wilder and Cassie
Fairbanks
Born Feb. 24, 1867
Died June 4, 1884

Notes:
--Wilder, son of Jonathan Wilder Fairbanks, q.v., and Catherine Margaret Eisenbrey
--Wilder m. May 20, 1866, Catherine Jane "Cassie J." VanNess
--Wilder m. April 16, 1873, Sarah Jacobus

--1850 Census: Glens Falls, Warren Co., NY: Jonathan W. Fairbanks, age 42, b. VT, mason; Catharine M., age 45, b. PA; Joseph H., age 12 b. NY; Philip E., age 10 b. NY; Wilder, age 7, b. NY
--1860 Census: Pequannock Twp., Morris Co., NJ: Jonathan W. Fairbanks, age 52, b. VT, farmer; Catherine M., age 55, b. PA; Wilder, age 18, b. NY; Joseph H., age 22, b. NY; Harriet Pike, age 24, b. NY
--1870 Census: Pompton Plains P.O., Pequannock Twp., Morris Co., NJ: John Fairbanks, age 62, farmer; Catherine, age 65; Wilder, age 28, works on farm; Mary, age 3; Joseph P., age 9 months; 1 domestic; all b. "New Jersey"
--1880 Census: Pequannock Twp., Morris Co., NJ: Wilder Fairbanks, age 38 b. NY, brick mason; Sarah, age 40 b. NJ; Mary E., age 13 b. NJ; Joseph P., age 10 b. NJ; Bertha E., age 4 b. NJ

--1895 NJ State Census: Pequannock Twp., Morris Co., NJ: Wilder Fairbanks, Jr.; Sarah; Bertha; Wilder Fairbanks, Sr.
--1900 Census: Pequannock Twp., Morris Co., NJ: Wilder Fairbanks, age 58, b. Feb. 1847, m.27 yrs. b. "NY", house carpenter; Sarah, age 60 b. Oct. 1839, NJ, 1 born 1 living; Bertha, age 23, b. June 1876, age 23, b. NJ, bookkeeping

- - - - -

FRANCISCO

Francisco, ANDREW b. (abt. 1798)
(Neafie, p.7) d. January 17, 1853
(NJ Will #14355G,1853)

Andrew Francisco
Died Jan. 17, 1853
In his 54th year

wife, MARIA* (Speer) b. (abt. March 1, 1801)
(inscriptions, p.139) d. June 19, 1849

Maria
wife of
Andrew Francisco
died June 19, 1849
aged 48 years, 3 months
& 18 days

Notes:
--Andrew, son of John Francisco and Marietje Stager
--Andrew m. abt. 1822, Maria Speer, dau. of Richard Speer and Sarah Stagg

--1840 Census: Caldwell Twp., Essex Co., NJ: Andrew Francisco, 7 persons

--1850 Census: Caldwell Twp., Essex Co., NJ: <u>Andrew</u> Francisco, age 50, farmer; Richard, age 23, farmer; Mariah age 21; George age 18, farmer; Josiah age 16, farmer; William, age 13, farmer; John H., age 1(grandson); (adj. to Henry Francisco)

- - - - -

Francisco, CALVIN   b. 1828 (July)
(monument)   d. 1904

Calvin Francisco
1828 - 1904
-
His Wife
Harriet L.
1834 - 1890

wife, HARRIET L. (Jacobus) b. 1834
(monument)   d. 1890

Notes:
--Calvin, son of Henry Francisco, q.v. and Sarah Courter
--Harriet, dau. of Henry T. Jacobus and Mary .....
--1850 Census: Caldwell Twp., Essex Co., NJ: Henry Francisco, age 53, farmer; Sarah, age 50; Peter, age 27, farmer; <u>Calvin</u>, age 22; Catherine J., age 16; Harriet Ann, age 10; Elisabeth, age 20; all b. New Jersey
--1850 Census: Caldwell Twp., Essex Co., NJ: Henry T. Jacobus age 39, farmer; Mary, age 39; Amarintha, age 19; <u>Harriet</u>, age 16; Mary E., age 12; Sarah M., age 10; Leah E., age 8; Charles, age 5; George, age 3; Henrietta age 7 months; all born NJ (adj. to Leah Jacobus, age 72)
--1860 Census: Caldwell Twp., Essex Co., NJ: <u>Calvin</u> Francisco, age 31, farmer; <u>Harriet</u>, age 26; Sarah, age 59; Henry J., age 7; Sarah, age 4; Milton, age 1; all b. NJ

--1870 Census: 7 Wd., Newark, Essex Co., NJ: Calvin Francisco, age 42, huckster; Harriet L., age 36; Henry, age 17; Sarah, age 14; Milton, age 11; Sarah, age 70, at home; all b. New Jersey

--1880 Census: Newark, Essex Co., NJ: Calvin Francisco, age 55, butter merchant; Harriet L., age 45; Henry J., age 26, son, bookkeeper; Sarah, age 22, dau., hat trimmer;all b. New Jersey; 2 boarders

--1900 Census: 4 Wd. Newark, Essex Co., NJ: Sarah Demarest, age 42, b. Mar. 1858, widow, boarding house; Calvin Francisco, age 71, b. July 1828, father, widower; Edwin Francisco, age 18, nephew; also: boarders

- - - - -

Francisco, Henry*   b. (abt. 1798)
                          d. (January 15, 1885?)

wife, MARIA (Courter)
(Neafie, p.17)   b. (June 1, 1806)
(monument)   d. November 27, 1870

In
Memory of
Maria
wife of
Jacob Jacobus, Dec.d
and late wife of
Henry Francisco
who died
Nov. 27, 1870
aged
61 years 7 months
and 26 days

Notes:

--(?)NJ Death Record: "Mary Francisco, b. c.1796; d. June 26, 1847, age 51, married. spouse Henry Francisco"
--(?)NJ Death Record: "Henry Francisco b. c.1801, d. Jan. 15, 1885, Newark; age 84 years 10 months, widowed"
--Maria, dau. of Thomas C. Courter and Elizabeth Gould
--Maria Courter, m. #1, Dec. 30, 1828, Jacob Jacobus, q.v.
--Maria Courter, m. #2, Henry Francisco

--1850 Census:Caldwell Twp., Essex Co., NJ: Henry Francisco, age 52, farmer; James, age 22, farmer; Mariah, age 19; Eliza, age 17; Euphemia, age 19; all b. New Jersey
--1860 Census: Caldwell Twp., , Essex Co., NJ: Henry Francisco, age 62, no occupation listed; Maria, age 54; Harriet Jacobus, age 20; all b. New Jersey
--1880 Census: Newark, Essex Co., NJ: Sarah M. Williams, age 49, widow; Henry M. Williams, age 21, son, carpenter; Lizzie V. Williams, age 16, dau.; Henry "Francesco", age 80, father, widowed; all b. New Jersey

- - - - -

Francisco, HENRY   b. (abt. 1797)
(Neafie, p.20)   d. May 14, 1852
(monument)
(NJ Will #14204G,1852)

In
Memory of
Henry Francisco
Who died
March 14th, 1852
Aged 55 years

wife, SARAH (Courter)
(Neafie, p.20)   b. November 29, 1800
(monument)   d. January 15, 1888

Sarah Courter
wife of
Henry Francisco
Born Nov. 29, 1800
Died Jan. 15, 1888

Notes:
--Henry, son of Josiah Francisco and Sarah Jacobus
--Henry m. September 1818, Sarah Courter, dau. of Peter Courter and Maria Mead

--1850 Census: Caldwell Twp., Essex Co., NJ: <u>Henry</u> Francisco, age 53, farmer; <u>Sarah</u>, age 50; Peter, age 27, farmer; Calvin, age 22; Catherine J., age 16; Harriet Ann, age 10; Elizabeth, age 20; all b. New Jersey
--1860 Census: Caldwell, Essex Co., NJ: Calvin Francisco, age 31, farmer; Harriet, age 26; <u>Sarah</u>, age 59; Henry J., age 7; Sarah, age 4; Milton, age 1; all b. NJ
--1870 Census: 7 Wd, Newark, Essex Co., NJ: Calvin Francisco, age 42, huckster; Harriet L., age 36; Henry, age 17; Sarah, age 14; Milton, age 11; <u>Sarah</u>, age 70; all b. NJ
--1880 Census: Newark, Essex Co., NJ: Herbert Ehlors, age 40, b. Prussia, hat & ... store; Hattie, age 38, b. NJ; Jetta, age 11, b. NJ; <u>Sarah</u> Francisco, age 79, b. NJ widow, mother-in-law; 1 servant

- - - - -

Francisco, Henry*   b. October 8, 1835
(monument)   d. April 20, 1892

Henry Francisco
Born
Oct. 8, 1835
Died Apr. 20, 1892
-
Mary R. Van Ness

His Wife
Born Mar. 30, 1837
Died Apr. 4, 1926

wife, MARY R. (Van Ness) b. March 30, 1837
(monument)   d. April 4, 1926

daughter, ZILLAH   b. (abt. May 29, 1859
(Neafie, p.14)   d. December 20, 1861

Zillah
Daughter of
Henry and Mary R.
Francisco
Died Dec. 20, 1861
Aged 2 yrs. 6 mos. 21 days

daughter, LOUISA   b. (abt. September 8, 1866)
(Neafie, p.14)   d. March 30, 1871

Louisa
Daughter of
Henry and Mary R.
Francisco
Died March 30, 1871
Aged 4 years 6 months
and 22 days

Notes:
--Henry, son of Peter Francisco, q.v., and Abigail Gould
--Henry m. June 13, 1857, Mary Roome VanNess, dau. of Isaac J. Van Ness and Anne Roome

--1850 Census: Caldwell Twp., Essex Co., NJ: Peter Francisco, age 39, farmer; Abigail age 40; Elizabeth age 17; Henry age 15, farmer; Joanna, age 13; Marcus, age 11;

Rachel age 9; Josiah, age 7; Susan age 5; Ellen age 3; Sally Gould, age 50; all b. New Jersey; George Griffith, age 57, b. England, laborer

--1850 Census: Caldwell Twp., Essex Co., NJ: Isaac J. Vanness, age 36, farmer; Ann, age 37; Mary R., age 12; John, age 11; Caroline, age 10; Jane, age 7; Jacob Bush, age 50, laborer; all b. New Jersey

--1860 Census: Caldwell Twp., Essex Co., NJ: Henry Francisco, age 24, farmer; Mary R., age 23; Zillah, age 1; Michael, age 19, laborer; all b. New Jersey

--1870 Census: Caldwell Twp., Essex Co., NJ: Henry Francisco, age 33; Mary, age 32; Bertha, age 8; George, age 6; Louisa, age 3; all b. NJ

--1880 Census: Caldwell Twp., Essex Co., NJ: Henry Francisco, age 44, farmer; Mary R., age 43; Bertha, age 18; George, age 16; Harry, age 8; Mary, age 5; Frank, age 3; all b. New Jersey

--1900 Census: Caldwell Twp., Essex Co., NJ: 'Trapo' (Frank) Francisco, b. March 1876, single, farmer; Harry, b. May 1871, single, brother, farmer; Mary, age 64, mother, widow, b. March 1836; Henry Comfort, age 33, boarder, b. NY, farm labor

--1910 Census: Caldwell Twp., Essex Co., NJ: Mary Francisco, age 73, widow, 7 born 4 living, retired own income; Harry Francisco, son, single age 37, laborer odd jobs

- - - - -

Francisco, JOHN J. b. September 21, 1806)
(Neafie, p.13) d. April 5, 1880
(monument)
(NJ Will #19901G, 1880)

(Neafie)
John J. Francisco
Died Apr. 5, 1880
Aged 73 years 5 mos

& 15 days

(monument)
John J. Francisco
Born Sept. 21, 1806 Died April 5, 1880

-

His Wife
Rebecca Sindle
Born March 9, 1803 Died Jan. 10, 1873

wife, REBECCA (Sindle)	b. March 19, 1803
(Neafie, p.13)	d. January 10, 1873
(monument)	

(Neafie)
Rebecca
Wife of
John J. Francisco
Died Jan. 10, 1873
Aged 69 years
10 mos.

dau., HESTER	b. March 27, 1833
(monument)	d. March 15, 1899

Hester Francisco
Born
March 27, 1833
Died March 15, 1899

dau., EMMA	b. June 15, 1845
(monument)	d. (1926)

Emma Francisco
Born June 15, 1845

Notes:
--John, son of Josiah Francisco, q.v., and Sarah F. Jacobus

--John m. April 29, 1827, Rebecca Sindle

--1850 Census: Caldwell Twp., Essex Co., NJ: John J. Francisco, age 43, farmer; Rebecca, age 44; Hester, age 17; John, age 13; Emma, age 3; 2 laborers; adj. to Peter Francisco, age 39; all b. New Jersey

--1860 Census: Caldwell, Essex Co., NJ: John J. Francisco, age 53, farmer; Rebecca, age 54; Hetta, age 25, seamstress; John, age 23, laborer; Margaret, age 19; Emma, age 15; all b. New Jersey

--1870 Census: Caldwell, Essex Co., NJ: John 'G' Francisco, age 63, farmer; Rebecca, age 64; John, age 33, farmer; Emma age 20; Hester, age 37; all b. New Jersey

--1880 Census: Caldwell, Essex Co., NJ: John Francisco, age 43, 'single' farmer; Hester, age 47, sister; Emma, age 34, sister

--1900 Census: 4Wd, Montclair, Essex Co., NJ: Margaret Stagg, age 58; Emy Stagg, dau., age 22, clerk; Warren Stagg, son, age 17, bookkeeper?' Emma Francisco, boarder, age 54; John Francisco, boarder, age 63; all b. New Jersey

--1920 Census: 1Wd, East Orange, Essex Co., NJ: Margaret Stagg, age 78 widow; Warren Stagg, age 36, sgl. salesman advertising?; Harry, age 49, machinist unemployed; Emma Francisco, age 74, sister, single; Ralph H. Stagg, age 22, grandson, motorman trolley railway; all b. NJ

- - - - -

Francisco, JOSIAH   b. (November 23, 1767)
(Neafie, p.20)   d. November 18, 1842
(inscriptions, p.139)
(monument)
(NJ Will #13199G, 1842)

In
Memory of
Josiah Francisco

who died
Nov. 18th, 1842
Aged 74 Years
11 Months & 25 days

wife, SARAH F. (Jacobus)   b. (abt. March 7, 1775)
(Neafie, p.20)   d. February 14, 1834
(inscriptions, p. 139)
(monument)

In
Memory Of
Sarah Francisco
wife of
Josiah Francisco
who departed
this life
February 14th, 1834
Aged 58 years
11 Months and 7 days

Notes:
--Josiah, son of Henry Francisco and Margaret DeBaun
--Josiah m. August 9, 1794, Sarah F. Jacobus

--1830 Census: Caldwell Twp., Essex Co., NJ: <u>Josiah</u> "Francesco". 9 persons

- - - - -

Francisco, MARCUS   b. (abt. 1840)
(Neafie, p.14)   d. March 12, 1873
(NJ Will #17861G, 1873)

Marcus Francisco
Died March 23, 2873

Aged 33 years
Also his infant child

wife, Martha Louisa * (Wilson)
                       b. (abt. February 1840)
                       d. (betw. 1900 - 1910)

Infant   b. (1873)
                       d. (1873)

Notes:
--Marcus was son of Peter Francisco, q.v., and Abigail Gould
--Marcus m. 1866, Martha Louisa Wilson, dau. of Rev. Joseph Wilson and Mary Ann Taylor

--1850 Census: Caldwell Twp., Essex Co., NJ: Peter Francisco, age 39, farmer; Abigail age 40; Elizabeth age 17; Henry age 15, farmer; Joanna, age 13; Marcus, age 11; Rachel age 9; Josiah, age 7; Susan age 5; Ellen age 3; Sally Gould, age 50; all b. New Jersey; George Griffith, age 57, b. England, laborer
--1850 Census: Caldwell Twp., Essex Co., NJ: Joseph Wilson, age 53, b. England, clergyman 'R. Dutch Ch.'; Mary Ann, age 44, b. PA; Benjamin F., age 14, b. NY; Martha L., age 12, b. NY; Sarah G., age 6, b. NJ; Rebecca J., age 2, b. NY; Rosa McKenna, b. Ireland
--1860 Census: Caldwell Twp. Essex Co., NJ: Abba Francisco, age 50, farmer; Joanna, age 21; Marcus, age 20; Susan, age 14; Ellen age 12; Stephen, age 9; all b. NJ; 1 farm laborer
--1860 Census: Caldwell Twp., Essex Co., NJ: Rev. J. Wilson, age 63, b. England, R.D. Clergyman; Mariann, age 55 b. PA; Martha L., age 22, b. NY; Sarah G., age 16, b. NJ; Rebecca J., age 12, b. NY

--1870 Census: 8Wd, Newark, Essex Co., NJ: Mark Francisco, age 30, b. NJ, vinegar maker; Louisa, age 26, b. 'NJ'
--1870 Census: Caldwell Twp., Essex Co., NJ: Joseph Wilson, age 73, b. England, clergyman; Mary A., age 65, b. PA; Sarah G. age 24, b. NJ; Rebecca J., age 22, b. NY
--1880 Census: Brooklyn, Kings Co., NY: Martha L. Francisco, age 41, widow, b. NY, father b. England, mother b. PA, dress making; Reuben Francisco, son, age 8, b. NJ; R. J. Wilson, age 36, sister, single, b. NY, seamstress
--1900 Census: Montclair, Essex Co., NJ: Ruben Francisco, b. Oct. 1871, age 28, b. NJ, father NJ, mother NY, dairy business; Louisa Francisco, mother, widow, b. Feb. 1840, NY, father b. England, mother b. PA; Jennie Wilson, aunt, b. Jan. 1852, age 48, single, b. NY, father b. England
--1910 Census: Montclair, Essex Co., NJ: Rubin Francisco, age 38, single, b. NJ, clerk at milk co.; Rebecca J. Wilson, age 45, b. NY, no occupation

- - - - - -

Francisco, MILTON	d. 1858
	d. 1927
first wife, Annie*	b. (abt. 1858)
	d.
daughter, IDA BELL (Neafie, p.14)	b. January 22, 1879
	d. July 31, 1885

Ida Bell
daughter of
Milton and Annie
Francisco
Born Jan. 22, 1879
Died July 31, 1885

Notes:
--Milton, son of Calvin Francisco and Harriet L. Jacobus

--1860 Census: Caldwell, Essex Co., NJ: Calvin Francisco, age 31, farmer; Harriet, age 26; Sarah, age 59; Henry J., age 7; Sarah, age 4; Milton, age 1; all b. New Jersey
--1870 Census: 7Wd, Newark, Essex Co., NJ; Calvin Francisco, age 42, huckster; Harriet L., age 36; Henry age 17; Sarah, age 14; Milton, age 11; Sarah, age 70
--1880 Census: Newark, Essex Co., NJ: "Menlton" Francisco, age 24, coffin polisher; Anna, age 22; 'Cleo' (Ida), age 1; all b. New Jersey
--1895 NJ State Census: 2Wd, East Orange, Essex Co., NJ: Milton Francisco; Anna E.; Edwin; Harold
--?1900 Census: 35Wd., Philadelphia, PA: Milton Francisco, age 42, b. Nov. 1857 NJ, m. 1 yr., farmer; Sarah, age 49, b. May 1851, b. NJ
--?1910 Census: Montgomery Co., PA: Milton G. Francisco, age 55, servant; at res. of Jos. S. McCoulough
--?1920 Census, p.3B, Radnor Twp., Delaware Co. PA: Milton G. Francisco, age 61 b.NJ, widower, boarder

- - - - -

Francisco, PETER b. (April 8, 1811)
(Neafie, p.20) d. January 4, 1855
(NJ Will #14702G, 1855)

(Neafie)
Peter Francisco
Died Jan. 4, 1855
Aged 43 years 8 mos.
26 days

(monument)
Peter Francisco
Born Apr. 3, 1812 Died Jan. 4, 1855
Abigail

Born Nov. 3, 1809(?) Died Nov. 24, 1899(?)
Sarah
Born Nov. 13, 1837 Died June 20,. 1835
Josiah
Born July 3, 1844 Died July 1, 1858

-

wife, Abigail* (Gould) b. (November 3, 1809)
(monument) d. (May 24, 1896)

daughter, SARAH b. November 18, 1830
(Neafie, p. 20) d. January 20, 1835
(inscriptions, p. 139)

Sarah
daughter of
Peter and Abigail G.
Francisco
Born Nov. 18, 1830
Died Jan. 20, 1835
Aged 4 yrs. 2 mos. 2 days

son, JOSIAH b. (abt. July 9, 1844)
(Neafie, p.20) d. July 1, 1858

Josiah Francisco
Died July 1, 1858
Aged 13 years, 11 months
& 22 days

Notes:
--Peter, son of Josiah Francisco, q.v. and Sarah Jacobus
--Peter m. October 31, 1829, Abigail Gould; dau. of Josiah Gould and Elizabeth Colyer

--1850 Census: Caldwell Twp., Essex Co., NJ: Peter Francisco, age 39, farmer; Abigail age 40; Elizabeth age 17;

Henry age 15, farmer; Joanna, age 13; Marcus, age 11; Rachel age 9; <u>Josiah</u>, age 7; Susan age 5; Ellen age 3; Sally Gould, age 50; all b. New Jersey; George Griffith, age 57, b. England, laborer
--1860 Census: Caldwell Twp., Essex Co., NJ: <u>Abba</u> Francisco, age 50, farmer; Joanna, age 21; Marcus, age 20; Susan, age 14; Ellen age 12; Stephen, age 9; all b. NJ; 1 farm laborer
--1870 Census: Caldwell Twp., Essex Co., NJ: <u>Abigail</u> Francisco, age 60; Susan age 24; Ella, age 22, school teacher; Stephen age 19, farmer; all b. New Jersey; and 1 farm laborer
--1880 Census: Caldwell Twp., Essex Co., NJ: Stephen Francisco, age 29, b. NJ, milkman; Lydia, age 30 b. NY, parents b. NJ, wife; Wellington P., age 4, son, b. NJ; <u>Abbey</u>, age 60, b. NJ, mother, retired; Susan age 34, sister, b. NJ, dressmaker; 2 farm laborers; 2 servants

- - - - -

Francisco, PETER   b. (abt. August 30, 1823)
(Neafie, p.15)   d. July 23, 1862
(NJ Will #15616G, 1862)

Peter Francisco
Died July 23, 1862
Aged 38 years, 10 mos.
& 23 days

wife, Elizabeth* (Jacobus)   b. (abt. 1830)
    d. (October 8, 1892)

Notes:
--Peter H., son of Henry Francisco, q.v., and Sarah Courter
--Peter m. June 16, 1849, Elizabeth Jacobus, dau. of Jacob Jacobus, q.v., and Maria Courter
--Elizabeth, b. c.1830; d. Oct. 8, 1892, Caldwell; age 62, widow

--1850 Census: Caldwell Twp., Essex Co., NJ: Henry Francisco, age 53, farmer; Sarah, age 50; Peter, age 27, farmer; Calvin, age 22; Catherine J., age 16; Harriet Ann, age 10; Elizabeth, age 20; all b. New Jersey
--1860 Census: Caldwell Twp., Essex Co., NJ: Peter H. Francisco, age 36, farmer; Elizabeth, age 30; Sarah H. age 7; Frank, age 1; all b. New Jersey
--1870 Census: Caldwell Twp., Essex Co., NJ: Elizabeth 'Francies', age 41 Barney H. Francisco., age 18, farmer; Jane, age 16; Frank, age 11; a.. b. New Jersey
--1880 Census: Caldwell Twp., Essex Co., NJ: Elizabeth Francisco, age 50, widow, farmer; Henry B., age 28, farmer; Jane S., age 26; Frank, age 21; all b. New Jersey

- - - - -

Francisco, William   See: Pearce Burial Ground
wife, Harriet

- - - - -

GARRABRANT

Garrabrant, Abraham A.*   b. (abt. September 1833)
                            d. (aft. 1910)

first wife, SARAH JANE (Riker)
(Neafie, p.5)   b. (abt. November 28, 1839)
                            d. May 20, 1875

Sarah Jane
wife of
Abraham A. Garabrant
Died
May 20, 1875
Aged 35 years 5 months

and 22 days

son, infant b. (abt. May 7, 1859)
(Neafie, p.4) d. May 28, 1859

*Infant Son
Aged 21 days
Children of
Abraham A. and Sarah J.
Garabrant*

son, IRA b. (abt. May 10, 1860)
(Neafie, p.4) d. March 14, 1863

*Aged 2 yrs. 10 mos. 4 ds.
Children of
Abraham A. and Sarah J.
Garabrant*

Notes:
--Abraham A., son of Abraham Garrabrant and Sarah .....
--Abraham m. July 4, 1858, Sarah Jane Riker, daughter of John Riker, q.v., and Ann Smith
--?Abraham m. #2, aft. 1875, Martha ..... (Stager?); b. abt. Feb. 1836; d. bef. 1900.
--?Abraham Garrabrant b. Sept. 11, 1837; d. Nov. 20, 1912; bur. Old Burying Ground, Brookdale, Essex Co., New Jersey

--1850 Census: Bloomfield Twp., Essex Co., N: Sarah Garrabrant, age 49; Abram, age 16, laborer; Ellen, age 14; Rachel A., age 12; Henry, age 9; 'Garet', age 6; Cornelius, age 3; all b. New Jersey
--1850 Census: Acquackanonk Twp., Passaic Co., NJ: John Riker, age 44, hotel keeper; Ann, age 41; Ellen, age 21; Hester A., age 13; Sarah J., age 10; all b. NJ; 7 'lodgers?'

--1860 Census: Little Falls P.O., Acquackanonk Twp., Passaic Co., NJ: <u>Abram</u> 'Garribrant' age 25, farmer; <u>Sarah</u>, age 21; William, age 1 month

--1870 Census, p.237, Little Falls, Passaic Co., NJ: <u>Abr. A.</u> Garrabrant, age 36, wagonmaker; <u>Sarah J.</u>, age 30; Emma, age 7; Thos. R. "Marr" (Morrell), age 40; Hester A. Marr, age 33; Susan Marr, age 12; Abr. VanRiper, age 21, farm labor; all b. 'NJ'

--??1870 Census: Little Falls, Passaic Co., NJ: Catherine Riker, age 70, keeping house; Jane? Smalley; Chas. H. Smalley; Susan Smalley; George Smalley; <u>Martha</u> Stager, age 32; Lorena Stager, age 10; Jenny Stager, age 9; John Stager, age 7; Mary Stager, age 4; Julia B. Stager, age 2; John Haslem, age 13, farm labor; all b. NJ

--1871-1873: <u>A. A.</u> Garrabrant: Surveyor of Highways, Little Falls

--1879-1883: Paterson City Directories: <u>Abram A.</u> Garrabrant: wheelwright

--1880 Census: Little Falls, Passaic Co., NJ: <u>Martha</u> "Garabrant" age 40, keeping house; <u>Abram</u> Garabrant, age 46, wheelwright; Emma Garabrant, age 17; Bertha Garabrant, age 10; 'Lorena' Stager, age 20, wks. carpet factory; John Riker, age 17, wks. carpet factory; Mary Riker, age 14, works carpet factory; Jennie Riker, age 12, wks. carpet factory (prob. children of James and Henrietta Riker); Lizzie Youngs, age 6 'at home'; Lillie Youngs, age 3, 'at home' (children of John and Eliza Jane Youngs); all b. New Jersey

--1895 NJ State Census: Little Falls, Passaic Co., NJ: <u>Abram</u> A. Garrabrandt; <u>Martha</u> Garrabrants

--1900 Census: Little Falls, Passaic Co., NJ: <u>Abraham A.</u> 'Garrabraut' b. September 1833, m. 18 yr., wheelwright; <u>Martha</u> b. Feb. 1836, 6 born 6 living; both b. NJ

--1910 Census: Little Falls, Passaic Co., NJ: Emma Stinson, age 47, widow, 10 born 8 living; William, age 27, weaver at carpet mill; Robert, age 21, weaver at carpet mill; Eva, age 25; Stella, age 17; Herbert, age 19, weaver at carpet mill;

Ethel age 12; Helen, age 8; <u>Abraham A.</u> Garrabrant, age 76, father, widower; all b. NJ

- - - - -

GILBERT

Gilbert, LESLIE (monument)	b. 1842 d. 1907
wife, Margaret E.*	b. (1841) d.

Leslie Gilbert
1842-1907

Notes:
Served: <u>Civil War:</u> Co. B., 1st Reg't, NJ Inf. and US Navy
--1880 Census: 2 Dist. Caldwell, Essex Co., NJ: <u>Leslie</u> Gilbert, age 39 b. OH, father b. Ireland, mother b. NJ, bank clerk; Margaret E., age 38 b. NY, parents b. NJ
--1900 Census: Caldwell Twp., Essex Co., NJ: <u>Leslie</u> Gilbert, age 58, b. Apr. 1842, m.34 yr. b. OH, father b. Ireland, mother b. NJ, treasurer of binding co.; Margaret E., age 58, b. July 1841, 3 born 3 living, b. NY, parents b. NJ

- - - - -

GOODRICH

Goodrich, Bethuel*	b. (September 10, 1821) d. (May 24, 1885)
first wife, Sarah* (Tilman)	b. (abt. 1823) d. (bef. 1857)
second wife, Mary C.* (Jacobus)	

                    b. (abt. 1833)
                    d. (December 8, 1899)

son, JUDSON P.   b. (abt. October 10, 1866)
(Neafie, p.8)   d. April 10, 1868

*Judson P.
Son of
Bethuel and Mary C.
Goodrich
Died Apr. 10, 1868
Aged 1 year and 5 months*

Notes:
--Bethuel served: Civil War, Co. F, 1st NJ Regiment
--Bethuel, son of Cyprian Goodrich and Anna DeCue
--Bethuel m. February 1, 1843, Sarah Tilman
--Bethuel m. January 4, 1857, Mary C. Jacobus, dau. of Peter Jacobus, q.v., and Eliza Ann Oliver

--1850 Census: Byram Twp., Sussex Co., NJ: Bethuel Goodrich, age 28; Sarah, age 27; William C., age 3; all b. New Jersey
--1860 Census: Caldwell, Essex Co., NJ: Bethuel Goodrich age 38, tobacco seller; Mary C., age 27; William C., age 14; Lucy A., age 8; Charles L., age 2; Frank L. age 1; Edgar Williams, age 8; all b. New Jersey
--1870 Census: 1 Wd., Newark, Essex Co., NJ: Bethuel Goodrich, age 48, tobacco pedlar; Mary C., age 35; 'Jeremiah' age 24, clerk in store; Lucy, age 18; Charles L., age 13; Frank W., age 11; Elmer E., age 9; George L., age 6; "Leopold C., son" age 4; all b. New Jersey
--1880 Census : Newark, Essex Co., NJ: "Bethual Goadrick" age 58 b. NJ, father b. VT, mother b. NJ, clerk in store; Mary C., age 47; Charles L., age 22, works tobacco; Elmer E., age 18, works tobacco; George L., age 15, cotton works; "Cora L., daughter" age 9; Sarah Rearson, age 51, domestic help;

all b. New Jersey
--1890 Veterans Schedule, Newark, NJ: "<u>Bethens</u> Goodrich" Co. F, 1st NJ Reg't.
--1891 Newark City Directory: <u>Mary C.</u> Goodrich, widow of Bethuel

- - - - -

HALL

Hall, Ogden*
    b. (September 17, 1801)
    d. (May 3, 1857)

wife, Maria* (VanSaun Neafie)
    b. (April 21, 1815)
    d. (October 15, 1875)

son, JAMES THEODORE   b. (August 31, 1839)
(Neafie, p.1)   d. May 3, 1840
(inscriptions, p. 139)

James Theodore
son of
Ogden & Maria Neafie Hall
Died May 3, 1840
aged 8 months, 3 days

Notes:
--Ogden Hall, b. September 17, 1801, East Haddam Connecticut; son of Sylvester Hall and Margaret .....
--Ogden Hall m. Dec. 7, 1838, Maria VanSaun Neafie, dau. of John Richard Neafie and Sarah Doremus
--Maria, sister of Catherine Eugenia Neafie who m. George VanNess, q.v.
--members Little Falls, Reformed Church
--Capt. Major Dey built a one story stone house in Little Falls..."In 1848 April 10 the date of the spring election that

year this house was burned to the ground being occupied at the time by Ogden Hall and family." (*Preakness and the Preakness Ref. Church. p.33* George W. Labaw. NY. 1902)

--1840 Census: Acquackanonk Twp., Passaic Co.,NJ: Ogden Hall; adj. to John R. Neafie
--1848, Little Falls, New Jersey
--1850 Census: Acquackanonk, Passaic Co., NJ: John "K. Nafie", age 59 farmer; Sarah, age 53; Aaron B., age 28, teamster; Emeline, age 20; Eugenia age 17; Jeptha H., age 14, all b. New Jersey
--1860 Census: 9Wd, Dist. 4, New York City: George 'Vanhees' (VanNess) age 26 b. NY, silversmith; 'Virginia' age 24 b. NJ; Alice age 4 b. NY; Emeline age 2 months b. NY; Maria Hall, age 43, b. NJ
--1870 Census: 9Wd, Dist. 14, New York City: John McGilvery, age 38, b. Ireland, tailor; Sarah 29 b. NJ; John 9 b. NY; Ogden 5, b. NY; James age 1 b. NY; Maria Hall, age 55, b. NJ (Adj. to Stephen and Sarah Nafie family)

- - - - -

HAMMA

Hamma, William*	b. (November 15, 1817)
	d. (April 4, 1900)
	(bur. Ref. Church Cemetery Montville, N.J.)
wife, Lucinda* (Pier)	b. (March 5, 1820)
	d. (Janaury 2, 1889)
	(bur. Ref. Church Cemetery Montville, N.J.)
son, DAVID H. (Neafie, p.18)	b. (abt. July 9, 1842)
	d. January 29, 1851

David H. Hamma
Died Jan. 29, 1851
Aged 8 years 6 months
and 20 days
Children of
William and Lucinda Hamma

son, JOHN   b. (abt. Feb. 1851)
(Neafie, p.18)   d. August 23, 1851

John Hamma
Died Aug. 23, 1851
Aged 6 mos.
Children of
William and Lucinda Hamma

Notes:
--William, son of Cornelius Hamma and Maria VanNess
--William m. Lucinda Pier, dau. of John I. Pier and Sarah ...

--1850 Census: Pequannock Twp., Morris Co., NJ: William 'Hamm' age 33, b. NJ, farmer; Lucinda, age 27, b. NJ; David, age 7 b. NJ; Mary A., age 4, b. NJ; 1 labor; 1 domestic
--1860 Census: Bridgewater Twp., Somerset Co., NJ: William Hamma, age 42, b. NJ, farm laborer; Lucinda, age 36; Mary A., age 14; Arthur, age 8 months
--1870 Census: Montville, Morris Co., NJ: William Hamma, age 53, b. NJ, farmer; Lucinda, age 47, b. NJ; Arthur age 10, b. NJ; William Kearney, age 73, b. NJ, farm laborer
--1880 Census: Montville, Morris Co., NJ: William "Hammia" age 63, farmer; Lucinda, age 57
--1895 NJ Census: Montville, Morris Co., NJ: Arthur W. Hamma, Emma J.; Maude A.; Floyd L; Bessie O; William Hamma

- - - - -

HENNIE

Hennie, Frederick C. *   b. (October 29, 1867)
                            d. (1945)

first wife, IDA (Demarest) b. November 26, 1869
(Neafie, p.12)   d. December 6, 1892
(another monument)   (Laurel Grove Mem. Park,
                            Totowa, New Jersey)

Ida Demarest
wife of
F. C. Hennie
Born Nov. 28, 2869
Died Dec. 6, 1892

Notes:
--Frederick, son of Christian Hennie and Christina Young
--Frederick m. #1, aft. 1880, Ida Elizabeth Demarest, dau of John Demarest and Maria E. Garrison
--Frederick m.#2, Sept. 20, 1896, Jane C. Hutton

--1870 Census: Wayne Twp., Passaic Co., NJ: James M. Demarest, age 50, farmer; Sarah, age 50; John, age 27; Maria, age 25; Ida, age 1 month; George, age 23; Hannah, age 21; Lyman, age 16; all b. NJ
--1880 Census: Wayne Twp., Passaic Co., NJ: John 'Demerest' age 37 b. NJ, laborer; Mariah E., wife, age 34, b. NY, parents b. NJ; Ida, dau., age 10, b. NJ; Monroe James, age 7, b. NJ; Charles, son, age 4 b. NJ
--1900 Census: Totowa Borough, Passaic Co., NJ: F. C. Hennie, b. October 1867, m.13 (3) yr. b. NY, parents b. Switzerland, station agent; Jennie C. b. Nov. 1868 England, parents b. England; Roy, b. Nov. 1888 NJ; Hazel b. Oct. 1899 NJ; adj. to Samuel Ruddrick, age 64 b. England, r.r. gateman

--1910 Census: Little Falls, Passaic Co., NJ: Fred C. "Hennis" age 40, m. #2 for 13 years, b. NY, parents b. Germany, telegraph operator; 'Jennie', age 40, m. #2 for 13 years, b. England, 4 born, 3 living; Roy Bosman, age 21, b. NJ, bookkeeper at insurance co.; Hazel, age 10, b. NJ; F. Claire, age 6, b. NJ

--1920 Census: Little Falls, Passaic Co., NJ: Fred C. Hennie, age 52, b. NY, parents b. Switzerland, mgr. coal business; 'Fannie' C., age 51, b. Ireland, parents b. Englnad; Hazel M., age 20, b. NJ, stenographer at water factory; Fred C., age 15, b. NJ

--1930 Census: Little Falls, Passaic Co., NJ; Frederick C. Hennie, age 62, b. NJ, father b. Scotland, mother b. NJ, coal dealer; Jane C. age 60, b. NY, parents b. Switzerland

- - - - -

HILL
HILLIKER

Hill, John*	b. (abt. 1849)
	d. (bef. 1895)
wife, Jennie E.* (Jacobus)	b. (abt. 1850)
	d. (aft. 1920)
dau., BLANCHE E.	b. 1869
(monument)	d. 1888 (August 20)
Hilliker, GEORGE	b. 1826
(monument)	d. 1896 (June 30)

George Hilliker
1826 - 1896

-

Blanche E. Hill
1869 - 1888

Notes:
--Blanche, granddaughter of Thomas Jacobus, q.v. and Sarah C. (Hilliker) Jacobus; niece of George Hilliker
--Death record: Blanche E. Hill, b. 1870 d. Aug. 20, 1888, Wayne, NJ; aged 18 years 8 months

--1850 Census: Wayne Twp., Passaic Co., NJ: Thomas Jacobus, age 34, carpenter; Sarah age 31; Jane, age 5
--1860 Census: Wayne Twp., Passaic Co., NJ: Thomas Jacobus, age 36, b. NJ, farmer; Sarah, age 35, b. NY; Jane, age 12, b. NJ; George, age 8, b. NJ; James, age 6, b. NJ; Laura, age 4, b. NJ
--1870 Census: Wayne Twp., Passaic Co., NJ: Sarah C. Jacobus, age 40, b. NY; George W., age 19; Jas. J., age 17; Samuel A., age 14; Marilla, age 8; all children b. NJ; adj. to Jno W. Hill, age 23, b. NY, carpenter; Jennie E. Hill, age 22, b. NY; Blanche A. Hill, age 3 months b. NY
--1875 NY State Census: Ramapo, Rockland Co., NY: John W. Hill, age 28; Jane, age 27; Blanch, age 6
--1880 Census: Haverstraw, Rockland Co., NY: John Hill, age 31, b. NY, farm labor; Jennie, age 30 b. NY; Blanche E., age 10, b. NJ; Grace E., age 8, b. NJ; Frank, age 3, b. NY; Ellis, age 1, b. NY
--1895 NJ State Census: Wayne Twp., Passaic Co., NJ: Mrs. Jennie E. Hill; Sarah C. Jacobus; Frank Hill; Ellis Hill; Nettie Hill
--1900 Census: Wayne Twp., Passaic Co., NJ: Jennie Hill, age 50, b. Dec. 1849, widow, 4 born 3 living, b. NY, parents b. NY, stenographer; Nettie, dau., age 11 b. April 1889 NY
--1910 Census: Wayne Twp., Passaic Co., NJ: Jennie E. Hill, age 61, widow, 5 born 4 living, b. NY, father b. NJ, mother b. NY; Nettie, age 21, b. NY, father b. NJ, mother b. NY, sales lady at dept. store
--1920 Census: Wallkill, Orange Co., NY: Percy G. Roe, age 38, b. NY, switchman C... RR; Etta, age 39, b. NY; Bernice

E., b. NY age 6; Jenny Hill, age 70, mother-in-law, widow, b. NY
--?Monument: Jennie E. Hill "1848-1914": Laurel Grove Memorial Park, Totowa, Passaic Co., NJ

--George, prob. brother of Sarah C. (Hilliker) Jacobus, wife of Thomas Jacobus, q.v.
--Death record: George W. Hilliker b. c.1828; d. June 30, 1896, Wayne, Passaic Co., NJ; age 68 years 11 months; b. US; single, seaman; res. 15 years

- - - - -

HOPKINS

Hopkins, Henry T. with, Catherine — See: Pearce Burial Ground

- - - - -

HOPPER

Hopper, Hassell* b. (March 15, 1772)
  d. (before October 1844)

widow, ANN (Dey) b. (abt. October 18, 1773)
(Neafie, p.12) d. October 18, 1844
(monument)
(inscriptions, p. 139)

Ann Dye
widow of
Hassell Hopper
died Oct. 18th, 1844
aged 71 years

Notes:
--Hassel, son of John Hendrick Hopper and Feytje Doremus.
--Hassel m. March 5, 1796, at Caldwell, Ann Doremus Dey, dau. of John Dey and Jane Doremus
--?1830 Census: Saddle River, Bergen Co., NJ: "Anny" Hopper: 1 male age 10-14; 1 female age 10-14; 1 female age 50 - 59

- - - - -

HOWE

Howe, Amos*   b. (February 19, 1830)
                       d. (June 16, 1908))

wife, Julia Matilda (Cruse)
                       b. (June 17, 1823)
                       d. (June 15, 1916)

son, JAMES ELI   b. April 19. 1852
(Neafie, p.6)   d. August 5, 1852

Esther Cook
Died June 30, 1852
Aged 66 years
also her great grandson, James E.
infant son of Amos and Julia
Died Aug. 11, 1852
Aged 4 months

Notes:
--Amos, son of Eli Howe and Jane Elizabeth Cook, dau. of Henry Francis Cook, q.v., and Esther .....
--James, son of Amos, is buried with his great-grandmother, Esther Cook, wife of Henry Francis Cook, q.v.

--1870 Census: 17Wd, Salt Lake City, Salt Lake Co., Utah Territory: Amos Howe, age 40 b. NY, freighter; Julia, age 45, b. England; Edgar, age 15, b. MO; George, age 12, b. MO; Charles, age 10 b. MO
--1880 Census: Salt Lake City, Salt Lake Co., UT: Amos Howe, age 50 b. NY, machinist foreman; Julia, age 56, b. England; Geo. Edw., age 21 b. MO, machinist; Charles R., age 19 b. MO, moulder; 1 servant
--1900 Census: 3Wd, Salt Lake City, Salt Lake Co. UT: Amos Howe, b. February 1830, b. IN, parents b. NY, mfg. iron & brass; Julia, b. June 1823, England; 1 servant
--1910 Census: 3Wd, Salt Lake City, Salt Lake Co. UT: Julia C. Howe, age 87, widow, b. England, 6 born 3 living; 1 servant

- - - - -

HUSK

Husk, Abram widow, Esther	See: Pearce Burial Ground

- - - - -

Husk, Marcus E.*	b. (March 7, 1850) d. (1938) bur. (Prospect Hill Cemetery, Caldwell, N.J.)
wife, Lavenia* (Ryerson)	b. (July 1848) d. (1914) bur. (Prospect Hill Cemetery, Caldwell, N.J.)
daughter, FLORENCE E. (Neafie, p. 17) (monument)	b. (abt. March 19, 1879) d. December 19, 1887

Florence E. Husk
Died Dec. 29, 1887
Aged 8 years 9 months
and 10 days
At Rest
Gone
But Not Forgotten

Notes:
--Marcus, son of Abraham Husk, and Esther Crane
--Marcus m. Nov. 24, 1870, Lavinia, dau. of Peter F. Ryerson, q.v., and Elizabeth Dod
--?Marcus m. #2, Louisa or Carrie; see 1930 Census

--1850 Census: Caldwell Twp., Essex Co., NJ: Abraham Husk age 48, farmer; Esther, age 46; Marcus, age 4 months; 9 other children; all b. NJ
--1850 Census: Wayne Twp., Passaic Co., NJ: Peter F. Ryerson, age 31, b. NJ, wheelwright; Elizabeth, age 30; 'Lavina' age 3; 4 other children; all b. New Jersey
--1860 Census: Caldwell, Essex Co., NJ: Esther Husk, age 56, farmer; William, age 19; Abba, age 14; Thomas, age 12; Marcus, age 10; 1 laborer; all b. New Jersey
--1860 Census: Caldwell Twp., Essex Co., NJ: Peter F. Ryerson, age 42, farmer; Elizabeth, age 40; Lavinia, age 13; 7 other children
--1870 Census: Kearney, Hudson Co., NJ: Marcus Husk, age 22, carpenter; 'Leana' age 21; Charlotte, age 1; Henry, age 18, carpenter; all b. New Jersey
--1880 Census: Newark, Essex Co., NJ: 'Mark' Husk, age 30, carpenter; Lavenia, age 33; Peter, age 10; Wilber, age 7; 'Florence' age 1; ... N. Gilliland, age 22, nephew, brickmason; Wilber Ryerson, age 20, brother-in-law; all b. New Jersey
--1900 Census: 8Wd, Newark, Essex Co., NJ: Marcus E. Husk b. March 1850, m.31 yr, b. NJ, carpenter; Lavenia, b.

July 1848 NJ; Wilbur C. Ryerson, b. March 1873, brother-in-law, carpenter;
--1910 Census: 8Wd, Newark, Essex Co., NJ: Marcus E. Husk, age 60, m. 40 yr. b. NJ, carpenter builder; Lavenia, age 63 b. NJ
--1920 Census: 5Wd. East Orange, Essex Co., NJ: Marcus Husk, age 69, b. NJ, retired; "Louisa", age '53', b. NJ; also two 'friends"
--1930 Census: 11 Wd. Newark, Essex Co., NJ: "Markus" Husk, age 80, b. NJ, retired; "Carrie", age 63, wife, b. NJ

- - - - -

Husk, Richard   See: Pearce Burial Ground
wife, Anna A.

- - - - -

Husk, Stephen   See: Pearce Burial Ground
wife, Rachel

- - - - -

Husk, WILLIAM   b. January 7, 1841
(Neafie, p. 9)   d. August 19, 1889

William Husk
Born Jan. 7, 1841
Died Aug. 29. 1889

wife, Rachel Ann* (Jacobus)
                b. (abt. 1845
                d. (aft 1930?)

Notes:
--William, son of Abraham Husk, q.v., and Esther Crane

--William m. Rachel Ann Jacobus, dau. of Thomas G. Jacobus, q.v., and Emeline Vanderhoof

--1850 Census: Caldwell Twp., Essex Co., NJ: Abraham Husk, age 48, farmer; Esther, age 46; Stephen, age 19, farmer; Eliza, age 16; Lucetta, age 16; John, age 14; Richard, age 11; William, age 9; Alfred, age ; Abby R., age 5; Thomas, age 3; Marcus, age 4 months; all b. New Jersey
--1850 Census: Caldwell, Essex Co., NJ: Thomas G. Jacobus, age 35; Emeline, age 29; Rachel Ann, age 8
--1860 Census: Caldwell, Essex Co., NJ: Esther Husk, age 56, farmer; William, age 19; Abba, age 14; Thomas, age 12; Marcus, age 10; Harry Campbell, age 20, laborer; all b. New Jersey
--1860 Census: Caldwell, Essex Co., NJ: Thos. Jacobus, age 44; Emeline, age 40; Rachel A., age 18
--1870 Census: Beaver Twp., Polk Co., Iowa: Wm. Husk, age 29, farmer; Rachel, age 28; Estella age 6; Frank, age 1; all b. New Jersey
--1880 Census: Caldwell, Essex Co., NJ: Thomas G. Jacobus, age 65, farmer; Emeline, age 60; William Husk, age 39, son-in-law, farmer; Rachel Ann Husk, age 35, daughter; Estella Husk, age 15, granddaughter; Frank Husk, age 10, grandson; Henry VanWart, age 57, farm labor; all b. NJ
--1900 Census, Caldwell Twp., Essex Co, NJ: Frank Husk, age 31, farmer; Lottie E., age 31; 5 children; Rachel A., age 58, mother, age 58, b. Jan. 1842, widow; all b. NJ
--1910 Census: 2 Wd., Paterson, Passaic Co., NJ: Frank Husk, age 41, mgr. beef house; Lottie, age 41; 7 children; Rachel A. Husk, age 65, mother, widow; all b. NJ
--1920 Census: 7Wd, Paterson, Passaic Co,. NJ: Frank Husk, age 51, wid., butcher; Ida, age 17, dau,; Clarence, age 16, son, Mildred, age 13, dau.; Rachel A. Husk, age 77, mother, widow; all b. New Jersey
--?1930 Census, West Paterson, Passaic Co., NJ: Robert Neubold, age 28, sign painter; Ida, age 28; Frank, age 8;

Lois, age 4; <u>Rachel</u> Husk, age 88 (grand?) mother-in-law; all b. New Jersey

- - - - -

JACOBUS

Jacobus, CORNELIUS R.   b. April 28, 1807
(Neafie, p.12)   d. May 11, 1869
(monument)

Cornelius R. Jacobus
Born
Apr. 28, 1807
Died May 11, 1869
Rest In Peace

wife, ANN (Hopper)   b. April 24, 1817
(monument)   d. January 28, 1902

Ann Hopper
Wife of
Cornelius R. Jacobus
Born
Apr. 24th, 1817
Died
Jan. 28th, 1902

daughter, MARY C.   b. October 30, 1843
(Neafie, p.12)   d. April 13, 1847
(inscriptions, p. 139)
(monument)

Mary C.
daughter of
Cornelius and Ann Jacobus
Born October 30. 1843

Died April 13 1847

Notes:
--Cornelius Jacobus m. Feb. 1, 1835, Anna Hopper
--1850 Census, Wayne Twp., Passaic Co., NJ: <u>Cornelius R.</u> Jacobus, age 42, farmer; <u>Ann</u>, age 36; Ann S., age 14; Jane, age 11; Peter R., age 50; all b. NJ
--1860 Census, Wayne Twp., Passaic Co., NJ: <u>Cornelius R.</u> Jacobus, age 52, farmer; <u>Ann</u>, age 45; Jane, age 20, house keeper; Jeremiah Berdan, age 30, farmer; Ann Berdan, age 23; Lizzy Berdan, age 5; Cornelius Berdan, age 8 months; all b. New Jersey
--1870 Census, Wayne Twp., Passaic Co., NJ: Geo. R. Berdan, age 34, farmer; Jane, age 30; Chas. C., age 2; <u>Ann</u> Jacobus, age 55; all b. New Jersey
--1880 Census, Wayne Twp., Passaic Co., NJ: Jeremiah R. Berdan, age 49, farmer; Anna S. Berdan, age 43; Elizabeth Hopper, age 24, daughter; Richard P. Berdan, age 4, son; <u>Ann</u> Jacobus, age 65, mother-in-law; all b. New Jersey
--1900 Census, Wayne Twp., Passaic Co., NJ: Richard Berdan, age 24, farmer; Lily, age 22; Ada, age 6 months; Anna S., age 63, mother b. Nov. 1836, widow; <u>Anna</u> Jacobus, age 86, grandmother, age 86 b. "Aug. 1813", widow; all b. New Jersey

- - - - -

Jacobus, Garrett*	b. (November 9, 1776)
	d. (bef. 1830?)
wife, RACHEL (Dey) (Neafie, p.11)	b. (abt. December 17, 1779)
	d. October 5, 1868

Rachel Day
wife of
Garrett Jacobus
Died Oct. 5 1868

In the 90th year
of her age

Notes:
--Garret, son of James/Jacobus Jacobus and Maria Sisco
--Garret m. February 10, 1798, Rachel Dey, dau. of John Dey and Jane Doremus

--1830 Census: Caldwell Twp., Essex Co., NJ: <u>Rachel</u> Jacobus: 3 persons; (same page as Cornelius Dey)
--1840 Census: Caldwell Twp., Essex Co., NJ: <u>Rachel</u> Jacobus (same page as Cornelius Dey)
--1850 Census: Caldwell Twp., Essex Co., NJ: Daniel A. Vanderhoof, age 20, farmer; Margaret, age 29; Mary M., age 10 months: <u>Rachel</u> Jacobus, age 69; all b. New Jersey
--1860 Census: Caldwell, Essex Co., NJ: "Dun" Vanderhoof, age 30, farmer; Margaret, age 41; Margaret M., age 11; <u>Rachel</u> Jacobus, age 80; Jacob Jacobus, age 42, laborer; all b. New Jersey

- - - - -

Jacobus, Jacob*   b. (abt. 1805)
                          d. (bef. 1850)

wife, MARIA (Courter)
(Neafie, p.17)   b. (abt. June 1806)
(monument)   d. November 27, 1870

In
Memory of
Maria
wife of
Jacob Jacobus, Dec.d
and late wife of
Henry Francisco
who died

Nov. 27, 1870
aged
61 years 7 months
and 26 days

daughter, HARRIET   b. (abt. October 9, 1830
(Neafie, p.18)   d. January 25, 1861

Harriet
daughter of Jacob and Maria
Jacobus
Died Jan. 25, 1861
Aged 30 years 3 mos.
and 16 days

son, JOTHAM   b. (abt. April 18, 1832)
(Neafie, p.18)   d. July 15?, 1862

Jotham Jacbous
Died July 15(?), 1862
Aged 30 years. 2 months
and 27 days

Notes:
--Jacob, son of Aaron Jacobus
--Jacob m. December 30, 1828, Maria Courter, dau. of Thomas C. Courter and Elizabeth Gould
--Maria m. #2, aft. 1850, Henry Francisco, q.v.

--1850 Census: Caldwell Twp., Essex Co., NJ: Mariah Jacobus, age 45; Angeline, age 18; Jotham, age 16, carpenter; Harriet, age 10; all b. New Jersey
--1850 Census: Caldwell Twp., Essex Co., NJ: Henry Francisco, age 52, farmer; James, age 22, farmer; Mariah, age 19; Eliza, age 17; Euphemia, age 19; all b. New Jersey

--1860 Census: Caldwell, Essex Co., NJ: Henry Francisco, age 62, no occupation listed; Maria, age 54; Harriet Jacobus, age 20; all b. New Jersey

- - - - -

Jacobus, James G. See Pearce Burial Ground
wife, Sarah

- - - - -

Jacobus, JAMES O. b. (abt. April 1835)
(Neafie, p.8) d. June 10, 1868
(monument)

James O. Jacobus
Died June 10, 1868
Aged 33 years 1 month
& 12 days

wife, Hetty Ann* (VanNess)
  b. (abt. 1836)
  d. (1905)

Notes:
--James Oliver Jacobus, son of Peter Jacobus, q.v., and Eliza Ann Oliver
--James m. March 20, 1858, Hetty Ann (Hester) VanNess, dau. of Peter VanNess and Sarah Ann VanHouten
--Hetty/Hester m. #2, Peter F. Ryerson, q.v., son of Francis Ryerson and Margaret Doremus

--1850 Census: Caldwell Twp., Essex Co., NJ: Peter Jacobus, age 40, farmer; Eliza Ann, age 43; Mary C., age 17; James O., age 15, farmer; Martha W.?, age 13; Sarah, age 11; Emma H., age 9; Julia A., age 7; Delia A., age 4; William C., age 1; Daniel Vanderhoof, age 21, laborer; all b. New Jersey

--1850 Census: Caldwell Twp., Essex Co., NJ: Peter VanNess, age 28, shoemaker; Sally Ann age 37; Henry age 17, tobacconist; Hetty Ann age 14; Martha J. age 12; Harriet E. age 10; Phebe Louisa age 7; Josephine age 5; Charlotte A., age 1; Henry T. VanNess age 76, farmer

--1860 Census: Caldwell, Essex Co., NJ: Jas. "D" Jacobus, age 25, clerk; Hetty A., age 24; Marcus J., age 1; Martha W. age 23, seamstress; all b. NJ

--1870 Census: Caldwell, Essex Co., NJ: Hetty A. Jacobus, age 33; Lewis P. age 8; Sarah A., age 6; Jacob VanNess, age 21, cigar maker; Albert Campbell, age 16, works at tobacco factory; all b. New Jersey

--1880 Census: Port Royal, Caroline Co., VA: Peter F. Ryerson, age 63, b. NJ, farmer; Hettie A., wife age 44, b. NJ; George C., age 26, son, b. NJ brick mason; Ada B., age 7, dau. b. NJ; Herbert age 8, son, b. NJ; Ella M., age 4, dau., b. NJ; Earnest, son, age 2, b. VA; 3 other persons

--1900 Census: Port Royal, Caroline Co., VA: Hettie Ryerson, age 63, b. June 1836 NJ, widow, farmer (post mistress); Earnest V., age 21, b. VA, farm labor; Hattie L. Marshall, age 16, b. VA, granddaughter; 1 farm laborer

- - - - -

Jacobus, JOHN J.   b. (abt. 1780)
(Neafie, p.2)   d. November 18, 1850
(NJ Will #13951G, Inv.)

John J. Jacobus
Died Nov. 18, 1850
In his 70th year

wife, SARAH (Van Riper?)   b. (abt. February 1783)
(Neafie, p.2)   d. June 26, 1847
(inscriptions, p.139)

Sarah

wife of John J. Jacobus
died June 26, 1847
aged 64 years, 4 months
& 18 days

Notes:
--1840 Census: Caldwell Twp., Essex Co., NJ: John J. Jacobus, 2 persons
--1850 Census: Caldwell Twp., Essex Co., NJ: Cornelius Paxton, age 37, shoemaker; Abigail J. Paxton, age 38; John J. Jacobus, age 66, farmer; all b. NJ

- - - - -

Jacobus, PETER b. (October 1811)
(Neafie, p. 11) d. February 28, 1884
(NJ Will #21363G, 1884)

Peter Jacobus
Died Feb. 28, 1884
Aged 73 years

first wife, ELIZA ANN (Oliver)
(Neafie, p.11)) b. (abt. 1807)
 d. August 5, 1854

Eliza Ann
wife of Peter Jacobus
Died Aug. 5, 1854
In her 54th year

son, WILLIAM C. b (abt. June 1, 1848)
(Neafie, p.8) d. June 1, 1865

William C.
son of Peter and Eliza Jacobus
Died June 1, 1865

Aged 16 yrs. 5 mos. \
and 26 days

Notes:
--Peter, son of Peter D. Jacobus and Rachel Egberts
--Peter m. March 8, 1832, Eliza Ann Oliver, dau. of William Oliver and Mary .....
--Peter m. October 7, 1855, Rachel Mead

--1850 Census: Caldwell Twp., Essex Co., NJ: Peter Jacobus, age 40, farmer; Eliza Ann, age 43; Mary C., age 17; James O., age 15, farmer; Martha W.?, age 13; Sarah, age 11; Emma H., age 9; Julia A., age 7; Delia A., age 4; William C., age 1; Daniel Vanderhoof, age 21, laborer; all b. New Jersey
--1860 Census: Caldwell, Essex Co., NJ: Peter Jacobus, age 50, farmer; Rachel, age 56; Emma, age 17; Deliah age 13; William age 11; Margaret E. age 18, milliner; all b. NJ
--1870 Census: Caldwell, Essex Co., NJ: Peter Jacobus, age 59, farmer; Rachel, age 64; Sarah, age 30, seamstress; all b. NJ
--1880 Census: Caldwell, Essex Co., NJ: Peter Jacobus, age 70, farmer; Rachel, age 78; Ellen Ward, age 15, servant

- - - - -

Jacobus, RALPH b. (abt. September 1818)
(Neafie, p.10) d. February 5, 1875
(NJ Will #18515G, 1875)
(monument)

Ralph Jacobus
Died February 5th, 1875
Aged 56 Years
& 5 months
Asleep in Jesus Blessed Sleep

Sarah Jacobus
Born Jan. 30, 1818
Died Dec. 30, 1899
His Wife

wife, SARAH   b. January 30, 1818
(monument)   d. December 30, 1899

son, JOHN A. (R.?)   b. (abt. January 4, 1844)
(Neafie, p.10)   d. October 4, 1874

John A.
Died Oct. 4, 1874
Aged 30 years, 9 months
Son of Ralph and Sarah
Jacobus

son, THOMAS E.   b. (abt. July 1837)
(Neafie, p.10)   d. June 11, 1838
(inscriptions, p.139)

Thomas E.
Died June 11, 1838
Aged 10 months & 17 days
Son of Ralph and Sarah
Jacobus

Notes:
--?Sarah Jacobus, widow, age 80: d. Newark, NJ, December 30, 1898 (NJ Death Record)

--1850 Census: 9Wd, Dist. 3, New York City: Ralph Jacobus, age 31, charcoal; Sarah age 31; Ann age 11; Caroline age 9; John age 6; all b. New Jersey
--1860 Census: 1Wd, Newark, Essex Co., NJ: Ralph Jacobus age 41, provisions?; Sarah 41; Anna E. age 21; Carrie age 19; John R. age 16; Agnes Baldwin age 19; all b. New Jersey

--1870 Census: 1Wd, Newark, Essex Co., NJ: <u>Ralph</u> Jacobus age 51 butcher; <u>Sarah</u> age 51; Anna A. age 30; <u>John R.</u> age 27, butcher; Levena age 18; all b. NJ
--1880 Census: Newark, Essex Co., NJ: <u>Sarah</u> Jacobus age 62, widow, b. NJ; Anna, age 40, single, daughter b. NJ

- - - - -

Jacbous, Samuel B.   See: Pearce Burial Ground
wife, Marietta

- - - - -

Jacobus, THOMAS   b. 1812
(monument)   d. 1865

Thomas Jacobus
1812 - 1865
-
Sarah C. Hilliker
His Wife
1822 - 1898

wife, SARAH C. (Hilliker)   b. 1822
(monument)   d. 1898 (September 25)

Notes:
--see above: George Hilliker (brother?) and Blanche E. Hill (granddaughter)

--1850 Census: Wayne Twp., Passaic Co., NJ: <u>Thomas</u> Jacobus, age 34, carpenter; <u>Sarah</u> age 31; Jane, age 5
--1860 Census: Wayne Twp., Passaic Co., NJ: <u>Thomas</u> Jacobus, age 36, b. NJ, farmer; <u>Sarah</u>, age 35, b. NY; Jane, age 12, b. NJ; George, age 8, b. NJ; James, age 6, b. NJ; Laura, age 4, b. NJ

--1870 Census: Wayne Twp., Passaic Co., NJ: Sarah C. Jacobus, age 40, b. NY; George W., age 19; Jas. J., age 17; Samuel A., age 14; Marilla, age 8; all children b. NJ; adj. to Jno W. Hill, age 23, b. NY, carpenter; Jennie E. (Jacobus) Hill, age 22, b. NY; Blanche A. Hill, age 3 months b. NY
--1880 Census: Wayne Twp., Passaic Co., NJ: Sarah C. Jacobus, age 56, widow, b. NY, parents b. NY; Irving son, age 25, b. NJ, father b. NJ, mother b. NY, silversmith; Ida, age 23, dau-in-law, b. NY, parents NY; Laura, age 21, dau. b. NJ; Rilla H., dau. age 18, b. NJ
--1895 NJ State Census: Wayne Twp., Passaic Co., NJ: Mrs. Jennie E. Hill; Sarah C. Jacobus; Frank Hill; Ellis Hill; Nettie Hill

- - - - -

Jacobus, Thomas G.* b. (abt. 1814)
 d. (January 25, 1898)

wife, EMELINE (Vanderhoof)
(Neafie, p.10) b. December 15, 1819
(monument) d. April 29, 1882

*In
Memory of
Emiline Vanderhoof
wife of
Thomas G. Jacobus
Born Dec. 15, 1819
Died April 29, 1882
Aged 52 yrs. 4 mos.
and 14 days*

Notes:
--Thomas G. m. November 17, 1838, Emeline Vanderhoof

--Death Index: "Tho's S Jacobus" b. c.1814 Caldwell; d. January 25, 1898, Caldwell, Essex Co., NJ; Age 84 years; widowed

--1840 Census: Caldwell Twp., Essex Co., NJ: Thos. Jacobus; (adj. to 'Tina' Vanderhoof; near John, Peter A. John A. and Cornelius Vanderhoof)
--1850 Census: Caldwell Twp., Essex Co., NJ: <u>Thomas G.</u> Jacobus, age 35; <u>Emeline</u>, age 29; Rachel Ann, age 8
--1860 Census: Caldwell, Essex Co., NJ: <u>Thos.</u> Jacobus, age 44, farmer; <u>Emeline</u>, age 40; Rachel A., age 18
--1870 Census: Caldwell, Essex Co., NJ: *Thomas G.* Jacobus, age 53, farmer; <u>Emeline</u>, age 50; Maria Vanderhoof, age 55; all b. New Jersey
--1880 Census: Caldwell, Essex Co., NJ: <u>Thomas G.</u> Jacobus, age 65, farmer; <u>Emeline</u>, age 60; William Husk, age 39, son-in-law, farmer; Rachel Ann Husk, age 35, daughter; Estella Husk, age 15, granddaughter; Frank Husk, age 10, grandson; Henry VanWart, age 57, farm labor; all b. NJ

- - - - -

Jacobus, WILLIAM S. b. March 19, 1824
(Neafie, p.8) d. May 16?, 1884

William S. Jacobus
Born Mar. 19, 1824
Died May 16?, 1884
Aged 60 years and 2 months

wife, MARGARET V. (Vanderhoof)
(Neafie, p.8) b. December 13, 1823
  d. November 19, 1899?

Margaret V.
wife of
William S. Jacobus

Born Dec. 13, 1823
Died (blank)

-

daughter, EMELINE   b. October 4, 1855
(Neafie, p.8)   d. (blank)

child, INFANT   b.
(Neafie, p.8)   d.

-

Emeline
Born Oct. 4, 1855
Died (blank)

-

Infant
(no dates)

-

Children of
William S. and Margaret
Jacobus

Notes:
--?William, son of James Jacobus and Sarah Vanderhoof
--William m. November 19, 1844, Margaret Vanderhoof
--?Margaret Jacobus, b. c,1824, d. Nov. 19, 1899, Caldwell Boro, Age 75 years; widow

--1850 Census: Caldwell Twp., Essex Co., NJ: William Jacobus, age 26, farmer; Margaret, age 26; John R. age 2; Cyrus Williams, age 18, laborer; all b. NJ
--1860 Census. Caldwell Twp., Essex Co., NJ: William S. Jacobus, age 36, farmer; Margaret age 36; John R., age 12
--1870 Census: Caldwell Twp., Essex Co., NJ: William 'T' Jacobus, age 46, farmer; Margaret, age 46; John R., age 21, brick mason; Sarah L., age 20

--1880 Census: Caldwell Twp., Essex Co., NJ: William S. Jacobus, age 56, farmer; Margaret, age 56; John R., age 32, mason; Sarah L., age 31; William B., age 2
--1895 NJ State Census: Caldwell Twp., Essex Co., NJ: Margaret Jacobus; John R. Jacobus; Sarah Jacobus; Willie Jacobus

- - - - -

Jacobus, Zenas Egbert*   b. (abt. 1848)
                                      d. (aft. 1910)

first wife, Mary J.* (VanNess)
                                      b. (abt. 1844)
                                      d. (June 28, 1892)

daughter, ANNIE R.   b. (abt. August 16, 1872)
(Neafie, p.20)   d. July 8, 1873

Annie R.
infant of
Zenas E. and Mary J.
Jacobus
Died July 8, 1873
Aged 10 months and 22 days

Notes:
--Zenas, son of Jacob E. Jacobus, and Rebecca Ann Sindle
--Zenas m. #1, Mary Ann VanNess, dau. of Jacob Smith VanNess and Lydia Zeliff
--?Mary J. Jacobus, b. c.1844 d. June 28 1892, age 48; Newark, NJ
--Zenas m. #2, abt. 1897, Annie E. ..... (? widow of Edward H. Bailey, res. Newark, who d. bef. May 1887)

--1850 Census: Caldwell Twp., Essex Co., NJ: Jacob E. Jacobus, age 36, carpenter; Rebecca Ann, age 31; Mary C.,

age 13; Hester M., age 11; Ann Eliza, age 8; James W., age 6; Zenas E., age 2; all b. New Jersey
--1860 Census: Caldwell, Essex Co., NJ: Jacob E. Jacobus, age 46, laborer; Rebecca A., age 41; Anna E., age 18; James W., age 16; Zenas E., age 12; Sarah E., age 6
--1870 Census: 5Wd, Newark, Essex Co., NJ: "Ferris" E. Jacobus, age 22, b. NJ, carpenter; Mary J., age 25, b. NJ
--1900 Census: 4Wd, Newark, Essex Co., NJ: "Zemes" E. Jacobus, b. 1856, m. 5 yr, b. NJ, carpenter; Annie E., age 50, b. May 1850 NJ
--1910 Census: 4Wd, Newark, Essex Co., NJ: Zenas E. Jacobus, age 62, m. #2 for 13 yrs. b. NJ, house carpenter; Anna E., age 60, m. #2, for 13 yr., 4 born 2 living, b. NJ, parents b. England; Steven A. Wells, age 23, m. 1 yr, b. NJ, parents NJ, driver paint supplies; Esther Wells, age 19, m. 1 yr, b. NJ, parents b. NJ

- - - - -

KANOUSE

Kanouse, THEODORE BALDWIN
(monument)   b. February 28, 1842
       d. October 23, 1922

Kanouse
Theodore B. Kanouse
Born Feb. 28, 1842
Died Oct. 23, 1922

wife, MARY ELIZABETH VANDERHOOF
(monument)   b. November 2, 1845
       d. July 19, 1921

Kanouse
Mary E. Vanderhoof
Wife of T. B. Kanouse

Born Nov. 2, 1845
Died July 19, 1921

son, FRANK   b. July 24, 1867
(monument)   d. October 3, 1882

K
Frank Kanouse
Born July 24, 1867
Died Oct. 3, 1882

son, PETER   b. May 5, 1865
(monument)   d. April 1, 1884

K
Peter Kanouse
Born May 5, 1865
Died Apr. 1, 1884

Notes:
--Theodore served: Civil War. Pvt. Co. H, 26 Reg't, NJ Inf.
--Theodore, son of John Kanouse and Elizabeth Hedden Baldwin
--1850 Census: Orange, Essex Co., NJ: John Kanouse, age 43, b. NJ, hatter; Elizabeth, age 32, b. NJ; Edward M., age 10, b. 'NY'; Theodore B., age 8, b. 'NY'; John T. age 6, b. NJ; Ann A, age 1, b. NJ; Cloe, age 68, b. CT
--1860 Census: Orange, Essex Co., NJ: John Kanouse, age 53, hatter; Elizabeth, age 41; Theodore, age 18, blacksmith apprentice; Anna, age 11; Ida, age 8; Emma, age 8; Clorinda, age 77; all b. NJ
--1870 Census: Caldwell Twp., Essex Co., NJ: Theodore Kanouse, age 28, blacksmith; Elizabeth, age 23; Peter, age 4; Frank, age 3; 'no name' (Emma?), age 1 month; all b. NJ
--1880 Census: Caldwell Twp., Essex Co., NJ: Theodore Kanouse, age 35, blacksmith; Mary E., age 34; Peter, age 15,

works on farm; Frank, age 12; E. ... (Emma?) dau., age 10; Susan, age 8; Theodore, age 4; Mary, age 8 months; all b. NJ
--1895 Census: Caldwell Twp., Essex Co., NJ: Theodore Kanouse; Mary E.; Theodore Jr.; Elizabeth; Harry
--1900 Census: Caldwell Twp., Essex Co., NJ: Theodore B. Kanouse, b. Feb. 1845, farmer; Mary E., age 54, b. Nov. 1845; Theodore J., age 24, b. Dec. 1875, mason; Mary E., b. Sept. 1879; Harry, age 17, b. June 1882; all b. NJ
--1910 Census: Caldwell Twp., Essex Co., NJ: Theodore B. Kanouse, age 68, farmer; Mary E., age 66
--1920 Census: Caldwell Twp., Essex Co., NJ: Theodore B. Kanouse, age 77, farmer; Mary, age 73

- - - - -

KENT

Kent, George M.* b. (August 1847)
 d. (bef. 1930)

first wife, SARAH E. (Ryerson)
(Neafie, p.16) b. (abt. March 8, 1847)
 d. November 28, 1870

Sarah E
wife of George Kent
daughter of
Paul V. and Sarah Ryerson
Died Nov. 28, 1870
Aged 23 years 8 months
and 20 days

Notes:
--George, son of John J. Kent and Jane .....
--George m. #1 Sarah E., dau. of Paul F. Ryerson, and Sarah E. Drew

--George m.#2, abt. 1873, Elmira Durling, dau. of Theodore Durling and Maria ..... (Asenath?)

--1850 Census: Caldwell Twp., Essex Co., NJ: John J. Kent, age 29, farmer; Jane, age 25; George, age 4; Hamilton, age 2; George, age 20, farmer; Casiah, age 57; all b. NJ
--1850 Census: Vernon Twp., Sussex Co., NJ: Paul F. Ryerson, age 32, carpenter; Sarah, age 28; Ira, age 8; Ebenezer, age 5; Sarah, age 3; Peter, age 1; all b. NJ
--1850 Census, Hardyston, Sussex Co., NJ: Theodore Durling, age 27, miller; Maria, age 26, b. NJ; Almira, age 4; Sidney, age 2; all b. New Jersey
--1860 Census: Caldwell, Essex Co., NJ: John J. Kent, age 39, farmer; Jane, age 35; George, age 13; Hamilton, age 11; Martha A., age 5; Munson, age 4 months; all b. NJ
--1860 Census, p.614, Meads Basin, Wayne Twp., Passaic Co., NJ: Paul F. Ryerson, age 41, b. NJ, farmer; Sarah, age 37, b. NJ; Sarah, age 13, b. NJ; 6 other children
--1870 Census, p.123, Caldwell, Essex Co., NJ: George Kent, age 23, b. NJ, cigar maker; Sarah, age 23, b. NJ
--1870 Census: 1 Wd. Paterson, Passaic Co., NJ: Theodosia Derling, age 18, b. NJ, at school; "Elvira" Derling, age 23, b. NJ, works at silk mill
--1880 Census: Paterson, Passaic Co., NJ: George Kent, age 33, b. NJ, cigar maker; Elmira, age 32; Jennie, age 6; George, age 2; all b. New Jersey
--1895 NJ State Census: Paterson, Passaic Co, NJ: George Kent; Elmira; Jennie; George; John; Bertha
--1900 Census: 3Wd, Paterson, Passaic Co., NJ: George Kent, b. August 1847, m.27 yr. b. NJ, grocery salesman; Elmira b. Feb. 1848 NJ; Jennie b. Feb. 1875, school teacher; John, b. Dec. 1880 NJ, grocery salesman; Bertha b. August 1884 NJ
--1910 Census: 4Wd, Paterson, Passaic Co., NJ: George Kent, age 63 m. #2 at age 37, bookkeeper at jute mill; Elmira, age 61, m. #1, at age 37; John, age 29, inspector at gov't house; Bertha, age 25; Stewart R. Brown, son-in-law,

widow, age 35, b. NJ, travelling salesman; Eleanor Brown, granddau. age 7 b. NJ; Stewart Brown, grandson, age 3, b. NJ
--1920 Census: 4Wd, Paterson, Passaic Co., NJ: George Kent, age 73, b. NJ, receiving clerk at jute mill; Elmira, age 71 b. NJ; John W., age 38, investigator for State Labor Bureau
--1930 Census: Paterson, Passaic Co., NJ: John W. "Kart" age 49, m. #1, at age 39, b. NJ, works labor dept. State of NJ: Louise age 40 m. at age 30 b. NY;Elmira, age 82, m. at age 25, b. NJ; Madlyn 'Alenaner', age 20, stepdau. b. NY, teacher;

- - - - -

Kent, GEORGE S.   b. October 27, 1829
(monument)   d. September 7, 1898

George S. Kent
Oct. 27, 1829
Sept. 7, 1898
-
Elizabeth A. His wife
Sept. 2, 1832
Jan. 12, 1928

wife, ELIZABETH A.   b. September 2, 1832
(monument)   d. January 12, 1928

Notes:
--George, son of Isaac Kent, q.v. and Casiah Sindle
--George m. aft. 1850, Elizabeth A. .....

--1850 Census: Caldwell Twp., Essex Co., NJ: John J. Kent, age 29, farmer; Jane Kent, age 25; George Kent, age 4;

Hamilton Kent, age 2; George Kent, age 20, farmer; Cassiah Kent, age 57; all b. NJ
--1860 Census: Caldwell Twp., Essex Co., NJ: George Kent, age 30, farmer; Elizabeth, age 27; Isaac N., age 6; Charles V., age 4; Kesiah Kent, age 68; all b. NJ
--1870 Census: Caldwell Twp., Essex Co., NJ: George S. Kent, age 40, farmer; Elizabeth A., age 38; Isaac N., age 16, works on farm; Charles W., age 14; Sarah J., age 8; all b. NJ
--1880 Census: Caldwell Twp., Essex Co., NJ: George S. Kent, age 50, farmer; Elisabeth A., age 47; Sarah Jane, age 18; all b. NJ (adj. to I. Newton Kent)
--1895 Census: Caldwell Twp., Essex Co., NJ: George S. Kent; Elizabeth A. Kent; Edward Francisco; Sarah Jane Francisco; George K. Francisco
--1900 Census: Caldwell Twp., Essex Co., NJ: Edward Sisco, age 39, b. June 1860 NJ, carpenter; Sarah, age 38 b. Dec. 1861 NJ; Geo. K, age 12, b. Oct. 1887 NJ; Elizabeth Kent, age 67, b. Sept. 1832, mother-in-law, widow, b. NY, parents b. NY
--1910 Census: Caldwell Twp., Essex Co. NJ: Frank E. Kent, age 34, farmer; Zelda, age 34; Dorothy, age 4; Neriana, age 3; Elizabeth A., age 78, widow, grandmother; Maud, age 20' Charles Miller, age 34, hired man; all b. NJ
--1920 Census: Caldwell Twp., Essex Co., NJ: Elizabeth Kent, age 87, widow, b. NY, parents b. NY

- - - - -

Kent, ISAAC   b. (abt. January 1791)
(Neafie, p.18)   d. February 4, 1838
(inscriptions, p. 139) (d. February 14, 1838)
(NJ Will #12891G, Inv. 1838)

Isaac Kent
Died Feb. 4, 1838
Aged 47 years, 1 month
& 2 days

wife, CASIAH (Keziah Sindle)
(Neafie, p.18) b. (abt. February 8, 1793)
(monument) d. September 1, 1869

Casiah Sindle
wife of
Isaac Kent
Died Sept. 1, 1869
Aged 76 years, 6 months
& 24 days

Notes:
--1830 Census: Caldwell Twp., Essex Co., NJ: <u>Isaac</u> Kent, 9 persons: (adj. Josiah Francisco; near Christopher and Thomas Sindle)
--1840 Census: Caldwell Twp., Essex Co., NJ: <u>Keziah</u> Kent: 5 persons (adj. to William Kent and Richard Van Ness)
--1850 Census: Caldwell Twp., Essex Co., NJ: John J. Kent, age 29, farmer; Jane, age 25; George, age 4; Hamilton, age 2; George, age 20, farmer; <u>Cassiah</u>, age 57; all b. NJ
--1860 Census: Caldwell, Essex Co., NJ: George Kent, age 30, farmer; Elizabeth, age 27; Isaac N., age 6; Charles V., age 4; <u>Keziah</u>, age 68; all b. NJ

- - - - -

Kent, ISAAC NEWTON b. November 8, 1858
(monument) d. December 24, 1903

Isaac Newton Kent
Born Nov. 6, 1858 Died Dec. 24, 1903
-
Ida Surrena Bush, His Wife
Born Nov. 16, 1857 Died Feb. 7, 1904
-

Jesse Elmer Kent
Born Feb. 23, 1879 Died Sept. 11, 1885
Arthur Kent
Born Jan. 25, 1882 Died July 15, 1897

wife, IDA SURRENA (Bush)
(monument)   b. November 16, 1857
                                    d. February 7, 1904

son, JESSE ELMER   b. February 23, 1879
(Neafie, p.15)   d. September 11, 1885
(monument)

Jesse Elmer
son of
Isaac N. and Ida S. Kent
Died Sep. 11, 1885
Aged 6 years 6 months
19 days

ARTHUR   b. January 25, 1882
(monument)   d. July 15, 1897

Notes:
--Isaac, son of George S. Kent, q.v., and Elizabeth A. .....
--Isaac m. January 12, 1875, Ida Surrena Bush, dau. of Thomas H. Bush, q.v., and Margaret Jane Jacobus

--1860 Census: Caldwell Twp., Essex Co., NJ: George Kent, age 30, farmer; Elizabeth age 27; Isaac N., age 6; Charles V., age 4; Keziah, age 68; all b. New Jersey
--1860 Census: Wallkill, Orange Co., NY: Thomas H. Bush, age 26, tobacconist; M. J., age 23; Walter, age 4; Ida, age 1; Rachel, 11 months; all b. New Jersey
--1870 Census: Caldwell Twp., Essex Co., NJ: George S. Kent, age 40, farmer; Elizabeth A., age 38; Isaac 'W', age

16, works on farm; Charles W., age 14; Sarah J., age 8; all b. New Jersey
--1870 Census: Caldwell Twp., Essex Co., NJ: Peter Vanderhoof, age 61, stone mason; Margaret J. Vanderhoof, age 33; Ida I. Bush, age 12; Rachel Bush, age 10; Georgianna Bush, age 7; Lottie Vanderhoof, age 1; all b. NJ
--1880 Census: Caldwell Twp., Essex Co., NJ: I. Newton Kent, age 26, segar maker; "Iola" age 22; Frank E., age 4; Jesse E., age 1; all b. NJ; adj. to George Kent, age 50
--1900 Census: Caldwell Twp., Essex Co., NJ: Isaac Kent, b. November 1853, m. 25 yrs., farmer; Ida S. b. November 1857; Maud, b. November 1889; Frank E. b. Jan 1876, butcher; Zelda, b. March 1876, daughter-in-law; all b. NJ

- - - - -

Kent, John I.*   b. (abt. March 1821)
                       d. (aft. 1910)

wife, Jane* (Bush)   b. (abt. December 1825)
                       d. (aft. 1900)

daughter, MARY JANE   b. September 5, 1851
(Neafie, p.18)   d. October 24, 1855

Mary Jane
daughter of
John I. and Jane Kent
Born Sept. 5, 1851
Died Oct. 24, 1855

Notes:
--John, son of Isaac Kent, q.v., and Keziah Sindle
--John m. October 1, 1844, (Effie?) Jane Bush, dau. of Henry C. Bush and Mary Van Riper?

--1850 Census: Caldwell Twp., Essex Co., NJ: John I. Kent, age 29, farmer; Jane, age 25; George, age 4; Hamilton, age 2; George, age 20, farmer; Cassiah, age 57; all b. NJ
--1860 Census: Caldwell, Essex Co., NJ: John I. Kent, age 39, farmer; Jane, age 35; George, age 13; Hamilton, age 11; Martha A., age 5; Munson, age 4 months; all b. NJ
--1870 Census: Caldwell, Essex Co., NJ: John I. Kent, age 49, farmer; Jane, age 45; Hamilton, age 21; Abby H., age 19; Martha, age 15; Munson, age 10; all b. NJ; adj. to George S. Kent, age 60; and William Kent, age 53
--1880 Census: Caldwell, Essex Co., NJ: John I. Kent, age 59, farmer; Jane, age 54; Munson, age 20
--1900 Census: Caldwell Twp., Essex Co., NJ: John 'J' Kent, age 79, b. March 1821, m. 55 yrs., b. NJ, carpet weaver; Jane, age 74, b. Dec. 1895, NJ, 5 born 3 living
--1910 Census: Caldwell Twp., Essex Co., NJ: John I. Kent, age 89, widower, b. NJ, retired own farm

- - - - -

KIERSTEAD

Kiersted, AARON W. b. (abt. 1798)
(Neafie, p.4) d. March 25, 1855

Aaron W. Kiersted
Died March 25, 1855
Aged 56 yrs. 11 mos.
& 16 days

wife, Sarah* (Pier) b. (abt. 1800)
  d. (aft. 1870)

Notes:
--Aaron Williams Kierstead, son of John Aaron Kierstead, q.v., and Polly Williams
--Aaron m. Dec. 5, 1818, Sarah Pier

--1840 Census: Caldwell Twp., Essex Co., NJ: Aaron W. Kiersted: 7 persons
--1850 Census: Caldwell Twp., Essex Co., NJ: Aaron W. Kierstad, age 52, farmer; Sarah, age 50; Catherine M., age 15; Nancy S., age 50 (sister); all b. New Jersey
--1860 Census: Caldwell, Essex Co., NJ: Robert L. Stagg, age 41, farmer; Margaret, age 36; James C., age 16; Mary L., age 11; Aaron E., age 7; Sarah Kierstead, age 60; Nancy Stager, age 60; John McMahan age 19 b. NY; Robert McMahan, age 4 b. NY
--1870 Census: Caldwell, Essex Co., NJ: Robert L. Stagg, age 51, farmer; Margaret H., age 46; Aaron E., age 17; Sarah Kierstad, age 60

- - - - -

Kiersted, JOHN A.,ESQ. b. (abt. August 1769)
(Neafie, p.3) d. February 3, 1851

John A. Kiersted, Esq.
Died Feb. 3, 1851
Aged 81 years 5 months
& 14 days

wife, POLLY WILLIAMS
(Neafie, p.3) b. (abt. May 19, 1767)
  d. February 5, 1836

Polly Williams
wife of
John Kiersted, Esq.
Died Feb. 5, 1836
Aged 68 years 8 months
& 20 days

Notes:
Served: War of 1812: Capt. of Essex Co. Inf.
--John, son of Aaron Kierstead and Lanna (Eleanor) Colyer
--John Aaron Kierstead m. October 6, 1791, Polly Williams; (widow of ..... Freeman?)

--?1840 Census: South Ward, Newark, Essex Co., NJ: John A. Kiersted. 8 persons
--1850 Census: Caldwell Twp: Thomas J. Keirstead, age 46, farmer; Margaret S., age 46; John S., age 22, mason; Joseph, age 20, mason; George, age 6; John A., age 83; all b. New Jersey

- - - - -

Kiersted, Thomas J.*	b. (February 13, 1804)
(NJ Will #19959G, 1880)	d. (November 12, 1879)
wife, Margaret* (Stager)	b. (abt 1804)
	d. (bef. November 1879)
daughter, SOPHIA	b. (abt. August 1832)
(Neafie, p.3)	d. November 20, 1837
(inscriptions, p.140)	

Sophia
daughter of
Thomas J. & Margaret Kiersted
Died Nov. 20. 1837
Aged 5 years, 3 months
& 2 days

Notes:
--Thomas Jefferson Kierstead, son of John Aaron Kierstead and Mary "Polly" Williams
--Thomas m. Dec. 25, 1824, Margaret, dau. of Henry Stager

--"T.J. Kiersted' b. c.1804; d. Nov. 12, 1879, Caldwell; aged 75 years 3 mos.; widowed" (NJ Death Record)

--1840 Census: Caldwell Twp., Essex Co., NJ: <u>Thomas J.</u> Kiersted: 6 persons
--1850 Census: Caldwell Twp., Essex Co., NJ: <u>Thomas J.</u> Kierstead, age 46, farmer; <u>Margaret S.</u> age 46; John S., age 22, mason; Joseph age 20, mason; George, age 6; John A., age 83; all b. New Jersey
--1860 Census: Caldwell Twp., Essex Co., NJ: <u>Thomas J.</u> "Keirstead" age 56, farmer; <u>Margaret</u> 57; George, age 16; all b. NJ
--1870 Census: Caldwell Twp., Essex Co., NJ: <u>Thomas J.</u> Kierstead, age 64, farmer; <u>Margaret</u> age 62; George C. age 24, farmer; Eliza L., age 20; Lillian age 1 month; all b. NJ

- - - - -

KUSSMAUL

Kussmaul, JOHN   b. May 8, 1809
(Neafie, p.10)   d. December 18, 1888
(NJ Will #22815G, 1888)

John Kussmaul
Born May 8, 1809
Died Dec. 18, 1888

wife, SOPHIA D. (Durr)   b. August 9, 1815
(Neafie, p.10)   d. June 6, 1866

Sophie D.
wife of
John Kussmaul
Born Aug. 9, 1818
Died June 6, 1866

son, JOHN A.　　　　　　b. August 6, 1840
(Neafie, p.11)　　　　　　d. May 27, 1858

John A. Kussmaul
Born Aug. 6, 1840
Died May 27, 1858
Aged 17 yrs. 9 mos.
& 21 days

Notes:
--John m. June 13, 1836, Sophia Dorothea Durr

--1850 Census: Caldwell, Essex Co., NJ: John Kussmaul, age 40, b. Germany, cooper; Sophia , age 33, b. Germany; Augustin J., age 10, b. NJ; Lewis age 8, b. NJ; Mary, age 6, b. NJ; Peter, age 4, b. NJ; Sophia L., age 9 months b. NJ
--1860 Census: Caldwell, Essex Co, NJ: John 'Kushman' age 52, b. Wurttemberg, farmer; Sophia, age 45 b. Wurttemberg; Lewis F. age 18; Mary A., age 15; Sophia, age 10; Peter S., age 12; Henrietta, age 8; children b. NJ
--1870 Census: Caldwell, Essex Co., NJ: John Kussmaul, age 61, b. Wurttemberg, farmer; Louis F., age 27, b. NJ, farmer; Pauline, age 23, b. Wurttemberg, keeping house; Mary, age 25, b. NJ; Peter, age 23, b. NJ, carpenter; Henrietta age 18, b. NJ; Frederic, age 9, b. NJ
--1880 Census: Caldwell, Essex Co., NJ: John Kussmaul, age 71, b. Wurttemberg, farm labor; William Gould, age 32, son-in-law, b. NJ, brick layer; Mary A. Gould, age 35, daughter, b. NJ, parents b. Wurttemberg

- - - - -

Kussmaul, LOUIS F.　　　　b. September 27, 1842
(monument)　　　　　　　　d. April 28, 1913

wife, PAULINE　　　　　　　b.
(monument)　　　　　　　　d.

Notes:
Served: Civil War: Co. C, 7 Regt. NJ Vol. Infantry; U.S. Navy
--1890 Veterans Schedule, Caldwell, Essex Co., NJ: Louis Kussmaul, Pvt. C Co. 7 Reg't.

- - - - -

LAWRENCE

Lawrence, ANNA   b. (abt. 1814)
(Neafie, p.6)   d. January 23, 1855

Anna Lawrence
Died Jan. 23, 1855
Aged 41 years

Notes:
--reported adj. to Martha Louise Van Duyne, dau. of Peter Van Duyne. q.v.
--??1850 Census, 13Wd, NY, NY: James Vansteenbergh, age 42 b.NY; James, age 10; Adeline age 9; George age 6; Joseph, age 4; Anna Lawrence, age 43, b. NJ
--(James Vansteenbergh m. Dec. 12, 1830, Sally Crum, Seventh Presb. Church, New York City)

- - - - -

Lawrence, OREN S.   b. 1838 (August)
(gov't stone)   d. 1907
(monument)

O. S. Lawrence
Co. D
4 R.I. Inf

Oren S. Lawrence
1838 - 1907
-
Sarah E. Baker, his wife
1841 - 1891

wife, Sarah* (Baker)   b. 1841
                                 d. 1891

Notes:
--Served: Civil War: "Oren 'Orrin' S. Lawrence; Co.D; 4th R.I. Infantry;wounded 9/17/1862 at Antietam"
--Oren, son of Jeremiah S. Lawrence and Clarissa Keach
--"Oren S. Lawrence, age 28, m. Sarah Baker, age 29, Nov. 3, 1868 at Newark, NJ"

--1850 Census: Glocester, Providence Co., RI: Jeremiah S. Lawrence, age 37, farmer; Clarissa, age 36; Orin S., age 9; 5 other children; Chloe Eddy, age 69; all b. Rhode Island
--1860 Census: Glocester, Providence Co., RI: Jeremiah S. Lawrence, age 47, stone cutter; Clarissa, age 43; Orin S., age 20, farm labor; Emily M.,age 17; servant; Lawson J., age 15, farm labor; Ezra S., age 13, farm labor; Chloe Eddy, age 81; all b. Rhode Island (Adj. to Arnold Eddy family)
--1870 Census: Newark, Essex Co., NJ: Orin L. Lawrence, age 31, b. RI, blacksmith; "Louisa", age 37, b. NJ; Clara, age 5, b. NJ; Frank, age 3, b. NJ
--1880 Census: Caldwell Twp., Essex Co., NJ: Orrin Lawrence, age 39 b. RI, blacksmith; Sarah, age 42, b. NJ; Clara, age 16, b. NJ; Francis, age 13, b. NJ, works in blacksmith shop
--1890 Veterans of Civil War Schedule, Caldwell, Essex Co., NJ: James O.S. Lawrence, Pvt. Co. D, 4th Rhode Island Volunteers
--1900 Census: Caldwell Twp., Essex Co., NJ: Frank Lawrence, age 34, b. Oct. 1865, m.3 yrs. b. NJ, father RI, mother NJ, blacksmith; Carrie, age 33 b. Nov. 18 1866, b. NJ

parents b. NJ; Frank Jr., age 4 months, b. May 1900 NJ; Orrin S. Lawrence, father, widower, age 62, b. Aug. 1837, b. RI, parents b. RI, blacksmith

- - - - -

MANDEVILLE

Mandeville, Hendrick* b. (abt. 1770)
                                       d. (bef. 1850)

first wife, Esther* (Pier) b.
                                        d. (bef. 1812)

second wife, MARY (Jacobus)
(Neafie, p.4) b. (abt. April 17, 1781)
                                        d. February 20, 1853

Mary Jacobus
wife of
Henry I. Mandeville
Died Feb. 20, 1853
Aged 71 years 10 months
& 3 days

daughter, SARAH b. (September 19, 1813)
(Neafie, p.4) d. April 21, 1834

Sarah Mandeville
Died April 21, 1834
Aged 20 years, 7 months
& 12 days

son, RALPH b. (February 16, 1818)
(Neafie, p.4) d. August 25, 1835
(inscriptions, p.140)

Ralph Mandeville
Died August 25, 1835
Aged 17 years, 6 months
& 9 days

son, DANIEL	b. (abt. August 20, 1820)
(Neafie, p.4)	d. August 24, 1835
(inscriptions p. 140)	

Daniel Mandeville
Died August 24, 1835
Aged 15 years & 4 days

Notes:
--Hendrick, son of John Mandeville and Geertry Van Ness.
--Hendrick m. April 1788, Esther Pier.
--Hendrick m. abt. 1812, Maria Jacobus, dau. of Abr. Jacobus and Leah Mandeville

--?1830 Census: Pequannock Twp., Morris Co., NJ: Henry Mandeville, 5 persons: near Isaac H. Mandeville
--?1840 Census: Pequannock Twp., Morris Co., NJ: Mary Mandeville: 1 person; adj. to Jacob I. Mandeville
--1850 Census: Wayne Twp., Passaic Co., NJ: Simon S. VanNess, age 49, farmer; Jane, age 50; Benjamin, age 12; Mary Mandeville, age 70; all b. New Jersey

- - - - -

Mandeville, JOHN H.	b. (abt. October 1790)
(Neafie, p. 15)	d. January 22, 1846
(inscriptions, p.140)	

John H. Mandeville
Died January 22, 1846
in his 56th year

wife, ELIZABETH (Mourison)
(Neafie, p.15) b. (abt. 1798)
 d. April 30, 1879

> *Elizabeth Mandeville*
> *Died Apr. 30, 1879*
> *In the 82nd year*
> *of her age*

?daughter, JULIA b. (abt. 1829)
(Neafie, p.15) d. April 26, 1862

> *Julia Mandeville*
> *Died Apr. 26, 1862*
> *Aged 33 years*

daughter, KATE b. (abt. 1841)
(Neafie, p.15) d. May 4, 1870

> *Kate Mandeville*
> *Died May 4, 1870*
> *Aged 29 years*

Notes:
--John, son of Hendrick Mandeville, q.v., and Esther Pier

--1850 Census: Pequannock Twp., Morris Co., NJ: Christian Mandeville, age 27; Elizabeth, age 52; Elizabeth, age 16; Margaret A., age 12; Catherine, age 9; John 'Morrison', age 20; all b. New Jersey
--1860 Census: Pequannock Twp., Morris Co., NJ: Elizabeth 'Mandervill' age 62; Hester, age 33; Catherine, age 19; all b. New Jersey
--?1860 Census: 3 Wd. Newark, Essex Co., NJ: Charles Jackson, age 28, b. England, tailor: Elizabeth, age 24, b. NJ; Francis, age 3, b. NJ; Ella, age 3, b. NJ; Julia Mandeville, age 30, b. NJ

--1870 Census: South Orange, Essex Co., NJ: Job B. Tillou, age 55, farmer; Hettie Tillou, age 40; Mary Tillou, age 62; Amanda Kierstead, age 9; Elizabeth Mandeville, age 70; all b. NJ

- - - - -

MANNING

Manning, CHARLES J.   b. March 20, 1777
(monument)   d. March 3, 1859

Charles J. Manning
Mar. 20, 1777
March 3, 1859
-
Hester Sorey
His wife
March 28, 1787
Aug. 17, 1858

wife, HESTER SUREY   b. March 28, 1787
(monument)   d. August 17, 1858

Notes:
--Charles Johnson Manning m. London, England, Aug. 22, 1815, Hester Surey/Shurey
--1840 Census: Caldwell Twp., Essex Co., NJ: Charles Manning: 4 persons. (adj. John F. Post and Henry Francisco)
--1850 Census: Caldwell Twp., Essex Co., NJ: Charles Manning, age 73, b. England, tailor; Hester Manning, age 64, b. England

- - - - -

Manning, JAMES   b. December 3, 1815
(monument)   d. December 30, 1899

M
James Manning
December 3, 1815
December 30, 1899

-

Charity Mandeville
His wife
August 22, 1819
January 10, 1898

-

Mary A. Manning
September 4 1863
November 24, 1921

wife, CHARITY MANDEVILLE
(monument)   b. August 22, 1819
                        d. January 10, 1898

Manning, MARY A.   b. September 4, 1863
(granddaughter)   d. November 24, 1921
(monument)

Notes:
--James Johnson Manning, son of Charles Manning, q.v.
--James m. abt. 1840, Charity Mandeville, dau. of John H. Mandeville, q.v. and Elizabeth Mowerson/Mourison

--1850 Census: Caldwell Twp., Essex Co., NJ: James Manning, age 33, b. England, farmer; Charity, age 29 b. NJ; Charles age 9, John age 7; Elizabeth, age 4; William E., age 1
--1860 Census: Caldwell Twp., Essex Co., NJ: James Manning, age 42, b. England, farmer; Charity, age 41; b. NJ; Charles age 19, b. NJ; John, age 17, b. NJ; Elizabeth 15, b. NJ; William E., age 10 b. NJ; Mariann age 7 b. NJ; Louisa age 4, b. NJ

--1870 Census: Caldwell Twp., Essex Co., NJ: James Manning, age 54, b. England, farmer; Charity, age 50 b. NJ; John, age 28 b. NJ, lawyer; William, age 18, farm labor; Mary A., age 16, b. NJ; Louisa, age 13; all children b. NJ
--1880 Census: Caldwell Twp., Essex Co., NJ: James Mannning, age 64, b. England, farmer; Charity, age 60, b. NJ; William, son, age 30 b. NJ, works on farm; Louisa, age 21, dau., b. NJ

- - - - -

MASTENBROCK
(Mastenbroek)

Mastenbrock, C.s* b. (abt. 1800)
 d. (bef. 1870?)

wife, MARTYNTJE (Witte) b. (abt. September 28, 1825)
(Neafie, p.2) d. December 28, 1853
(inscriptions, p. 14)

*Martyntje Witte
vrouw van C.s Mastenbrock,
K.Z. stief den 28 December 1853
in den Ouderdom van 28 Jany 2 Maanden*
(age 28 years, 2 months)

Notes:
--1850 Census, p.159&160, New Barbadoes Twp., Bergen Co., NJ: "Craynus Masterbook", age 50, laborer; Maria, age 47; Lyndert age 15, laborer; John, age 12; Adrianna age 9; William, age 5; Martha age 46; all b. Holland
--?1860 Census, 9Wd., Milwaukee, Wisconsin: Daniel Bogerman (Bogortman), age 29, b. Holland, mason; Catharina, age 27, b. Holland; Nicholas, age 2, b. Wisconsin; Cryn, age 1, b. Wisconsin; Cryn Mastenbrook, age 57, b. Holland

--?1870 Census, 2Wd. Paterson, Passaic Co., NJ: Daniel Bogartman, age 38, b. Holland, brick & stone mason; Cathrine, age 37, b. Holland; Nicholas, age 11, b. Wisc.; William, age 9, b. Wisc.; Mary, age 8, b. Wisc.; Nelly, age 5, b. NJ; Katty, age 2, b. NJ; Bella, age 7 mos. b. NJ

- - - - -

McCORD

McCord, ANDREW (monument)
b. 1814
d. 1888 (July 17)

Andrew McCord
Born 1814
Died 1888
71 Yrs.

-

His Wife
Sarah
McCord
Died 1901
81 Yrs.

wife, SARAH (monument)
b. (abt. 1821)
d. 1901

son, ANDREW (Neafie, p.10) (monument)
b. April 3, 1860
d. November 22, 1879

Andrew
son of
Andrew and Sarah
McCord
Born Apr. 3, 1860
Died Nov. 22, 1879

Notes:
--1850 Census: Greenwich, Warren Co., NJ: Andrew McCord, age 35, b. NY, brickmaker; Sarah age 29, b. NJ; Margaret, age 10 b. NJ; Jane, age 6, b. NJ; Thompson, age 3, b. NJ; Ellen, age 2 b. NJ., James, age 4 mos., b. NJ
--1860 Census: Wayne Twp., Passaic Co., NJ: Andrew McCord, age 42, b. NY, sup't. canal; Sarah, age 38 b. NJ; Margaret, age 20, tailoress; Thompson, age 14; Ellen, age 13; George, age 9; Elizabeth age 5; Josephine, age 3; Andrew, age 11 months; Peter Riker, age 26
--1870 Census: Wayne Twp., Passaic Co., NJ: Andrew "McCoy", age 50 b. NY, canal foreman; Sarah age 48, b. NJ; Margaret, age 29; Thomas, age 23, works on canal; Ellen, age 21; George, age 19; Elizabeth, age 17; Josephine, age 14; Andrew, age 9; Emma, age 7; Sarah Kelly, age 4; Elizabeth Kelly, age 2; all children b. NJ
--1880 Census: Wayne Twp., Passaic Co., NJ: Andrew McCord, age 60 b. NY, parents NY, overseer of canal; Sarah, age 57 b. NJ, parents NJ; Ellen, dau.,age 26; Emma, dau., age 17; Mable Stewart, dau., age 7;
--1885 NJ Census: Wayne Twp., Passaic Co., NJ: Andrew McCord; Sarah McCord; Emma McCord

- - - - -

McCord, Thomas* b. (January 1848)
 d. (1917)
 (bur. Laurel Grove Mem. Park, Totowa, NJ)

first wife, MARY ELIZABETH
(Neafie, p.10) b. (abt. 1846)
(monument) d. July 5, 1870

Mary Elizabeth
wife of

Thomas McCord
Died July 5, 1870
Aged 24 years

Notes:
--Thomas, son of Andrew McCord, q.v., and Sarah .....
--Thomas m. #1, Mary Elizabeth .....
--Thomas m. #2, abt. 1892, Ella J. Banker, dau. of Thaddeus Banker and Susan D. .....

--1850 Census: Greenwich, Warren Co., NJ: Andrew McCord, age 35, b. NY, brickmaker; Sarah age 29, b. NJ; Margaret, age 10 b. NJ; Jane, age 6, b. NJ; Thompson, age 3, b. NJ; Ellen, age 2 b. NJ., James, age 4 mos., b. NJ
--1860 Census: Wayne Twp., Passaic Co., NJ: Andrew McCord, age 42, b. NY, sup't. canal; Sarah, age 38 b. NJ; Margaret, age 20, tailoress; Thompson, age 14; Ellen, age 13; George, age 9; Elizabeth age 5; Josephine, age 3; Andrew, age 11 months; Peter Riker, age 26
--1870 Census: Wayne Twp., Passaic Co., NJ: Andrew "McCoy", age 50 b. NY, canal foreman; Sarah age 48, b. NJ; Margaret, age 29; Thomas, age 23, works on canal; Ellen, age 21; George, age 19; Elizabeth, age 17; Josephine, age 14; Andrew, age 9; Emma, age 7; Sarah Kelly, age 4; Elizabeth Kelly, age 2; all children b. NJ
--1880 Census: Montgomery, Orange Co., NY: Thaddeus W. Banker, age 47 b. NY, farmer; Susan D., age 43 b. NY; Ella J., age 8 b. NY; 3 older children
--1895 NJ State Census: Wayne Twp., Passaic Co., NJ: Thomas McCord; Ella McCord
--1900 Census: Wayne Twp., Passaic Co., NJ: Thomas McCord, age 57, b. January 1848, NJ, m. 8 years, travelling salesman; Ella, age 27, b. August 1872, wife, b. New York
--1910 Census: Wayne Twp., Passaic Co., NJ: Thos. 'McCard', age '54' m.#2 for 18 yr., b. NJ, father b. NY, mother b. NJ, coal salesman; Ella J. age 37, b.NY, parents b. NY

--1920 Census: Wayne Twp. Passaic Co., NJ: Ella J. McCord, age 46, widow, b. NY; Susan D. Banker, mother, widow, age 80, b. NY
--1930 Census: Wayne Twp., Passaic Co., NJ: Ella J. McCord, age 57, widow, b. NY, parents b. NY; "Siras F.", age 63, brother b. NY, labor odd jobs

- - - - -

McCORMICK

McCormick, HUGH   b. May 5, 1783
(Neafie, p.21)   d. October 12, 1852

Hugh McCormick
Born County Down, Ireland
May 5, 1783
Immigrated to America, 1816
Died at Pompton Plains, NJ
October 12, 1852

(inscriptions, p.140)

Hugh McCormick
Born at Kircubbin,
County of Down, Ireland
May 5, 1783
Died in hope at Pompton Plains
October 12, 1852

(monument)

Hugh McCormick
In
Memory of
Hugh McCormick
Born at Kircubbin
County of Down, Ireland
May 5th, 1783

Emmigrated to America in
1816
Died in hope at
Pompton Plains
Oct. 12, 1852

wife, JEAN (Welsh)	b. August 23, 1784
(Neafie,)	d. August 13, 1849
(inscriptions, p.140)	

Jean Welsh,
wife of
Hugh McCormick
born at Grandshaw,
County of Down, Ireland
August 23, 1784
Died in the Faith at Fairfield
August 13, 1849

Notes:
--Hugh, bapt. May 6, 1783 at the Presbyterian Church, Kircubbin, County Down, Ireland; son of John McCormick.
--Jean, bapt. August 23, 1784, Kircubbin, County Down, Ireland, daughter of Robert Welsh.

--1850 Census: Pequannock, Morris Co., NJ: Garret C. Schenck, age 43, b. NJ, clergy; Jane 26 b. NY; Eleanor age 15 b. NJ; Lafayette G. age 10 b. NJ; Sarah Ann age 8 b. NJ; Mary D. age 2 b. NJ; David age 7 months b. NJ; Hugh McCormick, age 67, b. Ireland; Mary O'Brian, age 22, b. Ireland

- - - - -

MEAD
Meade

Mead, THOMAS H. b.
(monument) d. January 20, 1914

T. H. M.

Notes:
Served: CIVIL WAR Pvt. Co. A. 13th Regt. NJ Inf.
See: *Roster of the Officers & Men of the 13th Regiment, NJ Volunteers, Co. A.*

- - - - -

Mead, WILLIAM b. (abt. September 19, 1801)
(Neafie, p.16) d. July 30, 1849
(inscriptions, 140)
(monument)

William Mead
Died
July 30, 1849
Aged 47 years,
10 months
& 11 days

wife, RACHEL (Van Ness) b. January 28, 1804
(Neafie, p.16) d. March 23, 1883
(monument)

Rachel Van Ness
Wife of
William Mead
Born Jan. 28, 1804
Died March 23, 1883

son, THOMAS b. (abt. April 29, 1834)
(inscriptions, p.140) d. October 3, 1836

Thomas
son of
William and Rachel Mead
Died October 3, 1836
Aged 2 years, 5 months
& 4 days

Notes:
--William, son of Peter 'Meet' and Maria VanBuren
--William P. Mead m. Jan. 1, 1824, Rachel VanNess, dau. of David Van Ness, q.v., and Ellen Vanderhoof
--Rachel m. #2, Peter D. Jacobus

--1850 Census: 16 Wd, Dist. 3, New York City: Rachel Mead, age 45 b.NJ; Peter, age 25, NJ, carpenter; David age 20 b. NJ, mason; Abraham 17 b. NJ, mason; Thomas, age 12 b. NJ; Margaret E., age 8 b. NY; Mary J., age 22? b. NY; (adj. to Wilson Jacobus, age 28, mason and John age 33, carpenter)
--1860 Census;: Caldwell Twp., Essex Co., NJ: Peter Jacobus, age 50, farmer; Rachel age 56; Emma age 17; Delilah age 13; William age 11; Margaret E. age 18, milliner; all b. NJ
--1870 Census: Caldwell Twp., Essex Co., NJ: Peter Jacobus, age 59, farmer; Rachel, age 64; Sarah, age 30, seamstress; all b. NJ
--1880 Census: Caldwell Twp., Essex Co., NJ: Peter Jacobus, age 70, farmer, b. NJ; Rachel, age 78, b. NJ; adj. to A. C. Mead, age 75, farmer, b. NJ

- - - - -

MILLER

Miller, Isaac S.   See: Van Ness Burial Ground
wife, Elenor

MORRELL

Morrell, THOMAS R.   b. (February 22, 1830)
(Neafie, p.3)   d. April 23, 1886

Thomas R. Morrell
Died Apr. 23, 1886
Aged 56 years, 1 mos.
& 1 day

wife, Esther Ann* (Riker)   b. (abt. 1835)
    d. (April 29, 1898)

son, WILLIAM   b. (abt. April 30, 1855)
(Neafie, p.5)   d. November 16, 1856

William
son of Thomas H.
and Esther Ann Morrell
Died Nov. 16, 1856
Aged 18 months
& 16 days

Notes:
--Thomas, son of Francis Asbury Morrell and Mary Griffith of Parsippany, Morris Co., NJ
--Thomas m. March 23, 1855 at Little Falls: Esther, daughter of John Riker, q.v., and Ann Smith

--1850 Census: Paterson, Passaic Co., NJ: Thomas Morrell, age 20 b. 'NJ' boarder, school teacher; Theodore Morrell, age 18, b. 'NJ', boarder, clerk

--1850 Census: Acquckanonk, Passaic Co. NJ: John Riker, age 44; Ann age 41; Ellen, age 21; Hester A., age 13; Sarah J. Riker; 6 other persons

--1860 Census: Acquackanonk Twp., Passaic Co., NJ: Thomas Morrell, age 31, occupation....., b. NY; Hester, age 22, b. NJ; Susan, age 2, b. NJ; (adj. to John VanPelt and Ellen (Riker) VanPelt

--1870 Census: Little Falls, Passaic Co., NJ: Abr. A. Garrabrant, age 36, wagonmaker; Sarah J., age 30; Emma, age 7; Thos. R. "Marr" (Morrell), age 40; Hester A. "Marr", age 33; "Susan Marr", age 12; Abr. VanRiper, age 21, farm labor; all b. 'NJ'

--1880 Census: Little Falls, Passaic Co., NJ: Thomas Morrell, age 51, b. NY, hotel keeper; Ester, age 45, b. NJ, parents b. NJ; Susan, age 20, b. NJ, father b. NY, mother b. NJ

--1895 NJ State Census: Little Falls, Passaic Co., NJ: Esther A. Morrell; Susan Stinson; May Stinson; John J. Fox; George Riker

- - - - -

OGILVIE

Ogilvie, JAMES GLAEN   b. August 26, 1792
(Neafie, p.3)   d. August 5, 1832
(inscriptions, p.140

Rev. James Glaen (sic) *Ogilvie*
Pastor of
The Reformed Dutch Church
Fairfield, N.J.
Died Aug. 5, 1832
Born at New York Aug. 26, 1794 (1792)

wife, ELIZABETH W. (Wilson)
(Neafie, p.3)   b. (abt. 1794)

d. October 25, 1870

Elizabeth W. Wilson
wife of
Rev. James Glaen Ogilvie
Died Oct. 25, 1870
Aged 76 years

Notes:
--See: Pastors: Fairfield Reformed Church
--"Glaen": usually spelled "Glean"

--"Ogilvie, James Glaen(sic) b. 1794 (sic). lic. 1826. Montville 1826-7; Missionary at Little Falls and Fairfield 1827-9; Fairfield 1828-32 d. August 5(sic), from injuries received by being thrown from his horse." (*Manual of the Reformed Church in America.* Edward T. Corwin, D.D., NY, 1902)

--James, b. New York City: born August 26, 1792; bapt. Oct. 14, 1792, First Presb. Church, NYC; son of Anthony Ogilvie and Elizabeth Cowdrey. Anthony and Elizabeth were m. June 22, 1791, St. George's Church, Hempstead, LI. She died Dec. 24, 1795, 'much beloved'.

--1795 July - Nov.: NYC: Yellow Fever Epidemic Deaths: John Ogilvie, house carpenter; Anthony Ogilvie, painter and glazier; Widow Ogilvie; Isaac Ogilvie, mariner
--1795 December 9: NYC: Anthony Ogilvie, painter and glazier; d. intestate : Adm. to widow, Elizabeth, Dec. 9, 1795
--(she died: December 24, 1795)
--1795 December 31: NYC. Anthony Ogilvie, painter and glazier; Adm. to father, Thomas Ogilvie
--James Glaen Ogilvie, grandson of "Thomas Ogilvie m. Abigail Glean, NY, May 3, 1764." (NY Marriage Record)

--1798, February: James Ogilvie 'grandson'; in the Will of Jonathan Cowdrey, Sr.,NY.; receives 1/3 of the estate with his brother, Thomas Cowdrey Ogilvie.

--James Glaen Ogilvie desecendant(?) of: "Anthony Glean, Esq. (1751-1842), a hero of the American Revolution who served as a Naval Officer in the Continental Army, and who stood with some measure of distinction among those men invited to join General George Washington on the day of his triumphal entry into New York City on November 25, 1783 for among them, he is reputed to have been "the man who fired the first gun, which took effect, at the British fleet, when it came to New York; and the man who hoisted the first American flag, when the British troops departed from it."

--1825, September 15: "James G. Ogilvie, chaplain (Presbyterian) U.S. Navy. This is the last appearance on Records of the Navy Department."

--1830 Census; Caldwell Twp., Essex Co., NJ: James G. Ogilvie: 1 male age 30-40; 1 male age 10-15; 1 female age 30-40

--1850 Census: Dist. 2, New York City: Eliza Ogilvie, age 55 b. NY; Ed Ogilvie, age '26' b. NY; Mary Kelly age 75, b. NY; Mary Gorman, age 25, b. Ireland

--1860 Census: Caldwell Twp., Essex Co., NJ: Henry 'Dry' age 45 b. NJ, farmer; Susan age 46 b. NJ; Samuel age 17 b. NJ; Mary age 12, b. NJ; Jane Berry, age 42, b. NJ; A. E. Ogilvie, age 42, b. NY, music? teacher; Elizabeth Ogilvie, age 60, b. NY

--1870 Census: Caldwell Twp., Essex Co., NJ: E. Anthony C. Ogilvie, (q.v.) age 49, b. NY, broker; Mary M. age 23, b. NJ, keeping house; Susan E., age 3 b. NJ; Jane B. age 5 months b. NJ; Elizabeth Ogilvie, age 85(?), b. NJ; Jane Berry, age 50 b. NJ

- - - - -

Ogilvie, E. ANTHONY C. b. (December 1819)
(Neafie, p.3) d. April 1, 1871
(NJ Will #17399G, 1871, Inv.)

Anthony Ogilvie
Died April 1, 1871
Aged 51 years 4 months

wife, Mary Margaret* (Dey) b. (October 24, 1846)
   d. (aft. 1920)

Notes:
--Edward Anthony C. (Cowdrey?) Ogilvie, son of James Glaen Ogilvie, q.v., and Elizabeth Wilson
--E. Anthony m. December 30, 1864, Paterson, Mary Margaret Dey, dau. of Henry Dey and Susan Berry.
--Mary Margaret m. #2, November 2, 1878, George Herman Winans, son of Abner Winans Jr. and Elizabeth Ann Conrad

--1830 Census: Caldwell Twp., Essex Co., NJ: James G. 'Oglevie': 1 male age 30-40; 1 male age 10-15; 1 female age 30-40
--1850 Census: 7Wd, Dist. 2, New York City: Eliza Ogilvie, age 55 b. NY; Ed Ogilvie, age '26' b. NY; Mary Kelly age 75, b. NY; Mary Gorman, age 25, b. Ireland
--1860 Census: Caldwell Twp., Essex Co., NJ: Henry 'Dry'(Dey) age 45 b. NJ, farmer; Susan age 46 b. NJ; Samuel age 17 b. NJ; Mary age 12, b. NJ; Jane Berry, age 42, b. NJ; A. E. Ogilvie, age 42, b. NY, music? teacher; Elizabeth Ogilvie, age 60, b. NY
--1870 Census: Caldwell Twp., Essex Co., NJ: E. Anthony C. Ogilvie, age 49, b. NY, broker; Mary M. age 23, b. NJ, keeping house; Susan E., age 3 b. NJ; Jane B. age 5 months b. NJ; Elizabeth Ogilvie, age "85", b. NJ; Jane Berry, age 50 b. NJ

--1880 Census: Caldwell Twp., Essex Co., NJ: George H. Winans, age 23, b. NJ, hatter; Mary M. age 33 b. NJ; Susan E. Ogilvie age 13, dau. b. NJ, father b. NY, at school; Jane B. Ogilvie age 10 dau., b. NJ, father b. NY, at school; Jane Berry, age 61, single, aunt, b. NJ, housekeeping; 1 boarder
--1900 Census: 8Wd, Newark, Essex Co., NJ; Mary 'Winnans' b. Oct. 1846, b. NJ, widow, 6 born 6 living; Mark, b. July 1881, son, single, shipping clerk; Bessie b. Dec. 1883 NJ; Grace b. Nov. 1885 NJ; Florence b. Jan. 1888; Susan Ogilvie b. Dec. 1867, dau., single; Jennie Ogilvie, b. July 1868, dau., single; Jane Berry b. Nov. 1817, NJ, aunt, single
--1910 Census: 8Wd, Newark, Essex Co., NJ: Mary M. 'Wimsus', age 63, widow, b. NJ; Grace G. age 24, dau. single b. NJ; Florence M. age 22, dau. single b. NJ; 1 boarder
--1920 Census: 8Wd, Newark, Essex Co., NJ: Mary M. Winans, age 73, widow b. NJ; Susan E. Ogilvie age 52, dau. single b. NJ, father b. NY; Grace B. Winans, age 30, dau. single. b. NJ, nurse; Florence M. Winans, age 33, dau., single, b. NJ, teacher
--1930 Census: Newark: Susan E. Ogilvie age 63, single, b. NJ, father b. NY, mother b. NJ

- - - - -

OSBORNE

Osborne, JACOB   b. (abt. 1825)
(Neafie, p.11)   d. April 11, 1891
(monument)
(gov't stone)

Jacob Osborne
Co. B, 1 Regt. NJ Vols.
Died April 11, 1891
Aged 66 years

wife, MARY   b. (abt. 1832)

(Neafie, p.11) d. December 31, 1874
(monument)

> *Mary*
> *wife of*
> *Jacob Osborne*
> *Died Dec. 31, 1874*
> *Aged 42 years*

Notes:
--Served: <u>Civil War:</u> Co. B., 1 Regt. N.J. Vols.

--?1840 Census: Pompton Twp., Passaic Co., NJ: Jacob Osborn. two persons
--1850 Census: Lodi Twp., Wastenaw Co., MI: <u>Jacob M.</u> Osborn, age 27, b. NJ, farmer; <u>Mary</u>, age 18 b. NY; 'Juliana' age 9 months, b. Michigan
--1860 Census: Boonton, Hanover Twp., Morris Co., NJ: <u>Jacob</u> "Orsborns", age 35, b. Morris Co., laborer; <u>Mary</u>, age 25, b. NY; Julia, age 10 b. MI; Irene, age 8 b. MI; Edward, age 6, b. Morris Co.; William, age 4, b. Morris Co., Francis, age 1, b. Morris Co.
--1870 Census: Rockaway Twp., Morris Co., NJ: <u>Jacob</u> Osborn, age 46 b. NJ, laborer; <u>Mary</u>, age 37 b. NY; Juliana M., age 20, b. MI, mason; Susy J., age 18, b. MI; Edwin, age 16, b. NJ, laborer; William W., age 13, b. NJ, laborer; George F., age 10, b. NJ; Arminna, age 4, b. NJ; Nora, age 2 b. NJ
--1890 Veterans Schedule: Wayne, Passaic Co., NJ: Jacob Osborn.

- - - - -

PEARCE
PIERCE

Pearce, Edward   See: Pearce Burial Ground
wife, Hannah

- - - - -

Pierce, Francis   See: Pearce Burial Ground
wife, Sarah

- - - - -

Pierce, Joseph   See: Pearce Burial Ground
wife, Nancy

- - - - -

Pearce, Mark   See: Pearce Burial Ground
wife Ellen M.

- - - - -

Pierce, Reuben   See: Pearce Burial Ground
wife, Emeline

- - - - -

Pierce, William   See: Pearce Burial Ground
wife, Roba

- - - - -

Pierce, William Jr.   See: Pearce Burial Ground
wife, Amelia

- - - - -

PIER
Peer

Pier, DAVID   b. (abt. 1768)
(Neafie, p. 19)   d. April 4, 1838
(inscriptions, p. 140)   (d. April 1, 1838)
(NJ Will #12907G, 1838)

David Pier
Died April 1, 1838
in the 71st year
of his
age

wife, SARAH (Berry)   b. (abt. September 9, 1770)
(Neafie, p.19)   d. March 16, 1850

Sarah
Wife of
David Pier
Died March 16, 1850
Aged 79 years 6 months
& 7 days

Notes:
--?1830 Census: Caldwell Twp., Essex Co., NJ: David Pier: 5 persons

- - - - -

Pier, David*   b. (abt. 1813)
(Neafie, p.18)   d. May 3, 1880
(NJ Will #20024G, 1880)

David Pier
Died May 3, 1880
Aged 67 years

first wife, HESTER* (Dods)
(Neafie, p.18)   b. (abt. April 29, 1819)
(inscriptions, p. 140)   d. August 20, 1848

Hester Dods
Wife of
David Pier
Died Aug. 20, 1848
Aged 29 years, 3 months
& 22 days

second wife, ELIZABETH (Smith)
(Neafie, p.18)   b. (abt. 1820)
     d. March 15, 1851

Elizabeth S.
Wife of
David Pier
Died March 15, 1851
Aged 30 years, 7 months
& 23 days

third wife, Rachel A.*(Hyler) b. (abt. 1822)
(NJ Will #25611G, 1894)   d. (May 24, 1893)

daughter, SARAH ANN   b. (abt. September 13, 1853)
(Neafie, p.18)   d. January 27, 1862

Sarah Ann
Daughter of
David and Rachel Pier
Died Jan. 27, 1862
Aged 8 years 4 months
& 14 days

Notes:

--David, son of John I. Pier, q.v., and Sarah .....
--David m. #1, Hester Dods
--David m. #2, Elizabeth Smith
--David m. #3, Rachel Ann Hyler
--Death Record: "Rachel A. Pier, b. c.1822 d. May 24, 1893, Caldwell; widowed"

--1850 Census: Caldwell Twp., Essex Co., NJ: John J. Pier, age. 60, shoemaker; Sarah age 61; David, age 37; Eliza age 30; John A., age 9; all b. NJ
--1850 Census, Pequannock, Morris Co., NJ: Jacob H. "Hiler", age 28, carpenter; Rachel A., age 27; Sarah Jane, age 2; all b. New Jersey
--1860 Census: Caldwell Twp., Essex Co., NJ: David "Peri" age 47, farmer; Rachel age 37; John A., age 19; Sarah A., age 7; Willard age 4; Anthony, age 1; all b. New Jersey (adj. to Francis 'Peri')
--1870 Census: Caldwell Twp., Essex Co., NJ: David "Pur" age 57, farmer; Rachel A., age 47; 'William' age 14; Anthony O. age 11; 'Elmer' age 8; all b. NJ; adj. John A. Pier, age 29, teacher and Sarah C. Pier, age 22
--1880 Census: Caldwell Twp., Essex Co., NJ: Rachel A. Pier, age 57, widow; Willard, age 23, hatter; Ogilvee A. age 21, farmer; Elmira, age 18, daughter; all b. New Jersey
Aug. 1867, 6 born 4 living; Clyde E. (Clyde Ogilvie Pier, b. Oct. 9, 1890) b. Oct. 1888; Elsie E. b. Dec. 1891; Norman A. (Norman Allen Pier, b. Jan. 8, 1897); Leroy E., b. Aug. 1899; all b. NJ
--1885 Census: Caldwell Twp., Essex Co., NJ: George E. Pier; Rachel A. Pier; Myra Pier; George E. Pier

- - - - -

Pier, FRANCIS	b. (September 25, 1794)
(Neafie, p. 20)	d. June 10, 1861

Francis Pier

June 10, 1861
In his 67th year

wife, ELIZABETH (Van Ness)
(Neafie, p.21)   b. (abt. 1798)
                      d. February 9, 1861

Elizabeth
wife of
Francis Pier
Died Feb. 9, 1861
In her 63rd year

son, ISAAC F.   b. (February 12, 1820)
(Neafie, p.20)   d. January 7, 1843
(inscriptions)

Isaac F. Pier
son of Francis and Elizabeth
Pier
died January 7, 1843
aged 23 years, 10 months
& 19 days

daughter, RACHEL J.   b. (abt. April 24, 1824)
(Neafie, p.20)   d. July 31, 1854

Rachel J.
Died July 31, 1854
Aged 30 years, 3 mos.
& 7 days
(m. Henry Dodd, q.v.)

Notes:
--Francis, son of Isaac Pier and Maria Post
--Frances m. May 14, 1815, Elizabeth Van Ness, dau. of William Van Ness

--1850 Census: Pequannock Twp., Morris Co. NJ: Francis 'Peer' age 55, farmer; Elizabeth age 52; Richard J. age 26; David, age 18, laborer; Munson, age 13; Richard, age 10; all b. New Jersey
--1860 Census: Pequannock Twp., Morris Co., NJ: Francis 'Peer' age 65, farmer, b. Essex Co.; Elizabeth age 62, b. Essex Co.; David, age 28, farmer, b. Morris Co.; Richard, age 20, farmer, b. Morris Co.; Mary E., age 9; Francis Dodd age 6 (grandson?)

- - - - -

Pier, FRANCIS J. b. (abt. 1819)
(Neafie, p.15) d. December 29, 1885

Francis J. Peer
Died Dec. 19, 1885
In his 67th year

wife, Catherine* (Francisco)
 b. (abt. December 1827)
 d. (July 17, 1900)

Notes:
--Francis, son of James Pier, q.v., and Mary .....
--Francis m. July 1846, Catherine Francisco

--1850 Census: Caldwell Twp., Essex Co., NJ: James J. Pier, age 50, mason; Catherine, age 24; Mary Jane, age 16; John, age 10; James, age 3; John, age 1; Francis, age 29, farmer; all b. NJ
--1860 Census: Caldwell Twp., Essex Co., NJ: Francis 'Peri', age 41, mason; Catharine, age 32; James F., age 13; John W., age 11; Mary C., age 9; all b. NJ (adj. to David Pier)

--1860 Census: 3Wd, Newark, Essex Co., NJ: <u>Francis</u> Peer, age 35, mason, boarder, b. New Jersey
--1870 Census: Caldwell, Essex Co., NJ: <u>Francis</u> Pier, age 48, brick mason; <u>Catherine</u>, age 42; John W., age 21, brick mason; Mary, age 19, seamstress; all b. NJ
--1880 Census: Dist. 2, Caldwell, Essex Co., NJ: <u>Francis</u> Peer, age 59 b. NJ, brick mason; <u>Catherine</u>, wife, age 53, b. NJ
--1895 NJ Census: Montclair, Essex Co., NJ: Melvin Sigler; Mary Sigler; 4 Sigler children; <u>Catherine</u> Pier
--1900 Census: Montclair, Essex Co., NJ: Melvin Sigler, age 49, feed & grain; Mary C. Sigler, age 49, b. Oct. 1850; Ella Sigler, age 19, dau.; Alice P. Sigler, age 11, dau.; <u>Catherine</u> "Peer", age 72, b. Dec. 1827, mother-in-law, widow; Harry I. Peer, age 23, nephew, timekeeper at stone quarry; all b. NJ

- - - - -

Pier, Isaac J.*   b. (abt. May 1857)
                         d. (aft. 1940)

first wife, Anna Jane (Harris)*b. (abt. 1860)
                         d. (bef. 1896)

second wife, Adella L. Condit*
                         b. (October 12, 1874)
                         d. (aft. 1940)

son, CLYDE C.   b. (abt. December 17, 1882)
(Neafie, p.21)   d. January 27, 1885

Clyde C.
Died Jan. 27, 1885
Aged 2 years 1 month
&10 days
Children of
Isaac and Anna I. Pier

son, CHARLES V. b. (abt. January 25, 1885)
(Neafie, p.21) d. January 31, 1885

Charles V.
Died Jan. 31, 1885
Aged 6 days
Children of
Isaac and Anna J. Pier

Notes:
--Isaac, son of William Pier and Eliza J. VanNess
--Anna Jane, dau. of Andrew Harris and Jenny ...
--Isaac m. #2, abt. 1896, Adella J. Condit, dau. of Franklin I. Condit and Mary J. Thomas

--1860 Census: Caldwell Twp., Essex Co., NJ: Isaac "Peri", age 60, farmer; Margaret, age 58; William, age 26, laborer; Anna E., age 24; Rachel A., age 5; Isaac, age 3; Sarah M., age 28; Anna E., age 23; all b. New Jersey
--1870 Census: Caldwell Twp., Essex Co., NJ: Isaac Pier, age 70; Margaret, age 68; William, age 38, farmer; Eliza J. age 35; Isaac, age 13; Charles, age 4; all b. NJ
--1870 Census: Caldwell Twp., Essex Co., NJ: Elijah Harris, age 57, b. NJ farmer; Jemima, age 57, b. NJ; Andrew Harris, age 26, b. NJ, farmer; Jenny, age 27, b. NJ; Ira James, age 17, b. NJ; Henry E., age 12, b. PA; Anna J., age 10, b. NJ; Ida J., age 6, b. NJ; Luther, age 1 month, b. NJ
--1880 Census: Caldwell Twp., Essex Co., NJ: Isaac Pier, age 23, farmer; Annie Jane, age 20, b. NJ
--1880 Census: Hanover Twp., Essex Co., NJ: Susan R. Condit, age 54, widow, b. NJ, father b. NY, mother b. NJ; Selwyn, age 27, son, b. NJ, mason; Mary, age 19, dau., b. NJ; Daniel, age 18, son, b. NJ; Clarence, age 15, son, b. NJ; Adella, age 5, granddaughter b. PA, father b. NJ, mother b. England

--1900 Census: 7Wd, Newark, Essex Co., NJ: Isaac J. Pier, age 43, b. May 1857, NJ, parents NJ, teamster; Adela b. Oct. 1874 PA, father NJ, mother b. England; Herbert, age 13, b. April 1887 NJ; Hilda, age 3, b. Oct. 1896 NJ
--1910 Census: 8Wd. Newark, Essex Co., NJ: Isaac Pier, age 53, b. NJ, driver laundry wagon; Della, age 35, b. PA, father b. NJ, mother b. England; Kenneth, age 2, b. NJ
--1940 Census: 9 Wd. Newark, Essex Co., NJ: Isaac Pier, age 84, b. NJ; Della, age 56, b. NJ, landlady rooming house boarders

- - - - -

Pier, James I.* b. (abt. 1799?)
 d. (aft. 1850?)

wife, MARY (Dey) b. October 21, 1794
(Neafie, p.15) d. July 18, 1847
(inscriptions, p. 140)

Mary
wife of James Pier
Died July 18, 1847
Aged 52 years 8 months
& 28 days

Notes:
--James m. Mary Dey, dau. of John Dey
--?1840 Census: Caldwell Twp., Essex Co., NJ: James Pier, 6 persons; adj. to John, Isaac, and David Pier
--?1850 Census: Caldwell Twp., Essex Co., NJ: James I. Pier, age 50, mason; Catherine, age 24; Mary Jane, age 16; John, age 10; James, age 3; John, age 1; Francis, age 29, farmer; all b. NJ

- - - - -

Pier, JOHN I. b. (abt. May 10, 1789)
(Neafie, p.18) d. May 10, 1860
(monument)
(NJ Will #15389G, 1860)

> *John I. Pier*
> *May 10th 1860*
> *Aged 71 years*
> *and 29 days*

wife, SARAH
(Neafie, p.18) b. (abt. January 5, 1789)
  d. June 9, 1853

> *Sarah*
> *Wife of*
> *John I. Pier*
> *Died June 9, 1853*
> *Aged 64 years, 5 months*
> *& 4 days*

Notes:
--?John, son of Isaac Pier and Maria Post

--1850 Census: Caldwell Twp., Essex Co., NJ: John Pier, age 61, shoemaker; Sarah, age 61; David, age 37; Eliza, age 30; John A., age 9; all b. New Jersey

- - - - -

Peer, JOHN W. b. 1848
(monument) d. 1910

> *John W. Peer*
> *1848 - 1910*

His Wife
Jane C. Zeek
1852 - 1896

wife, JANE C. (Zeek) b. 1852 (October 18, 1851)
(monument) d. 1896 (February 11, 1895)

Notes:
--John W., son of Francis J. Pier, q.v.
--Jane Caroline Zeek, 'b. Oct. 18, 1851, Bloomfield NJ; dau. of Abraham Zeek (q.v.) and Elizabeth." (NJ Birth Record)
--Jane C. Pier "b. abt.1853. d. Feb. 11, 1895, Verona, NJ; age 42, married" (NJ Death Record)
--1850 Census: Caldwell Twp., Essex Co., NJ: James J. Pier, age 50, mason; Catharine, age 24; Mary Jane, age 16; John, age 11; James, age 3; John W., age 1; Francis, age 29, farmer; all b. New Jersey
--1860 Census: Caldwell Twp., Essex Co., NJ: Francis 'Peri', age 41, mason; Catharine, age 32; James F., age 13; John W., age 11; Mary C., age 9; all b. NJ
--1860 Census: Bloomfield, Essex Co.,NJ: Abraham 'Lemek', age 40, farmer; Elizabeth, age 40; Helen age 21; Emma, age 19; Thomas age 17; Mary,age 13; Jane, age 12; Mark, age 9; Ellen, age 7; Clara, age 4; all b. NJ
--1870 Census: Caldwell Twp., Essex Co., NJ: Francis Pier, age 48 b. NJ, brick mason; Catharine, age 42, b. NJ; John W., age 21, b. NJ, brick mason; Mary, age 19, b. NJ, seamstress
--1880 Census: 2 Dist. Caldwell Twp., Essex Co., NJ: 'James' W. Peer, age 29 b. NJ, brick mason; Jane C., age 28, b. NJ; Harry, son, age 3 b. NJ; adj. to Elizabeth "Zeke", age 60, b. NJ
--1900 Census: 2Wd. Bloomfield, Essex Co., NJ: John W. Pier, age 48 b. Nov. 1851, NJ, widower, mason; boarder at res. of Henry Crane, mason

- - - - -

Pier, OGILVIE b. January 9, 1859
(monument) d. June 8, 1902

Ogilvie Pier
Born Jan. 9, 1859
Died June 8, 1902

Notes:
--Anthony Ogilvie Pier, son of David Pier, q.v., and Rachel A. Hyler
--Member, Little Falls Reformed Church
--1860 Census: Caldwell Twp., Essex Co., NJ: David "Peri" age 47, farmer; Rachel age 37; John A., age 19; Sarah A., age 7; Willard age 4; Anthony, age 1; all b. New Jersey
--1870 Census: Caldwell Twp., Essex Co., NJ: David "Pur" age 57, farmer; Rachel A., age 47; 'William' age 14; Anthony O. age 11; 'Elmer' age 8; all b. NJ; adj. John A. Pier, age 29, teacher and Sarah C. Pier, age 22
--1880 Census: Caldwell Twp., Essex Co., NJ: Rachel A. Pier, age 57, widow; Willard, age 23, hatter; Ogilvee A. age 21, farmer; Elmira, age 18, daughter; all b. New Jersey
--1900 Census: Caldwell Twp., Essex Co., NJ: A. 'Ogleri' Pier b. Jan 1859, m.10 yr, farmer and hatter; Louisa, wife, b. Aug. 1867, 6 born 4 living; Clyde E. (Clyde Ogilvie Pier, b. Oct. 9, 1890) b. Oct. 1888; Elsie E. b. Dec. 1891; Norman A. (Norman Allen Pier, b. Jan. 8, 1897) b. Jan. 1897; Leroy E. b. Aug. 1899; all b. NJ

- - - - -

Pier, Simeon D. See: Pearce Burial Ground
wife, Caroline

Pier, William* b. (abt. May 18, 1833)
  d. (aft. 1910)

wife, Eliza J.* (Van Ness)   b. (October 3, 1835)
                             d. (aft. 1910)

dau., RACHEL A.   b.
(monument)   d. (no date)
(Neafie, p.21)

In Memory of
Rachel A. Pier
Aged 12 yrs. 4 mos.
& 11 ds.

son, RICHARD   b.
(monument)   d. (no date)
(Neafie, p.21)

Richard Pier
Aged 2 years 11 mos.
& 13 ds.

Notes:
--William, son of Isaac Pier and Margaret Riker
--William, m. Eliza J. Van Ness, dau. of Richard Van Ness and Rachel Stagg
--1850 Census: Caldwell Twp., Essex Co., NJ: Isaac Pier, age 50, farmer; Margaret, age 48; James, age 25, blacksmith; Thomas, age 23; Sarah M., age 21; William, age 18, farmer; Ann E., age 14
--1860 Census: Caldwell Twp., Essex Co., NJ: Isaac Pier, age 60, farmer; Margaret, age 58; William, age 26, laborer; Anna E., age 24; Rachel A., age 5; Isaac, age 3; Sarah M., age 28; all b. NJ
--1870 Census: Caldwell Twp., Essex Co., NJ: Isaac Pier, age 70, farmer; Margaret, age 68; William, age 38, farmer; Eliza J., age 35; Isaac, age 13; Charles, age 4; all b. NJ
--1880 Census: Caldwell Twp., Essex Co., NJ: Margaret 'Peer', age 78; William, age 48, farmer; Eliza J., age 44;

Charles, age 13, works on farm; William, age 6; adj. to Thomas Pier
--1900 Census: Caldwell Twp., Essex Co., NJ: William Pier, age 67, b. May 1833, farmer; Eliza J., age 64, b. Oct. 1835; William H., age 37 b. July 1872, farmer
--1910 Census: Caldwell Twp., Essex Co., NJ: William Pier, age 76, m.52 years, farmer; Eliza J., age 74, 5 born 3 living; William H., age 33, farm laborer; all b. NJ

- - - - -

POST

--Statement by John Neafie: This is a large family ... "Not a living Post, male or female, that we have met, can tell, or tell positively, who his or her great grandfather was."(*Preakness and the Preakness Ref. Church. A History. 1695-1902*) George W. Labow. New York. 1902)

- - - - -

Post, Cornelius Henry*   b. (abt. April 1820)
(monument)   d. (September 17, 1905)
    bur. (Laurel Grove Mem. Park Totowa, Passaic Co., NJ)

Cornelius H. Post
Died Sept. 27, 1905
Age 85 years

wife, Leah Maria* (Ryerson) b. (July 20, 1823)
(monument)   d. (December 12, 1893)
    bur. (Laurel Grove Mem. Park Totowa, Passaic Co., NJ)

Leah M. Ryerson
wife of

Cornelius H. Post
Died December 12, 1893
In her 71st year

son, INFANT   b. (abt. February 1848)
(Neafie, p.2)   d. April 2, 1848
                        bur. Fairfield Ref. Church

Infant Son
of Cornelius H. Post
and
Leah M. Post
Died April 2, 1848
Aged 6 weeks

Notes:
-- Cornelius Henry, son of Francis C. Post, q.v.
--Cornelius Henry m. May 10, 1847, Leah Maria Ryerson, dau. of Nicholas Ryerson and Mary Jacobus

--1850 Census: Pequannock Twp, Morris Co. NJ: Francis C. Post, age 63 farmer; Mariah age 54; Henry age 30, farmer; Leah M. age 27; Catherine Berry, age 18; all b. NJ
--1860 Census: Pequannock Twp., Morris Co., NJ: Cornelius H. Post, age 40, b. Morris Co., farmer; Lea, age 37, b. Passaic Co.; Abram, age 7, b. Morris Co.; Mary C., age 1, b. Morris Co.; William Button, age 16, b. Passaic Co.; Eliza Button, age 18, b. Passaic Co.; Charles Hicks, age 15, b. Essex Co.
--1870 Census: Pequannock Twp., Morris Co., NJ: Cornelius H. Post, age 50 b. NJ, farmer; Leah, age 47; Abraham, age 17; Mary C., age 13; Eliza Button, age 27, b. NJ
--1880 Census: Pequannock Twp., Morris Co., NJ: C. H. Post, age 60, farmer; Leah, age 56, wife; Abram, age 27, son, farm labor; Lara C., age 24, daughter-in-law; Eliza Button, age 39, housekeeper

--1900 Census: Pequannock Twp., Morris Co., NJ: Cornelius H. Post, age 80, b. Apr 1820, farmer; Abraham, age 47, b. Oct. 1852, farmer; Mary C., age 43, b. Oct. 1856; Laura C., age 44, b. July 1855, dau-in-law; Eva B., age 18, granddau. b. Apr. 1883, music teacher; Myrtle A., age 11, graddau. b. Mar. 1889; Eliza Button, age 60, b. Sept. 1839, NJ, father b. England, mother b. NJ, servant; Halmagh H. Ryerson, age 31, b. NJ, farm laborer

--1905 NJ State Census: Cornelius H. Post, age 85; Abram 52; Laura 49; Mary 48; Blanche 22; Myrtle 167; Eliza Button 65; Halmagh 'Rogers'(Ryerson) 34; Jeremiah Ackerman 19

- - - - -

Post, FRANCIS   b. 1783 (?)
(monument)   d. 1838
(NJ Will #11992G, Inv.1839)

Francis Post
1783 - 1838
-
Rachel Gould
His wife
1787 - 1853

wife, RACHEL GOULD   b. 1787 (January 31)
(monument)   d. 1853

Notes:
--Are the dates on this monument correct?
--??Francis Johannes Post, son of Johannes F. Post and Antje Rutan ("Johannes Post, Antye Rattan: francoos b. 12 Oct. bp. Nov. 9, 1788" Old Church at Totowa)
--Francis m. Feb. 1811, Caldwell: Rachel Gould, dau. of Josiah Gould and Elizabeth Colyer

--?1850 US Census Mortality Schedule: Caldwell Twp., NJ: "Rachel Post, age 66, widow, d. March. Caldwell Twp., Consumption"

- - - - -

Post, FRANCIS C. b. (1787-1788)
(Neafie, p. 1) d. April 30, 1851
(NJ Will #3408N, 1851)

Francis C. Post
Died Apr 30, 1851
Aged 64 years, 3 months
& 25 days

first wife, MARY (Jacobus) b. (abt. September 29, 1791)
(Neafie, p.1) d. October 14, 1836
(inscriptions, p. 141)

Mary Jacobus
wife of
Francis C. Post
Died October 14, 1836
Aged 45 years & 15 days

Notes:
--?Francis, son of John Francis Post and Mary Neafie
--Francis C. Post and wife: burial reported adj. to Catherine E. Neafie, wife of George Van Ness, q.v. and James Theodore, son of Ogden and Maria Neafie Hall, q.v.
--Francis m. #1, Mary Jacobus
--?Mary, dau. of Cornelius II. Jacobus and Abigail Gould
--?Francis m. #2, aft. 1836, Mariah .....

--"Marretje Nefie of Saddle River Twp., Bergen Co., dau. of Cornelius, bapt at Acquackanonk NJ May 22, 1768; m. John Francis Post: children: Francis b. May 12, 1788, bapt.

Totowa; Cornelius b. Aug. 20, 1790, bapt. Acquackanonk; Aultje b. July 29, 1793, bapt. Acquackanonk" (*Joannes Nevius & His Descendants.* A. Van Doren Honeyman. Plainfield, NJ. 1900)

--1830 Census: Pequannock Twp., Morris Co., NJ: Francis C. Post, 7 persons: (Adj. Simeon Doremus, Francis Neafie; Cornelius Neafie and J. VanWart)
--1840 Census: Pequannock Twp., Morris Co., NJ: Francis C. Post. 7 persons (adj. Sarah Van Ness and Nicholas Van Duyne)
--1850 Census: Pequannock Twp, Morris Co. NJ: Francis C. Post, age 63 farmer; Mariah age 54; Henry age 30, farmer; Leah M. age 27; Catherine Berry, age 18; all b. NJ
--?1860 Census: Acquackanonk Twp., Passaic Co., NJ: Ann Alyea, age 46; Richard, age 23, farmer; William age 18; Maria Post, age 65; all b. New Jersey
--?1870 Census: 4 Wd. Paterson, Passaic Co., NJ: Ann Alyea, age 55; Maria Post, age 76; (adj. A. A. Doremus)
--?1880 Census: Paterson, Passaic Co., NJ: A. A. Doremus, age 61, builder; Sarah, wife, age 59; Ann Alyea, age 66, widow, boarder; Mary Post, age 85, widow, boarder; Sarah Rome, age 76, widow, boarder
--?NJ Death Record: Maria Post, b. c.1794, d. Sept. 10, 1882; Pequannock, age 88, 'widow'

- - - - -

Post, JAMES F. (monument)	b. 1812 (June 25) d. 1890
wife, SARAH J. (Ryerson) (monument)	b. 1818 d. 1892
son?, JAMES, JR. (monument)	b. 1855 d. 1893

son?, C. HENRY (monument)	b. 1853 d. 1898

Notes:
--James, b. June 25, 1812, bapt. Pompton Ref. Church, son of Francis C. Post, q.v., and Mary Jacobus

--1850 Census: Pequannock, Morris Co., NJ: James F. Post, age 37, carpenter; Sarah Jane, age 28; Francis, age 9; Sarah, age 6; Bernard, age 2; (adj. to Francis C. Post and Barney Budd)
--1860 Census: Boonton PO, Pequannock Twp., Morris Co., NJ: James F. Post, age 49 b. Morris Co., farmer; Jane, age 39 b. NJ; Francis, age 19 b. Morris Co., Sarah, age 16, b. Morris Co.; Bernard, age 12, b. Morris Co., James, age 4, b. Morris Co.; Henry age 3 months, b. Morris Co., adj. to Cornelius H. Post
--1870 Wayne Twp., Passaic Co. NJ: James F. 'Past', age 58, farmer; Sarah J., age 48; Burnett, age 10; James F., age 14; Henry, age 10; all b. NJ
--1880 Census: Pequannock Twp., Morris Co., NJ: James F. Post, age 67, farmer; Sarah J., age 60; James, age 24, miller; Cornelius H., age 21, dentist; adj. to Cornelius H. Post.
--1885 NJ Census: Pequannock Twp., Morris Co., NJ: James F. Post; Sarah Jane Post; Cor. H. Post; at res. of Jacob and Susan Budd

- - - - -

QUICK

Quick, John J.* Rev.	b. (September 7, 1810) d. (June 19, 1886) (bur. Michigan)
wife, Deborah* Tunison	b. (November 7, 1805)

d. (April 28, 1871)
(bur. Traverse City Cemetery
Traverse City, Michigan)

daughter, MARY b. (abt. September 27, 1847)
(Neafie, p.2) d. July 13, 1848

Mary
Daughter of
John J. and Deborah Quick
Died July 13, 1848
Aged 9 mos. & 16 days

Notes:
--Pastor, q.v., of the Fairfield Reformed Church from 1845 to 1849
--John, son of James Quick and Mary Hagaman
--John m. July 31, 1839, Deborah Tunison, dau. of PhilipTunison and Susanah Brown

--1850 Census: Greenbush Twp., Rensselaer Co., NY: John Quick, age 40, b. NJ, pastor; "Tarissen" age 43 b. NY; Susan age 9 b. NY; Peter age 6, b. NJ; Mary, age 1 month, b. NY
--1860 Census: Root Twp., Montgomery Co., NY: John J. Quick, age 49, b. NJ, Ref. Dutch clergyman; "Taborah" age 47 b. NJ; Susan, age 18, b. NY; Peter, age 16, b. NY; Mary, age 10, b. NY; Susan "Tmson" age 78, b. NJ
--1870 Census: Traverse City, Grand Traverse Co., MI: John Quick, age 60, b. NJ, farmer; Deborah, age 54, b. NJ; Susan, age 28, b. NY, no occupation; Peter, age 26, b. NJ, teaching school; Mary, age 22, b. NY, teaching school
--1880 Census: Reeder Twp., Missaukee Co., MI: John J. Quick, age 65 b. NJ, farmer; Peter I., age 35, b. NJ, farmer; Susie, age 30, b. NJ

- - - - -

RIKER

Riker, HENRY H. b. (abt. March 1777)
(Neafie, p.5) d. June 5, 1854

Henry H. Riker
Died June 5, 1854
In his 77th year

first wife, SARAH (VanNess)
(Neafie, p.5) b. (abt. 1777)
(inscriptions, p. 142) d. January 5, 1844

Sarah Van Ness
Wife of
Henry H. Riker
Died January 5, 1844
in the 68th year
of her age

Notes:
--Henry, son of Hendrick Riker and Christina Vincent
--Henry H. Riker m. April 13, 1800, Sarah Van Ness; dau. of Thomas E. Van Ness and Margaret Francisco.
--Henry m. #2, after 1844, Eliza Randolph, widow of Wm. H. Doremus

--1850 Census: Caldwell Twp: <u>Henry H.</u> Riker, age 72, b. NJ, farmer; <u>Eliza,</u> age 50 b. NY; Letitia Doremus age 18 b. NJ

- - - - -

Riker, Isaac* b. (abt. 1773)
 d. (abt. 1822)

wife, CATHARINE(Berry)

(Neafie, p.16)   b. (December 14, 1780)
(inscriptions, p. 141)   d. December 5, 1842
(monument)

> *Sacred*
> *To the*
> *Memory of*
> *Catherine*
> *Wife of Isaac Riker*
> *Died Dec. 5, A.D.1842*
> *Aged 61 years, 11 months,*
> *& 5 days*

Notes:
--Isaac, son of John Riker, q.v., and Leah Riker
--Isaac m. June 14, 1801, Catherine Berry, daughter of Samuel Berry and Susanna Courter; by Rev. John Duryee

- - - - -

Riker, ISAAC   b. (June 17, 1817)
(Neafie, p.12)   d. October 26, 1874
(monument)

> *Isaac Riker*
> *Born Jun 16, 1818*
> *Died Oct. 26, 1874*

wife, JANE (Paxton)   b. March 23, 1819
(Neafie, p. 12)   d. February 1, 1893
(monument)

> *Jane Paxton*
> *Wife of*
> *Isaac Riker*
> *Died Feb. 1, 1893*
> *Born March 23, 1819*

daughter, MARY ANN b. (abt. January 26, 1839)
(Neafie, p.16) d. March 17, 1840
(inscriptions, p.141)

Mary Ann
Daughter of
Isaac and Jane Riker
Died Mar. 17, 1840
aged 1 year, 1 month
& 20 days

Notes:
--Isaac, son of Isaac Riker, q.v. and Catharine Berry
--Isaac m. March 17, 1838, Jane Paxton, (?dau. of Hendrick Paxton and Marretje Post)
--NJ Death: "Isaac Riker, b. c.1816 Montville; d. age 58; Nov. 26, 1874, Little Falls. Innkeeper, son of Jno. Riker and Cath."
--?Jane m. #2, John R. Jacobus

--1850 Census; Acquackanonk Twp., Passaic Co. NJ: Isaac Riker age 32, carriage maker; Jane age 28; John age 11; Henry age 10; Obediah age 8; Samuel? G. age 5; Jane age 3; 'Zachariah' age 1; David Pow, age 45, laborer; all b. NJ
--1860 Census; Paterson, Passaic Co. NJ: Isaac Riker, age 44, hotelkeeper; Jane 40; Henry 19, bartender; Obidiah age 17; Jane, age 13; Saml. age 14; Isaac age 11; Lydia age 9; Emma age 7; Thomas age 4; all b. NJ
--1870 Census; Little Falls, Passaic Co. NJ: Isaac Riker, age 54, hotel keeper; Jane age 43; Obediah age 29; Mary age 21; Catherine age 3; Henry age 30, painter; Thomas age 13; Lydia age 18; Emma age 16; Samuel Riker, age 56; all b. NJ; 1 servant
--1880 Census; Little Falls, Passaic Co., NJ: John R. Jacobus, age 62, b. NJ, tinsmith; Jane P. Jacobus, age 62, b.

NJ, wife; Thomas Riker, age 22, son, b. NJ; Charles Fish, age 3, b. NY, father b. Germany, mother b. NJ

- - - - -

Riker, Isaac H.*　　　　　　b. (March 31, 1818)
　　　　　　　　　　　　　　d. (August 3, 1899)

wife, MARY ANN (DeHart)
(Neafie, p.14)　　　　　　　b. October 1, 1817
　　　　　　　　　　　　　　d. (September 27, 1901)

Mary A. De Hart
Wife of Isaac H. Riker
Born Oct. 1817
Died Sept. 27, 1901

son, EPHRAIM　　　　　　　b. May 20, 1844
(Neafie. p. 5)　　　　　　　　d. February 15, 1862

Ephraim
Born May 20, 1844
Died Feb. 15, 1862
Children of Isaac H. and Mary A. Riker

daughter, SARAH AGNES　　b. May 24, 1859
(Neafie, p.5)　　　　　　　　d. August 23, 1861

Sarah Agnes
Born May 24, 1859
Died Aug. 23, 1861
Children of Isaac H. and Mary A. Riker

dau. MARY E.　　　　　　　b. June 23, 1852
(Neafie, p.14)　　　　　　　d. February 19, 1884

Mary E.
Daughter of
Isaac H. and Mary A.
Riker
and wife of
Wilber E. Woodruff
Born June 23, 1852
Died Feb. 19, 1884

Notes:
--See: Wilber Woodruff
--Isaac, son of Henry H. Riker, q.v., and Sarah VanNess
--Isaac m. January 9, 1840, Mary Ann DeHart, dau. of William DeHart and Agnes Van Houten

--1850 Census: Caldwell Twp., Essex Co., NJ: Isaac H. "Reker" age 32; Mary Ann, age 32; William H., age 9; Ephraim, age 7; Martin, age 3; all b. NJ
--1860 Census: Caldwell, Essex Co., NJ: Isaac Riker, age 42, mason; Mariann, age 42; William H., age 18; Ephraim, age 16; Martin, age 13; Mary E., age 8; Susan A., age 1
--1870 Census: Caldwell, Essex Co., NJ: Isaac H. Riker, age 52, stone mason; Mary A., age 52; Henry, age 28, teacher; Mary E., age 18
--1880 Census: Caldwell, Essex Co., NJ: Isaac H. Riker, age 62, farmer; Mary A., age 62; William H., age 38, justice of the peace; Mary E., age 25
--1900 Census: 4Wd, East Orange, Essex Co., NJ: William H. Riker, b. August 1843, m. 10 yrs., cigar mfr.; May C. b. Feb. 1852; William A., b. Aug. 1891; Mary E., b. October 1817, mother, widow; Sarah A. Cuglar, sister-law, b. March 1860; 1 servant

- - - - -

Riker, JOHN b. (November 10, 1805/6)
(Neafie, p.5) d. May 12, 1853
(monument) d. (May 22, 1853)

John Riker
Died May 12, 1853
Aged 46 years, 6 months
& 12 days

wife, ANN (Smith) b. (abt. September 5, 1809)
(Neafie, p. 5) d. February 14, 1855
(monument)

Ann Smith
Wife of John Riker
Died Feb. 14, 1855
Aged 45 years, 5 months
& 9 days

Notes:
--John, son of Isaac Riker and Catherine Berry
--John m. Dec. 1826, Ann Smith
--1850 Census: Acquackanonk Twp., Passaic Co., NJ: John Riker, age 44, hotel keeper; Ann, age 41; Ellen, age 21; Hester A., age 13; Sarah J., age 10; 6 'lodgers'

- - - - -

Riker, John I. See: Van Ness Burial Ground
wife, Leah

- - - - -

Riker, OBADIAH b. October 29, 1842
(Neafie, p. 16) d. August 6, 1872

Obadiah Riker
Born Oct. 29, 1842
Died Aug. 6, 1872

wife, Mary* (Clark) b. (abt. 1849)
d. (December 31, 1893)

Notes:
--Served: Civil War. Cpl/ Sgt. Co. E. 25 Regt. NJ Vols. "Obadiah Riker, Sgt. Discharged at Eckington US Army General Hospital, Washington DC Jan 19, 1863. Disability"
--Draft Registration. June 1863: "Obadiah Riker. Age 21. Res. Paterson. Bar tender. previous service, (pvt.) 70th NY Vol."
--Obadiah, son of Isaac Riker, q.v., and Jane Paxton
--"Mary L. Riker b. 1848 d. Dec. 31, 1893. widow. Paterson, NJ" (Death Record)
--1850 Census: Acquackanonk Twp., Passaic Co. NJ: Isaac Riker age 32, carriage maker; Jane age 28; John age 11; Henry age 10; Obediah age 8; Samuel? G. age 5; Jane age 3; 'Zachariah' age 1; David Pow, age 45, laborer; all b. NJ
--1860 Census: Paterson, Passaic Co. NJ: Isaac Riker, age 44, hotelkeeper; Jane 40; Henry 19, bartender; Obidiah age 17; Jane, age 13; Saml. age 14; Isaac age 11; Lydia age 9; Emma age 7; Thomas age 4; all b. NJ
--1870 Census: Little Falls, Passaic Co. NJ: Isaac Riker, age 54, hotel keeper; Jane age 43; Obediah age 29; Mary age 21; Catherine age 3; Henry age 30, painter; Thomas age 13; Lydia age 18; Emma age 16; Samuel Riker, age 56; all b. NJ; 1 servant
--1891-93 Paterson City Directory: Mary Riker, widow of Obadiah. 20 Washington St., Paterson

- - - - -

Riker, Samuel*　　　　　b. (June 22, 1814)
　　　　　　　　　　　　d. (January 11, 1880?)

first wife, Jane* (Cyphers)　b. (January 21, 1813)
　　　　　　　　　　　　d. (October 31, 1855)

daughter, CATHERINE　　b. (abt. March 8, 1840)
(Neafie, p.16)　　　　　　d. July 23, 1840
(inscriptions, p. 141)
(monument)

In
Memory
of
Catharine
Daughter of
Samuel and Jane Riker
who died July 23,
1840 Aged 4 months,
15 days

Notes:
--Samuel, son of Isaac Riker, q.v., and Catharine Berry
--?Samuel died Jan. 11, 1880, Paterson, NJ
--Samuel m. #1, July 1834, Jane Cyphers, dau. of George Cyphers and Trientje Van Duyne; Samuel and Jane were members of the Little Falls Ref. Church
--Samuel m. #2, March 6, 1856, Abigail Louisa Francisco. (She m. #1, abt. 1849, David J. Hubbs)
--?NJ Death Record: "Samuel Riker b. c.1813; d. Jan. 11, 1880, Paterson; age 67, married"

--1850 Census: Acquackanonk Twp.Passaic Co. NJ: Samuel Riker, age 35, stage proprietor; Jane age 36; Isaac, age 12; John H. age 8; Catharine J. age 4

--1850 Census: 12Wd, New York City, NY: David J. Hubbs, age 22, b. NY, cutter; <u>Abby L.</u> Hubbs, age 18 b. NJ; Charles A. Hubbs, age 10 months b. NJ
--1860 Census: Little Falls, Acquackanonk Twp, Passaic Co., NJ: <u>Samuel</u> Riker, age 48, hotel keeper; <u>Abigal</u> age '46' (38?); Isaac 23; John 18, bartender; Jane 14; Samuel age 3; Abigal, age 1; Charles 'Huls' (Charles A. Hubbs) age 11; John 'Huls' (John Hubbs) age 6; all b. New Jersey
--1870 Census: Little Falls, Passaic Co. NJ: Isaac Riker, age 54, hotel keeper; Jane age 43; Obediah age 29; Mary age 21; Catherine age 3; Henry age 30, painter; Thomas age 13; Lydia age 18; Emma age 16; <u>Samuel</u> Riker, age 56; all b. NJ; 1 servant

- - - - -

ROMAINE

Romaine, Abraham L.* b. (abt. 1840)
　　　　　　　　　　　d. (aft. 1910)

first wife, SERENA LUINA b. (abt. October 28, 1843)
(Neafie, p.14)　　　　　　d. October 16, 1861

Serena Luina
Wife of
Abraham L. Romaine
Died Oct. 16, 1861
Aged 17 years. 11 months
&18 days

Notes:
--Served: <u>Civil War.</u> Cpl. Co. C NY 127th Inf. Regt.; transferred to Co. G. U.S. Veteran Reserve Corps, 18th Inf. Regt.
--Abraham, son of Ralph A. Romaine, q.v. and Martha .....
--Abraham m. #2 Sarah .....

--1850 Census: 9Wd, New York City: Ralph Romeyn age 30 b. NJ, grocer; Martha, age 29, b. NJ; <u>Abraham</u>, age 10 b. NY; John, age 7, b. NY; John, age 7, b. NY; Mary, age 2 b. NY; John Post, age 23, b. NJ, grocer; Abraham Post, age 20, b. NJ, mason

--1860 Census: 20 Wd., New York City: Ralph A. Romaine, age 41, b. NJ, builder; (Martha) age 40 b. NJ; <u>Abraham</u>, age 20 b. NY, apprentice carpenter; Jno. W., age 18, b. NY, clerk; Mary M., age 12, b. NY; Rachel A., age 9, b. NY

--1870 Census: 9Wd. Paterson, Passaic Co., NJ: <u>Abraham</u> 'A' Romaine, b. NY, RR ticket agent; <u>Sarah</u>, age 25, b. Wash. DC; Nellie, age 2, b. NJ; Martha, age 1, b. NJ

--1880 Census, Acquackanonk Twp., Passaic Co., NJ: <u>Abram L.</u> Romaine, age 39 b. NY, RR Clerk; <u>Sarah</u>, age 38 b. Washington; Nellie, age 12 b. NJ; Martha age 10 b. NJ; Rachel age 8 NJ; Catherine age 7 b. NJ; Florence age 4 b. J; Mary E. age 11 months b. NJ

--1900 Census: Manhattan NY: <u>Abraham</u> Romaine, lodger, age 59, b. May 1841 b. NY, parents b. NY, clerk

--1910 Census: 3Wd. Meridan, New Haven Co., CT: William I. Bradley, age 46 b. CT, metal turner at silver factory; Martha Bradley, age 40 b. NJ; <u>Abraham L.</u> Romaine, age 68, father-in-law, widower, own income

- - - - -

Romaine, JOHN A.   b. (abt. July 14, 1821)
(Neafie, p.13)   d. March 29, 1877

Brother
John A. Romaine
Died
March 29, 1877
aged
55 years 8 months
& 15 days

Notes:
--?brother of Ralph A. Romaine

- - - - -

Romaine, RALPH A. b. (abt. 1820)
(monument) d. 1897

Martha
Wife of
Ralph A. Romaine
Died July 27, 1879
Aged 59 Yrs.

-

Ralph A. Romaine
1819 - 1897

wife, MARTHA b. (abt. 1820)
(Neafie, p.14) d. July 27, 1879
(monument)

Notes:
--1850 Census: 9Wd, New York City: Ralph Romeyn age 30 b. NJ, grocer; Martha, age 29, b. NJ; Abraham, age 10 b. NY; John, age 7, b. NY; Mary, age 2 b. NY; John Post, age 23, b. NJ, grocer; Abraham Post, age 20, b. NJ, mason
--1860 Census: 20 Wd., New York City: Ralph A. Romaine, age 41, b. NJ, builder; (Martha) age 40 b. NJ; Abraham, age 20 b. NY, apprentice carpenter; Jno. W., age 18, b. NY, clerk; Mary M., age 12, b. NY; Rachel A., age 9, b. NY
--1880 Census: NYC: Ralph A. Romaine, age 69, widower; boarder; b. NJ, parents b. NJ; carpenter
--1895 NJ State Census: Ralph A. Romaine; at res. of Lucas and Mary Van Ness
--NJ Death Record: Martha Romaine, b. c.1821; d. July 27, "1880", Paterson NJ; age 59, married

--NJ Death Record: Ralph A. Romaine, b.c1817; d. June 25, "1896", Paterson, NJ; age 79; widowed; builder

- - - - -

RYERSON

Ryerson, GEORGE C.   b. September 4, 1852
(Neafie, p.17)   d. March 16, 1892
(NJ Will #24705G, 1892)
(monument)

George C. Ryerson
Born Sept. 4, 1852
Died March 16, 1892

-

Matilda Hill
His wife
Born Jan. 12, 1854
Died March 22, 1884

first wife, MATILDA (Hill)   b. January 12, 1854
(Neafie, p.17)   d. March 22, 1884
(monument)

daughter, LULU J.   b. January 11, 1883
(Neafie, p.17)   d. July 21, 1892
(monument)

Lulu J. Ryerson
Born Jan. 11, 1883
Died July 21, 1892

Notes:
--George, son of Peter F. Ryerson, q.v., and Eliza Dods
--George m. #1, Matilda "Tillie" Hill
--George m. #2, Mary .....

--1850 Census: Wayne Twp., Passaic Co., NJ: Peter F. Ryerson, age 31, wheelwright; Elizabeth, age 30; John D., age 9; Francis, age 7; James N., age 5; Lavinia, age 3; Henry D., age 7 months; Margaret, age 56; all b. New Jersey
--1860 Census: Caldwell Twp., Essex Co., NJ: Peter F. Ryerson, age 42, farmer; Elizabeth, age 40; Francis, age 17; James N., age 15; Lavinia, age 13; Henry, age 10; George, age 8; Christiana, age 5; Ella J.,age 3; Wilbur C. age 8 months; all b. New Jersey
--1870 Census: Caldwell Twp., Essex Co.,NJ: Peter F. Ryerson, age 52, wagon maker; Eliza, age 49; Henry, age 20, wheelwright; George, age 17; Anna, age 15; Ella J., age 12; William C., age 10; all b. New Jersey
--1880 Census: Port Royal, Caroline Co,. VA: "Peterson" Ryerson, age 63, b. NJ, farmer; Hettie A., age 44, wife, b. NJ; George C., age 26, b. NJ, brick mason; Ada B., age 7 b. NJ; Herbert, age 8, b. NJ; Ella M., age 4, b. NJ; Earnest age 2, b. NJ; Alice Marchal, age 15 dau-in-law; Calvin C. Marchal, age 20, son-in-law, farmer, b. VA; Tillie Ryerson, age 25, dau-in-law, b. Europe
--1885 Census: 10Wd. Newark, Essex Co., NJ: George Ryerson, age 20-60; Mary Ryerson, age 20-60; Lulu Ryerson, age 0-4
--1885 Census: 10Wd. Newark, Essex Co., NJ: George Ryerson, age 20-60; Mary Ryerson, age 20-60; Lulu Ryerson, age 0-4

- - - - -

Ryerson, Peter F.*	b. (November 4, 1817)
	d. (August 17, 1885)
first wife, ELIZA (Dods) (Neafie, p. 17)	b. (July 13, 1820)
	d. February 5, 1871

Eliza Dods
wife of
Peter F. Ryerson
Died Feb. 5, 1871
Aged 50 years 6 months
& 23 days

Notes:
--Peter, son of Francis Ryerson and Margaret Doremus
--Peter m. #1, August 31, 1839, Eliza Dods. dau. of John Dod and Maria Van Houten
--Peter m. #2, Hettie A. (Hester Ann) Van Ness, widow of James O. Jacobus, q.v.

--1850 Census: Wayne Twp., Passaic Co., NJ: Peter F. Ryerson, age 31, wheelwright; Elizabeth, age 30; John D., age 9; Francis, age 7; James N., age 5; Lavinia, age 3; Henry D., age 7 months; Margaret, age 56; all b. New Jersey
--1860 Census: Caldwell Twp., Essex Co., NJ: Peter F. Ryerson, age 42, farmer; Elizabeth, age 40; Francis, age 17; James N., age 15; Lavinia, age 13; Henry, age 10; George, age 8; Christiana, age 5; Ella J., age 3; Wilbur C. age 8 months; all b. New Jersey
--1870 Census: Caldwell Twp., Essex Co.,NJ: Peter F. Ryerson, age 52, wagon maker; Eliza, age 49; Henry, age 20, wheelwright; George, age 17; Anna, age 15; Ella J., age 12; William C., age 10; all b. New Jersey
--1880 Census: Port Royal, Caroline Co,. VA: "Peterson" Ryerson, age 63, b. NJ, farmer; Hettie A., age 44, wife, b. NJ; George C., age 26, b. NJ, brick mason; Ada B., age 7 b. NJ; Herbert, age 8, b. NJ; Ella M., age 4, b. NJ; Earnest age 2, b. NJ; Alice Marchal, age 15 dau-in-law; Calvin C. Marchal, age 20, son-in-law, farmer, b. VA; Tillie Ryerson,age 25, dau-in-law, b. Europe
--1900 Census: Port Royal, Caroline Co., VA: "Hattie" Ryerson,age 63, b. June 1836 widow, b. NJ, parents b. NJ, farmer; Earnest V., son, age 21, b. June 1879, b. VA, parents

b. NJ, farm labor; Hattie L. Marshall, age 16, granddau. b. VA, father b. VA, mother b. NJ; Arthur French, age 18, black, servant, b. VA, parents b. VA, farm labor

- - - - -

SANFORD
(Sandford)

Sanford, PETER   b. (May 11, 1783)
(Neafie, p.19)   d. April 11, 1870
(NJ Will #17161G, 1870)

Peter Sanford
Died April 11, 1870
Aged 86 years
& 11 months

wife, LUCINDA (Bush)   b. (May 24, 1786)
(Neafie, p.19)   d. August 8, 1844
(inscriptions, p. 141)

Lucinda
wife of Peter Sanford
died August 8, 1844
Aged 61 years, 2 months
& 15 days

Notes:
--Peter, son of Peter Sanford and Neeltje Van Ness who married January 18, 1783 at Acquackanonk.
--Peter Sanford Jr. m. April 28, 1805, Lucinda Bush, dau. of Henry H. Bush and Ann Doremus

--?1840 Census: Caldwell Twp., Essex Co., NJ: Peter 'Sandford'; 5 persons

--1850 Census: Caldwell Twp. Essex Co., NJ: Peter 'Sandford' age 64, farmer; Sarah Vanness age 30; Abraham Reeves, age 69; all b. New Jersey
--1860 Census: 7Wd, Newark, Essex Co., NJ: David H. Vreeland, age 23, carpenter; Charlotte A. Vreeland age 23; Henrietta Vreeland age 9 months; Theodore Vreeland, age 9 months; Peter Sanford, age 78; 4 boarders; all b. New Jersey

- - - - -

SCHOONMAKER

Schoonmaker, John*   b. (December 8, 1791)
                      d. (aft. 1870)

wife, JEMIMA (Berry) b. (March 9, 1795)
(Neafie, p.)   d. February 3, 1839
(inscriptions, p.141)
(monument)

In
Memory of
Jemima, wife
of
J. Schoonmaker
Who died Feb. 3,
1839 Aged 43 years
and 11 months

Notes:
--John Schoonmaker, bapt. January 1, 1792, son of Daniel Schoonmaker and Elizabeth Post
--John m. May 15, 1814, Acquackanonk, Jemima Berry, daughter of Samuel Berry and Susanna Courter
--1855: NJ State Assemblyman: Little Falls, Passaic Co., NJ
--1850 Census: Acquackanonk Twp., Passaic Co., NJ: Daniel Schoonmaker, age 26, farmer; Sarah age 27; David age 5

months; John age 59, carpenter; all b. New Jersey; 1 farm hand
--1870 Census: Acquackanonk Twp. Passaic Co. NJ: S. V. A. Mandeville, age 47, b. NJ, stair builder; Susan age 47 b. NJ; James B. age 23, b. NJ, stair builder; Emma, age 18, b. NY; Millard F. age 16, b. NY; Jno. Schoonmaker, age 79, b. NJ

- - - - -

SHACKLETON

Shackleton, Johann	b. (abt. 1845?)
	d.
wife, ... (Colyer)	b.
	d.
son GEORGE L. (Neafie, p.9)	b. (July 14, 1882)
	d. December 16, 1882

George L. Shackleton
Died Dec. 16, 1882
Aged 5 months
& 2 days

Notes:
--Birth record: "George 'N' Shackleton, b. July 14, 1882, Passaic; son of 'Johannthe' Shackleton and ..... Colyer"
--Death record: "George 'H' Shackleton b. c.1882; d. Dec. 16, 1882, age 5 mos.; father b. England"
--?1880 Census: Paterson, Passaic Co., NJ: George 'Shackletes', age 35, married, b. England, saloon keeper; 5 boarders
--?1900 Census: 3Wd. Paterson, Passaic Co., NJ: John W. Shackleton, age 27, b. July 1872 NJ, parents b. England;

Anna, age 24 b. Feb. 1876, NJ, m.1 year; John F. age 4 months b. Feb. 1900, b. NJ, parents b. NJ

- - - - -

SHERMAN

Sherman, SADIE   b. (abt. 1822)
(monument)   d. May 27, 1838

Sadie Sherman
Died May 27 1838
Aged 16 years

Notes:

- - - - -

SHURTE

Shurte, DAVID   b. (abt. January 6, 1799)
(Neafie, p. 8)   d. June 9, 1859(?)
(NJ Will #704P, 1860)

David Shurte
Died June 9, 1859
Aged 61 years 4 months
& 3 days

first wife, Annaatje/Hannah* (Van Houten)
         b. (1791) (April 1798?)
         d. (1811)

second wife, Margaret* (Vanderhoof)
         b.
         d.

third wife, Jane* (Hopper)   b. (abt. 1802)
                             d. (aft. 1880)

Notes:
--See: William Stratton
--David, son of Christian Shurte and Margaret Demarest
--David m. Feb. 22, 1818, Essex Co., Annaatje Van Houten
--David m. Dec. 5, 1819, Fairfield, NJ, Peggy Vanderhoof
--David m. May 21, 1829 at Pomptain Plains, NJ;
Jane Hopper

--1840 Census: Manchester Twp., Passaic Co., NJ: David Shurt: 5 persons
--1850 Census: Wayne Twp., Passaic Co., NJ: David Shurte, age 51; Jane, age 48;
--1860 Census: Wayne Twp., Passaic Co., NJ: David Shuart, age 61, b. NJ, no occupation listed; Jane, age 56, b. NJ; Jane Stratton, age 11, b. NY; William Smith, age 10, b. Rhode Island; Mary Post, age 14, b. NJ
--1870 Census: Wayne Twp., Passaic Co., NJ: "James" Shuart, age 50; female, keeps house, b. NJ; Jenny Stratton, age 21 b. NJ; William Smith, age 19, b. Rhode Island
--1880 Census: Wayne Twp., Passaic Co., NJ: Jane Shurte, age 79, widow, b. NJ, parents b. NJ

- - - - -

SIMONSON

Simonson, Isaac*   b. (abt. September 14, 1811)
(NJ Will #22524G, 1887)   d. (May 8, 1887)
                              (bur. Prospect Hill Cemetery)

wife, Ann* (Sanford)   b. (July 22, 1815)
                              d. (February 27, 1889)
                              (bur. Prospect Hill Cemetery)

daughter, LUCINDA JANE   b. (abt. 1836
(inscriptions, p.141)   d. October 13, 1842

Lucinda Jane
Daughter of
Isaac and Ann Simonson
Died October 13, 1842
Aged 6 years, 4 months
& 19 days

Notes:
--Isaac, son of John Simonson and Fanny Lines
--Isaac married September 19, 1833, Ann Sanford, daughter of Peter Sanford, q.v., and Lucinda Bush

--1850 Census: Caldwell Twp., Essex Co., NJ: Isaac Simonson age 39, farmer; Ann age 35; John H. age 10; Sarah M. age 7; Charles S., age 3, all b. NJ; adj. to Anthony Simonson
--1860 Census: Caldwell Twp., Essex Co., NJ: Isaac Simonson age 47, farmer; Ann age 43; John H. age 20, apprentice; 'Susan' M. age 16; Charles 'T' age 12; adjacent to Fanny Simonson, age 71; all b. New Jersey
--1870 Census: Caldwell Twp., Essex Co., NJ: Isaac Simonson, age 58, farmer; Ann age 54; Andrew L. Parkhurst, age 31, carpenter; Sarah M. Parkhurst age 26; Willie A. Parkhurst, age 2 months; all b. New Jersey
--1880 Census: Caldwell Twp., Essex Co., NJ: Isaac Simonson, age 67 b. NJ; farmer; Ann wife age 64 b. NJ; Charles S., son, single, age 33, b. NJ, country store

- - - - -

SINDLE

Sindle, Christopher*   b.
                           d. (before March 18, 1793)

wife, Rebeckah * b.
 d. (aft. March 18, 1793)

Notes: Abstract of Will: Included for interest:
Signed: June 14, 1792; Proved: March 18, 1793
"Sindle, Christopher, of Horse Neck, Essex Co.: Wife, Rebeckah; Eldest daughter, Catlinetje (wife of Peter All); Children: Catlinetje, Elizabeth (wife of John 'Stigs'), George (eldest son), Mary, John, Jacob and Thomas." (*Calendar of Wills - 1791-1795*)

Sindle, CHRISTOPHER b. (abt. 1778)
(Neafie, p.17) d. January 31, 1833
(inscriptions, p.141
(monument)
(NJ Will #12453G, 1833 Inv.)

In Memory of
Christopher Sindle
Who died the 31st January
1833
Aged 55 years

Friends or Physicians could not save,
This mortal body from the grave,
Nor can the grave confine it here,
When Christ in judgment shall appear.

wife, Sarah* (Supenor) b. (abt. 1801)
 d. (November 10, 1850?)

Notes:
--Interment reported adj. to "Maria, wife of Jacob Jacobus (q.v.) dec'd and late wife of Henry Francisco"
--Christopher, son of George Sindle?; son of Christopher?

--Christopher m. Nov. 3, 1821 at Pompton Plains: Sarah Supenor
--Sarah, dau. of Christopher Supenor and Mary (Simonson)

--1830 Census: Caldwell Twp., Essex Co., NJ: Christopher Sindle. 4 persons: adj. Thos. Sindle and David Pier
--?1830 Census: Caldwell Twp., Essex Co, NJ: Sarah Sindle. 2 persons: 1 female b. 1790-1800; 1 female b. 1800-1810; adj. John Zeliff, Cornelius Yorks; John R. Nafie
--1850 Census: Caldwell Twp., Essex Co., NJ: Christopher Supenor, age 87, carpenter, b. NY; <u>Sarah Sindle,</u> (dau.) age 49 b. NJ; Ellen M. (Martha Ellen Sindle) Jacobus, age 22, b. NJ; Edward J. Jacobus, age 21, b. NJ, hatter; James L. Jacobus, age 1 month b. NJ

- - - - -

Sindle, CHRISTOPHER T.   b. (abt. 1800)
(Neafie, p.10)   d. May 2, 1886
(monument)
(NJ Will #2881P, 1886)

Father
Christopher T. Sindle
Died
May 2, 1886
In the 86th Year
Of his age

wife, CATHERINE (Post)   b. (February 19, 1804)
(monument)   d. October 29, 1894

Mother
Catherine Post
Beloved wife of
Christopher T. Sindle
Died

Oct. 29, 1894
In the 89th Year
of her age

son, GEORGE   b. (abt. December 12, 1838)
(Neafie, p.4)   d. September 12, 1847
(inscriptions, p.141)

George
son of
Christopher & Catharine Sindle
Died Sept. 12, 1847
aged 8 years & 9 months
Children of
Christopher and Catherine Sindle

daughter, CATHARINE   b. (abt. January 7, 1847)
(Neafie, p.4)   d. September 17, 1847
(inscriptions, p.141
(monument)

Catharine
daughter of
Christopher and Catharine
Sindle
Died
Sept. 17th, 1847
Aged 8 months
& 10 days

Notes:
--Christopher m. June 1825 Catharine Post, dau. of John Post & Marretye Vreeland
--Death Certif.: "Christopher T. Sindle. Died May 2, 1886, age 85, Essex Co.; res. Little Falls; father: Thomas Sindle; mother, Catherine Sindle"

--1830 Census: Caldwell Twp., Essex Co., NJ: Christopher T. Sindle. 5 persons; adj. John Riker, near John Personett
--1840 Census: Caldwell Twp., Essex Co., NJ: Christopher T. Sindle, 7 persons; adj. to Thomas Sindle
--1850 Census: Caldwell Twp., Essex Co., NJ: Christopher T. Sindle, age 49, farmer; Catharine, age 44; Thomas, age 24, miller; Rachel age 22; Francis, age 20; Caroline age 15; Christopher age 8; Stephen, age 6; adj. to Thomas Sindle age 79, farmer; and Catharine Sindle, age 75; all b. New Jersey
--1860 Census: Little Falls, Acquackanonk Twp., Passaic Co., NJ: Christopher Sindle, age 55, miller; Catharine age 53; Christopher, age 19, farmer; Stephen age 16, farmer; all b. NJ
--1870 Census: Little Falls, Passaic Co., NJ: "Christ Scudal" age 68, carpenter; Catherine 62; Christopher age 28, works grist mill; Emily, age 26; Amelia, age 9; Ada, age 6; Stephen, age 26, works grist mill; Anna age 22; Harry, age 4; Lilian, age 1; William Mass, age 24, works grist mill; all b. New Jersey
--1880 Census: Little Falls, Passaic Co., NJ: Christopher Sindle, age '88', carpenter; Catherine, age 75; Christopher, son, divorced, age 37, works in grist mill; Stephen, son, married, age 35, works in grist mill; Anna A. Sindle, daughter-in-law, age 32, b. NJ, works in grist mill; Lillian Sindle, granddaughter age 12; Fredrick Sindle, grandson, age 5; Harry S. Sindle, grandson, age 3; William Story, age 25, servant, all b. New Jersey
--1885 NJ Census: Little Falls, Passaic Co., NJ: Christopher T. Sindle, over 60; Catherine, over 60; Stephen, age 20-60; Anne, age 20-60; Elisabeth age 5-20; Frederick age 5 - 20; Frederick, age 5-20; Harry,age 5-20; Charles C., age 5-20

- - - - -

Sindle, FRANCIS   b. 1830
(monument)   d. 1915 (April 22)

1830 Francis Sindle 1915

His Wife
1831 Angeline Jacobus 1888

1869 Stephen Sindle 1875

1871 Frank Sindle 1875

SINDLE

first wife, ANGELINE (Jacobus)	
(monument)	b. 1831
	d. 1888
STEPHEN	b. 1869
(monument)	d. 1875
	d. (December 22, 1874)
FRANK	b. 1871
(monument)	d. 1875
son, HENRY F.	b. February 13, 1862
(monument)	d. February 12, 1921

Henry F. Sindle
Born Feb. 13, 1862
Died Feb. 12, 1921

Notes:
--Francis, son of Christopher T. Sindle, q.v.
--Francis m. #1, Feb. 12, 1852, Angeline Jacobus, dau. of Jacob Jacobus and Mariah Courter?
--Francis m. #2, Dec. 1896, Harriet Van Riper, dau. of John Van Riper and Charity ....

--1850 Census: Caldwell Twp., Essex Co., NJ: Christopher T. Sindle, age 49, farmer; Catharine, age 44; Thomas, age 24, miller; Rachel age 22; Francis, age 20; Caroline age 15; Christopher age 8; Stephen, age 6; (adj. to Thomas Sindle age 79, farmer; and Catharine Sindle, age 75; all b. New Jersey)

--1850 Census: Caldwell Twp., Essex Co., NJ: Mariah Jacobus, age 45; Angeline, age 18; Jotham age 16, carpenter; Harriet, age 10; all b. NJ

--1860 Census: Caldwell Twp., Essex Co., NJ: Frances Sindle, age 28, farmer; Angeline, age 28; Mary C., age 6; George, age 4 months; Eliza Jacobus, (dau. of James J. Jacobus) age 16; all b. NJ

--1870 Census: Caldwell Twp., Essex Co., NJ: Francis 'Lindle', age 38, farmer; Angeline, age 36; Mary, age 16; Henry age 13; Carrie, age 2; all b. New Jersey

--1880 Census: Caldwell Twp., Essex Co., NJ: Francis Sindle, age 48, farmer; Angeline, age 46; Henry F., age 20, working on farm; Carrie, age 11; all b. NJ

--1900 Census: North Caldwell Boro, Essex Co., NJ: Francis "Single", age..., b. Dec. ..., NJ, farmer; Harriet, age 59, b. Apr. 1841, NJ, 3 born 2 living; Henry, age 39, b. Feb. 1860, single, b. NJ, miller

--1910 Census: Caldwell Boro, Essex Co., NJ: Francis Sindle, age 80, m. 15 yrs. retired, own income; Harriet, age 69; both b. NJ

--1910 Census: Cedar Grove, Essex Co., NJ: Essex Co. Hospital for the Insane: Henry F. Sindle, Inmate, age 48, single, b. NJ, wood turner

--1920 Census: Cedar Grove, Essex Co., NJ: Essex Co. Hospital for the Insane: Henry F. Sindle, inmate, age 58, single, b. NJ

- - - - -

Sindle, GEORGE b. July 13, 1802
(Neafie, p.7) d. May 16, 1872
(monument)
(NJ Will #17710G, 1872 Inv.)

George Sindle
Born July 13, 1802
Died May 18, 1872

-

Nelly Sandford
Born May 11, 1807
Died June 11, 1858

first wife, NELLY (Sandford)
(Neafie, p.7) b. May 5, 1807
(monument) d. June 11, 1858

Notes:
--George m. February 26, 1825, Nelly Sandford
--George m. #2, Nov. 5, 1865, Margaret Cadmus, dau. of Peter Cadmus and Elisabeth .....

--?1840 Census: Caldwell Twp., Essex Co., NJ: Geo. 'Snidle'; 6 persons; adj. to Polly VanNess and Wm. Smith
--1850 Census: Caldwell Twp., Essex Co., NJ: George Sindle, age 48, farmer; Nelly, age 43; Peter S., age 24, carpenter; Thomas H., age 19, blacksmith; Isaac S., age 16, farmer; Harriet A., age 11; all b. NJ
--1850 Census: Caldwell Twp., Essex Co., NJ: Peter Cadmus, age 67, farmer; Elisabeth, age 65; Margaret, age 39; Sarah C., age 23; William, age 35, farmer; Sarah, age 32; and 7 other persons
--1860 Census: Caldwell Twp., Essex Co., NJ: George Sindle, age 57, farmer; Harriet, age 20
--1860 Census: Caldwell Twp., Essex Co., NJ; Margaret Cadmus, age 48; at res. of Anthony Cadmus

--1870 Census: Caldwell Twp., Essex Co., NJ: George "Lindle", age 67, farmer; Margaret, age 59; (adj. to Isaac S. Sindle and Peter S. Sindle)
--1880 Census: Caldwell Twp., Essex Co., NJ: William Cadmus, age 62, farmer; Sarah, wife, age 63; Abbey Ryerson, age 30, dau., dressmaker; Henry C. Ryerson, age 30, son-in-law, wheelwright; Nellie E. Ryerson, age 4, granddau.; Lucy B. Ryerson, age 1, granddau.; Ella R. Cadmus, age 24, dau. at school; Ida Cadmus, dau., age 19, at home; Margaret Sindle, age 69, sister, widow (d. Dec. 1882): all born NJ

- - - - -

Sindle, (George) MILTON   b. September 16, 1853
(Neafie, p.10)   d. May 12, 1881

Milton Sindle
Born Sept. 16, 1853
Died May 12, 1881

wife, ...   b.
   d.

Notes:
--Reported interred adj. to Christopher T. Sindle
--George Milton Sindle, son of Thomas H. Sindle and Rachel Ann Dulhagen
--"Geo. M. Sindle, b. c1854; d. May 12, 1881, Caldwell; Age 27 yrs., married" (death record)
--?"Milton Sindle of Fairfield m. Anna Louisa Cook of Little Falls: m. February 14, 1872, Ref. Church Little Falls"
--?"Milton Sindle, age 20 m. Annie Cook, age 18; May 15, 1872, at Little Falls, NJ"

--1850 Census; Caldwell Twp., Essex Co., NJ: John Dulhagen, age 46, farmer; Mary, age 48; Rachel Ann, age 16; James, age 14; David age 9; all b. NJ
--1860 Census: Caldwell Twp., Essex Co., NJ: Thomas H. Sindle, age 28, blacksmith; Rachel, age 26; George M., age 6; Ann Sandford, age 6 (Ann Sandford same as Ann Cook in 1870 Census?)
--1870 Census: Caldwell Twp., Essex Co., NJ: Thomas H. Sindle, age 36, blacksmith; Rachel, age 34; George M., age 17; E. Jane, age 9; Isaac Lester age 4 months; all b. NJ
--?1870 Census: Little Falls, Passaic Co., NJ: John E. Vreeland, 48, no occ.; Rachel A., age 50; John H., age 21, carpenter; Ellen, age 19; Eliza age 12; Ann Cook? age 16; all b. NJ
--1880 Census: Caldwell Twp., Essex Co., NJ: (census date: June 11, 1880); George M. Sindle, age 26, segar maker; Rachel A. (?), age 27; Ida May, dau., age 8; Alfred, (Fred Milton Sindle, b. Nov. 7, 1874) age 4; John Dulhagen, age 75, grandfather; all b. New Jersey; (adj. to Thomas H. Sindle, age 49)

- - - - -

Sindle, ISAAC b. November 4, 1834
(monument) d. September 26, 1896

Isaac S. Sindle
Born
Nov. 4, 1834
Died Sept. 26, 1896
We shall meet again
-
Catharine J., his wife
Born Dec. 25, 1837
Died July 5, 1914

wife, CATHARINE J.   b. December 25, 1837
(monument)   d. July 5, 1914

Notes:
--Isaac S., son of George Sindle, q.v. and Nelly Sanford

--1850 Census: Caldwell Twp., Essex Co., NJ: George Sindle, age 48, farmer; Nelly, age 43; Peter S., age 24; Thomas H., age 19; Isaac S. age 16; Harriet A., age 11
--1860 Census: Caldwell Twp., Essex Co., NJ: Isaac S. Sindle, age 25, farmer; Catherine, age 22
--1870 Census: Caldwell Twp., Essex Co., NJ: Isaac 'Lindle' age 35, farmer; Catherine, age 30; Malinda, age 9; all b. NJ
--1880 Census: Caldwell Twp., Essex Co., NJ: Isaac Sindle, age 45, farmer; Catherine J., age 40; Malinda, age 19;
--1900 Census: Caldwell Twp., Essex Co., NJ: Charles N. W. Kent, age 44, cigar maker; Malinda, age 39 b. March 1861; Catherine Sindle, age 65, b. Dec. 1834, mother-in-law, widow
--1910 Census: Caldwell Twp., Essex Co., NJ: Charles V. W. Kent, age 54, farmer; Malinda, age 49; Catherine J. Sindle, age 72, widow, 1 born 1 living

- - - - -

Sindle, PETER S.   b. February 9, 1826
(Neafie, p.7)   d. February 10, 1889
(monument)
(NJ Will #23779G, Inv. 1890)

Peter S. Sindle
Born Feb. 9, 1826
Died Feb. 10, 1886

-

Eleanor Smith
His wife
Born Nov. 9, 1829

Died Oct. 16, 1907

wife, ELEANOR (Smith)
(Neafie, p.7)   b. November 9, 1829
(monument)   d. October 16, 1907

son, CHARLES W.   b. May 15, 1858
(Neafie, p.7)   d. January 10, 1885
(monument)

*Charles W.
Son of
Peter S. &
Eleanor Sindle
Born May 19, 1853
Died Jan. 10, 1889*

Notes:
--Peter, son of George Sindle, q.v., and Nelly Sandford
--Peter Sandford Sindle m. December 25, 1855, Eleanor Smith, dau. of Garret Smith and Mary C. .....

--1850 Census: Caldwell Twp., Essex Co., NJ: George Sindle, age 48, farmer; Nelly, age 43; Peter S., age 24, carpenter; Thomas H., age 19, blacksmith; Isaac S., age 16, farmer; Harriet A., age 11; all b. NJ
--1850 Census: Wayne Twp., Passaic Co., NJ: Garret Smith, age 27, shoemaker; Mary C. Smith; Ellen Smith, age 20; Benjamin Parsels, age 18, b. NY, shoemaker
--1860 Census: Caldwell Twp., Essex Co., NJ: Peter S. Sindle, age 34, carpenter; Elenor, age 31; Charles W., age 2
--1870 Census: Caldwell Twp., Essex Co., NJ: Peter S. Sindle, age 45, carpenter; Ellen, age 41; Charles W., age 12; all b. NJ
--1880 Census: Caldwell Twp., Essex Co., NJ: Peter S. Sindle, age 54, carpenter; "Ellenann", age 50' Charles W., age 22, at home; all b. NJ

- - - - -

Sindle, Stephen* b. (abt. October 1843)
 d. (1908)

wife, Anna A.* (Yorks) b. (abt. 1847)
(Anna Augusta Yorks) d. (May 9, 1898)

son, HARVEY b. (abt. 1866)
(monument) d. June 15, 1872

Harvey
son of
Stephen & Anna
Sindle
Died June 15, 1872
Aged 6 years

Notes:
--Stephen, son of Christopher T. Sindle, q.v.
--Stephen m. Oct. 1865, Acquackanonk Twp., NJ, Anna A. Yorks, dau. of Cornelius Yorks and Abigail Jane Wells

--1850 Census:Caldwell Twp., Essex Co., NJ: Christopher T. Sindle, age 49, farmer; Catharine, age 44; Thomas, age 24, miller; Rachel age 22; Francis, age 20; Caroline age 15; Christopher age 8; Stephen, age 6; adj. to Thomas Sindle age 79, farmer; and Catharine Sindle, age 75; all b. New Jersey
--1860 Census:Little Falls, Acquackanonk Twp., Passaic Co., NJ: Christopher Sindle, age 55, miller; Catharine age 53; Christopher, age 19, farmer; Stephen age 16, farmer; all b. NJ
--1860 Census: Acquackanonk Twp., (Little Falls P.O.) Passaic Co., NJ: Cornelius York, age 48 b. NJ, farmer; Abigail, age 35 b. CT; Corintha, age 15, b. NJ; Ann, age 13, b. NJ; Emma, age 9, b. NJ; Margaret, age 5, b. NJ; Milton,

age 3, b. NJ; Frederick, age 1, b. NJ; Elsie York, age 81, b. NJ
--1870 Census: Little Falls, Passaic Co., NJ: "Christ Scudal" age 68, carpenter; Catherine 62; Christopher age 28, works grist mill; Emily, age 26; Amelia, age 9; Ada, age 6; Stephen, age 26, works grist mill; Anna age 22; 'Harry', age 4; Lilian, age 1; William Wass, age 24, works grist mill; all b. New Jersey
--1880 Census: Little Falls, Passaic Co., NJ: Christopher Sindle, age '88', carpenter; Catherine, age 75; Christopher, son, divorced, age 37, works in grist mill; Stephen, son, married, age 35, works in grist mill; Anna A. Sindle, daughter-in-law, age 32, b. NJ, works in grist mill; Lillian Sindle, granddaughter age 12; Fredrick Sindle, grandson, age 5; 'Harry' S. Sindle, grandson, age 3; William Story, age 25, servant, all b. New Jersey
--1900 Census: Little Falls, Passaic Co., NJ: Stephen Sindle, age 56, b. Oct. 1843, widower, felt mfr.; Charles, age 18, b. Sept. 1881, son; Lillian 'Wannem' (Warman), dau., age 31, b. Oct. 1865; Nelson 'Wannem', age 42, bookkeeper; all b. NJ

- - - - -

Sindle, THOMAS C.   b. December 1, 1826
(monument)   d. April 10, 1897

Thomas C. Sindle
Born
Dec. 1, 1826
Died
April 10, 1897
-
His wife
Henrietta Speer
Born
Oct. 12, 1827

Died
Nov. 10, 1898

-

SINDLE

wife, HENRIETTA (Speer)   b. October 12, 1827
(monument)   d. November 10, 1898

son, THOMAS T.   b. May 17, 1859
(monument)   d. July 17, 1875

Thomas T.
Son of
Thomas C. & Henrietta
Sindle
Born
May 17, 1859
Died
July 17, 1865

dau., CECELIA   b. Oct. 24, 1864
(monument)   d. Oct. 8, 1916

Cecelia Sindle
Born
Oct. 24, 1864
Died
Oct. 8, 1916

Notes:
--Thomas Christopher Sindle, son of Christopher T., q.v., and Catherine Post
--Thomas m. Aug. 1849, Henrietta Speer, dau. of Tunis T. Spier and Jemima Miller

--1840 Census: Caldwell Twp., Essex Co., NJ; Thos. "Smale" 4 persons: adj. Christopher T. Sindle

--1850 Census: Caldwell Twp., Essex Co., NJ: Christopher T. Sindle, age 49, farmer; Catharine, age 44; Thomas, age 24, miller; Rachel age 22; Francis, age 20; Caroline age 15; Christopher age 8; Stephen, age 6; adj. to Thomas Sindle age 79, farmer; and Catharine Sindle, age 75; all b. New Jersey

--1860 Census: Caldwell Twp., Essex Co, NJ: Thomas Sindle, age 33, miller; Henrietta, age 31; Catherine, age 9; Laura, age 6; Anna, age 4; Thomas, age 2; Thos. M. Speer, age 23, laborer; all b. NJ

--1870 Census: Caldwell Twp., Essex Co., NJ: Thomas C. "Lindle", age 43, saw mill & farmer; Henrietta, age 42; Catherine, age 19; Laura, age 16; Anna, age 14; Thomas T., age 12; Cecelia, age 5; Mary E., age 4; all b. NJ; also, Frank W. Cook, age 18, b. 'Germany', farm labor

--1880 Census: Caldwell Twp., Essex Co., NJ: Thomas C. Sindle, age 53, miller; Henrietta, age 53; Anna, age 24; Cecelia, age 18; all b. NJ; also two boarders

--1900 Census: North Caldwell, Essex Co., NJ: Robert Sanderson, age 35, b. Oct. 1856, b. NJ, parents b. Ireland; mfr. & farmer; Anna, age 44, b. Mar. 1856, b. NJ, parents b. NJ; Ethel H., age 15, b. Nov. 1884; Thomas C., age 12, b. Oct. 1887; Cecelia Sindle, age 35, b. Oct. 1864, single, sister-in-law, b. NJ

--1910 Census: North Caldwell, Essex Co., NJ: Robert Sanderson, age 53, wood turner; Anna, age 53; Ethel H., age 24; Thomas C., age 22; Celia Sindle, age 45, single, sister-in-law; all b. NJ

- - - - -

SLINGERLAND

Slingerland, Peter* b. (February 18, 1833)
  d. (December 10, 1900)

wife, MARY ANN (Vanderhoof)
(Neafie, p.11) b. (abt. February 28, 1837)

d. June 30, 1868

Mary A. Vanderhoof
wife of
Peter Slingerland
Died June 30, 1868
Aged 31 years, 4 mos.

Notes:
--Peter, son of John P. Slingerland and Hester Mandeville
--Peter m. abt. June 1860, Mary Ann Vanderhoof, daughter of Cornelius A. Vanderhoof, q.v., and Eliza Kierstead

--1850 Census: Pequannock Twp., Morris Co., NJ: John Slingerland, age 63; Hester, age 57; Effy, age 26; Charity age 20; Peter, age 17, farmer; all b. NJ
--1860 Census: Pequannock Twp., Morris Co., NJ: John Slingerland, age 72, farmer; Peter age 27; Charity age 29; Mary A., age 24; Philip Redding, age 10; all b. NJ
--1870 Census: Pequannock Twp., Morris Co., NJ: Peter Slingerland, age 34, farmer; Charity, age 36, keeps house; Irene, age 8, at school; George G. VanNess, age 33, farmer; all b. New Jersey
--1880 Census: Pequannock Twp., Morris Co., NJ: Peter Slingerland, age 45, b. NJ, farmer; Irena, age 18, dau., b.NJ
--1900 Census: Pequannock Twp., Morris Co., NJ: Peter Slingerland, age 67, widower, b. February 1833, NJ, farmer; Irene, age 38, daughter, b. March 1863 NJ

- - - - -

SMITH

Smith, Elias
wife, Cornelia

See: Smith Burial Ground

SPEER
Spear, Spier

Speer, Cornelius   See: Pearce Burial Ground

- - - - -

Speer, GEORGE E.(Ellis)   b. November 4, 1852
(Neafie, p. 11)   d. (June 24, 1907)

George E. Speer
Born Nov. 4, 1852
Died (no date)

wife, SARAH E.   b. April 19. 1855
(Sarah Estelle Springsteen)   d. November 8, 1881
(Neafie, p.11)

Sarah E. Springsteen
wife of
Geo. E. Speer
Born Apr. 19, 1855
Died Nov. 8, 1881

Notes:
--George, son of Thomas T. Speer, q.v., and Hettie Stiles
--Sarah was dau. of Abraham Springsteen

--1860 Census: Caldwell, Essex Co., NJ: Thomas 'F' Speer, age 29, teamster; Hetta, age 27; George E., age 7; Hannah M. Cadmus, age 15; all b. New Jersey
--1870 Census: Caldwell, Essex Co., NJ: Thomas T. Speer, age 40, farmer; Hettie, age 37; George E., age 17, bookkeeper; Annie M., age 1; Mary Murphy age 17,

domestic servant; John Kincaid, age 21, teamster; all b. New Jersey
--1870 Census: 9Wd, New York City: Abram Springsteen, age 48 b. NY, clerk of court; Mary J., age 48 b. NY; Wm. E., age 21, clerk; Sarah E., age 15; Oscar, age 12; Jane Coe age 80; Harriet Coe, age 54, milliner; Sarah Coe; all above b. NY; 4 boarders b. CT
--1880 Census: Newark, Essex Co., NJ: Mary J. Springsteen, age 58 b. NY; Oscar Springsteen, age 23 b. NY; George Speer, age 29, son-in-law b. NJ, bookkeeper; Sarah Speer, age 25 b. NJ, parents b. NY, daughter; Ada Speer, age 1 b. NJ, granddaughter
--1900 Census: 4Wd, Newark, Essex Co., NJ: George E. "Shear" widower b. Nov. 1852 NJ, insurance clerk; Ada J. Ellis b. April 1879, m. 1 yr, b. NJ, food demonstrator; boarders

- - - - -

Speer, Jane					See: Pearce Burial Ground

- - - - -

Speer, John Henry*			b. (September 24, 1842)
					d. (June 15, 1907)
					(bur. Prospect Hill, Cemetery Caldwell, New Jersey)

wife, RACHEL (Francisco)		b. July 5, 1842
(Neafie, p. 9)				d. March 5, 1873

Rachel Speer
Born July 5, 1842
Died March 5, 1873

Notes:
--John, son of William Burnett Speer and Jane Courter

--John m. Nov. 1865, Rachel Francisco, dau. of Peter Francisco, q.v. and Abigail Gould
--John m. #2, Alice K. Scott, dau. of .... Scott and Phyllis...., born Scotland

--1850 Census, p.78, Caldwell Twp., Essex Co., NJ: William B. Spear, age 43, farmer; Jane M., age 42; Lambert, age 20, farmer; Mary E., age 18; George, age 16, farmer; Oscar, age 14; Harriet Ann, age 12; Richard C., age 10; John Henry, age 8; Sarah E., age 6; Emma Irene, age 2; Jane A., age 1 month; 1 servant; 1 laborer
--1850 Census: Caldwell Twp., Essex Co., NJ: Peter Francisco, age 39, farmer; Abigail, age 40; Rachel, age 9; 7 other children; all b. NJ
--1860 Census, p.87&88, Caldwell, Essex Co., NJ: Jane Speer, age 51, farmer; Harriet, age 20, school teacher; Richard, age 19; John, age 17, farmer; Sarah, age 15; Jane, age 10
--1870 Census: Caldwell Twp., Essex Co., NJ: John H. "Spees", age 27, farmer; Rachel, age 27; Fred, age 1; Walter Jacobus, age 17, farm labor; all b. NJ
--1880 Census: Caldwell Twp., Essex Co., NJ: John H. Speer, age 37, farmer; Alice K., age 26; b. NJ, parents b. Scotland; Fred, age 12; Mary J., age 5; Charles R., age 2; Phillis Scott, age 60, mother-in-law, widow, b. Scotland; Euphemia Foster, age 30, b. NY, boarder

- - - - -

Speer, JOHN T.   b. January 15, 1783
(Neafie, p.2)   d. February 26, 1865
(monument)
(NJ Will #16216G, Inv.1865)

John T. Speer
Born Jan. 15, 1783
Died Feb. 26, 1865

wife, CAROLINE (Pier)
(Neafie, p.2)   b. November 4, 1786
(monument)   d. November 12, 1864

> *Caroline*
> *Wife of*
> *John T. Speer*
> *Born Nov. 4, 1786*
> *Died Nov. 12, 1864*

son, JOHN   b. (abt. November 9, 1824)
(Neafie, p.2)   d. March 9, 1832
(inscriptions, p.142)

> *John Speer*
> *son of*
> *John T. & Caroline Speer*
> *Died March 9, 1832*
> *aged 7 years, 3 months*
> *& 29 days*

Notes:
--John, son of Thomas Speer, q.v., and Maria Mourison
--John m. July 7, 1805, Caroline, dau. of Isaac Pier and Marretje Post

--1850 Census: Caldwell Twp., Essex Co., NJ: John T. Speer, age 65, farmer; Caroline, age 60; Peter J. age 23, farmer; Susanna, age 21; John P., age 9; all b. NJ; 1 laborer
--1860 Census: Caldwell Twp., Essex Co., NJ: John T. Speer, age 77, farmer; Caroline, age 74; Anna J. age 14; same house: Peter J. Speer, age 33, farmer; Susana age 31; James S. age 9; Seth W. age 7

- - - - -

Speer, John W. See: Pearce Burial Ground
wife, Elsie

- - - - -

Speer, JOSIAH b. (April 2, 1803)
(Richard Josiah Speer, Cpt., Mjr.)
(Neafie, p.17) d. March 28, 1877
(monument)
(NJ Will #19210G, 1877)

Our (father?)
Josiah Speer
Died March 28, 1877
Aged 74 years

wife, MARY ANN (Pearce)
(Neafie, p.17) b. October 11, 1804
(monument) d. January 18, 1894

Mary Ann Pearce
Wife of
Josiah Speer
Born Oct. 11, 1804
Died Jan. 18, 1894
With Long Life .....
Satisfied Thee

-

Rachel A. Crane
1828 - 1915

-

Frances Speer
1835 - 1913

daughter, ELLA ARAMINTA
(Neafie, p.17) b. .....
  d. .....

*Infant child
of Josiah and Mary Ann
Speer*

son, CHARLES   b. .....
(Neafie, p.17)   d. .....

*Infant child
of Josiah and Mary Ann
Speer*

dau. RACHEL A. (Crane)   b. 1828 (March)
(monument)   d. 1915

dau. FRANCES   b. 1835 (March)
(monument)   d. 1913

Notes:
--Josiah, son of Richard Speer, q.v., and Sarah Stagg
--Josiah m. 1825, Mary Ann Pearce, dau. of George Pearce and Rachel Riggs
--?Rachel Ann m. July 1877, John Duryea Crane. He d. April 1888
--1850 Census: Caldwell Twp., Essex Co., NJ: Josiah Spear, age 47, farmer; Mary Ann, age 46; Sarah, age 21; Rachel, age 19; William, age 17; Frances, age 15; Margaret, age 13; Richard, age 11; John, age 9; Charles, age 7; all b. New Jersey
--1860 Census: Caldwell Twp., Essex Co., NJ: Josiah Speer, age 57, farmer; Mariann, age 55; Rachel A., age 32; Margaret age 23, school teacher; John W., age 16; Charles, age '7'; all b. New Jersey
--1860 Census: Caldwell Twp., Essex Co., NJ: William H. Speer, age 30, laborer; Harriet, age 26; Mary, age 4; Harry W., age 1; Frances Speer, age 25, school teacher; all b. NJ

--1870 Census: Caldwell Twp., Essex Co., NJ: Josiah 'Spees' age 67, farmer; Mary A., age 65; Rachel, age 34, without occupation; Mahlon, age 32, brick mason; Frances, age 28, teacher; Charles, age 17, farm labor; all b. NJ
--1880 Census: Caldwell Twp., Essex Co., NJ: Mary Ann Speer, age 75, widow; Rachel, age 52, daughter, single; Frances, age 45, daughter, single
--1900 Census: Caldwell Twp., Essex Co., NJ: Rachel A. Crane, 72, b. March 1828, widow; Sarah M. Kent, sister, age 78 b. July 1826, widow; Frances Speer, sister, age 65, b. March 1835, single; all b. NJ
--1910 Census: Caldwell Twp., Essex Co., NJ: Rachel A. Crane, 82, b. NJ; retired, own income; Frances Speer, age 75, sister, single, b. NJ; retired, own income.

- - - - -

Speer, PETER b. October 8, 1786
(Neafie, p.19) d. February 28, 1872
(NJ Will #17717G, 1872)

Peter Speer
Born Oct. 8, 1786
Died Feb. 28, 1872

wife, HARRIET (Sandford)
(Neafie, p. 19) b. July 21, 1791
  d. June 17, 1873

Harriet
wife of Peter Speer and
daughter of
Wm. and Mary Sandford
Born July 21, 1791
Died June 17, 1873

Notes:

--Peter, son of Thomas Speer and Mary Mourison
--Peter m. Harriet Sandford, dau. of William Sandford and Mary Van Ness

--1850 Census: Caldwell Twp., Essex Co., NJ: Peter Speer, age 62, farmer, b. NJ; Harriet, age 59, b. NJ; Cornelius Mastenbrook, age 21, labor
--1860 Census: Caldwell Twp., Essex Co., NJ: Peter Speer, age 75, farmer; Harriet, age 69
--1860 Census: Little Falls, Acquackanonk Twp., Passaic Co., NJ: Peter Speer, age 74; Harriet, age 68; Adeline, age 44; Mary, age 22; Melvina, age 18; Henry Crane, age 34; Harriet Crane, age 24; Ines Crane, age 2; all b. NJ
--1870 Census: Caldwell Twp., Essex Co., NJ: Peter Speer, age 85, farmer; Harriet, age 82

- - - - -

Speer, PETER T. b. June 25, 1825
(Neafie, p.13)   d. July 23, 1890
(monument)

Peter T. Speer
Born June 25, 1825
Died July 23, 1890

-

Caroline, His Wife
Born Apr. 24, 1830
Died July 16, 1896

wife, CAROLINE (Van Duyne)
(Neafie, p.13)   b. April 24, 1830
(monument)   d. July 16, 1896

daughter, JULIA b. April 16, 1851
(Neafie, p.13) d. September 28, 1851

Julia Speer
Born Apr. 16, 1851
Died Sept. 28, 1851
Aged 5 months 11 days

son, WEBSTER T. b. November 21, 1852
(Neafie, p.13) d. February 5, 1860

Webster T. Speer
Born Nov. 21, 1852
Died Feb. 5, 1860
Aged 7 years 2 months
& 15 days

Notes:
--Peter, son of Tunis T. Speer, q.v., and Jemima Miller
--Peter m. October 25, 1848, Caroline VanDuyne, dau. of James A. Van Duyne and Catherine Doremus

--1850 Census: Caldwell Twp., Essex Co., NJ: Tunis T. Speer, age 53, farmer; Jemima age 53; Thomas T. age 28, farmer; Susan, age 15; Elias Miller, age 55, farmer; Peter T. Speer, age 34; Caroline Speer age 20; all b. New Jersey
--1860 Census: Caldwell, Essex Co., NJ: Peter T. Speer, age 34, surveyor; Caroline age 30; Daniel Courter, age 20, laborer; Fanny Jacobus, age 20; all b. New Jersey
--1870 Census: 2Wd, Newark, Essex Co., NJ: Peter T. Speer, age 40, agent steam engines; Caroline age 30; Lavinia age 9; Caroline age 3; Tunis T. age 72; Jemima age 73; all b. NJ
--1880 Census: Newark, Essex Co., NJ: Peter T. Speer, age 54, wood turning; Caroline 49; Lavinia 19; Carrie, age 13; Jemima, age 83, mother, widow; all b. NJ

- - - - -

Speer, RICHARD, MJR. b. (April 29, 1778)
(Neafie, p.5) d. August 3, 1838
(inscriptions, p.141)
(monument)

*In
Memory of
Maj. Richard Speer
who departed this life
August 3rd, A.D. 1838
Aged 60 years, 3 months
& 14 days*

wife, SARAH (Stagg) b. (February 13, 1782)
(Neafie, p.5) d. December 27, 1841
(inscriptions, p. 141)
(monument)

*In
Memory of
Sarah
wife of
Maj. Richard Speer
who departed this life
Dec. 27th, AD 1841
Aged 59 years
10 months & 24 days*

Notes:
Served: War of 1812: Mjr. General
--Richard, son of Thomas Speer, q.v., and Marrietje Mowerson
--Richard Speer m. May 19, 1798, Sarah Stagg

--1840 Census: Caldwell Twp., Essex Co., NJ; Richard Speer; 2 persons

-----

Speer, RICHARD A., Mjr. b. June 29, 1839
(monument) d. July 9, 1920

Richard Speer
Born June 29, 1839
Died July 9, 1920

-

Rachel Gould
His wife
Born Oct. 20. 18935
Died Nov. 8. 1923

first wife, JOANNAH (Francisco)
(Neafie, p.12)) b. (November 27, 1836)
(monument) d. February 4, 1865

Joannah
Wife of
Richard Speer
and daughter of
Peter & Abigail Gould
Francisco
Died Feb. 4, 1865
Aged 28 years 2 months
& 7 days

second wife, RACHEL (Gould)
(monument) b. October 20, 1835
d. Nov. 8, 1923

Notes:
--Richard, son of Josiah Speer and Mary Ann Pearce
--Richard m. #1, December 24, 1863, Joannah, dau. of Peter Francisco, q.v., and Abigail Gould

--Richard m. #2, 1868, Rachel Gould, dau. of Stephen J. Gould and Joanna Beach

--1850 Census: Caldwell Twp., Essex Co., NJ: Josiah Spear, age 47, farmer; Mary Ann, age 46; Sarah, age 21; Rachel age 19; William, age 17; Frances age 15; Margaret, age 13; Richard, age 11; John, age 9; Charles age 7; all b. New Jersey

--1850 Census: Caldwell Twp., Essex Co., NJ: Peter Francisco, age 39, farmer; Abigail age 40; Elizabeth age 17; Henry age 15, farmer; Joanna, age 13; Marcus, age 11; Rachel age 9; Josiah, age 7; Susan age 5; Ellen age 3; Sally Gould, age 50; all b. New Jersey; George Griffith, age 57, b. England, laborer

--1860 Census: 1Wd, Newark, Essex Co., NJ: Richd. Speer, age 21, mason, boarder, b. New Jersey

--1860 Census: Caldwell Twp., Essex Co., NJ: Abba Francisco, age 50, farmer; Joanna, age 21; Marcus, age 20; Susan, age 14; Ellen age 12; Stephen, age 9; all b. NJ; 1 farm laborer

--1860 Census: Caldwell Twp., Essex Co., NJ: Stephen J. Gould, age 59, farmer; Joanna, age 55; Rachel, age 24; 4 younger children

--1870 Census: Montclair, Essex Co., NJ: Richard Spear, age 31, bricklayer; Rachel, age 34; Mahon, age 37, stone mason; all b. New Jersey

--1880 Census: Parkersburg, Wood Co., West Virginia: Richard Speer, age 41, b. NJ, brick mason; Rachael, age 44, b. NJ; Stephen J., age 9, b. NJ; Frank, age 7, b. NJ

--1900 Census: Caldwell Boro, Essex Co., NJ: Richard Spear, b. June 1839, m.32 yr., real estate agent; Rachel, b. October 1835, 5 born 1 living; both b. New Jersey

--1910 Census: Caldwell Boro, Essex Co., NJ: Richard Spear, age 70, m. #2, for 41 yrs., mason; Rachel, age 74, m. #1 for 41 yrs.,, 5 born 1 living; all b. New Jersey

--1920 Census: Caldwell Boro, Essex Co. NJ: Richard 'S' 'Spear', age 80, b. NJ, retired contractor; 'Rachal' age 84, b. NJ; 1 housekeeper

- - - - -

Speer, THOMAS   b. (abt. 1753)
(Neafie, p.1)   d. June 26, 1829
(inscriptions, p. 141)
(NJ Will #12102G, 1829)

In
Memory of
Thomas Speer
who died June 26, A.D., 1829
in his 76th year

Let worms devour my roasting (sic) *flesh*
And crumble all my bones to dust:
My GOD shall raise my frame anew
At the revival of the just.

wife, MARIA (Mourison)
(Neafie, p.1)   b. (abt. 1758)
(monument)   d. October 31, 1846
(inscriptions, p.141)

In
Memory of
Maria
wife of
Thomas Speer
who departed this life
October 31, 1846
in the 88th year
of her age

Notes:
--verse source:"*New Jersey, a Guide to Its Present and Past*") (should read "wasting" flesh?)
--Thomas, son of Tunis Speer and Engeltje Cadmus
--Thomas Speer m. abt. 1777, Mary Mourison
--1787 Will of Teunis Spier: Executors: son, Thomas Spier and Richard Mourison

- - - - -

Speer, THOMAS M. (Mourison)
(Neafie, p. 2)   b. June 19, 1828
(gov't stone)   d. September 29, 1864
(NJ Will #16022G, 1864)

Thomas M. Speer
Died Sep. 28, 1864
Aged 36 years 3 months
& 10 days
-
Thomas M. Speer
Pvt. Btry E
1 NJ Arty

wife, Mary Jane* (Vanderhoof)
                b. (abt. 1833?)
                d.

Notes:
Served: Civil War: Battery E., 1 NJ Artillery
--Thomas M. Speer, son of John T. Speer, q.v., and Caroline Pier
--Thomas Mourison Speer m. Mary Jane Vanderhoof, April 23, 1862; Ref. Church, Little Falls, N.J.; dau. of Isaac Vanderhoof and Martha Riker
--1850 Census: Caldwell Twp., Essex Co., NJ: Isaac J. Vanderhoof, age 49, farmer Martha, age 32; Mary Jane, age

17; Susan Ann, age 14; Elizabeth, age 11; Martha, age 8; George, age 6; James H., age 1; all b. NJ
--1860 Census: Caldwell Twp., Essex Co., NJ: Thomas Sindle, age 33, miller; Henrietta age 31; Catherine age 9; Laura age 6; Anna age 4; Thomas age 2; Thos. M. Speer, age 23, laborer

- - - - -

Speer, THOMAS T.   b. November 23, 1829
(Neafie, p.8)   d. (November 21, 1908)

Thomas T. Speer
Born Nov. 23, 1829
Died (no date)

first wife, HETTIE (Stiles)   b. January 3, 1833
(Neafie, p.8)   d. August 2, 1894

Hettie Stiles
wife of Thos. T. Speer
Born Jan. 3, 1833
Died Aug. (?) 1894

Notes:
--Thomas, son of Tunis T. Speer, q.v., and Jemima Miller
--Thomas m. #1, bef. 1860, Hettie Stiles
--Thomas m. #2, abt. 1896, Catherine Kent, poss. dau. of Lyman B. Kent and Martha Paxton.

--1850 Census: Caldwell Twp., Essex Co., NJ: Tunis T. Speer, age 53, farmer; Jemima age 53; Thomas T. age 28, farmer; Susan, age 15; Elias Miller, age 55, farmer; Peter T. Speer, age 34; Caroline Speer age 20; all b. New Jersey
--?1850 Census: Hamilton Twp., Atlantic Co., NJ: Ephraim Stiles, age 56, farmer; Clarissa, age 47; Aquilla, age 16;

Hester age 15; Elisabeth, age 12; Amelia A., age 10; Thomas C., age 8; Mary, age 6; Clarissa, age 4; all b. NJ
--?1850 Census: Caldwell Twp., Essex Co., NJ: Lyman B. Kent, age 36, tobacconist; Martha, age 37; Catherine, age 6; Susan, age 4; 5 other children; all b. NJ
--1860 Census: Caldwell Twp., Essex Co., NJ: Thomas 'F' Speer, age 29, teamster; 'Hetta', age 27; George E., age 7; Hannah M. Cadmus, age 15; all b. New Jersey
--1870 Census: Caldwell Twp., Essex Co., NJ: Thomas T. Speer, age 40, farmer; Hettie, age 37; George E., age 17, bookkeeper; Annie M., age 1; Mary Murphy age 17, domestic servant; John Kincaid, age 21, teamster; all b. New Jersey
--1870 Census: Montclair, Essex Co., NJ: Warren S. Taylor, age 32, builder; Mary M., age 30; Nellie K. age 6; Frederick W., age 1; Martha, age 6 mos.; Catharine Kent, age 21, no occuption; all b. NJ
--1880 Census: Caldwell, (Essex Co. Penitentiary), Essex Co., NJ: Thomas T. Speer, age 50, warden; Hettie, age 47; Annie M., age 11; all b. New Jersey
--1880 Census: Montclair, Essex Co., NJ: Henry M. Rober, age 42, carpenter; Rachel A. (Kent), age 38; Jennie, age 18; Catharine Kent, age 34, single, (sister-in-law) boarder; all b. NJ
--1900 Census: 13Wd, Newark, Essex Co., NJ: Thomas "Speir" age 70, b. November 1829, m. 4 yrs. b. NJ, 'supt.'; Kate, age 56, b. March 1844, NJ
--1910 Census: 2Wd. Bloomfield, Essex Co., NJ: Kate E. Speer, age 65, b. NJ widow; 'Susian' Kent, sister, age 63, b. NJ, single
--1920 Census: Paterson, Passaic Co., NJ: Frank A. Geroe, age 37, driver oil supply truck; Mary E., age 34; William W., age 17; Catherine, age 15; Loretta, age 10; Catherine 'Spear' age 75, mother-in-law, widow; all b. New Jersey
--1930 Census: Paterson, Passaic Co., NJ: Mary Geroe, age 45, married; Catherine Speer, age 85, mother, widow;

Lauretta Geroe, age 19, dau. single, operator at telephone co.; all b. NJ

- - - - -

Speer, TUNIS T. b. August 10, 1796
(Neafie, p.13) d. November 26, 1872

Tunis T. Speer
Born Aug. 10, 1796
Died Nov. 26, 1872
Aged 76 years 3 mos.
& 16 days

first wife, JEMIMA (Miller)
(Neafie, p.13) b. October 28, 1796
  d. June 26, 1889

Jemima Miller
wife of
Tunis T. Speer
Born Oct. 28, 1796
Died June 26, 1889
Aged 92 yrs. 7 mos.
28 days.

daughter, ELIZABETH O. b. (abt. May 19, 1833)
(Neafie, p.1) d. April 2, 1841
(inscriptions, p. 142)

Elizabeth O.
Daughter of
T. S. & Jemima Speer
Died April 2, A.D., 1841
aged 7 years, 10 months
& 14 days

Notes:
--Tunis T. Speer, son of Thomas Speer, q.v., and Maria Mourison
--Tunis T. Speer m. Jemima Miller (?dau. of Philetas Miller and Joanna Kitchel)

--1850 Census: Caldwell Twp., Essex Co., NJ: <u>Tunis T. Speer</u>, age 53, farmer; <u>Jemima</u> age 53; Thomas T. age 28, farmer; Susan, age 15; Elias Miller, age 55, farmer; Peter T. Speer, age 34; Caroline Speer age 20; all b. New Jersey
--1860 Census: Caldwell Twp., Essex Co., NJ: <u>Tunis T. Speer</u>, age 63, farmer; <u>Jemima</u> age 63; Elias Miller, age 65
--1870 Census: 2Wd, Newark, Essex Co., NJ: Peter T. Speer, age 40, agent steam engines; Caroline age 30; Lavinia age 9; Caroline age 3; Tunis T. age 72; <u>Jemima</u> age 73; all b. NJ
--1880 Census: Newark, Essex Co., NJ: Peter T. Speer, age 54, wood turning; Caroline 49; Lavinia 19; Carrie, age 13; <u>Jemima</u>, age 83, mother, widow; all b. NJ

- - - - -

Speer, WILLIAM S.   b. (1811 - 1820)
                           d. (bef. 1850?)

wife, ADALINE STILES   b. November 26, 1815
(monument)   d. November 23, 1897
Inscription correct?

In
Memory of
Adaline Stiles
wife of
William S. Speer
Born Nov. 26, 1815
Died Nov. 23, 1897
Mother

daughter, EMMA M.   b. March 23, 1848

(Neafie, p. 19)   d. October 27, 1851

Emma M. Speer
Born March 23, 1840
Died Oct. 27, 1851
Daughter of
Wm. and Adaline
Speer

Notes:
--William, son of Peter Speer and Harriet Sandford
--Adaline, (? dau. of William Stiles and Mary Mourison)
--1840 Census: Acquackanonk, Passaic Co., NJ: William S. Speer: 1 male age 20-29; 1 female age 20-29; 3 females under age 5; 1 free colored female age 24 - 35
--1850 Census: Acquackanonk Twp., Passaic Co., NJ: Adaline Speer, age 34; Harriet, age 14; Mary, age 12; Emma M., age 10; Melvina A., age 8; all b. NJ; 1 laborer
--1860 Census: Little Falls, Acquackanonk Twp., Passaic Co., NJ: Peter Speer, age 74; Harriet, age 68; Adeline, age 44; Mary, age 22; Melvina, age 18; Henry Crane, age 34; Harriet Crane, age 24; Inez Crane, age 2; all b. NJ
--1880 Census: Little Falls, Passaic Co., NJ: Henry L. Crane, age 44, b.NJ, bark dealer; Harriet, age 44 b. NJ; Inez Crane, age 22 b. NJ; Adaline Speir, widow, age 64, b. NJ; Meddie Crane, age 8 b. NJ; 1 laborer
--1895 NJ Census: Little Falls: Adeline Speer (res. of Henry L. and Harriet (Speer) Crane

- - - - -

Speer, WILLIAM B.   b. May 31, 1807
(Neafie, p.5)   d. May 31, 1859
(monument)
(NJ Will #15286G, 1859)

*Memory
of
William B. Speer
Born May 31, 1807
Died May 31, 1859*

wife, JANE M.(Courter)   b. September 13, 1808
(Neafie, p.5)   d. February 21, 1864
(monument)

*In
Memory
of
Jane M. Courter
Wife of
William B. Speer
Born Sept. 13, 1808
Died Feb. 21, 1864*

son, OSCAR   b. (abt. October 7, 1835?)
(Neafie, p.5)   d. December 18, 1851

*Oscar
Died Dec. 18, 1851
Aged 16 years 2? months
& 11 days*

daughter, EMMA I. (Irene)   b. (abt. March 16, 1848)
(Neafie, p.5)   d. December 18, 1850

*Emma I.
Died Dec. 18, 1850
Aged 2 years 9 months
& 2 days*

Notes:
--William, son of Richard Speer, q.v., and Sarah Stagg

--Jane Maria, daughter of John Edward Courter and Elizabeth Cook

--1850 Census: Caldwell Twp., Essex Co., NJ: William B. Spear, age 43, farmer; Jane M., age 42; Lambert, age 20, farmer; Mary E., age 18; George, age 16, farmer; Oscar, age 14; Harriet Ann, age 12; Richard C., age 10; John Henry, age 8; Sarah E., age 6; Emma Irene, age 2; Jane A., age 1 month; 1 servant; 1 laborer

--1860 Census: Caldwell Twp., Essex Co., NJ: Jane Speer, age 51, farmer; Harriet, age 20, school teacher; Richard, age 19; John, age 17, farmer; Sarah, age 15; Jane, age 10

- - - - -

Speer, Zenas Crane* b. (August 7, 1828)
(monument) d. (February 2, 1920)
  (bur. Hillside Cemetery,
  Fairfield, NJ)

first wife, LUCINDA (VanNess)
(Neafie, p. 14) b. (abt. March 29, 1830)
  d. April 27, 1861

Lucinda
wife of
Zenas C. Speer
Died Apr. 27, 1861
Aged 31 years
& 29 days

second wife, Martha* (VanNess)
  b. (abt. 1833)
  d. (bef. 1900)

Notes:
--Zenas, son of John W. Speer and Elcie Bush

--Zenas m. #1 March 22, 1849, Lucinda VanNess, dau. of Robert VanNess, q.v., and Sarah Sandford

--Zenas m. #2, June 18, 1862, Martha VanNess

--1850 Census: South Ward, Newark, Essex Co., NJ: Zenas Spier, age 21, carpenter, b. NJ; Lucinda, age 20, b. NJ; Sarah C., age 7 mos. b. NJ

--1850 Census: Caldwell Twp., Essex Co., NJ: Cornelius Vanness, age 40, farmer; Mary, age 38; Martha, age 17; Isaac, age 14; Rachel Ann, age 10; Sarah E., age 8; Jane, age 5; John R., age 2; all b. NJ

--1860 Census: 7Wd, Newark, Essex Co., NJ: "Yernus" Speer, age 30, clerk; Lucinda, age 30; Catherine, age 10; John L., age 7; Sarah VanNess age 50; George Walter, age 22, mason; all b. New Jersey

--1860 Census: Caldwell Twp., Essex Co., NJ: John T. Vanness, age 31, carriage 'driver?'; Mary, age 31; Charles, age 8; Eliza, age 6; Ernst, age 1; Martha Vanness, age 25, dressmaker

--1870 Census: Amboy Twp., Lee Co., IL: Zenas Spear, age 41, b. NJ, carpenter; Martha, age 37, b. NJ; John, age 17, b. NJ, carpenter; William, age 6 bv. NJ; Horace, age 4, b. NJ; Lewis, age 2, b. IL

--1880 Census: Amboy Twp., Lee Co., IL: Zenas Speer age 52 b. NJ, farmer; Martha, wife, age 47 b. NJ; William son, age 16 b. NJ, farm hand; Harris, son, age 14, b. NJ; Lewis, son, age 11, b. IL; Frederick, son, age 2, b. IL

--1900 Census: 3Wd, East Orange, Essex Co., NJ: Matthias Wheaton b. Aug. 1845 m. 34 yr, b. NJ, butcher shop; Sarah C. b. Jan 1850 b. NJ; Jessie b. dau. b. May 1874 NJ; Grace D. dau., b. June 1883 NJ; Abby, age 36?, aunt, b. NJ; Zenas C. Speer, father-in-law b. August 1828 NJ

--1910 Census: 3Wd, East Orange, Essex Co., NJ: Edward C. Stasse, age 29, m. 14 yr., b. NJ, mgr. manufacturer's office; Grace W., age 28 b. NJ; Wilma W., dau.,age 3?; Virginia M., age 1 yr 6 mos.; Sarah Wheaton, age 60, widow, mother-in-law, b. NJ; Zenas C. Speer, age 82, widower, grandfather, b. NJ

- - - - -

STAGG

Stagg, AARON E. (Edward) b. (abt. September 1851
                                         d. (1930)

wife, LAURA (Sindle)   b. (abt. February 1854)
                                        d. (1923)

daughter, MARY L.   b. March 18, 1874
(Neafie, p.13)   d. April 19, 1875

Mary L.
Daughter of
Aaron E. and Laura Stagg
Born March 18, 1874
Died Apr. 19, 1875

Notes:
--Aaron, son of Robert L. Stagg, q.v., and Margaret Ann Kierstead
--Laura, dau. of Thomas C. Sindle and Henrietta Speer

--1860 Census: Caldwell Twp., Essex Co., NJ: Robert L. Stagg, age 41, farmer; Margaret, age 36; James C., age 16; Mary L., age 11; Aaron E., age 7; Sarah Kierstead, age 60; Nancy Stager, age 60; all b. New Jersey; also, John McMahan, age 19, b. NY; Robert McMahan, age 4, b. NY
--1870 Census: Caldwell Twp., , Essex Co., NJ: Robert L. Stagg, age 51, farmer; Margaret A., age 46; Aaron E., age 17; Sarah Kierstead, age 70; all b. New Jersey
--1870 Census: Caldwell Twp., Essex Co., NJ: Thomas C. 'Lindle', age 43, saw mill & farmer; Henrietta, age 42;

Catherine age 19; Laura, age 16; Anna, age 14; Thomas T., age 12; Cecelia, age 5; Mary E., age 4; all b. NJ; 1 farm laborer

--1880 Census: Caldwell Twp., Essex Co., NJ: Aaron E. Stagg, age 27, farmer; Laura, age 26; Thomas Archie, age 4, son; Margaret A., age 56, mother; all b. New Jersey; 1 laborer

--1900 Census: Caldwell Twp., Essex Co., NJ: Aaron Stagg, b. September 1851, m. 26 yr, farmer; Laura, b. Feb. 1854, 2 born 1 living; Thomas A., b. Feb. 1876, farm labor; all b. New Jersey

--1910 Census: Caldwell Twp., Essex Co., NJ: Aaron E. Stagg, age 56, m. 37 yrs. farmer; Laura, age 56, 2 born 1 living; Thomas A., age 38 m. 8 yr., butcher; Esther A., age 33, daughter-in-law, b. NY, parents NY; Allen E., age 5, grandson; Joseph A. Kierstead, age 80, widower, boarder; all b. New Jersey (except Esther A.)

--1920 Census: Caldwell Twp., Essex Co., NJ: Aaron E. Stagg, age 67, b. NJ, farmer; Laura, age 66, b. NJ; Thomas A., age 44, b. NJ, farmer; Esther A., age 43, b. NY, dau-in-law; Allan E., age 15, b. NJ, grandson; 1 servant; 3 boarders

- - - - -

Stagg, ROBERT L.   b. December 22, 1818
(Neafie, p.12)   d. February 16, 1875
(NJ Will #18632G, 1875)

Robert L. Stagg
Born Dec. 22, 1818
Died Feb. 16, 1875

wife, MARGARET A. (Kierstead)
(Neafie, p.12)   b. July 31, 1823
     d. May 23, 1893

Margaret A. Kiersted
wife of
Robt. L. Stagg
Born July 31, 1823
Died May 23, 1893

son, JAMES C.
(Served: Civil War)　　b. May 25, 1844
(Neafie, p.13)　　　　　d. June 22, 1865
(gov't. stone)

James C. Stagg
Born May 25, 1844
Died June 22, 1865
Co. D, 26 NJ Inf.

dau., MARY L.　　　　b. December 1(?), 1848
(Neafie, p.13)　　　　 d. December 3(?), 1867

Mary L. Stagg
Born Dec. 1, 1848
Died Dec. 2, 1867

Notes:
--Robert, son of James Stagg and Lydia Schoonmaker
--Robert m. September 5, 1841, Margaret Ann Kierstead, dau. of Aaron W. Kierstead, q.v.

--1850 Census: Caldwell Twp., Essex Co., NJ: Robert L. Stagg, age 31, b. NJ, shipping agent; Margaret Ann, age 27, b. NJ; James C., age 6, b. NY; Mary L., age 1, b. NJ; Aaron W. Kierstad, age 52, b. NJ, farmer; Sarh Kierstad, age 50 b. NJ; Catherine M. Kierstad, age 15, b. NJ; Nancy Kierstad, age 50, b. NJ
--1860 Census: Caldwell Twp., Essex Co., NJ: Robert L. Stagg, age 41, farmer; Margaret, age 36; James C., age 16; Mary L., age 11; Aaron E., age 7; Sarah Kierstead, age 60;

Nancy Stager, age 60; all b. New Jersey; also, John McMahan, age 19, b. NY; Robert McMahan, age 4, b. NY
--1870 Census: Caldwell Twp., Essex Co., NJ: <u>Robert L.</u> Stagg, age 51, farmer; <u>Margaret A.</u>, age 46; Aaron E., age 17; Sarah Kierstead, age 70; all b. New Jersey
--1880 Census: Caldwell Twp., Essex Co., NJ: Aaron E. Stagg, age 27, farmer; Laura, age 26; Thomas Archie, age 4, son; <u>Margaret A.</u>, age 56, mother; all b. New Jersey; 1 laborer

- - - - -

Stagg, THOMAS H. b. (abt. January 25, 1793)
(Neafie, p.2) d. November 25, 1864

Thomas H. Stagg
Died Nov. 25, 1864
Aged 70 years, 10 mos.
& 6 days

wife, FANNY (VanHouten)
(Neafie, p.2) b. (March 3, 1803)
(monument) d. December 13, 1884

Fanny Van Houten
wife of
Thomas H. Stagg
Died Dec. 13, 1884
Aged 81 years 10 months
and 10 days

son, JAMES b. (abt. January 10, 1831)
(Neafie, p. 13) d. June 23, 1833
(inscriptions, p.142)
(monument)

In memory of
James
son of
Thomas H. &
Fanny Stagg
who died June 23, 1833
Aged 2 years,
5 months
and 13 days

daughter, LEAH ANN   b. (abt. July 30. 1837)
(Neafie, p.2)   d. April 25, 1844
(inscriptions, p.142)
(monument)

In
Memory of
Leah Ann
Daughter of
Thomas H. & fanny stagg
who died
April 25, 1844
aged 6 years 8 months
and 26 days

daughter, MARY CATHARINE
(Neafie, p.2)   b. (abt. March 29, 1840)
(inscriptions, p. 142)   d. December 10, 1841

In
Memory of
Mary Catherine
daughter of
Thomas & Fanny Stagg
who died Dec. 10th, 1841
Aged 1 year 8 months
and 11 days

son, ABRAHAM BLAUVELT
(Neafie, p.2) b. (abt. August 8, 1841)
(inscriptions, p. 142) d. March 27, 1844

Abraham Blauvelt
son of
Thomas H. & Fanny Stagg
who died March 27, 1844
aged 2 years, 7 months
& 19 days

Notes:
--?Thomas, son of Henry Stagg and Leah Mandeville.
--Thomas m. March 31, 1827, Vrouwetje 'Fanny' Van Houten, dau. of Helmagh Van Houten and Lena Van Blarcom

--1850 Census: Wayne Twp., Passaic Co. NJ: Thomas H. Stagg, age 57, farmer; Fanny age 47; Ellen age 18; Elizabeth age 15; William H. age 11; John J. Post, age 21, laborer; all b. NJ
--1860 Census: Wayne Twp., Passaic Co. NJ: Thomas H. Stagg, age 67, farmer; Fanny age 57; Henry age 21, carpenter
--1870 Census: Wayne Twp., Passaic Co. NJ: Austin L. Stanley age 36, b. NY, carpenter; Elizabeth 35; Thomas E. 8; James C. 2; Fanny Stagg age 66; Sarah Linder?, age 14
--1880 Census: Wayne Twp., Passaic Co. NJ: Austin L. Stanley age 46, carpenter; Elizabeth age 45; Thomas E. age 18, clerk; James C. age 12; Bertrand A. age 8; Fannie Stagg, age 76, mother-in-law, widow; all b. New Jersey

- - - - -

Stagg, WILLIAM H. b. abt. 1838
(Civil War List) d. September 3, 1897

wife, Margaret Francisco *   b. abt. 1842
                              d.

Notes:
Served: Civil War Pvt. Co. I, 26th NJ Vol. Inf.
--Son of Thomas H. Stagg, q.v.
--1850 Census: Wayne Twp., Passaic Co. NJ: Thomas H. Stagg, age 57, farmer; Fanny age 47; Ellen age 18; Elizabeth age 15; William H. age 11; John J. Post, age 21, laborer; all b. NJ
--1870 Census: Montclair, Essex Co., NJ: William H. Stagg, age 30 b. NJ, carpenter; Margareth, age 28 b. NJ
--1880 Census: Wayne, Passaic Co., NJ: William H. Stagg, age 41, b. NJ, carpenter; Margaret, age 39; Harry, age 9; Mable age 6; Amy, age 2; all b. NJ
--1900 Census: 4Wd Montclair, Essex Co., NJ: Margareth Stagg age 58 b. Jan 1842, 4 born 4 living; Emy, age 22, b. Dec. 1877, clerk; Warren, age 17, b. May 1883, bookkeeper; Emma Francisco, age 54, b. June 1845, boarder; John Francisco, age 63 b. June 1836, boarder; all b. NJ
--1910 Census: 2Wd, Montclair, Essex Co., NJ: Margaret F. Stagg, age 68, widow, own income; Warren, age 26, song, single, trav. salesman lithograph house; Emma Francisco, age 64, sister, single, own income; all b. New Jersey
--1920 Census: 1Wd East Orange: Margaret Stagg, age 78 widow, b. NJ; Warren Stagg, age 36, son, single, b. NJ, salesman; Harry Stagg, age 49, son, married, b. NJ machinist unemployed; Emma Francisco, age 74, sister, single, b. NJ; Ralph H. Stagg, age 22, grandson, b. NJ, motorman trolley railway
--1925 Orange City Directory: Margaret Stagg, widow of William H., res. 10 N. Park; Warren Stagg, salesman, res. 10 N. Park

- - - - -

STANLEY

Stanley, Henry C.*   b. (July 17, 1821)
                            d. (January 7, 1908)

wife, CATHERINE (Riker)   b. (abt. May 1827)
                            d. (November 30, 1902)

daughter, ELLEN ANN   b. (abt. January 15, 1846)
(Neafie, p.4)   d. December 15, 1848
(inscriptions, p.142)
(monument)

Ellen Ann
Eldest
daughter of
Henry and Catharine Stanley
died Dec. 15, 1848
Aged 2 years
3 months
& 19 days

daughter, EMARINTHA   b. (abt. April 23, 1848)
(Neafie, p.4)   d. August 11, 1850
(inscriptions, p.142)

Emarintha
daughter of Henry Stanley
died August 11, 1850
aged 2 years, 3 months, 19 days

son, FRANK   b. (abt. December 21, 1853)
(Neafie, p.4)   d. February 27, 1855

Frank
son of
Henry and

Catharine Stanley
died Feb. 27, 1854?
Aged 1 year 2 months
and 6 days

son, WILLIAM WEBSTER b. (abt. December 29, 1857)
(Neafie, p.4)   d. April 21, 1862

William Webster
son of Henry and Catharine
Stanley
Aged 4 years 3 months
and 23? days

dau., MARY E.   b. (abt. February 6, 1870)
(Neafie, p.4)   d. April 24, 1875

Mary E.
daughter of
Henry & Catharine
Stanley
Died April 24, 1875
Aged 5 years 2 months
and 18 days

Notes:
--Henry, prob. son of Thomas Stanley who m. Dec. 31, 1817 Hannah Crane
--Henry, m. March 1845 at Little Falls, Catherine Riker, dau. of John Riker, q.v., and Ann Smith
--Members, Little Falls Ref. Church

--1830 Census: Caldwell Twp., Essex Co., NJ: Thos. Stanley
--1840 Census: Acquackanonk Twp., Passaic Co., NJ: Thomas Stanley

--1850 Census: Acquackanonk Twp. Passaic Co., NJ: Henry Stanley age 27, butcher; Catherine age 23; Emerantha, age 2; Jonathan Penost, age 21, butcher; all b. NJ
--1850 Census: Paterson, Passaic Co., NJ: Thomas Stanley, age 54, b. England, butcher; Hannah, age 54, b. NJ; Mary, age 17, b. NJ; William, age 17, b. NJ, butcher; Jeremiah, age 12, b. NJ; Peter Davenport, age 18, b. NY, butcher
--1860 Census: Acquackanonk Twp.Passaic Co., NJ: Henry Stanley age 40 b. NJ, farmer; Catherine age 34 b. NJ; John R., age 9 b. NJ; Henry age 6 b. NJ; William age 2 b. NJ; Jeremiah, age 24, b. NJ, (brother) stage driver; Eliza Nix, age 18, servant b. 'Germany'; Goline Doremus age 27, b. NJ, mason
--1870 Census: Little Falls, Passaic Co. NJ: Henry Stanley age 50 farmer; Catherine age 44; John 19; Henry 16; Amarentha 13; Mary 3; all b. NJ
--1880 Census: Little Falls, Passaic Co. NJ: Henry Stanley age 58 b. NJ, father b. England, mother b. NJ; Catherine age 52 b. NJ; Evaline age 20; Thomas age 85, b. England; Eliza Nix age 28, servant, b. NJ, parents b. Germany; Fanny Beach, boarder, b. NJ
--1885 NJ State Census: Henry Stanley; Catherine; George Barney; William Besset; Eliza Nix; Jane Nix
--1895 NJ State Census: Little Falls, Passaic Co., NJ: Henry Stanley; Catherine Stanley; Eliza Nix
--1900 Census: Little Falls, Passaic Co. NJ: Henry Stanley, b. July 1820 NJ, father b. England, m.56 years, farmer; Catherine b. May 1827, '8 born 2 living'; Eliza Nix b. July 1850 NJ, parents b. Germany, twister at carpet mill
--1905 NJ State Census: Passaic NJ: Evelyn (Stanley) DeMouth, age 44; Edwin DeMouth, age 23; Henry C. Stanley, age 83; Eliza Nix, age 57

- - - - -

STRATTON

Stratton, William Crapo* b. (December 14, 1823)
　　　　　　　　　　　　d. (May 2, 1898)

first wife, ANN ELIZA (Shurte)
(Neafie, p.8) 　　　　　b. April 25, 1830
　　　　　　　　　　　　d. January 12, 1856

Ann Eliza
Daughter of
David and Jane Shurte
wife of
Wm. C. Stratton
Born Apr. 25, 1830
Died Jan. 12, 1858

daughter, ELIZABETH 　b. February 12, 1851
(Neafie, p.9) 　　　　　d. January 23, 1856
(monument)

Elizabeth
daughter of
Wm. C. & Ann Eliza
Stratton
Born Feb. 12, 1851
Died Jan. 23, 1856

daughter, ANN ISABELLE b. April 4, 1853
(Neafie, p.9) 　　　　　d. September 8, 1856
(monument)

Ann Isabelle
daughter of
Wm. C. & Ann Eliza
Stratton
Born Apr. 4, 1853

Died Sept. 8, 1856

daughter, CAROLINE b. January 5, 1856
(Neafie. p.9) d. September 21, 1856
(monument)

Caroline
daughter of
Wm. C. & Ann Eliza
Stratton
Born Jan. 5, 1856
Died Sept. 21, 1856

Notes:
--William Crapo Stratton, son of Samuel Stratton and Eunice Crapo
--"William C. Stratton, b. Albany, NY, m. Nov. 11, 1847 at Medina, Orleans Co., NY, Anne Eliza Shuart, dau. of James Shuart and Mary Elizabeth 'Sofer'"; m. #2, bef. 1860, Lillie..... who died May 6, 1867. age 37. bur. City Cem., Sacramento, CA

--1850 Census: Wayne Twp., Passaic Co., NJ: William C. Stratton, age 26, b. NY, merchant; Ann E., age 20, b. NJ; Jane, age 1, b. NJ
--1850 Census: Village of West Troy, Watervliet, Albany, NY: Samuel Stratton, age 58, b. NJ, teacher; Eunice, age 52, b. NY
--1860 Census: Wayne Twp., Passaic Co., NJ: David Shuart, q.v., age 61, b. NJ, no occupation listed; Jane, age 56, b. NJ; Jane Stratton, age 11, b. NY; William Smith, age 10, b. Rhode Island; Mary Post, age 14, b. NJ
--1870 Census: Wayne Twp., Passaic Co., NJ: "James (Jane) Shuart", age 50, female, keeps house, b. NJ; Jenny "Sharltow" (Stratton), age 21 b. NJ; William Smith, age 19, b. Rhode Island

--1853: William C. Stratton: Postmaster, Little Falls, NJ
--1855: William C. Stratton: N.J. State Assemblyman
--1856-1859: William C. Stratton: California State Assemblyman rep. Placer County; Democratic Speaker 1859
--1860 Census: Sacramento, Sacramento Co. CA: W. C. Stratton, age 34, b. NY, State Librarian; Lillie, age 28 b. KY
--1861-1870: William C. Stratton: apptd. California State Librarian
--1870: law practice, Sacramento, California
--1873: Moved to Santa Barbara, CA where he died (*California State Library Foundation*, p.4)
--1898 May: "Judge William Crapo Stratton died at his home at Santa Barbara, CA after an illness of four years."

- - - - -

UNKNOWN

Unknown (vault)	b.
(Neafie, p.12)	d.

Notes:
"a vault with a large blue stone cover; no inscription"

- - - - -

VAIL

Vail, Henry*	b. (abt. October 1836)
	d. (December 2, 1901)
wife, Leah Ellen* (Budd)	
	b. (March 1841)
	d. (aft. 1916)
son, EARNEST B.	b. (abt. November 16, 1862)
(Neafie, p. 12)	d. June 30, 1863

Earnest B. Vail
Died June 30, 1863
Aged 7 mos. 14 ds.
Children of
Henry and Leah E. Vail

daughter, MELVA E. b. (abt. August 15, 1864)
(Neafie, p.12) d. January 5, 1866

Melva E. Vail
Died
Jan. 5, 1866
Aged 1 year 4 mos.
& 21 days
Children of
Henry and Leah E. Vail

Notes:
--Henry, son of John B. Vail, q.v.
--Henry m. abt. 1860, Leah Ellen Budd, dau. of Israel Budd, q.v.

--1850 Census: Williamsburg, Brooklyn, Kings Co., NY: John Vail, age 55, b. England, well digger; Sarah A., age 46, b. England 'deaf and dumb'; Sarah A., age 18, b. England; Henry, age 16, b. England; John S., age 10, b. NY; George R., age 6, b. NY; Mary McCracken,(m. Theo. MacCracken) age 21, b. England; Henrietta McCracken, (m. #1 James Riker; m. #2, John Condit) age 3, b. NY
--1860 Census: Meads Basin, Wayne Twp., Passaic Co., NJ: John Vail, age 59 b. England, farmer; Sarah Ann, age 57, b. England; Henry, age 24, b. England, farm labor; Leah Ellen, age 22, b. NJ; John, age 19 b. NY, farm labor; George, age 15, b. NY; Henrietta McCracken, age 13, b. NY; Frank McCracken, age 7, b. NY

--1870 Census: Wayne Twp., Passaic Co., NJ: Henry Vail, age 35, b. England, farmer; Ellen, age 29 b. NJ; Mary A., age 8 b. NJ; Louise E., age 8, b. NJ; Kate B. age 6 months, b. Dec., NJ; Sarah B., age 6 months b. Dec. NJ; Sarah A., age 69, b. England, 'blind & dumb'; Frank McCracken, age 18; Chas. Ackerman, age 18

--1880 Census: Wayne Twp., Passaic Co., NJ: Henry Vail, age 42, b. England, farmer; Leah L., age 39 b. NJ; Mary A., age 18 b. NJ; Louisa E., age 13, b. NJ; Kattie B., age 10 b. NJ; Sarah B., age 10 b. NJ; Fannie I., age 5, b. NJ; Lena J., age 3, b. NJ; Sarah A., age 81, b. England, mother, 'blind & dumb'; John W. Braddock, age 19, b. NJ, servant

--1895 NJ Census: Wayne Twp., Passaic Co., NJ: Henry Vail; Leah E., Mary; Louiza; Kate; Fanny; Lena

--1900 Census: Wayne Twp., Passaic Co., NJ: Henry Vail, b. October 1836 'NY', m. 40 yr. farmer; Leah L, b. March 1841 NJ; Mary, b. April 1861, NJ, house servant; Louisa, b. October 1865 NJ, nurse; Lena, b. September 1876 NJ, house servant; John S. Post, age 42, b. NJ, boarder, farm labor; Frank Andrews, age 50 b. Germany, servant, farm labor;

--1910 Census: 4Wd, Paterson, Passaic Co., NJ: Leah E. Vail, age 69, widow, b. NJ; Louise E., age 43, b. NJ, trained nurse; Kate B., age 40 b. NJ, dressmaker; Lena E., age 33, b. NJ; Thos. W. Randall, age 57, b. England, boarder, lawyer; Jennis S. Randall, age 60 boarder, b. NJ

- - - - -

Vail, JOHN B.	b. (abt. May 10, 1800)
(Neafie, p.12)	d. September 14, 1869
(monument)	
(NJ Will #1085P Inv. 1869)	

John B. Vail
Died
Sept. 14, 1869
Aged 69 years 4 months

and 4 days

wife, SARAH ANN   b. (abt. 1797)
(Neafie. p.12)   d. July 21, 1880
(monument)

Sarah Ann
widow of
John Vail
Died July 21, 1880
In Her 83rd Year

Notes:
--1850 Census: Williamsburg, Brooklyn, Kings Co., NY: John Vail, age 55, b. England, well digger; Sarah A., age 46, b. England 'deaf and dumb'; Sarah A., age 18, b. England; Henry, age 16, b. England; John S., age 10, b. NY; George R., age 6, b. NY; Mary McCracken, age 21, b. England, (m. Theo. MacCracken), Henrietta McCracken, age 3, b. NY
--1860 Census: Meads Basin, Wayne Twp., Passaic Co., NJ: John Vail, age 59 b. England, farmer; Sarah Ann, age 57, b. England; Henry, age 24, b. England, farm labor; Leah Ellen, age 22, b. NJ; John, age 19 b. NY, farm labor; George, age 15, b. NY; Henrietta McCracken, age 13, b. NY (m. James R. Riker; m. #2, John Condit) ; Frank McCracken, age 7, b. NY
--1870 Census: Wayne Twp., Passaic Co., NJ: Henry Vail, age 35, b. England, farmer; Ellen, age 29 b. NJ; Mary A., age 8 b. NJ; Louise E., age 8, b. NJ; Kate B. age 6 months, b. Dec., NJ; Sarah B., age 6 months b. Dec. NJ; Sarah A., age 69, b. England, 'blind & dumb'; Frank McCracken, age 18; Chas. Ackerman, age 18
--1880 Census: Wayne Twp., Passaic Co., NJ: Henry Vail, age 42, b. England, farmer; Leah L., age 39 b. NJ; Mary A., age 18 b. NJ; Louisa E., age 13, b. NJ; Kattie B., age 10 b. NJ; Sarah B., age 10 b. NJ; Fannie I., age 5, b. NJ; Lena J.,

age 3, b. NJ; <u>Sarah A.</u>, age 81, b. England, mother, 'blind, insane'; John W. Braddock, age 19, b. NJ, servant

- - - - -

VANDERHOOF

Van Derhuff, Aaron   See: Vanderhoof Burial Ground
wife, Jane

- - - - -

Vanderhoof, Cornelius A.*   b. (abt. 1809)
                                      d. (September 1, 1895)

wife, ELIZA (Kierstead)   b. (abt. 1812)
(Neafie, p.11)   d. March 15, 1875

Eliza Kiersted
wife of
Cornelius A.
Vanderhoof
Died March 15, 1875
in her 63rd year

Notes:
--Cornelius, son of Abraham J. Vanderhoof and Catherine Kierstead
--Cornelius m. January 16, 1836, Eliza Kierstead (?possible dau. of Isaac Kierstead and Mary Vreeland)

--1850 Census: Caldwell Twp., Essex Co., NJ: <u>Cornelius A.</u> Vanderhoof, age 40, mason; <u>Eliza</u>, age 37; Mary Ann, age 13; Charles R., age 10; all b. New Jersey
--1860 Census: Caldwell, Essex Co., NJ: <u>Cors.</u> Vanderhoof, age 52, farmer; <u>Eliza</u> age 48; Mariann age 23; Charles R.

(Raymond), age 21, laborer; (adj. to Daniel Vanderhoof, age 30)
--1870 Census: Caldwell Twp., Essex Co., NJ: <u>Cornelius A.</u> Vanderhoof, age 63, brick mason; <u>Eliza</u>, age 57; Charles, age 31, brick mason; 'Venus' Piearce, age 15, farm labor
--1880 Census: Caldwell Twp., Essex Co., NJ: <u>Corn.</u> A. Vanderhoof, age 73, farmer; Charles R., age 40, son; Martha Ann, age 26, dau.; Ada Eliza, age 3, granddaughter; all b. NJ
--1895 NJ Census: Caldwell Twp., Essex Co., NJ: Charles R. Vanderhoof; Martha Ann; <u>Cornelius A.;</u> Addie E.

- - - - -

Vanderhoof, Cornelius R.   See: Pearce Burial Ground

- - - - -

Vanderhoof, Henry P.   See: Pearce Burial Ground
wife, Rachel

- - - - -

Van Druff, Henry   See: Vanderhoof Burial Ground

- - - - -

Vanderhoof, John   See: Vanderhoof Burial Ground
wife, Phebe L.

- - - - -

Vanderhoof, Margaret   See: Vanderhoof Burial Ground

- - - - -

Vanderhoof, Maria   See: Vanderhoof Burial Ground

- - - - -

Vanderhoof, PETER A.   b. January 26, 1818
(Neafie, p. 10)   d. January 21, 1898
(NJ Will #27709G, 1898)

Peter A. Vanderhoof
Born Jan. 26, 1818
Died Jan. 21, 1898

wife, SUSANNA Y. (Crum)   b. September 12, 1818
(Susanna Youry Crum)   b. (September 12, 1819)
(Neafie, p.10)   d. April 12, 1891

Susanna Y.
Wife of
Peter A. Vanderhoof
Born Sept. 12, 1818
Died Apr. 12, 1891

Notes:
--Peter Abraham Vanderhoof, son of Abraham J. Vanderhoof and Catherine Kierstead
--Peter m. Susanna Youry Crum, dau. of John Crum and Martha Youry

--1850 Census: Caldwell Twp., Essex Co., NJ: Peter A. Vanderhoof, age 32, farmer, b. NJ; Susanna Y., age 32, b. NY; William H., age 10; Catherine A., age 7; Mary E., age 4; Catherine, age 75;
--1860 Census: Caldwell Twp., Essex Co., NJ: Peter Vanderhoof, age 42, b. NJ, farmer; Susan V., age 41, b. 'NJ'; William, age 20, b. NJ; Catherine A., age 18 b. NJ; Mary E., age 14, b. NJ
--1870 Census: Caldwell Twp., Essex Co., NJ: Peter 'H' Vanderhoof, age 53, b. NJ, farmer; Susannah, age 53, b. NY

--1880 Census: Dist. 2, Caldwell Twp., Essex Co., NJ: Peter A. Vanderhoof, age 62, b. NJ, farmer; Susana, age 66, b. NY, parents b. NY

--1895 NJ Census: Caldwell Twp., Essex Co., NJ: Peter A. Vanderhoof; Girardus Cable; Emma Cable; Norman Cable; Edna Cable

--Will: names daughter Elizabeth, wife of Theodore Kanouse; daughter Catherine Cables; Executors: grandsons Garardus and William H. Cables.

- - - - -

Vanderhoof, Richard See: Vanderhoof Burial Ground
wife, Emma

- - - - -

Vanderhoof, William* b. (abt. 1817)
(NJ Will #24777G, 1892) d. (December 19, 1891)
(see: Pearce Burial Ground)

wife, Jane* (Bush) b. (January 22, 1819)
d. (June 11, 1893)
(see: Pearce Burial Ground)

son, JOHN NELSON b. (abt. August 1, 1843)
(Neafie, p.5) d. November 20, 1845
(inscriptions, p.142)

John Nelson
son of
William and Jane
Vanderhoof
Died Nov. 20, 1845
Aged 2 years, 2 months
& 1 day

Notes:
--William m. September 20, 1838, Jane Bush, dau. of Henry J. Bush, q.v., and Jane Low.

--1850 Census: Caldwell Twp., Essex Co., NJ: William Vanderhoof, age 31, carpenter; Jane age 28; Harriet age 11; Charles H., age 2; Jane Mandeville, age 20; adj. to Henry P. Bush, age 52; all b. NJ
--1860 Census: Caldwell Twp., Essex Co., NJ: Wm. Vanderhoof, age 43, carpenter; Jane age 41; Henry C. age 11; all b. NJ
--1870 Census: Caldwell Twp., Essex Co., NJ: Wm. Vanderhoof, age 53, carpenter; Jane age 51; Chas. H. age 21; all b. NJ
--1880 Census: Caldwell Twp., Essex Co., NJ: William Vanderhoof, age 62, farmer, b. NJ; Jane, age 61 b. NJ

- - - - -

VAN DUYNE

Van Duyne, HENRY   b. abt. May 5, 1838
(Neafie, p.8)   d. December 6, 1868
(monument)

Henry VanDuyne
Died Dec. 6, 1868
Aged 31 years 7 mo.
& 1 day

wife, MARGARET JANE (Bowman)
(Neafie, p.8)   b. (abt. May 10, 1844)
(monument)   d. January 29, 1889

Mother
Margaret Jane
wife of

Henry Van Duyne
Died
Jan. 22, 1889
Aged
44 years 8 mo.
& 19 days

Notes:
--Henry, son of James A. VanDuyne, q.v., and Catherine Doremus
--Henry m. Apr. 27, 1862, Margaret Jane, dau. of James Bowman, q.v.
--Death record: Margaret J. Van Duyne "b. c.1841; d. Jan. 22, '1885' (1889), Wayne Twp., NJ; age 44 years and 8 months"
--Margaret Jane m. #2, June 5, 1872, Abraham Allen

--1850 Census: Wayne Twp., Passaic Co., NJ: Catharine VanDuyne, age 57; Giles, age 15; Sarah age 19; Henry, age '18', farmer; all b. NJ (adj. to Peter D. VanDuyne)
--1850 Census: Caldwell Twp., Essex Co., NJ: James Bowman, age 40, blacksmith; Ellen, age 36; Margaret J.,age 9; Peter, age 17, farmer; all b. New Jersey
--1860 Census: Meads Basin, Wayne Twp., Passaic Co., NJ: Catherine VanDuyne, age 61; Henry VanDuyne, age 22, farmer
--1860 Census: Caldwell Twp., Essex Co., NJ: James Bowman, age 50; Ellen, age 47; Margaret J., age 19; all b. New Jersey
--1870 Census: Wayne Twp., Passaic Co., NJ: Margret A. Van Dyne, age 29; James N., age 4; Geo. H., age 1; John Fourt, farm laborer; all b. New Jersey
--1880 Census: Wayne Twp., Passaic Co., NJ: Abraham Allen, age 38, farmer; Margaret J., age 40; James N. Van Duyne, age 13, stepson; George H. van Duyne, age 12, step son

- - - - -

Van Duyne, JAMES A.   b. (May 27, 1795)
(Neafie, p.6)   d. May 5, 1844
(inscriptions, p.142)

James A. Van Duyne
Died May 5, 1844
Aged 48 years, 11 months
& 8 days

wife, CATHARINE (Doremus)
(Neafie, p.6)   b. (October 6, 1798)
    d. August 13, 1873

Catherine Doremus
Widow of
Jas. A. van Duyne
Died Aug. 13, 1873
Aged 74 yrs 10 mos
and 7 days

Notes:
--James, son of Abraham Van Duyne and Catherine Mead
--Catharine, dau. of Peter G. Doremus and Catrina Van Wagenen

--1850 Census: Wayne Twp., Passaic Co., NJ: Catharine VanDuyne, age 57; Giles, age 15; Sarah age 19; Henry, age '18', farmer; all b. NJ (adj. to Peter D. VanDuyne)
--1860 Census: Meads Basin, Wayne Twp., Passaic Co., NJ: Catherine VanDuyne, age 61; Henry VanDuyne, age 22, farmer
--1870 Census: Wayne Twp., Passaic Co., NJ: Peter D. Van Duyne, age 49, farmer; Dorcas, age 46; Dorcas, age 18; Isaac

age 17; John, age 14; Anna, age 12; Catherine Van Duyne, age 72; all b. NJ

- - - - -

Van Duyne, Nicholas* b. September 20, 1838
 d. (aft. 1900?)

first? wife, RACHEL (VanNess)
(Neafie, p. 6) b. (December 19, 1840)
 d. February 19, 1884

*Rachel
Daughter of
John H. and C. M. van Ness
and wife of
Nicholas Van Duyne
Died Feb. 19, 1884
Aged 43 yrs. 3 mos.*

daughter, ESTHER C. b. (abt. August 18, 1863)
(Neafie, p.6) d. October 11, 1866

*Esther C.
Daughter of
Nicolas and Rachel
Van Duyne
Died Oct. 1, 1866
Aged 3 yrs. 1 month
and 23 days*

Notes:
--Nicholas, son of Nicholas Van Duyne and Hannah Vanderhoof
--Nicholas m. February 9, 1860, Rachel VanNess, dau. of John H. VanNess, q.v., and Catharine M. Cook

--1850 Census: Pequannock Twp., Morris Co., NJ: Nicholas Vanduyne, age 47, farmer; Hannah, age 48; Aaron, age 19, laborer; Catherine, age 16; Sarah L., age 14; <u>Nicholas</u>, age 11; all b. NJ

--1850 Census, p.94, Caldwell Twp., Essex Co., NJ: John H. VanNess, age 37, b. NJ, farmer; Catherine M., age 39 b. NY; <u>Rachel</u>, age 9, b. NJ; Benjamin F., age 7, b. NJ; George W., age 5, b. NJ; Laura L., age 3, b. NJ; Agnes B., age 1, b. NJ

--1860 Census: Pequannock Twp., Morris Co., NJ: Nicholas 'H' Vanduyne, age 58, b. Morris Co., farmer; Hannah, age 58, b. Morris Co.; <u>Nicholas</u>, age 22, b. Morris Co., farm labor; <u>Rachel</u>, age 20, b. Essex Co.; Jane, age 6, b. Morris Co.; Hanner M. Courter, age 11, b. NJ

--1870 Census: Montville, Morris Co., NJ: <u>Nicholas</u> VanDuyne, age 31, farmer; <u>Rachel</u>, age 29; Frank, age 9; Catharine, age 3; Harriet J. Cook, age 10, domestic servant

--1880 Census: Montville, Morris Co., NJ: <u>Nicholas K.</u> Van Duyne, age 41, farmer; <u>Rachel</u>, age 39; Frank, age 19, farmer; Catharine M., age 13; Frederick age 8; Jannie age 1; all b. NJ (adj. to Albert VanDuyne, age 43)

--1885 NJ Census: Montville, Morris Co., NJ: <u>Nicholas</u> Van Duyne; Frank; Catherine; Frederick; Jennie; Benjamin

--1900 Census: Acquackanonk Twp., Passaic Co., NJ; <u>Nicholus</u> Van Dyne age 63, b. Nov. 1836, m. 12 yr. b. NJ, farm labor; <u>Lucinda</u>, wife, age 46, b. Dec. 1853 NY, parents b. NY; Benjamin, son, b. Nov. 1881, NJ, father b. NJ, mother b. 'NY'

- - - - -

Van Duyne, PETER D.   b. (abt. 1822)
(Nealie, p.5)   d. May 7, 1871/1872
(monument)

Peter D. Van Duyne
Died May 7, 1871
Aged 50 years

wife, DORCAS (Kierstead)   b. (abt. 1825)
(Neafie, p.5)   d. December 21, 1893
(monument)

Dorcas Kierstead
wife of
Peter D. Van Duyne
Died Dec. 21, 1893
Aged 68 years

dau., MARTHA LOUISA
(Neafie, p.6)   b. (abt. February 25, 1852)
   d. May 20, 1853

Martha Louisa
Van Duyne
Died May 30, 1853
Aged 1 year 3 months
and 5 days

son, JOB   b. (abt. May 3, 1855)
(Neafie, p.6)   d. June 3, 1855

Job
Died June 3, 1855
Aged 1 month
Children of
Peter D. and Dorcas Van Duyne

son, SETH   b. (abt. November 25, 1860)
(Neafie, p.6)   d. August 25, 1861

Seth
Died Aug. 25, 1861
Aged 9 months
Children of

Peter D and Dorcas Van Duyne

son, SAMUEL   b. (abt. October 19, 1864)
(Neafie, p.6)   d. April 16, 1865

Samuel
Died Apr. 16, 1865
Aged 5 mos. & 22 (?) days
Children of
Peter D. and Dorcas van Duyne

Notes:
--Peter, son of James Van Duyne, q.v., and Catharine Doremus
--Peter D. Van Duyne m. November 25, 1846, Dorcas Kierstead, (?)dau. of Aaron O. Kierstead and Sarah Pier

--1850 Census: Wayne Twp., Passaic Co., NJ: Peter "C" Vanduyne, age 28, farmer; Dorcas, age 25; Sarah C., age 2; James, age 1; Peter Daniels, age 47, laborer, b. England; Jemima Riker, age 14; adj. to Catharine VanDuyne
--1860 Census: Mead's Basin PO., Wayne Twp., Passaic Co., NJ: Peter D. Vanduyne, age 38, farmer; Dorcas, age 35; Sarah, age 12; James, age 11; Dorcas, age 9; Jessie, age 6; Giles, age 3; Anna, age 2; all b. NJ (adj. to Catherine VanDuyne age 61 and Henry VanDuyne, age 72, farmer
--1870 Census: Wayne Twp., Passaic Co., NJ: Peter D. VanDuyne, age 49, farmer; Dorcas, age 46; Dorcas, age 18; Isaac age 17; John, age 14; Anna, age 12; Catherine, age 72; all b. NJ
--1880 Census: Newark, Essex Co., NJ: Dorcas "Van Clugore", age 55, keeping house; Annie Van Clugore, age 22; John A. Pier, age 39, no occupation; Sarah C. Pier, age 32; Lillian Pier, age 6; Frederic Pier, age 3; David S. Clark, age 52, b. NY, policeman

VAN HOUTEN

Van Houten, HENRY H.   b. (September 8, 1809)
(monument)   d. (October 10, 1885)

Henry H. Van Houten
Born
Sept. 9, 1809
Died
Nov. 10, 1896

wife, ELLEN (Pier)   b. September 27, 1817
(monument)   d. March 28, 1895

Ellen Van Houten
Born
Sept. 27, 1817
Died
March 28, 18895

son, JAMES F.
(Served: <u>Civil War)</u>
(Neafie, p.8)   b. September 14, 1838
(monument)   d. February 12, 1866
(gov't. stone)

James F.
son of
Henry H. & Ellen
Van Houten
He was a member of
Co. C, 13th Reg't. N.J. Vols
Died Feb. 12, 1866
Aged 27 years 4 mos.

& 29 days

Notes:
--Henry, son of Helmagh Van Houten and Lena Van Blarcom
--Henry m. October 10, 1835, Ellen Pier, dau. of James Pier and Mary Dey
--James F., son, served in the Civil War

--1850 Census: Wayne Twp., Passaic Co., NJ: Henry H. Van Houten, age 42, shoemaker; Ellen, age 32; Fanny, age 13; James, age 11; John H., age 9; Mary E., age 7; Leah C., age 4; all b. New Jersey
--1860 Census: Meads Basin P.O., Wayne Twp., Passaic Co., NJ: Henry Van Houten, age 51, shoemaker; Ellen, age 42; James, age 21, farm labor; Mary, age 17, tailoress; Leah Catherine, age 14; William, age 4; Emarintha, age 4 months; all b. New Jersey
--1870 Census: Wayne Twp., Passaic Co., NJ: Henry H. "Van Hanton: age 60 shoemaker; Ellen, age 53; Charles N., age 18; John W., age 14; Amarintha, age 10; all b. NJ
--1880 Census: Wayne Twp., Passaic Co., NJ: Henry H. Van Houten, age 70, shoemaker; Ellen, age 63; Emma, age 20; Michael Kenan, age 21, boarder, tinsmith

- - - - -

VAN NESS

Van Ness, AARON   b. December 8, 1797
(Neafie, p.7)   d. December 15, 1847
(nscriptions, p.143)

Aaron Van Ness
born December 8. 1797
died December 15, 1847
aged 50 years

wife, NANCY (Vanderhoof)
(Neafie, p.7)   b. (abt. 1799)
                                    d. February 16, 1864

Nancy Van Ness
Died Feb. 16, 1864
Aged 64 years

Notes:
--Aaron, son of Henry T. Van Ness, q.v. and Margaret Cadmus
--Aaron m. May 29, 1819, Nancy Vanderhoof

--1830 Census, Caldwell Twp., Essex Co., NJ: <u>Aaron</u> Van Ness adj. to Henry T. Van Ness
--1850 Census, Caldwell Twp., Essex Co., NJ: Cornelius Van Ness age 26, farmer; Phebe Ann age 26; Ann E. age 4; <u>Nancy</u> age 51; Margaret age 18; Henry Williams, age 17, farmer; all b. NJ
--1860 Census: Caldwell Twp., Essex Co., NJ: Cor.s A. Vanness age 36, farmer; Phebe J., age 36; Eliza age 13; <u>Nancy</u> age 66; Theodore age 2; John A. Van Houten, age 20, segar maker; all b. New Jersey

- - - - -

Van Ness, Benjamin H.*   b. (abt. September 13, 1837)
                                    d. (aft. 1920)

wife, Fanny*   b. (abt. November 1843?)
(Frances Jacobus)   d. (aft. 1920)

daughter, LIZZIE   b. (abt. June 20. 1867)
(Neafie, p. 10)   d. March 23, 1881

Lizzie
Died March 23, 1881

Aged 13 years 9 months
and 3 days
Children of Benjamin H.
and Fanny Van Ness

son, WELDON   b. (November 6, 1873)
(Neafie, p.10)   d. December 4, 1873

Weldon
Died Dec. 4 1873
Aged 28 days
Children of Benjamin H.
and Fanny Van Ness

Notes:
--(stones recorded by Neafie: next to Ralph Jacobus)
--Benjamin, son of Simon S. VanNess, q.v.
--Benjamin m. March 1862 at Caldwell, Fannie Jacobus

--1850 Census: Wayne Twp., Passaic Co., NJ: Simon S. van Ness, age 49, farmer; Jane, age 50; Benjamin, age 12; Mary Mandeville, age 70; all b. NJ
--1860 Census: Meads Basin, Wayne Twp., Passaic Co., NJ: Simon 'Than Ness' age 59, farmer; Jane, age 57; Benjamin, age 22, teacher at common school; Catherine, age 14
--?1860 Census: Caldwell Twp., Essex Co., NJ: Peter T. Speer, age 34; Caroline Speer, age 30; Daniel Courter, age 10; Fanny Jacobus, age 20 all b. NJ
--1870 Census: 8Wd, Newark, Essex Co., NJ: Benjamin VanNess, age 33, retail grocery; Fanny age 30; Mary Bell, age 6; Lizzie, age 3; all b. NJ; 2 clerks
--1880 Census:Newark, Essex Co., NJ: Benj. H. VanNess, age 41, sgt. of police; Fannie, age 41; Mabel age 16; Lizzie, age 13; Edna, age 3; all b. NJ
--1900 Census: 15 Wd. Newark, Essex Co., NJ: Benjamin Van Ness, age 59, b. Sept. 1841, m.32 years, 'secretary'?; Frances, wife, age 57, b. Nov. 1842, 4 born 2 living;

Mabelle, dau., age 40, b. Sept. 1880, insurance clerk; all b. NJ

--1905 NJ Census: Essex Co., NJ: Benjamin H. Van Ness, age 68; Frances age 67; Mabelle, age 37; I. Carl Mcclenathan age 35; Edna Mcclenathan age 28; Evart Mcclenathan, age 6; Phebe J. Foster, age 70

--1910 Census:15Wd, Newark, Essex Co., NJ: Benjamin H. VanNess, age 72, m.48 years, life insurance broker; Fannie, age 70; Mabelle, age 46; Edna MacLenathan, age 33, b. 13 yrs.; Evart C. MacLenathan, age 11, b. NJ, father b. NY

--1920 Census: 1Wd. Newark, Essex Co., NJ: Benjamin H. Vanness, age 82, real estate & insurance; Fanny, age 80; Mabelle Vanness, age 56, dau., ass't head, insurance co.; Edna Macclenahan, age 43, dau. office clerk jewelry factory; Evart L. Macclenahan, age 21, grandson, clerk importers; all b. NJ

- - - - -

Van Ness, CORNELIUS D. b. August 3, 1821
(monument)   d. October 3, 1898
(NJ Will #27710G,1898)

In
Memory of
Cornelius D. Van Ness
Born Aug. 3, 1821
Died Oct. 3, 1898

-

Harriet Jacobus
wife of
C.D. Van Ness
Born July 2, 1822
Died June 7, 1882

wife, HARRIET (Jacobus)
(Neafie, p.13)   b. July 2, 1822

(monument)   d. June 7, 1882

Notes:
--Cornelius, son of David VanNess, q.v., and Ellen Vanderhoof
--Harriet, dau. of John R. Jacobus and Sarah Vanderhoof

--1850 Census: Caldwell Twp., Essex Co., NJ: Cornelius D. VanNess, age 29, farmer; Harriet, age 28; Sarah Ellen, age 7; Hannah M., age 3; David, age 78, farmer; all b. New Jersey; Charles W. Richardson, age 52, b. VA, school teacher
--1860 Census: Caldwell, Essex Co., NJ: Cors. D. VanNess, age 39, coal merchant; Harriet, age 38; Sarah E., age 17; Hannah M., age 13; John S. age 7; Joseph W., age 4; all b. New Jersey
--1870 Census: Caldwell Twp., Essex Co., NJ: Cornelius Van Ness, age 49, farmer; Harriet, age 48; Hannah M., age 23; "Stiles" 17, apprentice mason; Wilson, age 15; all b. New Jersey
--1880 Census: Caldwell Twp., Essex Co., NJ: Cornelius D. VanNess, age 59, farmer; Harriet, age 58; J. Stiles, age 27, son, mason; Christiana, age 23, daughter-in-law; Zelda, age 4, granddaughter; all b. New Jersey
--1885 NJ Census: Caldwell Twp., Essex Co., NJ: Cornelius D. Van Ness; John S.; Annie; Zelda

- - - - -

Van Ness, CORNELIUS I.   b. (abt. 1810)
(Neafie, p.15)   d. (February 11, 1871)
(NJ Will #17454G, Inv. 1871)

Cornelius I Van Ness
Died Feb. 11, 1871
In his 61st year

first wife, MARY (Ryerson)

(Neafie, p.15)   ب. (April 17, 1812)
                              d. (March 13, 1851)

Mary
Wife of
Cornelius Van Ness
Died March 13, 1851
Aged 38 years 10 months
& 26 days

second? wife, SARAH   b. (abt. 1813)
(Neafie, p.15)   d. April 28, 1855

Sarah
Wife of
Cornelius I. van Ness
Died Apr. 28, 1855
Aged 42 years

third wife, Corintha* (Snyder) b. (abt. 1813)
(?NJ Will #26709G, 1896)   d. (October 9, 1889)

son, ISAAC   b. (abt. 1836)
(Neafie, p.15)   d. May 24, 1871

Isaac
Died May 24 1871
In his 35th year
Sons of
Cornelius and Mary
Van Ness

son, JOHN R.   b. (abt. 1847)
(Neafie, p.15)   d. September 18, 1864

John R.
Died Sept. 18, 1864

In his 17th year
Sons of
Cornelius I. and Mary
Van Ness

Notes:
--Cornelius, son of Isaac VanNess, q.v., and Sarah Jacobus
--Cornelius m. #1, abt. 1833, Mary Ryerson, dau. of John Ryerson and Rachel Jacobus; m. #2, aft. 1851, Sarah ....; m. #3, bef. 1860, Corintha .....
--"Cornelius Van Ness b. 1810, age 46, widowed, m. May 4, 1856, Essex Co. NJ: Catherine C. Snyder, "

--1850 Census: Caldwell Twp., Essex Co., NJ: Cornelius vanNess, age 40, mason; Mary, age 38; Martha, age 17; Isaac, age 14; Rachel Ann, age 10; Sarah E., age 8; James, age 5; John R., age 2; all b. New Jersey
--1850 Census: Caldwell Twp., Essex Co., NJ: Corintha H. Snyder, age 28, b. NJ; at res. of Enoch T. Shinn, innkeeper
--1860 Census: Caldwell Twp., Essex Co., NJ: Cornelius 'J' VanNess, age 50, farmer; Corintha age 46; Sarah E., age 17; James, age 15; John R., age 13; Mary, age 9; Sarah, age 72; all b. New Jersey
--1870 Census: Caldwell Twp., Essex Co., NJ: Cornelius 'J' VanNess, age 60, country merchant; 'Catherine', age 57; Mary, age 19; all b. New Jersey
--1880 Census: Montclair, Essex Co., NJ: Cornl. V. Bush, age 39, mason; 'Cornittia', age 14, daughter; Charles, age 13, son; Ernest, age 9, son; Newport (Lee Port), age 2, son; 'Cornitia' Vanness, age 66, widow, mother-in-law; all b. NJ
--1885 NJ Census: Caldwell, Essex Co., NJ: Corintha Vanness; 1 female over age 60

- - - - -

Van Ness, DAVID   b. (abt. 1772)
(Neafie, p. 17)   d. February 16, 1851

(monument)
(NJ Will #14147G, 1851)

> *Sacred*
> *To the memory of*
> *David Van Ness*
> *Who died Feb. 16, 1851*
> *Aged 81 years 8 mos.*
> *& 29 days*

wife, ELLEN (Vanderhoof)   b. (abt. August 18, 1779)
(Neafie, p. 17)   d. February 11, 1845
(monument)

> *wife of David Van Ness*
> *died February 11, 1845*
> *aged 65 years, 5 months & 24 days*

> -

> *Sacred*
> *to the memory*
> *of*
> *Ellen, wife of*
> *David Van Ness*
> *who died*
> *Feb. 11, 1845*
> *Aged 65 years, 5 mos.*
> *& 24 days*

Notes:
--David, son of Thomas E. Van Ness and Margaret Francisco
--David m. February 17, 1802, Ellen Vanderhoof, dau. of Henry Vanderhoof and Rachel Kierstead

--1840 Census: Caldwell Twp., Essex Co., NJ: <u>David</u> "Varness"; 3 persons

--1850 Census: Caldwell Twp., Essex Co., NJ: Cornelius D. Vanness, age 29, farmer; Harriet, age 28; Sarah Ellen, age 7; Hannah M. age 3; David, age 78, farmer; all b. NJ

- - - - -

Van Ness, EPHRAIM M.   b. 1836
(monument)   d. 1919 (May 16)

Ephraim M. Van Ness
1836 - 1919
His Wife Sarah J.
1841 - 1917

wife, Sarah J.* (Van Houten) b. 1841
d. 1917

Notes:
Served: Civil War. Co. A, 25th Reg. NJ Inf.
--son of John E. Van Ness, q.v.
--1850 Census: Wayne Twp., Passaic Co. NJ: John E. Van Ness, age 50, farmer; Margaret, age 48; Thomas, age 24, farmer; Munson, age 13; Martinus age 11; Emma age 9; John, age 6; all b. NJ (adj. Moses van Ness, age 26, farmer; Eliza, age 22)
--1860 Census: Meads Basin, Wayne Twp., Passaic Co., NJ: Margaret Van Ness, age 58; Thomas, age 33, farmer; Ephraim (Munson), age 24, farmer; Martinus, age 21, farmer; Harriet (Emma), age 17, tailoress; John, age 16
--1880 Census: Wayne Twp., Passaic Co., NJ: Ephraim M. Van Ness, age 43, b. NJ, farmer; Sarah J.,age 38, wife, b.NJ
--1900 Census. Wayne Twp., Passaic Co. NJ: E. Van Ness, age 63 b. June 1836, m. 37 years, farmer; Sarah,age 58 b. Oct. 1841, 0 born 0 living; both b. NJ; 1 farm laborer
--1910 Census: Wayne Twp., Passaic Co. NJ: Ephraim M. Van Ness, age 73, m.47 yrs. b. NJ, farmer; Sarah J., age 68, wife, b. NJ

Van Ness, EVART	b. 1765
(inscriptions, p. 142)	d. 1833
?wife, Lena* (Ryerson)	b.
	d. (bef. 1827)

Notes:
--Inscription for Evart is reported near William E. and Henry E. Van Ness
--?"William Ryerson m. July 26, 1735, his cousin Elizabeth, dau. of Joris and Hannah (Schouten)(Dey) Ryerson; she died between 1765 and 1772; ...children of William and Elizabeth: William, d. 1832, m. Ellen Cook; and LENA (d. bef. 1827) m. EVART Van Ness; child of Evart and Lena: John E. Van Ness" (and William E. Van Ness) (*Descendants of Rebecca Van Der Scheuren.* WikiTree.com)

Van Ness, EVERT H.	b. (September 24, 1772)
(Neafie, p.19)	d. August 28, 1862
(inscriptions, p.142)	
(monument)	

In
Memory of
Evert H. Van Ness
who died
August 28th, 1802
aged 89 years 11 months
and 4 days

wife, CAROLINE (Smith)	
(Neafie, p. 19)	b. (abt. October 8, 1778)

d. December 8, 1855

Caroline Smith
wife of
Evert H. Van Ness
Died Dec. 8, 1855
Aged 77 yrs. 2 mos.

Notes:
--Evert, son of Henry VanNess and Rachel Sandford
--Evert m. November 16, 1797, Pompton Ref. Church, Caroline "Caty" Smith, dau. of Jacob Smith

--1830 Census: Acquackanonk Twp., Essex Co., NJ: Evert H. Van Ness: 5 persons (adj. Abr. Vreeland and Cornelius Jacobus.)
--1850 Census: Little Falls, Acquackanonk Twp., Passaic Co., NJ: Evert H. VanNess, age 78, farmer; Caroline, age 73; Catherine, age 30; Wm. H., age 8; Catherine Slingerland, age 13; Eliza C. VanNess, age 1; all b. NJ
--1860 Census: Little Falls, Acquackanonk Twp., Passaic Co., NJ: "Evas" Van Ness, age 88; James, age 50, farmer; Jane, age 42; James, age 12; Elizabeth age 24; Sophia, age 22; all b. New Jersey

- - - - -

Van Ness, Francis* (NJ Will #25733G, 1894)	b. (December 7, 1812) d. (July 6, 1894) (June 7, 1894)
wife, Jane* (Speer)	b. (March 20, 1819) d. (November 16, 1895)
son, JAMES BENTLEY (Neafie, p.19) (inscriptions, p. 143)	b. (August 20, 1843) d. September 27, 1848

James Bently
son of
Francis and Jane Van Ness
Died September 27, 1848
Aged 5 years, 1 month
& 7 days

son, PETER   b. (February 12, 1846)
(Neafie, p.19)   d. October 11, 1847
(inscriptions, p.143)

Peter
son of
Francis and Jane Van Ness
Died October 11, 1847
Aged 1 year, 7 months, & 29 days

son, THOMAS HENRY   b. (May 6, 1848)
(Neafie, p.19)   d. September 11, 1849
(inscriptions, p.143)

Thomas Henry
son of
Francis and Jane Van Ness
Died September 11, 1849
Aged 1 year, 4 months & 5 days

Notes:
--Francis, son of Evert H. Van Ness, q.v., and Caroline Smith
--Francis m. Jane Speer, dau. of Tunis Speer, q.v. and Jemima Miller

--1850 Census: Acquackanonk Twp., Passaic Co.NJ: Francis Van Ness age 37 farmer; Jane age 31 b. NJ; Harriet age 9 b. NJ; Robert Simpson, age 12, b. Ireland

--1860 Census: Little Falls PO, Acquackanonk Twp., Passaic Co. NJ: Francis Van Ness, 47, farmer(?); Jane 40; 'Harrel' age 19; Isaac age 10; Evert age 8; Francis age 2; all b. New Jersey (adj. to 'Evas' Van Ness, age 88, et al.)

--1870 Census: Little Falls, Passaic Co.NJ: Francis Vanness age 57, farmer; Jane, age 50; Isaac M. age 19; 'Ernest' H. age 17; Frank age 12; Susan age 10; all b. NJ

--1880 Census: Newark, Essex Co., NJ: Francis Vanness age 68, works in coal yard; Jane age 62; Everett age 25, clerk at cigar store; Frank age 20, bookkeeper; Susan age 18; Thomas Pier, age 21, boarder, works at machine shop; all b. NJ

--1885 NJ State Census: 1Wd. Newark, Essex Co., NJ: Francis Vanness; Jane; Everett; Frank; Kitty; Susan; Mary Sparks

- - - - -

Van Ness, FRANCIS   b. (abt. 1840)
(monument)   d. 1893

Francis Van Ness
1845 - 1893

-

His wife
Malinda P.
1841 - 1859

-

Their children
Henry C.
1866 - 1866

Thomas Lester
1865 - 1869

wife, MALINDA P. (VanNess)
(Neafie, p.7)   b. (abt. 1841)
    d. March 7, 1869

*Malinda P.
wife of
Francis Van Ness
Died March 7, 1869
Aged 28 yrs. 3 mos.
& 21 days*

son, THOMAS LESTER   b. February 9, 1865
(Neafie, p.7)   d. April 16, 1869

*Thomas Lester
Born Feb. 9, 1865
Died Apr. 16, 1869
Children of
Francis and Malinda P.
Van Ness*

son, HENRY CLIFFORD   b. March 20, 1866
(Neafie, p.7)   d. July 31, 1866

*Henry Clifford
Born March 20, 1866
Died July 31, 1866
Children of
Francis and Malinda P.
Van Ness*

Notes:
--Francis, son of Henry J. (I.)VanNess, q.v., and Phebe Ann Speer
--Francis m.January 16, 1862, Malinda P. VanNess, dau. of Thomas VanNess and Martha M. .....

--1850 Census: Caldwell Twp., Essex Co., NJ: Henry J. Vanness, age 35, carpenter; Phebe Ann, age 33; Munson, age 13; Francis, age 10; Mary E., age 5; all b. NJ

--1850 Census: East Ward, Newark, Essex Co., NJ: Thomas Vanness, age 44, saddle tree maker; Martha M., age 44; Malinda P., age 9; Elizabeth Fisher, age 19
--1860 Census: Caldwell, Essex Co., NJ Henry J. VanNess, age 48, carpenter; Phebe A., age 45; Munson, age 23, carpenter; Francis, age 19, laborer; Mary E., age 15; Harriet, age 20
--1860 Census: Newark, Essex Co., NJ: Thos. Vanness, age 54, saddle tree maker; Martha M., age 53; Malinda P., age 19, 'canvas saddle tree'; all b. NJ
--1880 Census: Caldwell, Essex Co., NJ: "Henry I. Vanness, age 67; Frank, age 36, son, single, salesman; Catharine Ray, age 60

- - - - -

Van Ness, Garret*   b. (December 24, 1813)
                          d. (aft. 1900)

first wife, MARGARET (Doremus)
(Neafie, p.6)   b. (January 8, 1814)
(monument)   d. December 15, 1855

Margaret Doremus
Wife of
Garret Vanness
Died Dec. 15, 1855
Aged 41 years 11 months
and 7 days

Notes:
--Garret, son of Henry T. VanNess, q.v., and Margaret Cadmus
--Garret m. #1, Margaret Doremus, dau. of John Doremus and Margaret Vanderhoof
--Garret m. #2, Catherine Elizabeth Nafie

--1850 Census: Caldwell Twp., Essex Co., NJ: Garret Vanness, age 37, farmer; Margaret, age 36; Mary Jane, age 12; Aaron, age 1; all b. New Jersey
--1860 Census: Caldwell Twp., Essex Co., NJ: Garret Vanness, age 46, farmer; Elizabeth, age 34; Aaron, age 11; Horace, age 12; Jacob V., age 10
--1870 Census: Caldwell Twp., Essex Co., NJ: Garret Van Ness, age 55, saloon keeper; Elizabeth, age 42; Charles, age 4; Sarah Neafie, age 65; all b. NJ
--1880 Census: Caldwell Twp., Essex Co., NJ: 'Ganet' Vanness, age 66, works in garden; Elizabeth, age 54; Charles, age 13; all b. NJ
--1900 Census: Caldwell Twp., Essex Co., NJ: Stephen Husk, age 68, b. NJ, farmer; Rachel Husk, age 69, b. NY; Gilbert Husk, age 39, b. NJ, house painter; Garret Vanness, b. December 1813, b. NJ, widower, boarder

- - - - -

Van Ness, Garret   See: Vanderhoof Burial Ground
wife, Elizabeth

- - - - -

Van Ness, George*   b. (abt. 1834)
                                d. (May 16, 1890)
                                (In his 54th year)

first wife, CATHERINE E. (Neafie)
(Neafie, p.1)   b. (abt. July 3, 1833)
(monument)   d. August 7, 1865

Catherine E. Neafie
wife of
George Van Ness
Died Aug. 7, 1885
Aged 32 years 1 month

and 4 days

Notes:
--George VanNess m. May 11, 1854, Catherine Eugenia Neafie, dau. of John Richard Neafie and Sarah Doremus
--George m. #2, Josephine .....

--1850 Census:
--1850 Census: Acquackanonk Twp., Passaic Co., NJ: "John K. Nafie" age 59, farmer; Sarah, age 53; Aaron B., age 28, teamster; Emeline, age 26; Eugenia, age 17; Jeptha F., age 14; all b. New Jersey
--1860 Census: 9Wd, Dist. 4, NYC: George "Vanhees" age 26 b. NY, silversmith; "Virginia" age 24, b. NJ; Alice, age 4, b. NY; Emeline age 2 months b. NY; Mary Donnelly, age 35, b. Ireland, domestic; Maria Hall, age 43, b. NJ (see Ogden Hall)
--1870 Census: 4Wd, Brooklyn, Kings Co., NY: George "Van Niss" age 34 b. NY, works at silver manufactory; Josephine age 23 b. NY; Kate, age 2 b. NY; Alice, age 14, b. NY, at school; 3 boarders
--1880 Census: Brooklyn, Kings Co., NY: George "Vanep" age 44, b. NY, parents NY, silversmith; "Josafine", age 32 b. NY; Alice, age 22, b. NY; C. E., (Catherine Eugenia?), dau., age 12 b. NY; "Rosmer" son, age 2 b. NY

- - - - -

Van Ness, GEORGE WASHINGTON
(monument) b. February 18, 1845
d. November 3, 1927

George Washington Van Ness
February 18, 1845
November 3, 1927

first wife, SARAH JANE YOUNG

(monument)   b. April 20, 1844
d. May 12, 1901

*Sarah Jane Young
Wife of
George W. Van Ness
April 20, 1844
May 12, 1901*

Notes:
--George W., son of John H. Van Ness, q.v.
--George W. m. #1, Apr. 25, 1865, Sarah Jane Young, dau. of Andrew Young and Rachel (Van Ness)
--George W., m. #2, abt. 1902, Anna (Jacobus)
--1850 Census: Caldwell Twp., Essex Co., NJ: John H. VanNess, age 37, b. NJ, farmer; Catherine M., age 39 b. NY; Rachel, age 9, b. NJ; Benjamin F., age 7, b. NJ; George W., age 5, b. NJ; Laura L., age 3, b. NJ; Agnes B., age 1, b. NJ
--1860 Census: Caldwell Twp., Essex Co., NJ: John H. Vanness, age 46, b. NJ, farmer; "Mary E.", age 48, b. NY; Jane A., age 23, b. NJ; Benjamin F., age 17, b. NJ; George W., age 15, b. NJ; Laura L., age 13, b. NJ; Joseph W., age 1, b. NJ
--1860 Census: Pequannock, Morris Co., NJ: Andrew Young, age 46, shoemaker; Rachel, age 45; Mary E., age 18; Sarah J., age 16; George W., age 11; Sarah Young, age 80; all b. New Jersey
--1870 Census: Caldwell Twp., Essex Co., NJ: John H. Vanness, age 56, blacksmith; Catherine, age 57, b. NY; Jane, age 31, seamstress; George W., age 25, farmer; Sarah J., age 26; Andrew, age 1; Joseph W., age 11; Stephen Cook, age 9
--1880 Census: Caldwell Twp., Essex Co., NJ: John H. Vanness, age 66, retired farmer; Cathrine M., age 68, wife; Jane Ann, age 43, dau.; Joseph M., age 21, grandson, works on farm; Washington, age 35, son, farmer; Sarah J., age 35, daughter-in-law, Andrew, age 11, grandson; Mary Agnes,

age 5, granddaughter; Charles Pierce, age 17, works on farm; all b. New Jersey
--1900 Census: Caldwell Twp., Essex Co., NJ: George W. Vanness, age 55 b. Feb. 1844, m.33 yr. farmer; Sarah J., age 56, b. Apr. 1844, 2 born 2 living; John, age 31, b. Dec. 1868, single, farm laborer; all b. NJ
--1910 Census: West Caldwell, Essex Co., NJ: George W. Van Ness, age 64, m. #2 for 8 years, farmer; Anna, age 46, m. #1 for 8 yr.; Abram, age 19, nephew, farm labor
--1920 Census: West Caldwell, Essex Co., NJ: George W. Van Ness, age 74, farmer; Anna, age 55; both b. NJ

- - - - -

Van Ness, HENRY E.   b. (abt. May 11, 1798?)
(Neafie, p.19)   d. December 19, 1836
(monument)
(NJ Will #12834G, 1837 Inv.)

In
Memory
of
Henry E. Van Ness
Who Departed This life
Dec. 19, 1876
Aged 38 years 7 months
& 8 days

wife, HESTER (Francisco)
(Neafie, p.20)   b. (February 5, 1802)
(monument)   d. July 20, 1836

In
Memory
of
Hester Francisco
wife of

Henry H. Van Ness
who departed this life
July 20, 1836
Aged 34 years 4 mos.
& 25 days

Notes:
--Henry E. Van Ness, son of Evert H. VanNess, q.v., and Caroline Smith. (Bapt. Pompton Ref. Church)
--Henry E. Van Ness m. May 13, 1820, Hetty Francisco, daughter of Josiah Francisco, q.v., and Sarah F. Jacobus

--1830 Census: Acquackanonk, Essex Co., New Jersey: Evert H. Van Ness

- - - - -

Van Ness, HENRY H.   b. November 21, 1782
(Neafie, p.3)   d. June 13, 1867
(NJ Will #16579G, 1867)

Henry H. Van Ness
Born Nov. 21, 1782
Died June 13, 1867

wife, MARGARET (Bush)
(Neafie. p.3)   b. September 2, 1784(1781?)
    d. October 22, 1855

Margaret Bush
wife of
Henry H. Van Ness
Born Sept. 2, 1784
Died Oct. 22, 1855

Notes:
--See also: Isaac J. Van Wart

--Henry, son of Henry VanNess and Rachel Sandford
--Henry m. #2, before 1860, Maria .....
--1850 Census: Caldwell Twp., Essex Co., NJ: Henry H. Vanness, age 66, farmer; Margaret, age 64; Job Doremus, age 38, mason; Rachel Doremus, age 35; Susan, age 13; Warren, age 3; all b. New Jersey
--1860 Census: Caldwell Twp., Essex Co., NJ: Henry H. Vanness, age 77, farmer; Maria, age 51; Harriet, age 18

- - - - -

Van Ness, HENRY I. b. November 30, 1812
(Neafie, p.7) d. November 3, 1889
(monument)
(NJ Will #23399G, 1889)

Henry I. Van Ness
Born Nov. 30, 1812
Died Nov. 3, 1889
(Neafie)

Henry I. Van Ness
1812 - 1889

-

His wife
Phebe Ann Speer
1816 - 1873
(monument)

wife, PHEBE ANN (Speer)
(Neafie, p.7) b. (abt. June 22, 1818)
(monument) d. September 13, 1875

Phebe Ann Speer
wife of
Henry I. Van Ness
Died Sept. 13, 1875

Aged 57 years 2 mos.
and 22 days
(Neafie)

Notes:
--Henry, son of Isaac VanNess, q.v. and Sarah Jacobus
--Henry m. Phebe Ann Speer, dau. of Tunis Speer and Jemima Miller
--Will Vol J2-K2 Image 167: ment. dau. Mary E. Bush, wife of Henry M. Bush; son, William M. Van Ness; son Francis Van Ness

--1850 Census: Caldwell Twp., Essex Co., NJ: Henry J. Vanness, age 35, carpenter; Phebe Ann, age 33; Munson, age 13; Francis age 10; Mary E., age 5
--1860 Census: Caldwell Twp., Essex Co., NJ: Henry J. VanNess, age 48, carpenter; Phebe A., age 45; Munson, age 23, carpenter; Francis, age 19, laborer; Mary E., age 15; Harriet, age 20; all b. New Jersey
--1870 Census: Caldwell, Essex Co., NJ: Henry J. Van Ness, age 57, farmer; Phebe A., age 54; Munson, age 32, carpenter; Harriet, age 29; Malinda P., age 1; all b. NJ
--1880 Census: Caldwell, Essex Co,. NJ: Henry I. Vanness, age 67; Frank, age 36, son, single, salesman; Catharine Ray, age 60

- - - - -

Van Ness, Henry R.*	b. (April 17, 1800)
	d. (June 26, 1897)
wife, MARIA (Ryerson) (Neafie, p.13)	b. (January 24, 1802) d. April 5, 1881

Maria
Wife of
Henry R. Van Ness

Died Apr. 5, 1881
Aged 79 years, 2 mos.
and 11 days

Notes:
--Henry, son of Robert H. VanNess and Mary Jacobus
--Henry m. June 18, 1823, Maria Ryerson, dau. of Martin Ryerson and Ann Ackerman
--Henry and Maria, members of the Ref. Church at Little Falls.

--1850 Census: Acquackanonk Twp., Passaic Co,. NJ: Henry R. VanNess age 50, merchant; Maria, age 48; Lucas R., age 24, merchant; Mary P., age 21; Henry, age 1; all b. New Jersey
--1860 Census: Acquackanonk Twp., Passaic Co., NJ: Henry Van Ness, age '50' farmer; Mary, age '50' Rachel Garribrants, age 22; Monroe Schommake age 18; near: Lucas Van Ness, age 33, farmer; Mary, age 31; Henry, age 10; William, age 6; Hester Demarest, age 17, servant, all b. NJ
--1870 Census: Little Falls, Passaic Co., NJ: Henry R. VanNess age 70, country store; Maria, age 68; Lucas R. age 43; Mary, age 42; Henry, age 20; William, age 15; all b. New Jersey; 1 laborer b. Ireland
--1880 Census: Little Falls, Passaic Co., NJ: Henry R. VanNess, age 80, keeping store; Maria, age 78; both b. New Jersey

- - - - -

Van Ness, HENRY T.   b. (abt. 1775)
(Neafie, p.6)   d. January 19, 1860
(monument

Henry T. Van Ness
Died Jan. 19, 1860
In his 86th year

wife, MARGARET (Cadmus)
(Neafie, p.6) b. (abt. 1777)
(inscriptions, p.142) d. July 20, 1848
(monument)

> *Margaret Cadmus*
> *wife of*
> *Henry T. Van Ness*
> *Died July 20, 1848*
> *Aged 72 years*

Notes:
--Henry, son of Thomas Evert Van Ness and Margaret Francisco
--Henry T. Van Ness m. September, 1797, Margaret Cadmus

--1850 Census: Caldwell Twp., Essex Co., NJ: Peter VanNess, age 28, shoemaker; Sally Ann age 37; Henry age 17, tobacconist; Hetty Ann age 14; Martha J. age 12; Harriet E. age 10; Phebe Louisa age 7; Josephine age 5; Charlotte A., age 1; <u>Henry T.</u> VanNess age 76, farmer

- - - - -

Van Ness, Isaac* b. (March 25, 1785)
(?NJ Will #12186G, Inv.1830) d. (bef. 1850)

wife, SARAH (Jacobus)
(Neafie, p.15) b. (December 18, 1786)
  d. February 14, 1875

> *Sarah Jacobus*
> *wife of*
> *Isaac Van Ness*
> *Died Feb. 14, 1875*
> *Aged 87 years, 4 mos.*

and 21 days

Notes:
--Isaac, son of Henry VanNess and Rachel Sandford
--Sarah, dau. of Roelof Jacobus and Frances Riker

--1850 Census: Caldwell Twp., Essex Co., NJ: <u>Sarah</u> VanNess, age 63; William 'J', age 25, farmer; all b. NJ
--1860 Census: Caldwell Twp., Essex Co., NJ: Cornelius 'J' VanNess, age 50, farmer; Corintha age 46; Sarah E., age 17; James, age 15; John R., age 13; Mary, age 9; <u>Sarah</u>, age 72; all b. New Jersey
--1870 Census: Caldwell Twp., Essex Co., NJ: Wm. J. 'Van Nep' age 45, farmer; Maria, age 36; Judson, age 9; Aminda age 8; <u>Sarah</u> Van Ness, age 83; Michael Prout, age 24, b. NY, farm labor; Joseph Francisco, age 19, b. NJ, brick mason

- - - - -

Van Ness, Isaac   See: Van Ness Burial Ground

- - - - -

Van Ness, ISAAC D.   b. February 18, 1815
(Neafie, p.8)   d. November 7, 1885

Isaac D. Van Ness
Born
February 18, 1815
Died
November 7, 1885

wife, Mary Ann* (Pier)   b. (abt. November 22, 1817)
                         d. (January 9, 1899)

Notes:

--Isaac, son of David VanNess, q.v., and Ellen Vanderhoof

--1850 Census: Caldwell Twp., Essex Co., NJ: Isaac D. VanNess, age 35, shoemaker; Mary Ann, age 33; Sarah R., age 11; Lucinda, age 9; Mary L., age 3; all b. New Jersey
--1860 Census: Caldwell Twp., Essex Co., NJ: Isaac D. VanNess, age 45, hatter; Anna, age 43; Sarah R., age 21; Lucinda, age 19; Mary L, age 13; all b. New Jersey
--1899 Newark City Directory: Mary Ann, widow of Isaac D. Van Ness

- - - - -

Van Ness, ISAAC J. b. (August 4, 1813)
(Neafie, p.11) d. January 27, 1886
(monument)
(NJ Will #22210G, 1886)

Isaac J. Van Ness
Died
Jan. 27, 1886
In his 74th year
Weep not he is at rest.

-

Ann Rome (sic)
His wife
Died Jan. 26, 1892
Aged 80 years

first wife, Eliza Caroline* (Simonson)
                        b. (1815)
                        d. (February 13, 1835)

second wife, ANN (Roome)
(monument) b. (1815)
                        d. January 26, 1892

daughter, CARRIE　　　　b. (abt. November 5, 1841)
(Neafie, p.11)　　　　　 d. November 17, 1870
(monument)

> *Carrie*
> *Daughter of*
> *Isaaac and Ann*
> *VanNess*
> *Died*
> *Nov. 17th, 1870*
> *Aged 29 years*
> *and 12 days*

son, SAMUEL　　　　　b. (abt. February 1, 1847)
(Neafie, p.11)　　　　　 d. September 1, 1849
(inscriptions, p. 144(

> *Samuel*
> *son of Isaac J. and*
> *Ann Van Ness*
> *Died September 1, 1849*
> *Aged 2 years & 7 months*

son, CHARLES H.　　　b. April 13, 1854
(Neafie, p.11)　　　　　 d. May 6, 1856
(monument)

> *Charles H.*
> *Born Apr. 13, 1854*
> *Died May 6, 1856*

Notes:
--Isaac, son of Jacob Peter Van Ness and Mehetabel Cobb
--Isaac m. #1, June 12, 1834, Eliza Caroline Simonson; m. #2, May 14, 1836, Ann Roome

--1850 Census: Caldwell Twp., Essex Co., NJ: Isaac J. Vanness, age 36, farmer; Ann, age 37; Mary R. age 12; John age 11; Caroline, age 10; Jane, age 7; Jacob Bush, age 50, laborer; all b. New Jersey (adj. to Henry T(?) Vanness, age 35)

--1860 Census: Caldwell Twp., Essex Co., NJ: Isaac J. Vanness age 46, farmer; Ann age 47; Caroline, age 19, seamstress; Jane, age 17, seamstress; Isaac Conklin, age 63, laborer; all b. NJ

--1870 Census: Caldwell Twp., Essex Co., NJ: Isaac J. Van Ness, age 56, farmer; Ann age 56; Jane age 27; William Howard, age 13, farm boy

--1880 Census: Caldwell Twp., Essex Co., NJ: Isaac J. Vanness, age 66, farmer; Anne, age 67; James Roome, age 22, nephew, works on farm; (adj. to Henry T. Vanness, age 64)

--1895 NJ Census: Isaac J. Van Ness; Ann Van Ness

- - - - -

Van Ness, Jacob S.*	b. (abt. 1804)
(?NJ Will #22565G, 1887)	d. (abt. 1887)
wife, Lydia*	b. (abt. 1806)
	d. (aft. 1880)
daughter, SARAH	b. (abt. November 16, 1831)
(Neafie, p.20)	d. December 29, 1832

Sarah
Daughter of
Jacob S. and Lydia
Van Ness
Died December 29, 1832
Aged 1 year, 1 month
& 13 days

Notes:
--Jacob, son of Evert H. VanNess, q.v., and Caroline Smith

--1850 Census: 5Wd, Newark, Essex Co., NJ: Jacob Vanness age 45, grocer; Lydia, age 43; Ephraim J., age 23, dock builder; Caroline age 19; Peter F., age 16, clerk; Sarah M. age 14; Henry age 12; Mary L., age 9; Rachel A., age 8; William S., age 5; all b. New Jersey
--1860 Census: 5Wd, Newark, Essex Co., NJ: Jacob S. Vanness age 56, dock builder; Lydia age 54; 'Ephrim', age 30, carpenter; Henry age 22, paper carrier; Mary age 18; Rachel age 16; William, age 14; all b. NJ
--1870 Census: 5Wd, Newark, Essex Co., NJ: Lydia Vanness age 64 b. NJ; at res. of Catherine Walters, age 65 b. Ireland
--1870 Census: 5Wd, Newark, Essex Co., NJ: J. S. Vanness, age 66, dockbuilder
--1880 Census: Newark, Essex Co., NJ: Jacob S. Vanness age 77 b. NJ, dockbuilder; Lydia, wife, age 74 b. NJ; Lydia F. Vanness, granddaughter, age 18, b. Massachusetts, granddaughter (dau. of Henry and Sarah VanNess)

- - - - -

Van Ness, James* b. (July 4, 1810)
  d. (aft. 1880)

first wife, CATHARINE (VanHouten)
(Neafie, p.18) b. (December 29, 1807)
  d. August 7, 1849

Catharine Van Houten
wife of
James Van Ness
Died August 7, 1849
Aged 41 years, 7 months
& 8 days

daughter, ANN AMELIA b. (abt. June 9, 1845)
(Neafie, p18) d. August 1, 1849

Ann Amelia
Daughter of
J. & C. Van Ness
Died August 1, 1849
Aged 4 years, 1 month
& 23 days

Notes:
--James, son of Evert H. VanNess, q.v., and Caroline Smith
--James m. Catherine Van Houten, dau. of Johannes Van Houten and Sarah Mandeville.
--James m. bef. 1860, Jane Vedder

--1850 Census: Acquackanonk Twp., Passaic Co. NJ: James Vanness age 40, farming & sawing; Sarah C. age 16; Elizabeth age 14; Sophia, age 10; John age 8; James S. age 1; William Brower, age 15; all b. NJ
--1860 Census: Little Falls, Passaic Co. NJ: "Evas Van Ness" age 88; James age 50 farmer; Jane age 42; James age 12; Elizabeth age 24; Sophia age 22; John, age 18, farmer; (adj. to Francis Van Ness, age 47)
--1870 Census: Little Falls, Passaic Co., NJ: James Vanness age 59, farmer; Elizabeth age 34; Sophia, age 31; James, age 20
--1880 Census: Little Falls, Passaic Co., NJ: James Vanness, age 69, widower, farmer; Lizzie L. age 44; Sophia age 40; James Westervelt, age 14; Charles Westervelt, age 11; all b. New Jersey (children of Sarah C. Van Ness and Peter B. Westervelt)

- - - - -

Van Ness, JOHN E. b. (March 3, 1800)
(Neafie, p.1) d. April 24, 1854

John E. Van Ness
Died Apr. 24, 1854
Aged 54 years

wife, Margaret* (Kierstead)
b. (abt. 1802)
d. (aft. 1870)

son, WILLIAM A. b. (abt. December 7, 1833)
(Neafie, p.1) d. July 29, 1849

William A.
Son of
John E. and Margaret
Van Ness
Died July 29, 1849
Aged 15 years, 7 mos.
& 22 days

Notes:
--John E. Van Ness, son of Evart (?) VanNess, q.v., and Ellen (Lena) Ryerson.
--John E. VanNess m. December 17, 1820, Margaret Kierstead

--1850 Census: Wayne Twp., Passaic Co. NJ: John E. Van Ness, age 50, farmer; Margaret, age 48; Thomas, age 24, farmer; Munson, age 13; Martinus age 11; Emma age 9; John, age 6; all b. NJ (adj. Moses van Ness, age 26, farmer; Eliza, age 22)
--1860 Census: Meads Basin, Wayne Twp., Passaic Co., NJ: Margaret Van Ness, age 58; Thomas, age 33, farmer; Ephraim (Munson), age 24, farmer; Martinus, age 21, farmer; Harriet (Emma), age 17, tailoress; John, age 16
--1870 Census: Boonton, Morris Co., NJ: Margaret 'Vanney' age 68, b. NJ; Harriet, age 29; b. NJ

Van Ness, JOHN H.   b. (December 24, 1813)
(monument)   d. August 22, 1895
(NJ Will #26198G, 1895)

John H. Van Ness
Born Dec. 24, 1813
Died Aug. 22, 1885

wife, CATHERINE M. (Cook)
(monument)   b. February 14, 1811
     d. December 13, 1897

Catherine M. Cook
wife of
John H. Van Ness
Born Feb. 14, 1811
Died Dec. 13, 1897

daughter, AGNES BERNARD
(Neafie, p.6)   b. March 23, 1849
     d. March 17, 1858

Agnes Bernard
Died March 17, 1859
Aged 9 years 11 months
and 25 days
Children of
John H. and Catherine M.
Van Ness

daughter, ESTHER COOK   b. March 1, 1854
(Neafie, p.6)   d. December 11, 1856

Esther Cook
Died Dec. 11, 1856
Aged 2 years 9 months
and 11 days
Children of
John H. and Catherine M.
Van Ness

Notes:
--John Henry VanNess, son of Henry T. VanNess, q.v., and Margaret Cadmus
--John m. January 21, 1836, Catherine M. Cook, dau. of Henry Francis Cook and Esther .....

--1850 Census: Caldwell Twp., Essex Co., NJ: John H. VanNess, age 37, b. NJ, farmer; Catherine M., age 39 b. NY; Rachel, age 9, b. NJ; Benjamin F., age 7, b. NJ; George W., age 5, b. NJ; Laura L., age 3, b. NJ; Agnes B., age 1, b. NJ
--1860 Census: Caldwell Twp., Essex Co., NJ: John H. Vanness, age 46, b. NJ, farmer; "Mary E.", age 48, b. NY; Jane A., age 23, b. NJ; Benjamin F., age 17, b. NJ; George W., age 15, b. NJ; Laura L., age 13, b. NJ; Joseph W., age 1, b. NJ
--1870 Census: Caldwell Twp., Essex Co., NJ: John H. Vanness, age 56, blacksmith; Catherine, age 57, b. NY; Jane, age 31, seamstress; George W., age 25, farmer; Sarah J., age 26; Andrew, age 1; Joseph W., age 11; Stephen Cook, age 9
--1880 Census: Caldwell Twp., Essex Co., NJ: John H. Vanness, age 66, retired farmer; Catherine M., age 68; Jane Ann, age 43; Joseph M., age 21, grandson, works on farm; Washington, age 35, son, farmer; Sarah J., age 35, daughter-in-law; Andrew, age 11, grandson; Mary Agnes, age 5, granddaughter; Charles Pierce, age 17, laborer; all b. New Jersey

- - - - -

Van Ness, JOHN K.   b. August 28, 1843
(NJ Civil War Gravestones)   d. March 8, 1921
(monument)

In
Memory of
John K. Van Ness
Priv. 25 Regt. NJ Vols
Aug. 28, 1843
March 8, 1921

-

Sarah E. Van Ness
His wife
Dec. 17, 1843
May 27, 1908

-

Harriet Van Ness
Born July 3, 1871
Died June 28, 1892

wife, SARAH E.   b. December 17, 1843
(monument)   d. May 27, 1908

dau., HARRIET   b. July 8, 1871
(monument)   d. June 28, 1892

Notes:
Served: Civil War: Co. A, 25 Reg't. NJ Volunteers

--1870 Census: Boonton, Morris Co., NJ: John K. VanNess, age 26, r.r. labor; Sarah E., age 26 b. NJ; Melvill, age 2, b. NJ; Berton S., age 1 b. NJ
--1880 Census: Wayne Twp., Passaic Co., NJ: John K. VanNess, age 37 b. NJ, laborer; Sarah E., age 37; Melville,

age 13; Stiles B. age 10; Harriet age 8; Wallace M. age 7; Vonetta age 11 months; all b. NJ
--1900 Census: Wayne Twp., Passaic Co., NJ: John Van Ness, b. August 1842, m.31 yr. farmer; Sarah E. b. Dec. 1842; Vannetta b. July 1879, house servant; Louise, b. August 1882, house servant; all b. New Jersey
--1910 Census: Wayne Twp., Passaic Co., NJ: John K. VanNess, age 66, b. NJ, widower, farmer
--1920

- - - - -

Van Ness, JOHN R.　　　b. (May 7, 1806)
(Neafie, p. 4)　　　　　d. April 20, 1834
(monument)

John R. Van Ness
Died
April 20, 1834
Aged 27 years, 11 months
& 13 days

wife, Sarah* (Dodds)　　b. (Abt. 1805)
　　　　　　　　　　　d. (January 27, 1881)

Notes:
--John, son of Robert H. Van Ness and Mary Jacobus
--John Robert Van Ness, m. March 18, 1826, Sarah Dodds.

--1850 Census: Pequannock Twp., Morris Co., NJ: Sarah Vanness, age 45; Robert, age 23, farmer; Sarah C., age 17; Jacob, age 12; all b. New Jersey
--1860 Census: Pequannock Twp., Morris Co., NJ: Simon Van Ness, age 33, b. Morris Co., farmer; Leah M, age 29, b. Morris Co.,; Thomas, age 10, b. Morris Co.; Ella, age 7, b. Essex Co., ;Adelade, age 5, b. Essex Co.; Cornelia, age 3, b.

Essex Co.,; Emma L., age 1, b. Morris Co.; <u>Sarah</u>, age 55, b. Morris Co.,; Jacob, age 21, b. Morris Co.
--1870 Census: Parsippany P.O., Hanover Twp., Morris Co., NJ: Jacob Vanness, age 31, blacksmith; Nancy, age 29; Sarah, age 6; Louisa age 4; Robert, age 2; <u>Sarah</u>, age 65; all b. New Jersey
--1880 Census: Montville, Morris Co., NJ: Robert Van Ness, age 54, farmer; Harriet A., age 55, b. NJ, father NJ, mother NY; <u>Sarah</u>, age 74, mother, widow, b. NJ

- - - - -

Van Ness, JOHN R.   b. (April 13 1839)
(Neafie, p.11)   d. April 2, 1873
(monument)

John R. Van Ness
Died Apr. 2, 1873
In his 34th year

Safe in the arms of Jesus
Sweetly my soul shall rest.

Notes:
--John, son of Isaac J. VanNess, q.v.
--1850 Census: Caldwell Twp., Essex Co., NJ: <u>Isaac J.</u> Vanness, age 36, farmer; <u>Ann,</u> age 37; Mary R. age 12; <u>John age 11</u>; Caroline, age 10; Jane, age 7; Jacob Bush, age 50, laborer; all b. New Jersey (adj. to Henry T(?) Vanness, age 35)
--?1860 Census: 9Wd. Newark, Essex Co., NJ: Henry Vandine, age 45, carpenter; Eliza H. Vandine, age 42; <u>John</u> Vanness, age 22, carpenter; Emma Vanness, age 24; all b. New Jersey

- - - - -

Van Ness, J. (John) STILES b. October 25, 1852
(monument) d. July 30, 1932

J. Stiles Van Ness
Oct. 25, 1852

-

July 30, 1932
Annie Ryerson
His wife
Mar. 5, 1855
Feb. 13, 1936

-

Harriet Van Ness
July 7, 1898
Aug. 23, 1899

wife, ANNIE RYERSON b. March 5, 1855
(monument) d. February 13, 1936

dau.? HARRIET b. July 7, 1898
(monument) d. August 23, 1899

Notes:
--John Stiles, son of Cornelius D. Van Ness, q.v.
--1860 Census: Caldwell, Essex Co., NJ: Cors. D. VanNess, age 39, coal merchant; Harriet, age 38; Sarah E., age 17; Hannah M., age 13; John S. age 7; Joseph W., age 4; all b. New Jersey
--1870 Census: Caldwell Twp., Essex Co., NJ: Cornelius Van Ness, age 49, farmer; Harriet, age 48; Hannah M., age 23, "Stiles" 17, apprentice mason; Wilson, age 15; all b. New Jersey
--1880 Census: Caldwell Twp., Essex Co., NJ: Cornelius D. VanNess, age 59, farmer; Harriet, age 58; J. Stiles, age 27, son, mason; Christiana, age 23, daughter-in-law; Zelda, age 4, granddaughter; all b. New Jersey

--1885 NJ Census: Caldwell Twp., Essex Co., NJ: Cornelius D. Van Ness; John S.; Annie; Zelda

- - - - -

Van Ness, JOSEPH WILSON
(monument)   b. September 30, 1855
                           d. June 11, 1893

In
Memory of
J. W. Van Ness
Born
Sept. 30, 1855
Died
June 11, 1893

Notes:
--Joseph, son of Cornelius D. Van Ness, q.v.
--1860 Census: Caldwell, Essex Co., NJ: Cors. D. VanNess, age 39, coal merchant; Harriet, age 38; Sarah E., age 17; Hannah M., age 13; John S. age 7; Joseph W., age 4; all b. New Jersey
--1870 Census: Caldwell Twp., Essex Co., NJ: Cornelius Van Ness, age 49, farmer; Harriet, age 48; Hannah M., age 23; "Stiles" 17, apprentice mason; Wilson, age 15; all b. New Jersey
--1880 Census: Newark, Essex Co., NJ: Joseph W. Van Ness, age 23, teamster; Clara M., age 22; Paul M., age 1

- - - - -

Van Ness, Peter   See: Van Ness Burial Ground
wife, Harriet

- - - - -

Van Ness, ROBERT b. (abt. December 30, 1806)
(Neafie, p.19) d. July 30, 1836
(inscriptions, p. 143)
(NJ Will #12747G, 1836)

Robert VanNess
died July 30, 1836
aged 29 years, 7 months

wife, Sarah* (Sanford) b. (December 20, 1809)
                        d. (December 10, 1894)

son?, DAVID b. (abt. May 1, 1829)
(inscriptions, p.143) d. January 7, 1832

David
Died Jan. 7, 1832
Aged 2 yrs. 8 mos.
& 6 days

daughter, SARAH RACHEL b. (May 10, 1833)
(inscriptions, p.143) d. November 15, 1833

Sarah Rachel
daughter of
Robart (sic) *and Sarah VanNess*
died November 15, 1833
aged 6 months

son?, WILLIAM b. (abt. October 23, 1834)
(inscriptions, p.143) d. December 29, 1835

William
Died
Dec. 29. 1835
Aged 1 yr. 2 mos.
& 6 days

Notes:
--Robert, son of Isaac Van Ness, q.v., and Sarah Jacobus
--Robert m. December 31, 1828, Sally Sanford

--1860 Census: 7Wd, Newark, Essex Co., NJ: 'Yemus' Speer, age 30, clerk; Lucinda age 30; Catherine age 10; John L. age 7; Sarah Van Ness, age 50; George Walter, age 22, mason; all b. NJ
--1870 Census: 8Wd, Newark, Essex Co., NJ: Matthew Wheaton, age 25, factory foreman; Sarah age 21; Fredrick age 4; Robert, age 2; Matthew age 3 months; Sarah Vanness, age 60; all b. New Jersey
--1880 Census: Lake View, Cook Co., IL: Isaac R. Vanness age 46 b. NJ, book keeper; Carrie A.W., wife age 40 b. NY, parents NY; Lester T. age 21 b. NJ, clerk at drug store; Nellie G. B. Dau. age 18 b. NJ, clerk at printing co.; Sanford L. son age 16 b. IL, clerk in bakery; Carrie J. dau age 14 b. IL; Frank C. age 12 b. IL; Gardiner B. age 9 b. IL; Charles C. age 3 b. IL; Douglas M. age 1 b. IL; Sarah R. Vanness, mother widow, age 70 b. NJ

- - - - -

Van Ness, ROBERT	b. (May 13, 1826)
(Neafie, p. 17)	d. August 26, 1882
(gov't. stone)	

Co. A, 22 NJ Inf.

wife, Harriet* (Stiles)	b. (abt. 1829)
	d. (aft. 1880)
daughter, NETTIE M.	b. (abt. June 25, 1866)
(Neafie, p.17)	d. March 18, 1869

Nettie M.
Daughter of
Robert and Harriet
Van Ness
Died March 18, 1869
Aged 2 years, 8 mos.
& 21 days

Notes:
--Robert, served Civil War
--Robert, son of John Robert VanNess and Sarah Dodds
--Robert m. August 10, 1850, Harriet Stiles

--1850 Census: Pequannock Twp., Morris Co., NJ: Sarah VanNess, age 45; Robert, age 23, farmer; Sarah C., age 17; Jacob, age 12; all b. New Jersey
--1860 Census: Pequannock Twp., Morris Co., NJ: Robert VanNess, age 33, b. NJ, farmer; Harriet, age 33, b. NJ
--1870 Census: Montville, Morris Co., NJ: Robert VanNess, age 44, farmer; Harriet, age 46
--1880 Census: Montville, Morris Co., NJ: Robert VanNess, age 54, farmer; Harriet A., age 55; Sarah, age 74; all b. New Jersey

- - - - -

Van Ness, Robert   See: Van Ness Burial Ground

Van Ness, SIMON S.   b. (abt. August 1800)
(Neafie, p.10)   d. April 7, 1879
(monument)

Simon S. Van Ness
Died
April 7th, 1879
Aged 78 years 7 mos.
and 11 days

wife, JANE (Van Ness)   b. (August 3, 1802)

(Neafie, p.10)   d. August 5, 1890
(monument)

Jane
Wife of
Simon S. van Ness
Died
August 5, 1890
Aged 88 years
and 2 days

Notes:
--Simon, son of Simon I. Van Ness and Elizabeth Doremus
--Simon m. May 23, 1823, Jane Van Ness, dau. of Robert Van Ness, q.v.

--1850 Census: Wayne Twp., Passaic Co., NJ: Simon S. Van Ness, farmer; Jane, age 50; Benjamin, age 12; Mary Mandeville, age 70; all b. New Jersey
--1860 Census: Meads Basin, Wayne Twp., Passaic Co., NJ: Simon "Than Ness" age 59, farmer; Jane, age 57; Benjamin, age 22, teacher; Catherine, age 14; all b. NJ
--1870 Census: Wayne Twp., Passaic Co., NJ: Simon S. Van Ness, age 70; Jane, age 68
--1880 Census: Wayne Twp., Passaic Co., NJ: Jane Van Ness, age 77, widow

- - - - -

Van Ness, THOMAS   b. February 14, 1808
(Neafie, p.17)   d. January 19, 1887
(monument)
(NJ Will #22566G, 1887)

Thomas Van Ness
Born

Feb. 14, 1806
Died
Jan. 19, 1887

wife, MARTHA M. (Vincent)
(Neafie, p.17) b. (abt. 1806)
(monument) d. August 9, 1880

Martha M. Vincent
wife of
Thomas Van Ness
Born .... 1808(?)
Died Aug. 9, 1880

son, DAVID b. (abt. December 5, 1829)
(Neafie, p.17) d. January 7, 1832
(inscriptions, p.138)
(Monument)

David
Died
Jan. 7, 1832
Aged 2 years
8 months
& 6 days
Children of
Thomas & Martha M.
Van Ness

daughter, SARAH ELLEN b. (abt. October 7, 1831)
(Neafie, p. 16) d. April 14, 1840
(monument)

Sarah Ellen
Died Apr. 14, 1840
Aged 8 years
6 months

and 7 days
Children of
Thomas and Martha M.
Van Ness

son, WILLIAM   b. (abt. October 23, 1834)
(Neafie, p.17)   d. December 29, 1835
(inscriptions, p. 138)
(monument)

William
Died
Dec. 29th,
Aged 1 year
2 months
& 6 days
Children of
Thomas and Martha M.
Van Ness

daughter, PHEBE ANN   b. (abt. July 11, 1837)
(Neafie, p.16)   d. February 26, 1843
(monument)

Phebe Ann
Died Feb. 26 1843
Aged 5 years
6 months
and 15 days
Children of
Thomas and Martha M.
Van Ness

Notes:
--Thomas, son of David Van Ness, q.v.
--Thomas m. abt. 1822, Martha Vincent

--1850 Census: East Ward, Newark, Essex Co., NJ: Thomas Vanness age 44, saddle tree maker; Martha M. age 44; Malinda P., age 9; Elizabeth Fisher, age 19; all b. NJ
--1860 Census: 4Wd, Newark, Essex Co., NJ: Thos. Vanness, age 54, saddle tree maker; Martha M. age 53; Malinda P., age 19
--1880 Census: Newark, Essex Co., NJ: Thomas Vanness, age 74, flagman; Martha M. age 74

- - - - -

Van Ness, William E.   b. (January 22, 1770)
(Neafie, p. 19)   d. November 16, 1834
(monument)

In
Memory of
William Van Ness
who died November 16, 1834
aged 64 years, 9 months
and 23 days

first wife, Elizabeth* (VanBlarcom)
         b. (April 9, 1769)
         d. (bef. August 1810)

second wife, Catherine* (Post)
         b. (abt. 1766)
         d. (bef. November 1834)

Notes:
--William, son of Henry VanNess and Rachel Sanford
--William m. March 29, 1793, Elizabeth Van Blarcom, dau. of Peter Van Blarcom and Jennetje Van Horn
--William m. aft August 1810, Catherine Post.

--1830 Census:

--**Will** of William VanNess: date Nov. 1, 1834; proved Nov. 15, 1834: estate to two children: Peter W. VanNess and Elizabeth, wife of Francis Pier; Peter to have homestead being the west end of the farm and two meadows in the Little Piece meadow containing 14 acres; Peter W. VanNess, executor.

- - - - -

Van Ness, William E.* b. (May 23, 1805)
  d. (April 4, 1896)

first wife, MARIAH (Speer) b. (May 5, 1805)
(Neafie, p.1) d. August 25, 1832
(inscriptions, p. 142)
(monument)

*In
Memory of
Mariah
wife of
Willliam Van Ness
who died
August 25th, 1832
in the 27th year
of her age*

second wife, Lydia* (Yorks)
  b. (abt. 1806)
  d. (August 25, 1889)
  (bur. Cedar Grove Cemetery)

son, CHARLES b. (abt. October 20, 1839)
(Neafie, p.1) d. December 19, 1847
(inscriptions, p. 142)

Charles
Son of
Wm. E. & Lydia Van Ness
Died December 19, 1847
Aged 8 years, 1 month
and 29 days

Notes:
--?William E., poss. son of Evart Van Ness, q.v.
--William m. #1, Mariah, daughter of John T. Speer, q.v.
--William m. #2, Lydia Yorks, dau. of Garret Yorks and Elsje Doremus

--1850 Census: Caldwell Twp., Essex Co., NJ: William E. Vanness age 45, farmer; Lydia age 44; Peter age 25, farmer; Margaret Van Allen, age 23; Henrietta Van Allen age 3; all b. NJ;
--1860 Census: Caldwell Twp., Essex Co., NJ: William E. Vanness age 55, farmer; Lydia age 54; Henry, age 12, all b. NJ; adj. to William P. Vanness, age 35; and adj. to Henry H. Vanness, age 77, farmer)
--1870 Census: Caldwell Twp., Essex Co., NJ: William E. VanNess, age 64, farmer; Lydia, age 63; adj. to Peter Van Ness age 44
--1880 Census: Caldwell Twp., Essex Co., NJ: William E. Vanness age 75, farmer; Lydia, age 74; Fred Beider, age 12, b. NJ, parents b. Germany, works on farm

- - - - -

Van Ness, WILLIAM   b. (August 31, 1807)
(Neafie, p.19)   d. June 5, 1856

William Van Ness
Died June 5, 1856
Aged 48 yrs. 9 mos.
and 5 days

wife, Catherine* (Hopper)   b. (April 13, 1809)
(monument)   d. (October 7, 1896)
                      bur. (Laurel Grove Mem.Park,
                      Totowa, N.J.

Catherine
wife of
Wm. Van Ness
1809 - 1896

-

Francis W. Van Ness
1834 - 1908

daughter, ALMIRA A.   b. (abt. February 4, 1833)
(Neafie, p.19)   d. March 4, 1850

Almira A.
Daughter of
Wm. and Catherine
Van Ness
Died March 4, 1850
Aged 17 yrs. 26 days

Notes:
--William, son of Evert H. VanNess, q.v. and Caroline Smith
--William m. 1829, Catherine Hopper, dau. of Andries Hopper and Antje Mandeville.
--Catherine Hopper m. #2, Job Doremus, q.v.

--1850 Census: Acquackanonk Twp., Passaic Co., NJ: William Van Ness, age 42, wood turner; Catherine, age 41; Francis, age 16; Maria C., age 14; Elizabeth A., age 11; Emily, age 9; Louisa J., age 6; all b. New Jersey
--1860 Census: Little Falls, Passaic Co.NJ: "James" Doremus age 50, farmer; Catherine age '59'; Francis (Van

Ness) age 24, farm labor; Elizabeth age 20 (Van Ness); Emily (Van Ness) age 18; Jane age 16 (Van Ness); 'Wanan' (Warren) Doremus age 13; William Riese, 13; John Hopper, age 40, carpenter
--1870 Census: Little Falls, Passaic Co. NJ: "John" Doremus, age 59, mason; <u>Catherine</u>, age 61; Francis age 30, clerk at country store; 'Carry', female age 28; Jane, age 21; Frank Schroder age 11; all b. New Jersey
--1880 Census: Little Falls Twp.,Passaic Co. NJ: Job Doremus age 69, brick mason; <u>Catherine</u> age 71, wife; Janie Shaw age 14, servant; all b. New Jersey
--1885 NJ Census: Little Falls, Passaic Co. NJ: Joseph C. Cooke, age 20-60; Jane L. Cooke, age 20-60' Sara L. Cooke, age 0-4; <u>Catherine</u> Doremus, age over 60; Mary E. Hanlon
--1895 NJ Census: Little Falls, Passaic Co., NJ: Joseph C. Cooke; Jennie L. Cooke; Sara Louise Cooke; <u>Katherine</u> Doremus

- - - - -

Van Ness, WILLIAM I.   b. (abt. January 3, 1824)
(Neafie, p.15)   d. November 7, 1873
(NJ Will #18038G, 1873)

William I. Van Ness
Died Nov. 7, 1873
Aged 47 years 10 mos.
and 4 days

wife, Maria* (Stager)   b. (abt. 1834)
   d. (aft. 1880)

Notes:
--William, son of Isaac VanNess, q.v., and Sarah Jacobus
--William m. Maria Stager

--1850 Census: Caldwell Twp., Essex Co., NJ: Sarah VanNess, age 63; William 'J', age 25, farmer; all b. NJ
--1860 Census, p.88, Caldwell, Essex Co., NJ: William VanNess, age 34, farmer; Maria, age 28; 'Joseph', age 9; George, age 2; all b. NJ
--1870 Census: Caldwell Twp., Essex Co., NJ: William Van Ness, age 45,farmer ; Maria, age 36; 'Judson' age 9; 'Armondy', age 8; Sarah, age 83; Michael Prout, age 24, (b.NY)farm labor; Joseph Francisco, age 19, b. NJ, brick mason;
--1880 Census: Caldwell Twp., Essex Co., NJ: Maria VanNess, age 47, widow; Araminta, age 18, daughter; Grace G., age 8, daughter; all b. NJ; 2 boarders

- - - - -

Van Ness, WILLIAM M.   b. 1837 (April 8)
(monument)   d. 1907

William M. Van Ness
1837 - 1907
-
His wife
Harriet A. Speer
-
Their children
Willie
1876 - 1876
Jesse
1879 - 1879

wife, HARRIET A. (Speer)   b. 1839 (October 18)
(monument)   d. 1931 (January 2)

son, WILLIE   b. 1876
(monument)   d. 1876

child, JESSE   b. 1879
(monument)   d. 1879

Notes:
--William, son of Henry J. (I.) Van Ness, q.v.
--1860 Census: Caldwell Twp., Essex Co. NJ: Henry J. Vanness, age 48, carpenter; Phebe A., age 45; Monson, age 23, carpenter; Francis, age 19, labor; Mary E. age 15; Harriet, age 20; all b. NJ
--1880 Census: East Orange, Essex Co., NJ: Wm. 'H' Van Ness, age 41, b. NJ, cider maker; Harriet A., age 40; Malinda, age 1
--1900 Census: 1Wd. Orange, Essex Co.NJ: William Vanness, age 63, cider mill; Harriet, age 60; b. NJ

- - - - -

VAN ORDEN

Van Orden, John A.*   b. (abt. 1819)
                              d. (1887)
                              bur. (Boonton Avenue Cem. Boonton, Morris Co., NJ)

John A. VanOrden
1828 - 1887

first wife, ELIZA M.   b. (abt. September 15, 1817)
(Neafie, p. 16)   d. December 16, 1845
(inscriptions, p.143)

Eliza M.
wife, of
John A. Van Orden
Died December 16, 1845
Aged 28 years, 3 months
& 1 day

second wife, Caroline* (Vreeland)
      b. (abt. 1824)
      d. (aft. 1885)
      Bur. (Boonton Avenue Cem.,
      Boonton, Morris Co., NJ)

Caroline
wife of
John A. VanOrden
Died...
Aged...

son, JACOB EUGENE b. (abt. August 1844)
(Neafie, p.16)   d. November 15, 1844
(inscriptions, p. 144)

Jacob Eugene
son of
John A. and Eliza M.
Van Orden
Died Nov. 15, 1844
Aged 12 weeks

Notes:
--John m. #2, June 1, 1850, Caroline Vreeland

--1850 Census: Pequannock Twp., Morris Co. NJ: John A. Vanorden, age 31, b. NJ, blacksmith; Leander Vanorden, age 25, b. NJ, laborer
--1860 Census: Pequannock Twp., Morris Co. NJ; John A. Vanorden age 40, b. Morris Co., baker; Caroline age 36, b. Bergen Co.; Louis A. age 4 months, b. Morris Co.
--1870 Census: Boonton, Morris Co. NJ: John A. Vanorden, age 51, fire insurance agent; Caroline age 45; Cate, age 8; all b. NJ

--1880 Census: Boonton, Morris Co. NJ: John A. Van Orden age 60 b. NJ, blacksmith; Caroline, wife, age 56, b. NJ
--1885 NJ Census: Boonton, Morris Co., NJ: John A. VanOrden; Caroline Van Orden.

- - - - -

VAN PELT

Van Pelt, John* b. (September 21, 1829)
(monument) d. (February 4, 1899)
  bur. (Laurel Grove Mem. Park, Totowa, NJ)

John
Van Pelt
Born
Sept. 21, 1829
Died
Feb. 4, 1899
-
Ellen, his wife
Born April 14, 1829
Died Jan. 16, 1906

wife, Ellen* (Riker) b. (April 14, 1829)
(monument) d. (January 16, 1906)
  bur. (Laurel Grove Mem. Park, Totowa, NJ)

son, WILLIAM b. (abt. September 3, 1852)
(Neafie, p.4) d. October 22, 1852

William
Died Oct. 22, 1852
Aged 1 mo. 19 ds.

daughter, EMMA L. b. (abt. August 2, 1854)
(Neafie, p.4) d. February 2, 1856

> *Emma L.*
> *Died Feb. 2, 1856*
> *Aged 1 yr. 6 mos.*

son, CHARLES b. (abt. January 3, 1858)
(Neafie, p.4) d. January 18, 1864

> *Charles*
> *Died Jan 18, 1864*
> *Aged 6 yrs. 15 ds.*

dau.?, EVERDEAR b. (abt. June 6, 1860)
(Neafie, p.4) d. February 11, 1864

> *Everdear*
> *Died Feb. 11, 1864*
> *Aged 3 yrs. 8 mos. 5 ds.*

Children of John and Ellen Van Pelt

Notes:
--John m. Ellen Riker, dau. of John Riker, q.v., and Ann Smith

--??1850 Census: 8 Wd. Brooklyn, Kings Co., NY: Margaret Van Pelt, age 48; Magdelena, age 24; Walter, age 22, mason; John, age 20, mason; Francis, age 18, carpenter; Maria, age 15; Margaret A., age 12; 4 members Forbell family; all b NY
--1850 Census: Acquackanonk Twp., Passaic Co., NJ: John Riker, age 44, hotel keeper; Ann, age 41; Ellen, age 21; Hester A., age 13; Sarah J., age 10; 7 other (lodgers?)
--1860 Census: Acquackanonk Twp., Passaic Co., NJ: John Van Pelt, age 31, b. NY, farmer; Ellen, age 32, b. NJ; Charles, age 2, b. NJ

--1870 Census: Little Falls, Passaic Co., NJ: John Vanpelt, age 41, b. NY, carman; Ellen, age 41, b. NJ; Marietta, age 7 b. NJ; Walter, age 4, b. NJ; Harvey, age 1, b. NJ
--1880 Census: Little Falls, Passaic Co., NJ: John Vanpelt, age 50, b. NY, farmer; Ellen, age 51, b. NJ; Maryetta, age 16 b. NY; Walter, age 13, b. NJ; John, age 12, b. NY; David Bogert, age 22 b. NJ, boarder, works at carpet factory
--1885 NJ Census: Little Falls, Passaic Co., NJ: John VanPelt; Ellen; Etta; Walter; John; David Bogert; Walter Stewart; Wm. Trumbull; James Holmes
--1900 Census: Little Falls, Passaic Co., NJ: Ellen Van Pelt, b. April 1829, widow, 3 born 2 living, b. NJ; Etta Bogart, dau., b. October 1863, m.12 yr., 1 born 1 living, b. NY, father b. NY, mother b. NJ; David Bogart, age 43, b. October 1856, NJ, son-in-law; Arthur Bogart, b. July 1893, NJ, grandson; Lydia Garrabrant, b. June 1850, cousin, widow, 0 born 0 living

- - - - -

VAN WART

Van Wart, Isaac J.* b. (abt. 1807)
  d. (aft 1870)

first wife, ELIZABETH (VanNess)
(Neafie, p.3) b. (abt. March 27, 1811)
(inscriptions, p.144) d. December 28, 1831

Elizabeth
wife of Isaac J. Van Wart
and eldest daughter of
Henry H. and Margaret Van Ness
Died December 28. 1831
Aged 20 years, 9 months & 1 day

-

and also an infant son

*of Isaac J. & Elizabeth Van Wart
aged 24 hours*

second wife, Margaret* (VanNess)
                         b. (abt. 1813)
                         d. (bef. 1870)

INFANT SON   b. (December 28, 1831)
(Neafie, p.3)   d. December 28, 1831
(inscriptions, p. 144)

*and also an infant son
of Isaac J. & Elizabeth Van Wart
aged 24 hours*

Notes:
--Isaac m. #1, Elizabeth Van Ness, dau. of Henry H. Van Ness, q.v., and Margaret Bush
--Isaac m. #2, Margaret Van Ness, dau. of David Van Ness, q.v. and Ellen Vanderhoof

--1840 Census: Caldwell Twp., Essex Co., NJ: <u>Isaac</u> Vanwart
--1850 Census: Caldwell Twp., Essex Co., NJ: <u>Isaac</u> Van Wart age 43, carpenter; <u>Margaret,</u> age 38; David, age 14; Rachel age 12; Theodore age 9; William 4; Josephine 2; all b. NJ; adj. to Jacob F. VanNess, age 33
--1860 Census: Newark, Essex Co., NJ: <u>Isaac</u> "Vantowk" age 53, b. NJ, carpenter; <u>Margaret</u> age 47, b. NJ; Rachel age 21, b. NJ; William, age 14, b. NY; Josephine 12, b. NY; Adeline 9, b. NY;
--1870 Census: 8Wd, Newark: Isaac '<u>Vanworl</u>" age 66 b. NJ; Josephine age 22 b. 'NY'; Adelia, age 19, b. NJ

- - - - -

VanWart, William*   b. (abt. 1846)
                          d.

wife, ADELIAH A.   b. (abt. 1846)
(Neafie, p.7)   d. September 5, 1873

*Adeliah A.
Wife of
Wm. Van Wert
Died Sept. 5, 1873
Aged 27 years*

Notes:
--William, son of Isaac Van Wart, q.v.
--??William m. Delia Jacobus, dau. of Peter Jacobus and Eliza Ann Oliver; sister of John O. Jacobus, q.v.
--1850 Census: Caldwell Twp., Essex Co., NJ: Isaac Van Wart age 43, carpenter; Margaret, age 38; David, age 14; Rachel age 12; Theodore age 9; William 4; Josephine 2; all b. NJ
--1850 Census: Caldwell Twp., Essex Co., NJ: Peter Jacobus, age 40, farmer; Eliza Ann, age 43; Mary C., age 17; James O., age 15, farmer; Martha W.?, age 13; Sarah, age 11; Emma H., age 9; Julia A., age 7; Delia A., age 4; William C., age 1; Daniel Vanderhoof, age 21, laborer; all b. New Jersey
--1860 Census: Caldwell Twp., Essex Co., NJ: Peter Jacobus, age 50, farmer; Rachel, age 56; Emma, age 17; Deliah age 13; William age 11; Margaret E. age 18, milliner; all b. NJ
--1870 Census: Boonton, Morris Co., NJ: Wm VanWart, age 28 b. NY, house mason; Delia, age 25, b. NJ; Hurbert, age 8 months, b. NJ
--?1880 Census: San Francisco, San Francisco Co. CA: 'Hamm' (Hamilton?) Irvin, age 46, b. NJ, father b. NY, mother b. NJ, carpenter; Martha, age 43, b. NJ, parents NJ: Sophia, age 7 b. CA; William, age 5, b. CA; Fredrick age 3

b. CA; Etta, age 4 mos. b. CA; Herbert Van Wort, age 10, nephew, b. NJ, parents b. NJ

- - - - -

VREELAND

Vreeland, JOHN Jr. b. (abt. 1805)
(Neafie, p. 14) d. December 28, 1875

John Vreeland
Died Dec. 28, 1875
Aged 71 years, 8 mos.

wife, MARY JANE b. (abt. 1810)
(Neafie, p. 14) d. October 27, 1879

Mary Jane
Wife of
John Vreeland, Jr.
Died Oct. 27, 1879
Aged 69 years

son, ISAAC b. (abt. February 1838)
(Neafie, p.14) d. June 23, 1849
(inscriptions p.144)

Isaac R.(?)
Son of
John and Mary Jane
Vreeland
Died June 23, 1849
Aged 11 years, 4 months

A bud on earth too (sic) *bloom in Heaven*

Notes:

--1850 Census: Caldwell Twp., Essex Co., NJ: John Vreeland Jr. age 45, b. NJ, mason; Mary J., age 37 b. NJ
--1860 Census: Little Falls Twp, Passaic Co., NJ: John Vreeland, age 55, farmer; Mary, age 47
--1870 Census: Little Falls, Passaic Co. NJ: Jno. J. Vreeland age 65, mason; 'May' J. age 57; Mary Vanhouten, age 14, domestic servant; all b. New Jersey
--?1880 Census: Little Falls, Passaic Co. NJ: Mary Vreeland, age 66, widow, b. NJ

- - - - -

WILLIAMS

Williams, IsraelSee: Pearce Burial Ground

- - - - -

Williams, JepthaSee: Pearce Burial Ground
wife, Elizabeth
wife, Elizabeth

- - - - -

WILSON

Wilson, John L.*b. (abt. 1837)
d. (February 14, 1893)

first wife, ELIZABETH R. (Ryerson Van Houten)
(Neafie, , p.9)b. (abt. 1833)
(monument)d. July 7, 1874

Elizabeth R.
wife of
John L. Wilson
Died

July 7, 1824
Age 41 years

Gone But Not Forgotten

Notes:
--John m. #1, December 17, 1856, Elizabeth Ryerson VanHouten, dau. of Henry J. VanHouten and Ann Berdan Doremus
--John m. #2, Margaret VanHouten, dau. of Henry J. VanHouten and Ann Berdan Doremus. (Margaret m.#1, 1862, James Bogert.) (Margaret, widow of John L. Wilson, d. Nov. 7, 1901)

--1850 Census: Manchester Twp., Passaic Co., NJ: Henry J. VanHouten, age 40, farmer; Ann, age 41; <u>Elizabeth</u>, age 17; Richard, age 15, farm labor; <u>Margaret</u>, age 12; John, age 11; Sarah, age 8; George, age 5; Henry, age 3; all b. New Jersey
--?1850 Census: Acquackanonk Twp., Passaic Co., NJ: James B. Wilson, age 54, b. Scotland, farmer; Maria, age 7, b. NJ; Rebecca, age 15, b. NJ; Emma J., age 11, b. NJ; Robert King, age 23, b. Scotland, farm labor
--1860 Census: Manchester Twp., Passaic Co., NJ: <u>John</u> Wilson, age 23, farmer; <u>Elis.</u>, age 27; Wm., age 3; Henry, age 1; all b. NJ (adj. to Henry VanHouten, age 50, farmer, and his wife, Ann, age 50)
--1870 Census: Manchester Twp., Passaic Co., NJ: <u>John</u> Wilson, age 33, b. NJ, gardener; <u>Elizabeth</u>, age 37, b. NJ; William D., age 13, b. NJ; Henry V., age 11, b. NJ
--1880 Census: Manchester, Passaic Co., NJ: John L. 'Willson', age 43, b. NY, father b. Scotland, mother b. NJ, gardener; Margaret, age 42, b. NJ; Henry V., age 20, b. NJ; Mamie, age 10, b. NJ; 1 farm laborer
--1885 NJ Census: Manchester Twp., Passaic Co., NJ: John L. Wilson; Margaret; Mary B.
--1900 Census: Wayne Twp., Passaic Co., NJ: C. K. Berry, age 33, m. 12 yr. farmer; Mary Berry, b. July 1868; 4

children; Margaret Wilson, age 63 b. Feb. 1837, widow; 3 born 3 living; retired; 3 servants

- - - - -

WOODRUFF

Woodruff, David See: Pearce Burial Ground
wife, Ann

- - - - -

Woodruff, Wilbur E.* b. (March 1858)?
  d. (aft. 1900)

wife, MARY E. (Riker)
(Neafie, p.14) b. June 23, 1852
  d. February 19, 1884

Mary E.
Daughter of
Isaac H. and Mary A. Riker
And wife of
Wilber E. Woodruff
Born June 23, 1852
Died Feb. 19, 1884

Notes:
--Wilbur, son of David P.? Woodruff and Diana (Ann) Bush
--Wilbur m. August 1883, Mary Ellen Riker, dau. of Isaac H. Riker, q.v., and Mary Ann DeHart.

--1850 Census: Caldwell Twp., Essex Co., NJ: Peter Vanderhoof, age 41, farmer; Rachel, age 40; Garret W., age 14; Sarah M., age 10; Evalina C., age 7; Garrett Bush, age 60, farmer; Sarah Bush, age 63; Ann Woodruff, age 26; David Woodruff, age 1; all b. New Jersey

--1860 Census: Caldwell Twp., Essex Co., NJ: Peter Vanderhoof, age 51,b. NJ, farmer; Rachel, age 49 b. NJ; Sarah M., age 20, b. NJ; Evaline C., age 17 b. NJ; Diana Woodruff, age 34, b. NY; David Woodruff, age 11, b. NJ; Wilbur N.age 4, b. NJ

--1870 Census: Caldwell, Essex Co., NJ: David H. Woodruff, age 21, b. NJ, cigar maker; Wilbur E. Woodruff, age 13, b. NJ, works on r.r.; at res. of John Williams

--1880 Census: Dist. 2, Caldwell, Essex Co., NJ: David Woodruff, age 30 b. NJ, segar maker; Sarah J., wife, age 24 b. NJ; Louis H., son, age 4, b. NJ; Maybelle, dau., age 3, b. NJ; Daniel, son, age 10 mos., b. NJ; Wilbur E. Woodruff, brother, single, age 23, b. NJ, segar maker

--1900 Census: 11Wd, Newark, Essex Co., NJ: Wilbur Woodruff, age 42, b. March 1858, NJ, parents b. NJ, single, boarder, cigar maker

- - - - -

WRIGHT

Wright, DAVID M. (monument)	b. 1843 d. 1926
wife, Susan*	b. 1846 d. 1920

David M. Wright
of the Civil War
10 NJ Vols.
Born 1843 Died 1926
Susan, His Wife
Born 1846 Died 1920
Dead But Not Forgotten

Notes:
Served: Civil War Co. F. 10th Regt. NJ Inf.

--1860 Census: Rockaway Twp. Morris Co. NJ: William Wright, age 48 b. NJ blacksmith; Lucinda (nee Van Wagoner), age 38 b. NJ; David, age 16, b. NJ, apprentice; Catherine, age 14 b. NJ, 6 younger children all b. NJ
--1870 Census: 1 Wd. Paterson, Passaic Co., NJ: David Wright, age 26 b. NJ, carpenter; Susan, age 24 b. NY; Emma, age 2, b. NJ
--1880 Census: Paterson, Passaic Co., NJ: David M. Wright, age 36, b. 'Holland', wheelwright; Susan, age 24, b. NY; Emma, age 11 b. NY; Sadie age 9 b. NJ; Walter, age 6, b. NJ
--1900 Census: 4 Wd. Paterson, Passaic Co. NJ: David Wright, age 56 b. May 1844 b. NY, parents NY, carpenter; Susan, age 54, b. Nov. 1846 NY; Walter, age 25, b. May 1875 NY, clerk; Ada, age 19, dau. b. Oct. 1880 NJ, cashier; Avery, age 12, son b. May 1888 NJ
--1910 Census: 11 Wd, Paterson, Passaic Co. NJ: David M. Wright, age 66, m.41 yr. b. NY, father NY, mother NJ; wheelwright at loco. works; Susan, age 64, 5 born 5 living, b. NY, parents b. NJ; Walter, age 35 b. NJ, clerk at grocery; Avery, age 21 b. NJ, draftsman at loco. works
--1920 Census: 5 Wd, Paterson, Passaic Co. NJ: David Wright, age 77 b. NY, parents NY, no occup; Walter, age 40, son, b. NJ, grocer; Avery, age 35, son, b. NJ, drafsman at machine co.

- - - - -

ZEEK

Zeek, ABRAHAM b. June 30, 1814
(Neafie, p. 9) d. January 16, 1879
(monument)

Our Father
Abraham Zeek
Born June 30, 1814
Died Jan. 16, 1879

Beloved .....

wife, ELIZABETH (Sigler)
(Neafie, p.9)   b. March 18, 1820
                 d. January 9, 1888

Elizabeth Sigler
wife of
Abraham Zeek
Born March 18, 1820
Died Jan. 9, 1888

Notes:
--Abraham m. Feb. 1838, Elizabeth, dau. of Thomas Sigler and Hetty Egbertson

--?1830 Census: Acquackanonk Twp., Essex Co., NJ: William 'Zack"?; 11 persons; adj. to Joseph Gould
--1840 Census: Bloomfield, Essex Co., NJ: Abr. Zeek; 5 persons
--1850 Census: Bloomfield, Essex Co., NJ: Abraham "Leek", age 35, tailor; Elizabeth, age 31; Helen M., age 11; Leah A., age 9; Marcus, age 1; Mary E., age 5; Thomas E., age 7; all b. New Jersey
--1860 Census: Bloomfield, Essex Co.,NJ: Abraham 'Lemek', age 40, farmer; Elizabeth, age 40; Helen age 21; Emma, age 19; Thomas age 17; Mary,a ge 13; Jane, age 12; Mark, age 9; Ellen, age 7; Clara, age 4; all b. NJ
--1870 Census: Caldwell Twp., Essex Co., NJ: Abraham Zeek, age 55, farmer; Elizabeth, age 50; Ella, age 17; Clara, age 14; Henry, age 8; all b. New Jersey
--1880 Census: Caldwell Twp., Essex Co., NJ: Elisabeth 'Zeke' age 60, widow; Harry Irvin Zeke, age 17, works on farm; (adj. to "James" (John?) W. Peer, q.v.)

- - - - -

ZELIFF

Zeliff, Henry* b. (abt. 1837)
(?NJ Will #23855G, 1890) d. (May 4, 1889)

wife, Jane* (Miller) b. (February 1842)
  d. (1912)

son, WILLIAM H. b. April 16, 1867
(Neafie, p.4) d. July 9, 1871

William H. Zeliff
Born Apr. 16, 1867
Died July 9, 1871

dau., EMMA MAY b. July 23, 1876
(Neafie, p. 4) d. June 3, 1877

Emma May Zeliff
Born July 23, 1876
Died June 3, 1877

Notes:
--Henry, son of John Zeliff, q.v., and Jane VanNess

--1850 Census: Acquackanonk Twp., Passaic Co., NJ:
John Zeliff, age 56, wheelwright; Jane, age 56; James, age 17, blacksmith; Lydia, age 19; David, age 15; Henry, age 12; John Oliver, age 21, blacksmith; all b. New Jersey
--?1850 Census: Pequannock Twp., Essex Co., NJ: Garret Miller, age 32, laborer; Pheby, age 25; Albert, age 0; Jane, age 8; Garret, age 5; Emeline, age 3; John, age 4 months
--1860 Census: 1 Wd., Newark, Essex Co., NJ: Henry Zeliff, age 22, carpenter; Jane, age 18
--1870 Census: 7Wd, Newark, Essex Co., NJ: Henry Zeliff, age 34, carpenter; Jane, age 28; Mary A., age 8; Garret, age 7; Sherman, age 6; William H., age 3; Winslow, age 10

months; Emeline Miller, age 21, works at rubber factory; all b. New Jersey
--1880 Census: Little Falls, Passaic Co., NJ: Henry Zeliff, age 43, b. NJ, carpenter; Jane, wife, age 39 b. NJ; Winslow, son, age 10; Freddie, age 8; Wilbert, age 6; Harry, age 2; all b. NJ
--1900 Census: 8Wd., Newark, Essex Co., NJ: Jane Zeliff, b. February 1841 NJ, widow; Harry, b. April 1878 NJ, mason; Walter, b. August 1882, NJ, bookkeeper
--1910 Census: 8Wd, Newark, Essex Co., NJ: Jane Zeliff, age 69, widow, b. NJ, 11 born 7 living, own income; Harry, age 33, single, b. NJ, undertaker; Wallace, age 28, single, b. NJ, plumber; Emma Battle, age 59, widow, lodger, b. England, dressmaker

- - - - -

Zeliff, JOHN   b. (abt. May 1, 1791)
(Neafie, p.4)   d. May 21, 1854

John Zeliff
Died May 21, 1854
Aged 63 years 20 days

wife, JANE (VanNess)   b. (abt. May 26, 1791)
(Neafie, p.4)   d. May 21, 1854

Jane Van Ness
Wife of
John Zeliff
Died May 21, 1854
Aged 62 yrs. 11 mos.
and 25 days

Notes:
--John, son of Peter Zeliff and Sarah Riker.

--John m. in 1818, Jane Van Ness, dau. of Simon Van Ness and Catherine Van Houten
--John and Jane were members of the Little Falls Ref. Church; "both killed instantly on Sabbath, May 21, 1854, as they returned from church, by being thrown out of the carriage"

--1850 Census, p.365, Acquackanonk Twp., Passaic Co., NJ: John Zeliff, age 56, wheelwright; Jane, age 56; James, age 17, blacksmith; Lydia, age 19; David, age 15; Henry, age 12; John Oliver, age 21, blacksmith; all b. New Jersey

- - - - -

Zeliff, Peter J.*   b. (abt. 1825)
                         d. (February 26, 1899)

wife, MARY E. (Vreeland)
(Neafie, p.14)   b. (abt. 1831)
                         d. April 23, 1891

Mary E.
wife of
Peter J. Zeliff
Died Apr. 23, 1891
Aged 60 years

son, GEORGE S.   b. (abt. 1856)
(Neafie, p.14)   d. September 20, 1879

George S.
Son of
Peter J. and Mary E.
Zeliff
Died Sept. 20, 1879
Aged 22 years

Notes:
--Peter m. Dec. 31, 1846, Little Falls: Mary Ellen Vreeland

--1850 Census: Acquackanonk Twp., Passaic Co., NJ: Peter Zeliff, age 23, blacksmith; Ellen, age 20; John, age 1; all b. New Jersey

--1860 Census: Acquackanonk Twp., Passaic Co,. NJ: Peter J. Zeliff, age 35, b. NJ, blacksmith; Mary, age 29, b. NJ; John, age '4', b. NJ; George, age 4, b. NJ

--1870 Census: Little Falls, Passaic Co., NJ: Peter J. Zeliff, age 45, blacksmith; Mary R., age 40; John N., age 20; Geo. S., age 14; Marilla, age 7; all b. NJ

--1880 Census: Little Falls, Passaic Co., NJ: Little Falls, Passaic Co., NJ: Peter J. Zeliff, age 54, b. NJ, farmer; Mary, wife, age 49 b. NJ; John V., age 30, b. NJ; Annie B., age 19 b. NJ; Marilla J., age 16, b. NJ

--1885 NJ Census: Little Falls, Passaic Co., NJ: Peter J. Zeliff; Mary E.; John V.; Mary J.; Annabelle; Dewitt Baldmer

- - - - -

PEARCE BURIAL GROUND
(Henry H. Pearce Burial Ground)

Please note:
--Below are listed <u>only those burials noted by John</u> <u>Neafie</u> in <u>1895</u>. For later details see: Hillside Cemetery at www.distantcousin.com. and the *Genealogical Magazine of New Jersey*, Vol. 49, p.55-60

Hillside Cemetery "also known as the Henry H. Pearce Burying Ground, is located on the north side of Horseneck Road in what was formerly the Gansegat section of Caldwell Township. It was first copied in 1933 by the late Rev. Warren Patten Coon, and recopied and checked on November 3, 1953, by Edwin A. Baldwin, the late Stephen C. Francisco and William Y. Pryor." *(Genealogical Magazine of New Jersey*, Vol. 49, pp.55-60)

Notes:
-- The 1895 Neafie report mentions "one large vault without any inscription" and "about a dozen rough stones unmarked". (Neafie, p.26)

BUSH

Bush, AMBROSE   b.
(Neafie, p.24)   d. March 21, 1887

Ambrose Bush
Died March 21, 1887
In his 74th year

wife, MARY JANE   b. May 31, 1816
(Neafie, p.24)   d. (March 27, 1896)

Mary Jane
Wife of
Ambrose Bush
Born May 31, 1816
Died . . . . .

- - - - -

Bush, HENRY I. b.
(Neafie, p.23) d. September 15, 1849

Henry I. Bush
Died Sept. 15, 1849
Aged 70 years 7 mos.

wife, JANE b.
(Neafie, p. 23) d. February 24, 1851

Jane
wife of Henry I. Bush
Died Feb. 24, 1851
Aged 71 yrs. 5 mos.

- - - - -

Bush, Monas I.* b.
  d.

wife, JANE b.
(Neafie, p.26) d. January 29, 1852

Jane
Wife of
Monas I. Bush
Died Jan. 29. 1852²
Aged 53 years.
Erected by her son, Nelson

- - - - -

Bush, THOMAS H.   b. May 5, 1834
(Neafie, p.24)   d. November 13, 1862

Thomas H. Bush
Born May 5, 1834
Died Nov. 13, 1862

Farewell wife and children dear

wife, Margaret J.*   b.
                         d.

dau., EMMEY JANE   b. December 14, 1860
(Neafie, p.24)   d. January 5, 1863

Emmey Jane
Daughter of
Thomas H.
and Margaret J. Bush
Born Dec. 14, 1880
Died Jan. 5, 1863

- - - - -

CAMPBELL

Campbell, William H.*   b.
                         d.

wife, Ellen*   b.
                         d.

son WALTER   b.
(Neafie, p.24)   d. September 22, 1857

Walter
Died Sept. 22, 1857
Aged 1 yr. 9 mos. 2 ds.
Child of Wm. H.
and Ellen Campbell

dau., JENNETTE   b.
                            d. August 16, 1864

Jennette
Died Aug. 16, 1864
Aged 6 yr. 9 mos. & 27 days
Child of Wm. H. and Ellen Campbell

- - - - -

COLE

Cole, John R.*   b.

                            d. (June 15, 1894

wife, Hannah M.* (Gilliland)
                            b.
                            d. (August 26, 1917)

dau. HATTIE ANN   b.
(Neafie, p.25)   d. December 30, 1856

Hattie Ann
Daughter of
John R. and
Hannah M. Cole
Died Dec. 30, 1856
Aged 2 yrs. 9 mos.
& 6 days

Cole, Richard* b.
 d.

widow, MARY b.
(Neafie, p.24) d. October 4, 1864

> *Mary*
> *Widow of Richard Cole*
> *Died Oct. 4, 1864*
> *Aged 62 yrs. 6 mos.*
> *24 ds.*
>
> *A tender mother*

COURTER

Courter, Charles* b. (April 9, 1843)
 d. (December 6, 1915)

wife, Mary Elizabeth Pierce*
 b. (July 22, 1844)
 d.

son, GEORGE b.
(Neafie, p.24) d. Febuary 17, 1867

> *George*
> *Died Feb. 17, 1867*
> *Aged 1 mo. 9 ds.*
> *Child of Charles and*
> *Mary Elizabeth*
> *Courter*

son, STEPHEN b.
(Neafie, p.24) d. July 21, 1872

Stephen
Died July 21 1872
Aged 7 months
Child of Charles and
Mary Elizabeth
Courter

Notes:
--Charles Courter, son of James Courter, q.v.
--?1850 Census: Caldwell Twp. (Verona), Essex Co., NJ:
James Courter, age 42, b. NJ, carpenter; Jane, age 40;
Charles age 7; Margaret Ann age 3; Ann Courter, age 83

- - - - -

Courter, James* b. (abt. 1808)
  d. (May 1850)

wife, JANE VAN RYPER b. (abt. 1808)
(Neafie, p.25) d. December 24, 1869

Jane Van Ryper
wife of
James Courter
Died Dec. 24, 1869
In her 61st year.

Notes:
--James Courter, son of John C. Courter and (Ann?)
--James Courter m. Oct. 1836, Jane Van Riper
--?1850 Census: Caldwell Twp. (Verona), Essex Co., NJ:
James Courter, age 42, b. NJ, carpenter; Jane, age 40;
Charles age 7; Margaret Ann age 3; Ann Courter, age 83

DOUGHERTY

Dougherty, Charles A.* b. (June 24, 1858)
                        d. (March 5, 1933)

first wife, BERTHA O. COURTER
(Neafie, p. 25)   b. January 15, 1869
                        d. May 2, 1892

Notes:
--Served: Civil War
--Bertha O. Courter, dau. of Charles Courter, q.v.
--Charles A. Dougherty m. #2, Ada E. Jacobus, dau. of Wm. G. Jacobus and Sarah Ann Courter
--Charles A. Doughtery m. #3, Loretta Cole
--1870 Census:Caldwell Twp. Essex Co., NJ: Charles Courter, age 26; Mary E., age 24; Bertha O., age 1;

FRANCISCO

Francisco, WILLIAM   b. (1837)
(Neafie, p.25)   d. August 23, 1889

Father
William Francisco
Died Aug. 23, 1889
In his 53rd year

wife, Harriet*   b. (1838)
                        d. (1902)

son, GEORGE   b.
(Neafie, p.25)   d. March 10, 1883

*George
Son of Wm. and Harriet
Francisco
Died March 10, 1883
Aged 4 yrs. 10 mos.
and 27 days*

- - - - -

HOPKINS

Hopkins, Henry T.*   b.
                            d.

wife, CATHERINE PARMER
(Neafie, p.23)   b.
                            d.

No Dates

son?, JOHN L.   b.
(Neafie, p.23)   d. May 22, 1871

*John L. Hopkins
Died May 22, 1871
Aged 22 yrs. 10 mos.
& 9 ds.*

- - - - -

HUSK

Husk, ABRAM   b.
(Neafie, p.24)   d. March 8, 1858

Abram Husk
Died March 8, 1859
Aged 55 yrs. 5 mos.
& 17 days

widow, ESTHER CRANE	b.
(Neafie, p.24)	d. February 13, 1869

Esther Crane
widow of
Abraham Husk
Died Feb. 13, 1869
Aged 64 years, 5 mos.
& 8 days

son, THOMAS O.	b. (1846)
(Neafie, p. 24)	d. Nov. 21, 1865

Thomas O.
Son of Abraham and Esther
Husk
Died Nov. 21, 1865
Agd 18 years 2 mos.
& 20 days

- - - - -

Husk, Richard*	b. (March 17, 1839)
	d. (December 4, 1919)
wife, Anna A.*	b. (September 14, 1841)
	d. (February 7, 1902)
dau. LAVENIA	b. December 23, 1868
(Neafie, p.24)	d. April 3, 1885

Lavenia
Born Dec. 23, 1868
Died Apr. 3, 1885
Child of Richard
and Anna A Husk

son ? FRANKY   b.
(Neafie, p.24)   d. Sept. 25, 1867

Franky
Died Sept. 25, 1867
Aged 7 months
Child of Richard and
Anna A. Husk

- - - - -

Husk, Stephen*   b. (December 10, 1831)
                       d.

wife, Rachel*   b. (September 16, 1830)
(Rachel M. Doremus)   d. (April 9, 1903)

son, GEORGE B. McCLELLAN
(Neafie, p.24)   b.
                       d. March 2, 1865

George B. McClellan,
son of Stephen and Rachel
Hust
Died March 2, 1865
Aged 11 months

- - - - -

JACOBUS

Jacobus, JAMES G. b.
(Neafie, p.25) d. August 22, 1888

James G. Jacobus
Died Aug. 22, 1888
In his 77th year

wife, SARAH BUSH b.
(Neafie, p.25) d. June 3, 1887

Sarah Bush
wife of
James G. Jacobus
Died June 3, 1887
In her 81st year.

- - - - -

Jacobus, Samuel B. b. (1844)
  d. (1903)

wife, MARIETTA VAN DUYNE
(Neafie, p.25) b. September 26, 1848
  d. December 2, 1876

Marietta Van Duyne
wife of
Samuel B. Jacobus
Born Sept. 26, 1848
Died Dec. 2, 1876

- - - - -

PEARCE
PIERCE

Pearce, EDWARD b. December 2, 1773
(Neafie, p.23) d. July 26, 1834

Edward Pearce
Born Dec. 2, 1773
Died July 26, 1834

-

Hannah
wife of
Edward Pearce
Born Apr. 13, 1778
Died Aug. 26, 1846

wife, HANNAH (Stagg) b. April 13, 1778
(Neafie, p.23) d. August 26, 1846

- - - - -

Pierce, Francis* b. (1850)
 d. (1929)

wife, Sarah*(Vanderhoof) b. (1853)
 d. (1934)

son?, BENNIE C. b.
(Neafie, p.23) d. December 1, 1881

Bennie C.
Died Dec. 1, 1881
Aged 3 yrs. 3 mos. 8 days
Child of
Francis and Sarah Pierce

dau., GERTIE b.
(Neafie, p.23) d. November 13, 1881

Gertie
Died Nov. 13, 1881
Aged 2 mos. 18 days
Child of Francis and Sarah
Pierce

- - - - -

Pierce, JOSEPH b. July 2, 1814
(Neafie, p.25) d. February 5, 1885

Joseph Pierce
Born July 2, 1814
Died Feb. 5, 1885

wife, NANCY BUSH b. Febuary 1, 1821
(Neafie, p.25) d. (June 4, 1893)

Nancy Bush
wife of
Joseph Pierce
Born Feb. 1, 1821
Died . . . . .

- - - - -

Pearce, Mark* b.
  d.

Pearce, ELLEN M. CARLTON
(Neafie, p.23) b.
  d. May 4, 1871

Ellen M. Carlton

wife of
Mark Pearce
Died May 4, 1871
Aged 30 years 11 mos.
and 16 days

dau., EVALINE (Neafie, p.23)	b. d. October 12, 1865

Evaline, daughter of
Mark and Mary E.
Pearce
Died Oct. 12, 1865
Aged 18 year 8 mos.

- - - - -

Pearce, Reuben*	b. d.
wife, EMELINE (Neafie, p. 26)	b. d. December 24, 1869

Emeline
Wife of Reuben Pearce
Died Dec. 24, 1869
Aged 31 years, 11 mos.
and 24 days

son ELBERT (Neafie, p.26)	b. d. January 15, 1868

Elbert
Died Jan. 15, 1868
Aged 1 month. 25 days
Child of Reuben and Emeline
Pearce

dau. EMELINE b.
(Neafie, p.26) d. August 11, 1870

> *Emeline*
> *Died Aug. 11, 1870*
> *Aged 9 months, 21 days*
> *Child of Reuben and Emeline*
> *Pearce*

- - - - -

Pierce, WILLIAM b.
(Neafie, p.25) d. May 17, 1867

> *William Pierce*
> *Died May 17, 1867*
> *In his 57th year*

wife, ROBA DAVIS b.
(Neafie, p.25) d. June 4, 1889

> *Roba Davis*
> *Wife of*
> *William Pierce*
> *Died June 4, 1889*
> *In her 80th year*

son, STEPHEN b.
(Neafie, p.25) d. August 15, 1869

> *Stephen*
> *Son of*
> *Wm. and Roba Pearce*
> *Died Aug. 15, 1869*
> *Aged 18 yrs. 1 mo.*
> *& 3 days*

Pierce, William Jr.* b.
 d.

wife, AMELIA DEBAUN b.
(Neafie, p.25) d. September 29, 1871

> *Amelia De Baun*
> *wife of*
> *William Pierce, Jr.*
> *Died Sept. 29. 1871*
> *Aged 18 yrs. 17 mos.*
> *and 19 days*

- - - - -

PIER

Pier, SIMEON D. b. December 21, 1817
(Neafie, p.25) d. May 17, 1888

> *Simeon D. Pier*
> *Born Dec. 21, 1817*
> *Died may 17, 1888*

wife, CAROLINE COLE b. March 10. 1821
(Neafie, p.25)1 d. December 30, 1891

> *Caroline Cole*
> *Wife of*
> *Simeon D. Pier*
> *Born March 10, 1821*
> *Died Dec. 30, 1891*

- - - - -

SPEER
SPEAR, SPIER

Speer, CORNELIUS b.
(Neafie, p.23) d. May 7, 1870

Cornelius Speer
Died May 7, 1870
Aged 51 years 5 mos.
& 12 days

- - - - -

Speer, JANE b.
(Neafie, p.23) d. December 15, 1870

Jane Speer
Died Dec. 15, 1863
In her 73rd year

- - - - -

Speer, JOHN W. b.
(Neafie, p.24) d. Feb. 7, 1858

John W. Speer
Died Feb. 7, 1858
Aged 59 yrs. 2 mos
& 26 days

wife, ELSIE BUSH b.
(Neafie, p.24) d. January 18, 1869

Elsie Bush
wife of
John W. Speer

Died Jan. 18, 1869
Aged 68 yrs. 9 mos.
& 9 days

- - - - -

VANDERHOOF

Vanderhoof, CORNELIUS R.
(Neafie, p.23)   b. (October 18, 1818)
       d. February 24, 1855

Cornelius R. Vanderhoof
Died Feb. 24, 1855
In the 38th year
of his age

- - - - -

Vanderhoof, HENRY P.   b.
(Neafie, p.23)   d. January 5, 1865

Henry P. Vanderhoof
Our only son
Died Jan. 5, 1865
Aged 21 years 8 mos.
& 8 days

- - - - -

Vanderhoof, Peter*   b.
       d. (January 29, 1894)

wife, RACHEL (Bush)   b. November 29, 1810
(Neafie, p.25)   d. May 23, 1864

Dearest Mother

*Rachel
Wife of
Peter Vanderhoof
Born Nov. 29, 1810
Died May 23, 1864*

- - - - -

Vanderhoof, WILLIAM   b.
(Neafie, p.25)   d. December 19, 1891

*William Vanderhoof
Died Dec. 19, 18891
Aged 75 years*

wife, JANE BUSH   b. January 22, 1819
(Neafie, p.25)   d. (June 11, 1893)

*Jane Bush
Wife of
Wm. Vanderhoof
Born Jan. 22, 1819
Died . . . . .*

- - - - -

WILLIAMS

Williams, HENRY   b.
(Neafie, p.23)   d. April 27, 1864

*Henry Williams
Died Apr. 26, 1864
Aged 30 yrs. 5 mos.*

- - - - -

Williams, ISRAEL b.
(Neafie, p.23) d. November 11, 1857

Israel Williams
Died Nov. 11, 1857
Aged 30 yrs. 4 mos.
& 15 days

- - - - -

Williams, JEPTHA b.
(Neafie, p.23) d. August 31, 1880

Jeptha Williams
Died Aug. 31, 1880
In the 81st year
of his age

first wife, ELIZABETH BUSH
(Neafie, p.23) b.
  d. September 15, 1854

Elizabeth Bush
wife of
Jeptha Williams
Died Sept. 15, 1854
In her 50th year

second wife, ELIZABETH b.
(Neafie, p.23) d. June 12, 1868

Elizabeth
Wife of
Jeptha Williams
Died June 12, 1868
Aged 70 years 2 mos.
& 12 days

- - - - -

WOODRUFF

Woodruff, David*	b
.	d.
wife, ANN BUSH	b.
(Neafie, p.26)	d. March 20, 1876

Our Mother
Ann Bush
Wife of
David Woodruff
Died March 20, 1876
Aged 52 years, 3 mos.
and 20 days

- - - - -

SMITH BURIAL GROUND

Notes:
--"Located on the farm of Cornelius Dey, at Fairfield, and adjoins the Vanderhoof Burial Ground. This is a very ancient burial place of the Smith family. The first ancestor, Elias Smith, was one of the first settlers of Horseneck, or Gansegat, now known as Fairfield - having settled soon after 1700." (Neafie, p.1)

--"Contains about 25 small rough, brown and grey stones without marks of any kind." (Neafie, p.28)

--"One brown stone which is in fragments, has the following inscription: (Neafie, p.28)

. . . . .d 10 d . . . . .
Weep not for me . . . .
die, I must die . . . .
And sink in deaths . . . . .
Weep not for me mo . . . . .
ause deths is right . . . . .
I go to the home of the blest.

(Weep not for me because I must die
And sink in death's coldness to rest;
Weep not for me because death is nigh
I go to the home of the blest.
(*Hymns for Children.* Publ. 1825. Boston)

- - - - -

Smith, ELIAS   b.
(Neafie, p.28)   d.

wife, CORNELIA JACOBUS b.
(Neafie, p.28)   d.

Notes:
"Elias Smith, the original owner of this property, and who is buried here, came from Middleburgh in Zeeland, Holland, and was married at the Dutch Church, New York City, Sept. 22, 1702 to Cornelia Jacobuz; born at the Bouwery (Stuyvesant's). He was living at Horseneck April 20, 1703 when he deeded property at Second River to Jacob Jacobson Van Winkle. This deed was acknowledged April 21, 1708. On October 20-1718 he was deeded 300 acres at Peckman's River, (Cedar Grove), acknowledged May 8, 1726." (Neafie, p.28)

"On November 11, 1695, the proprietors granted to Anthony Brockholst, Arent Schuyler, and Colonel Nicholas Bayard section 32, 4,000 acres of land, on the east side of

Pequannock and Passaic Rivers, one and a half miles wide, and running northerly from near Little Falls, up the Passaic River, along the Pompton River four and a half miles. This was then in Bergen County, now in Passaic. Both Schuyler and Brockholst located on the tract on the east bank of the Pompton River a little south of Pompton Lake. The purchase was made for mining purposes, but the grantees conveyed the greatest part of it December 17, 1701, to George Ryerson, John Meet, Samuel Berry, David Mandeville, and Hendrick Mandeville. They settled on portions of it and sold other portions to Elias Smith, Michael Vanderbeck, Thomas Juriansen (Van Reiper), Peter Van Zyle, Gerebrecht Gerrebrants, John Westervelt, Michael Hearty (Hartie), Casparus Schuyler, Dirk Van Reiper, Steven Bogert, Cornelius Van Horn, Garret Bertholf, Michael Demott, and Rolof Jacobs." (*Genealogical History of Hudson and Bergen Counties, N.J.*)

- - - - -

VANDERHOOF BURIAL GROUND

Notes:
--The 1904 inscription report refers to this cemetery as a "private cemetery near the Fairfield Reformed Church". (p.145)

--"One small grey stone" (Neafie, p.27)
--"One small brown stone. All marks obliterated."
--"a brown stone, about one foot square:

R. V. D.
Died Jan. the 11
A.D. 1823

-

A. V. D. - J. V. D.

(See Aaron and Jane Van Derhuff?)

- - - - -

Van Derhuff, Aaron* b.
 d.

wife, JANE VAN DUYNE b.
(Neafie, p. 27) d. July 2, 1831
(Inscriptions, p.145)

Jane Van Duyne
wife of
Aaron Van Derhuff
died
July 2, 1831
Aged 31 years
1 month
16 days

- - - - -

Van Druff, HENRY b.
(Neafie, p.27) d. January 29, 1821
(inscriptions p.145)

Henry Van Druff
who died 29th of
January A.D. 1821
Aged 91 years
3 months
and 29 days

- - - - -

Vanderhoof, John* b.
 d.

wife, Phebe L.*	b. d.
son, WILLIAM F. (Neafie, p.27)	b. d. Febuary 1, 1865

William F.
son of John and Phebe L.
Vanderhoof
Aged 12 years, 11 mos.
and 15 days

son, RICHARD U. (Neafie, p.27)	b. d. January 5, 1860

Richard U.
Son of John and Phebe L.
Vanderhoof
Died Jan. 5, 1860
Aged 2 years 9 mos.
and 11 days

- - - - -

Vanderhoof, MARGARET (Neafie, p.27)	b. November 29, 1788 d. October 19, 1856

Margaret Vanderhoof
Born Nove. 29, 1788
Died Oct. 19, 1856
Aged 67 years, 10 mos.
and 21 days

- - - - -

Vanderhoof, MARIA	b. (abt. 1811)

(Neafie, p.27)   d. March 14, 1875

Maria Vanderhoof
Died March 14, 1875
Aged 63 years 6 months
and 3 days

- - - - -

Vanderhuff, RICHARD   b. (abt. 1782)
(Neafie, p.27)   d. April 3, 1853

Richard Vanderhuff
Died April 3, 1853
Aged 71 yrs. 7 mos.
and 3 days

- - - - -

Vanderhoof, Richard*   b.
                                     d.

wife, EMMA M.   b. (abt. 1813)
(Neafie, p. 27)   d. December 17, 1858

EMMA M.
Wife of
Richard Vanderhoof
Died Dec. 17, 1858
Aged 25 years

- - - - -

VAN NESS

Van Ness, Garret*   b.
                                   d.

wife, Elizabeth*   b.
                        d.

son, GEORGE HENRY   b.
(Neafie, p.27)   d. August 31, 1862

George Henry
son of
Garret and Elizabeth Van Ness
Died Aug. 31, 1862
Aged 2 years, 7 mos. 15 days

- - - - -

VAN NESS BURIAL GROUND
(The Old Sindle Farm)

Notes:
--The Neafie report, 1895, calls this the Van Ness Burial Ground. The Inscriptions report, 1904, calls this 'the old Sindle Farm. River Road, Fairfield." (inscriptions p.136)

--"Note: - This graveyard has been entirely destroyed." (Neafie, p.1)
--"A dozen rough stones without marks." (Neafie, p.22)

- - - - -

--"illegible" (Neafie, p.22)

1776, October 22
is . . . . .

- - - - -

--"a brown stone" (Neafie, p.22)

A. R.
November 12, 1788

- - - - -

--"a brown stone" (Neafie, p.22)

$I + Z$
$L + Z$

- - - - -

ATKINSON

Atkinson, THOMAS   b.
(Neafie, p.22)   d. November 22, 1829
(inscriptions, p.136)

In
Memory of
Thomas Atkinson
who died
November 22nd, 1829
in the 25th year
of his age

- - - - -

MILLER

Miller, Isaac S.*   b.
    d.

wife, Elenor*   b.
    d.

son, EZEKIEL
(Neafie, p.22
(inscriptions, p.136)

b.
d. May 20, 1817

In
Memory of
Ezekiel
Son of Isaac S.
and Elenor Miller
Died May 20, 1817
Aged 11 months
and 20 days

- - - - -

RIKER

Riker, JOHN I.
(Neafie, p.22)
(inscriptions, p.136)

b. (September 10, 1741)
d. June 20, 1809

In
Memory
of
John I. Riker
who departed this life
June the 20th, in the year
of our Lord. 1809. Aged
67 years, 9 months and
10 days

first wife, LEAH (Riker)
(Neafie, p.22)
(inscriptions, p.136)

b.
d. March 8, 1803

In
Memory

of Leah, wife of John
I. Riker, who departed
this life, March the 8th in
the year of our Lord
1803, Aged 55 years 4
months & 14 days

Notes:
--See Rev. John Duryee, List of Pastors
--John Riker, bapt. Acquackanonk, NJ, son of Isaac Riker and Lena Bruyn
--John m. #1, Leah Riker, dau. of Abraham Riker and Aaltje Smith
--John m. #2, Catherine .....

"--The hamlet of Singac located in the extreme northwest corner of the township was as nearly as can be determined settled by John Riker who was the owner of most of the land in the immediate vicinity. His children were a son Isaac and three daughters among whom his property was divided, the son having the southwest side of the turnpike and the daughters the northeast. Isaac had three sons John, Samuel and Isaac of whom John became owner of the property. It was by him bequeathed to his daughters Mrs. Henry Stanley, Mrs. John Van Pelt, Mrs Thomas Morrell, and Mrs. A. A. Garrabrant who now own it." (*Hist. of Bergen and Passaic Counties, New Jersey.* (W. W. Clayton, Wm. Nelson. Everts & Peck. Philadelphia. 1882)

--Will signed: June 1, 1808; probate July 3, 1809
(Vol. A. #104-5)
"In the name of God Amen. I John Riker of the Township of Caldwell, County of Essex and State of New Jersey. Altho labouring under bodily infirmaties, but of sound understanding and memory. Blessed be God for it, considering that it is appointed unto all men once to die, and the time when being uncertain I have thought proper in oder to prevent altercations and disputes among my heirs touching the worldly estate wherewith it has pleased God to bless me in this life do make and ordain

this to be my last will and testament and I do hereby order all concerned to consider it as such . Imprimis I give and bequest my soul to God through the merits of our Lord Jesus Christ, and my body to the earth from whence it came, to be buried decently at the discretion of my Relations and Executors hereafter named.

Item: my will is and I do hereby order that my beloved wife <u>Catherine</u> be decently and well supported out of my estate and that <u>my four children</u> hereafter named, do bear their equal proportions towards her maintainance, that is to say, I give here two good milch cows to be at her disposal, a Bed and Bedding, and such articles of household furniture ...as may be necessary for her to keep house with, also her choice of one of the rooms in the house where I now live in, Fruit of all kinds growing on the Farm as she may want for her own use, one half of the garden, also six bushels of wheat, ten bushels of rye, fourteen bushels of Indiana corn, eight bushels of Buckwheat, pasture and fodder for two cows, fire wood for one fire, the grain to be furnished annually; also a pound of tea and fourteen pounds of sugar annually; the above articles to be furnished to my said wife so long and no longer that she remains my widow excepting the two cows which is her own property.

Item: my will is that all my just debts be paid out of my moveable property

Item: I give and bequeathe the use of my farm and buildings lying to the westward of the Turnpike road where it now run, to my <u>son Isaac</u> Riker during his natural life, including the land on the Bergen side to the westward of the Turnpike Road, after his decease my will is that <u>John</u> Riker, son of Isaac have the aforesaid land and buildings as his sole and exclusive property and at his own disposal, Provided nervertheless that my son Isaac shall have and I do hereby give him as his own property and at his own disposal two acres of said land adjoining the house and land where he now lives to run from the road to the River and provided that my Grandson John Riker shall pay to his two sisters Leah and Sally or their heirs the sum of seventy five dollars each whenever he shall become possessed of aforesaid property. I also give unto Isaac, my son under the aforesaid restrictions and limitations the half of the lott in Singack known by the name of the Taylor lott. he is to have that part of the lott nearest the River.

Item-I give to <u>my three daughters</u>, <u>Helena Kerstead</u>, <u>Sally Zeluff</u> and <u>Lydia Van Riper</u> the remainder of my farm lying to the eastward of the Turnpike duirng their natural lives to be divided equally among them according to the equity of the land. after their decease my will is that John Kerstead, son of Helena, and John Zeluff, son of Sally Zeluff, my daughters and the heirs of my daughter Lydia if she shall have any heir, the said land as their sole property and at their own disposal provided neverthe less that if the said John Kerstead and John Zeluff shall or either of them shall die without heirs then the said Estate to be divided equally among the surviving Brothers and Sisters as the law directs

Item. to my daughter Sally I give the use duing her natural life of a certain lott of land on Long Hill adjoining land of Peter Zeluff to run as far as a certain stone fence being a division fence of said lott, after her decease to be equally divided among her children, also her equal share with her sisters of my outlands at Singack not already mentioned under the aforesaid limitations and restrictions

Item. to my daughter Helen Kerstead I give the use of the remainder of the lot, on Long Hill with the exception of half an acre for a <u>Burying Ground</u> after her death to be equally divided among her Children, also her equal proportion of my out lands at Singack, given as above

Item: to my daughter Lydia, I give a certain lot in the great piece No. 4, containing about thirteen acres to be disposed off as she shall judge most proper; also her equal share of the outlands at Singack as aforesaid, after her decease the said land at Singack to be divided among the aforesaid heirs.

My will is that my moveable property of whatever kind or description be equally divided among my son and three daughters aforementioned or their heirs. Provided nevertheless that Lydia, the daughter of Sally Zeluff be paid the sum of seventy five dollars as soon as she shall be of lawfull age out of the said moveable property.

And I do hereby constitute and appoint my Son Isaac Riker, John Kerstead, Peter Zeluff and Peter Van Riper, Executors to this my Last Will and Testament in testimony whereof I have hereunto set my hand and seal this twenty first day of June in the year of our Lond One thousnad eight hundred and eight. Signed, sealed and declared by the Testator to be his last will and testament in presence of us. JOHN RIKER "LS"? in hand drawn circle Josiah Steel (NJ Probate. Essex County, Vol.A, p.209

- - - - -

Van Ness, ISAAC b.
(Neafie, p.22) d. September 25, 1830
(inscriptions, p.137)

In memory of
Isaac Vanness
who died
Sepember 25th 1830

Aged 50 Years
10 months and
2 days

- - - - -

Van Ness, PETER, Deacon   b. (September 2, 1730)
(Neafie, p.22)   d. August 4, 1820
(inscriptions, p.137)

In
Memory of
Deacon Peter Vanness
who died Agusut 4th 1820
in the 90th year
of his age.

His office made the Church his care:
Her interest was his daily prayer;
We trust he's gone to realms above,
There to enjoy his Savior's love.

wife, HARRIET   b.
(Neafie, p.22)   d. March 12, 1797
(inscriptions, p.137)

Sacred
to the memory of
Harriet, wife of
Peter Van Ness who
departed this life
March 12th 1797 in the
64th year of her age

Notes:
--Peter, son of Simon Van Ness and Hester Delamater.

Van Ness, ROBERT b. 1800
(Neafie, p.22) d. 1896

Note:
--"Robert, father of Henry P. Van Ness, -1800-1896- is buried here" (Neafie, p.22)

PASTORS

Fairfield Reformed Church
Fairfield, New Jersey
1762 - 1902

In the absence of church records these notes about the pastors of the Fairfield Reformed Church are included here.

"It is to be regretted that the old settlers did not keep diaries, for that habit, however it may be scorned in these days of the far-searching press, would have preserved to us valuable historical data, of which, through brief and scattering traditions, we now can hope to catch but a fading glimpse.(*Proceedings of the New Jersey Historical Society.* Vol. 6, p.227. Edison, NJ. 1921)

- - - - -

"Fairfield,NJ -- Fairfield. (Caldwell Township, Horseneck, Gansegat). Org. 1720; supplied 1720-62; pas, Cornelius Blauw, 1762-68; Hermanus Meyer, 1772-85; Matthew Leydt, 1779-80; John Duryee, 1801-17; Ava Neal, 1817-22; Abram J. Swits, 1822; Herman B. Stryker, 1823-26; missy, James G. Ogilvie, 1827-29; pas. 1829-32; Henry A. Raymond, 1833-35; Asahel Bronson, 1836038; JosephWilson, 1838-45; John J. Quick, 1845-49; Joseph Wilson, 1849-73; Elbert N. Sebring, 1873-77; ss, Mortimer Smith, 1877; pas. Philetus T. Pockman, 1878-80; James H. Owens, 1881-84; ss, Herman H. Shook, 1884-85; pas, Benjamin C. Miller, 1885-86; Lewis J. Lockwood, 1886-89; William E. Bogardus, 1890-92; ss, John W. Conklin, 1893-95; George H. Peeke, 1895-96; pas, Otto L. Mohn, 1897-1902; Charles B. Mitchell, 1903-05; Cornelius van der Mel, 1906-08; Robert R. Sutherland, 1908-15; William J. Miller, 1916-18; Lawrence L. Leaver, 1919-27; Leonard M. Braam, 1927-29; ss, Leland H.

Koewing, 1930-33; pas, 1933-34; George, Sr. Kroeze, 1938-41; Emil W. Geitner, 1942-48; ss, John H. Heinrichs, 1951-55; pas, William P. Green, 1957-63; John A. Hamersma, 1964-81; Ronald Svendsen, 1982-91; Mark K. Heijerman, 1991." *Historical Directory of the Reformed Church in America, 1628-1992.* Russell L. Gasero. 1992 (KEY: pas=pastor; missy=missionary; ss=stated supply)

- - - - -

Org. 1720   The 'twelfth oldest congregation of the Reformed Church in America'

- - - - -

1720 - 1761   Pulpit supplied by pastors from Acquackanonk and nearby places

- - - - -

1762 - 1768   Cornelius Blauw, Rev.
Matric. Groningen University, Holland 1749
b. Alkmaar, Holland 1722;
Ordained, Ref. Ch. 1762;
d. 1770, Hackensack, N.J.;
m. Margaret Lake, (1749-1825) daughter of Nicholas Lake and Maria Brevoort
(she m.#2, Elias Hubbard, son of James Hubbard and Altje Ryder)

"--Cornelius Blauw, matric. Groningen, 15, Sept. 1749; came to America, 1762; sett. Pompton Plains (Morris) N.J., Pequannock Chh., 1762-1768; Fairfield ('Cumberland', sic.,), N.J., Horseneck Chh., 1762-1768; Montville (Morris) N.J., Parsippany or Boonton Chh., 1762-1768; Paterson (Passaic) N.J., Totowa Chh., 1762-1768; Hackensack (Bergen) N.J.; 2nd Chh., 1768-1771; Schraalenburg (Bergen) N.J., 2nd or DuMont Chh., 1768-1771; Dutch Ref. (*The Colonial Clergy of the Middle*

Colonies. New York, New Jersey, and Pennsylvania. 1628 - 1776. Frederick Lewis Weis. Lancaster. 1938)

"Blauw, Cornelius. Matriculated at the University of Groningen, Sept 15,1749, for the study of Philosophy and Letters. He was from Alkmaar. Pompton Plains, Fairfield, Totowa, and Boonton, 1762-8, Hackensack, 2d, and Schraalenburgh, 2d, 1768-71.
He appears to have been a troublesome man of the Conference party, invading the congregations of others, accepting calls from the disaffected, and illegally administering the ordinances to them." (*Manual of the Reformed Church in America.*)

"The Rev Cornelius Blauw of the Conferentie. The Rev. Cornelius Blauw a Hollander of whom but little is known was called to the pastorate of the Churches of Totowa, Fairfield and Boonton by what was known in the Church of those days as the Conferentie party. He was installed pastor of these Churches in 1762 by the Rev. John Schuyler of Hackensack and the Rev. Johannes Ritzema of New York, two of the most ardent Conferentie ministers. He remained about five years when he removed to Hackensack to take charge of the Second Church there and after a three years ministry in 1771, finished his labors on earth to render an account of his stewardship to the great Judge of all. He lived at Two Bridges and having no carriage was taken to and from church by the more fortunate people. Towards the close of his life he fell into irregular and dissipated habits He is said to have been a good preacher but a quarrelsome man invading the congregations of others accepting calls from the disaffected and illegally administering the ordinances to them." (*The Pastor and the Church.* (Second Ref. Ch. at Paterson) Theodore W. Welles, D.D. NY 1896)

"Correspondence From America. Rev Joannes Kitzema to Rev.Winoldus Budde. July 5, 1764: "I would be glad to report better things of Domino Cornelius Blauw than I can truthfully do. Last fall he accepted a call to Fishkill and Poughkeepsie and to this day he leaves those two churches in doubt whether he will remain or go. This circumstance will I fear cause him trouble. At any rate he acts very faithlessly towards his own beloved congregations in New Jersey which have indeed above measure shown their love toward him. They have Increased his salary from eighty pounds to one hundred and twenty pounds. Such a thing has never before happened in this country to any minister. Moreover, some say that he gives himself up to greediness and serves his own belly. He preaches only once during the week closing with one catechetical sermon. He has become so fat that he is almost too lazy to move himself." (*Documents of the Assembly of the State of New York.* Vol. 30. Albany. 1907)

--"1770 Jan. 9. Blauw, Cornelius of Bergen Co., Int. Adm'rs. Mary Blauw (the widow) Johannes Demarest and Daniel Isaac Browne. Fellowbondsman- Lawrence Ackerman; all of Bergen Co. Witness. Matthies McDermott." (*Calendar of New Jersey Wills.* Lib. K, p.143)

"1773 June 12: Blauw, Barbard (sic) and Catherine of Bergen Co. Wards. Children of Cornelius Blauw of said co. Guardian - John Demarest of Hackensack, said co. File 1006B (*Calendar of New Jersey Wills.* Vol. 5, p. 48)

- - - - -

1772 - 1785 Hermanus Myer, Rev. D.D.
Grad: The Latin School, Bremen
Grad: Theol. Sem. of Groningen Univ.,
Holland. 1763 Ordained 1763
D.D. Rutgers College 1789
b. July 27, 1733, Bremen, Lower Saxony, son of Jacob Meyer and Rebecca Schlichting.
d. October 27, 1791, Pequannock, NJ
bur. Under the pulpit of the Pompton Plains Reformed Church, Pompton, NJ
m. May 1764, Rachel Hardenbergh, dau. of Col. Johannes Hardenbergh and Maria DuBois of Rosendale, NY

"--Hermann Meyer, D.D., b. Bremen, Germany, 27 July 1733, son of Jacob and Rebecca (Schlichting) Meyer; matric. Groningen, Holland, 6 Sept. 1747, in theol.; Ord. Groningen, Holland, 31 Mar. 1763; arriv. America, Oct. 1763; D. D., Rutgers, 1789; Prof. of Divinity, Rutgers, 1789-1791; Fellow of the German Soc., of Breman; sett. Kingston, (Ulster), N.Y., Chh. at Esopus, 2 Nov. 1763-Nov. 1772; Paterson (Passaic) N.J., Totowa Chh., 1772-1791; Fairfield ('Cumberland'?) N.J., Chh. at Horseneck, 1772-1785; Pompton Plains (Morris) N.J., Chh. at

Pequannock, 1772-1791; Montville (Morris) N.J., Parsippany or Boonton Chh., 1772-1791; all these chhs. were Dutch Ref.; Germ. Ref.; d. Pompton Plains, N.J., 27 Oct. 1791." (*The Colonial Clergy of the Middle Colonies. New York, New Jersey, and Pennslvania. 1628 - 1776.* Frederick Lewis Weis. Lancaster. 1938)

"The Rev Hermanus Meyer DD the Learned Divine: The pulpit of the Totowa Church seems to have been vacant after the removal of Mr Blauw in 1767 until 1772 unless as is not improbable their old pastor Domine Marinus resumed the duties of his ministry In November 1772 Totowa and Pompton together called the Rev Hermanus Meyer DD and he was installed as their pastor. Dr Meyer was born in Bremen Lower Saxony of good parentage July 27, 1733. He was a graduate of Groningen University Holland and was distinguished for his deep reading and learning, the warmth of his piety and the ardor of his evangelical preaching. His sermons were practical and pointed. On one occasion after preaching on the necessity of regeneration an officer of the Church met him and said Flesh and blood cannot endure such preaching. He quickly answered Flesh and blood cannot inherit the Kingdom of God. He came to this country with the Rev Jacob R Hardenbergh DD who was afterwards the first president of Queens now Rutgers College. When he was returning home from a visit to Holland he was almost immediately called to Kingston NY and for a time served the people with great acceptance but his marriage, April 17, 1764 with Rachel Hardenbergh, a daughter of Col Joannes Hardenbergh and Maria DuBois of Rosendale NY and sister of the Rev. Dr. Jacob R Hardenbergh one of the most ardent and influential members of the Coetus party together with his conscientious scruples in relation to the oath of allegiance to Great Britain which he was obliged to take renouncing allegiance civil or ecclesiastical to any other power caused great trouble. He thought he had abjured the authority of the Classis of Amsterdam Holland and so declared The Consistory of the Kingston Church was of the Conferentie party and greatly offended by these things closed the church doors against him and guarded the entrance with an armed sentinel. For several years previous to his receiving a call to Totowa he ministered in private houses.

"October 1784 he was appointed Professor of Hebrew and in 1786 Lector or Assistant to the Professor of Divinity in the Theological Seminary of the Reformed Church He received the degree of DD from Queens now Rutgers College in 1789 He died after a brief illness October 27, 1791 widely lamented and was buried under the pulpit of the Pompton Plains church. His remains have never been disturbed He was a profound scholar and had begun a new translation of the Old Testament but only completed the Psalms. It is said that his last sermon was from the text "He that hath the Son hath life' dwelling particularly on the last clause of the text 'hath life'. He had contemplated administering the Lord's Supper two weeks from that day but he was taken ill. During his sickness he sent for one of the elders and gave him directions about his funeral.

"He also remarked I meant to have administered the Lord's Supper next Sabbath but the Lord has intended otherwise and I shall not drink wine again until I drink it in my Father's Kingdom. As expressive of his pious sentiments he said after taking a little refreshment I have no more taste for what I once relished but the bread of heaven is provided for me. He was esteemed one of the most amiable of men a pious and faithful ambassador of Christ Few men stood higher in the opinion of the Church at large or were more generally beloved. It is reported, says Dr Duryea his thirtieth anniversary sermon, by some of the aged who remember him that in the latter part of his ministry he spoke often from the pulpit with streaming eyes and broken heart.

"The Church however during his ministry seems to have been in a feeble condition. Several causes may have contributed to this result among which the most powerful and influential were beyond all doubt the exciting events attending the struggle of the American colonies to achieve their independence and the severe and widespread financial distress which followed the dawning of peace. Liberty was proclaimed throughout all the land but the hosannas that greeted the proclamation came from many a poverty stricken home and were answered with a cry from despairing hearts for labor for the hand that had carried the musket and was now ready to toil. It required a long time for the country to recover from the effects of the war and the prevailing depression when the nineteen years pastorate of Dr Meyer was terminated by his death was probably the reason why the church at Totowa remained quiescent and so far as known for a period of eight years made no effort to secure a pastor.

"The period bounded by Dr Meyer's death and the call of another pastor to Totowa while leaving no record of spiritual activity was fraught with events of the greatest importance inaugurating influences far reaching and permanent tending to the church's future growth and prosperity When Dr Meyer closed his eyes in death the territory which had been the arena of his ministerial labors for nineteen years was a rural scene of exquisite beauty and loveliness a masterpiece of the adorable Creator."*(The Pastor and the Church or Rev. John H. Duryea, D.D. and the Second Reformed Church at Paterson, NJ. Rev. Theo. W. Welles, D.D., Ref. Church of America, NY, 1896)*

"Rev Hermanus MEYER DD. In November 1772 the people here united and in conjunction with the churches of Fairfield and Totowa called Dr Hermanus Meyer to be their pastor He removed here from Kingston and as near as we can ascertain commenced his labors here early in the year 1775. He took up his residence in the parsonage house at the Two Bridges where he remained until his death On his coming here the people appear to have laid aside their former dissentions and to have become united and harmonious Dr Meyer was born in Germany studied in one of the Holland Universities and came to this country in 1762 in company with Dr Jacob R Hardenberg whose sister he subsequently married The first sermon he preached in this country was at Raritan in the pulpit of his late travelling oompanion. He subsequently settled at Kingston Ulster County New York where he labored for some nine years but in consequence of his faithful presentation of divine truth it was too plain practical and pointed he became obnoxious to some of the influential men in the congregation so that finally he was deprived of his salary and excluded from the pulpit From there as we have noticed he came to the churches in this vicinity and continued to minister to the three churches to which he was called excepting for the latter part of his time when he gave up the regular service at Fairfield and preached alternately on the Plains and at Totowa until his death which occurred after a brief illness in October 1791 and after he had labored here for about nineteen years He was esteemed as one of the most amiable of men and a learned pious and faithful ambassador for Christ Few men stood higher in the opinion of the church at large or were more generally beloved.

"As evidence of the high standing of Dr Meyer he was appointed by the Synod in 1784 as Professor of Hebrew and in 1786 as Lecturer in Theology His name here was held in kind regard and grateful remembrance by the pious aged people who personally knew him and heard him preach Although distinguished as a man and as a preacher it yet seems his labors were awarded with little apparent fruit He is said to have spoken from the pulpit towards the latter part of his time of his small success and with tears streaming down his cheeks But the times in which he labored here were the dark and troublous days of the Revolutionary War Morals were then sunk to a low ebb and funeral occasions instead of being a time for solemn reflection too often became a scene of tippling or drunken revelry Some events connected with his last days are of a touching character and worthy of record The last sermon he preached was in the Plains church and on the words He that hath the Son hath life he that hath not the Son hath not life but the wrath of God abideth on him dwelling particularly on the first clause He had contemplated administering the Lord's Supper in two weeks from this time but he was taken sick and during his sickness he sent for one of the Elders of the church and gave him directions about his funeral He also remarked to him I meant to have administered the Lord's Supper next Sabbath but the Lord has intended otherwise I shall not drink the wine again until I drink it new in my Father's Kingdom As expressive of his pious sentiments when on his death bed he remarked on tasting wine I have no more taste for what I once relished but the bread of heaven is prepared for Me His remains as is well known lie entombed in front of the Plains Church pulpit and covered by a large brown stone slab with an appropriate inscription." (*Early Settlements and Settlers.* NJ Historical Society, p.75-79. Vol. IV, 1919)

--"John Ja. Mead, of Prequanock, Bergen Co., NJ to 'Manemanus Meyer, minister of same, L36.8, 11.5 acres. Signed John Ja Mead. Wit: Abraham Ryerse and Samuel Burham" (*Bergen County: Deed: May 25, 1781*)

"..... Dr Meyer died at his residence in Pekeney Pacquenack on the 27th of October 1791. His last words were 'Even so Come Lord Jesus'. His Funeral was attended not only by his own mourning people but by many from the neighbouring towns and especially by a large number of the clergy. ..... his remains were deposited under the pulpit of the Church in Pompton where he had been accustomed to stand to deliver his message ..... So much was he beloved by his people and so tenderly did they cherish his memory that when the old church was to be taken down in 1812 and a new one erected they would not consent to have his ashes disturbed. The wall on the West side was therefore left standing and was extended North and South so as to accommodate the width of the new building and thus leave the pulpit to occupy the same place in the new as in the old and keep it as it originally was exactly above his grave. His death cast a deep gloom over the churches." (*Annals of the American Pulpit: Lutheran, Reformed Dutch.* Vol IX. Wm. P. Sprague, D.D. NY 1869)

--Will of Hermannus Meier, Bergen Co.: signed Sept. 29, 1791 proved Dec. 7, 1791. File 2096B: ... "Wife Rachel, use of all real and personal during her widowhood; also my silver watch and certain books from my library. Of the 800 acres of Lot No. 19 of the Great or Hardenbergh Patent in Ulster Co. NY deeded to me by my father-in-law, Johannes

Hardenbergh; 50 acres in the center of said tract are to be deeded in trust to such persons belonging to the Reformed Dutch Church who shall form a congregation for the erection of a church, on said tract, and the 50 acres to be used for the support of the minister, except all rights of mines thereon, which shall be retained by my children.

To my 3 children, i.e., Maria (wife of Alexander P. Waldron); Rebecca (wife of Rev. Jeremiah Romejni) and Johannes Hardenbergh, the remainder of Lot no. 19 of the Hardenbergh Patent; also remainder of estate after my wife's decease to be equally divided between them.

To daughter, Maria, negro wench named Susannah and 20 of my sermons

To daughter Rebecca 20 sermons and books from library' Son, Johannes, remainder of library, writing desk and manuscripts; also negro boy, Moses, his riding mare, his bed, furniture etc. and L50 for finishing his studies.

Executors: wife Rachel, son, Johannes Hardenbergh and Roelof Jacobripe. Witn: Philip Dey, Richard Neafie, Daniel Woordin.

1791 Oct. 1, Codicil. To daughter Maria (wife of Alexander P. Waldron) L51.11, as an equivalent of dowry I have given my daughter Rebecca and in addition to dowry already given daughter Maria.

- - - - -

1779 - 1780 Matthew Leydt, Rev.
First graduate of Queen's College, Rutgers
A.B. Rutgers College. 1774
Licensed by the General Body. 1778, student under John H. Livingston, D.D.
Trustee Rutgers College 1783
b. March 4, 1753, son of Rev. Johannes Leydt and Syntje Slecht
d. November 24, 1783, Northampton, Bucks County, Pennsylvania.

bur. near First Ref. Church, Northampton

Note: "At a session of the General Synod of the Reformed Dutch Church, held at Albany, in June 1794, they resolved to locate their Divinity Hall in Flatbush. Their professor of divinity, the Rev. Dr. Livingston, had previously resided here, and had given instruction to such students in theology as put themselves under his charge. It is to be regretted that the General Synod of the church ever removed their Theological School from this place, and located it in (New Brunswick, abt. 1810) New-Jersey. "

"Leydt Matthew: son of Johannes Leydt b. 1754 Queens College 1775; studied under Hardenbergh; licensed by Gen Meeting of Mins and Elders 1778; Belleville and Gansegat 1779-80; North and South Hampton 1780-3; d Nov 24 1783. Elected a trustee of Queen's College 1783." *(Manual of the Reformed Church in America)*

"Letter XXXXV Matthew Light or Leydt was born March 4 1753 His father was the Reverend Johannes Leydt who was minister of the Dutch Reformed Church of New Brunswick from 1748 to 1783 a sturdy and active patriot and a devoted friend of learning he was one of the founders of Queen's College, a signer of the petition for the charter a solicitor of funds for the foundation and an original member of the Board of Trustees. Matthew Leydt, the son, after graduation from Queen's in the earliest group studied theology probably under Dr Hardenbergh and was licensed to preach in 1778 he was pastor at Belleville and Gansegat now Fairfield New Jersey 1779 80 and at North and South Hampton Pennsylvania from 1780 to 1783 In 1783 he was elected a trustee of Queen's College His death occurred in the same year November 24 1783 He is buried in the old graveyard at the place familiarly known as The Buck near which stood the first church building of the congregation of North Hampton." *(The John Bogart Letters.* Rutgers College. New Brunswick, NJ. 1914)

"--Johannes Leydt, b. Holland, 1718; ed. by Frelinghuysen and Goetschius; Trustee, Princeton, 1760-1760; original Trustee, Rutgers, 1770-1783; Ord. N. J., 1748; sett. New Brunswick (Middlesex) N.J., 27 Sept. 1748-1783; Six Mile Run (Somerset) N.J., at Franklin, 27 Sept. 1748-1783; Hillsborough (Sussex) N.J., 1766-1774; Conewago (Adams)Pa.; Chh. at Hunterstown, 1771-1771; Pres., Gen Synod, D. R.

Chhs., 1778; Dutch Ref.; d. Three Mile Run, Franklin, N.J., 2 June 1783m a. GS." (*The Colonial Clergy of the Middle Colonies.* F. L. Weis. Lancaster, 1938)

- - - - -

1801-1817 John Duryee, Rev.
Student of Dr. Peter Wilson (his brother-in-law) at Hackensack, N.J.
Student of Theology under John H. Livingston, D.D. at Erasmus Hall, NY
Ordained by The General Body 1784
Trustee. Rutgers College 1786
b. August 1, 1752, Bushwick, Kings Co., L.I., son of Joost Duryee and Catherine Schenck
d. October 2, 1836, near Little Falls, N.J.
bur. Old Burying Ground, First Presbyterian Church, Caldwell, NJ (Lockward, p.52)

-John m. #1: March 30, 1777 (Bible Record) Acquackanonk. "Johannes Duryee b. Long Eyland. res. Hackensack; to Maria Lee Brinckerhoff, widow (of Henry Brinkerhoff). b. New York. res. Hackensack. m. March 25, 1777" (*Dutch Ref. Ch. Records from New York and New Jersey.* Holland Society of New York) Mary Lee Brinckerhoff (b. 1749 d. Nov. 10, 1825, bur. Old Burying Ground, First Presbyterian Church, Caldwell, NJ); dau. of John Lee and (Jannetje De Groot?); widow of Hendrick Brinckerhoff (1744-1775).

--John m. #2, "February 25, 1828, at Stone House Plains, NJ, by J. G. Tarbele, minister: Rev. John Duryee to Wid. Mrs. Elenor Kierstead" (*Register of Dutch Ref. Church,*

Stone House Plains, N.J.) (see below)

Children of John Duryee and Mary Lee:
--Catherine, 1778-1815 NJ; m. Philip Isaac Schuyler
--John Lee, 1781-1854, NJ; m. .....
--George John, 1783-1871, NYC; m. Nancy Perry
--Henry Brinkerhoff, 1786-1854 NJ; m. Hester Dey
--Elizabeth, 1789-1882 NJ; m. Jared Freeman Harrison
--Jane Lee, 1791-1820 NJ; m. Mjr. Nathanial Samuel Crane

Revolutionary War
--April 1775: his father, Joost Duryee, of Bushwick signed with the revolutionary forces.
--John Duryee, Pvt., Capt. John Outwater's Company, Col. Theunis Dey's Regiment, New Jersey Militia; New Jersey State Troops
--John Lee, Joseph Lee and William Lee also served in Capt. Outwater's Company (*Jerseymen in the Revolutionary War: Essex County*"
--Declaration for Pension; Case #171709 of John Duryee of Essex Co.; Granted Jan. 27, 1833, Signed Hon. Theo. Felinghuysen, U.S. Senate

"That shortly after the commencement of the war he entered as a volunteer, as a soldier in the company of militia under the command of Captain (John) Outwater in the Regiment of Colonel (Theunis) Dey of the New Jersey militia that shortly after he enlisted he was with the regiment ordered to New York where he continued in acutual service with the regiment until the enemy captured New York and Long Island and they were evacuated by the American troops. After the retreat, the company of Captain Outwater was stationed on the line at Hackensack in Bergen county in the State of New Jersey. While there they assisted in covering the retreat of the American (baggage?) from New York across to Hackensack. And was once sent to escort Mrs. Washington, the wife of General Washington from Newark through Hackensack to Tappan. The exact date when he entered and left this service he cannot recollect. He was engaged in it he thinks about (blank) months. He was afterwards in actual service , a volunteer in the same company. In March 1781 (1780) on the 23 of which month while in an engagement with the enemy at (blank) he was taken prisoner and carried to the Sugar House in New York where he remained until the month of September following having been kept as a prisoner of war for six months when he was released by an exchange of prisoners. The scene of his service was first at New York and afterwards at Hackensack in New Jersey guarding the (goile/gaile/jail). Sylvester Marius whose affidavit is hereto annexed is a living witness of his service and Abraham Vanderbeck & Wilhelmus Eltinge are neighbors to whom he can refer for his character for veracity and for their belief of his services as a soldier of the revolution. He was born on the first of August 1752 at Long Island in Kings County; from there he removed to Hackensack in the year 1776 and resided at Hackensack during the war; at the time of his capture in 1781 (1780?) March 28 (23?) he resided there and had property destroyed and plundered by the enemy to the value of 'five?' thousand dollars. Since the war he has resided for fifteen years as a settled preacher at Raritan in Somerset county New Jersey for ten years at Fairfield in Essex co. N. Jersey and the remainder of the time he has been Missionary. He has no (proof) of his age except his family Bible and the Bible of his father which agree with the age above stated. He never received any discharge from the service." (*National Archives Microfilm Publications. Non Selected Records.* p.327-p.328) (note: Sylvester Marius and Abraham Vanderbeck also served in Capt. Outwater's Company)

--"A raid by British forces against Hackensack on March 23, 1780, resulted in the destruction by fire of the original courthouse structure. "When daylight came the few patriots who were left discovered that the raiders had taken off virtually every grown man in town, fifty or sixty in all. Among them were Abraham Haring, John Bant, Abraham Storms, John Van Antwerp, John Bogert, William Prevost, Henry Van Winkle, G. Van Wagenen, Morris Earl, JOHN DURIE, Jacobus Brouwer, William Brouwer, John Van Giesen, David Baldwin, Isaac Ver Valen, Peter Zabriskie, John Demarest, John Romeyn, Guiliam Bertholf, Jonathan Doremus, Christian Demarest, and five Negro slaves, Will, Jack, John, Venter and Hector. Some of them doubtless felt that the militia had been remiss in failing to have a patrol at Little Ferry through the night." (Glenn Valis. Web Page. Feb. 2002)

--"July 26, 1777" : "MRS. BRINKERHOF, now wife of JOHANNES DURYEE of Hackensack, said that John Zabriskie, now a prisoner, came to Peter Zabriskie's some time in January 1777 and related that he had taken a list of the Militia officers who had carried off the stores at Dr. Buskirk's etc near the New Bridge at the retreat of the Enemy from thence, etc. A young man student living at Mr. Isaac Van Giesen's in Hackensack was at New York on the Day that the above stores were conveyed off by the Militia and in the evening saw John Zabriskie's

Negro deliver a letter to a gentleman containing a detail of what had happened respecting the stores, and a list of the officers who commanded the militia as above." (*Correspondence of the Executive of New Jersey*, p.11; *Minutes of the Provincial Congress*, p.457; New Jersey State Library, Loose Manuscripts, Box 16; *Colonial Americans in Exile*. NY.

MINISTRY
--"Duryee John: b. 1760 (1752); studied theology under John H. Livingston D.D.; licensed by General Meeting of Ministers and Elders 1784; Raritan and Bedminster 1786-98; Bedminster 1798-1800; Pottersdam 1800-1801; Fairfield 1801- 1817; d 1836 Elected a trustee of Queens College (Rutgers) 1786." (*Manual of the Reformed Church of America*)

"Almost immediately after the death of Rev. T. F. Romeyn, the churches of Raritan and Bedminster called the Rev. JOHN DURYEA (sic) to be their pastor. He was born on Long Island, in 1760(sic), and received his academical education at Hackensack, under DR. PETER WILSON (his brother-in-law). He studied theology under Dr. Livingston, and was licensed by the General Synod, at an extra session, on May 18th, 1784, in New-York, and accepted the call from Raritan, which had given him, as the minutes state, October 14th, 1785. The first minute of consistory after his settlement is dated March 3d, 1786, and he continued to serve the church until 1799, when he resigned his charge." (*Forty Years at Raritan*. p.196)

"His ministry at Raritan was blessed in the beginning of it very much. The church increased from time to time by members on confession and by certificate. But in 1799 Mr Duryea resigned his charge. Dissatisfaction had grown up. He was never a student and was accustomed to preach without writing his sermons and did not satisfy the more intelligent portion of his people. But he was a good man loved to preach and did preach even in his old age. He had his work in providence and did it like a godly man. The final arrangements with Mr Duryea were effected on the 22d of October 1798. The consistory agreed to pay up all arrearages and allow him his salary until the 4th day of January with the use of the parsonage until May 1799. He continued to serve the church of Bedminster for another year and also preached occasionally in the vicinity of White House and Potters Town in Hunterdon County. Finally he received a call from Fairfield in Essex County where he resided for many years until he died finally at the Notch not far from Little Falls

Essex County in 1836. His remains rest in the cemetery attached to the Presbyterian Church at Caldwell, Essex County by the side of his daughter Mrs. Crane. He married late in life and left a widow surviving him. He had been without a pastoral charge for many years had given all his property to his children and was himself often in straitened circumstances but never in want. The Lord provided for him." (*Forty Years at Raritan. Eight Memorial Sermons.* Abraham Messler, D.D. New York, 1878)

--"When the invitation to preach (Bedminster Reformed Dutch Church) was extended to Mr Duryea the call was conveyed to him by John Vroom an explanation being made that there was but little money in the congregation but that all his temporal wants should be provided for. He preached several months without any payment being made whereupon after a regular morning sermon he thus addressed his people: You made certain promises to me if I would preach for you. Several sermons have been given and I have performed my part. A bargain thus made becomes a sacred contract. If you refuse you are a congregation of story tellers and you John Vroom are the biggest liar of them all ." (*Story of an Old Farm.* Andrew J. Mellick.)

"Rev. John 'Duryea' who was born in 1760 (1752) and having adopted the ministry as a profession studied with Dr Livingston and was licensed to preach in 1784. He was called to Raritan in 1785 where he remained until 1799. In 1801 he settled at Fairfield, Essex Co. which charge then embraced Little Falls and remained until 1817 when he removed to Little Falls and probably remained there until 1836 when his death occurred. After he had relinquished his charge he traveled on horseback and held service throughout the country at the various houses at which he received hospitality On these occasions a collection was invariably taken either for the dominie or the horse. "Mr 'Duryea' seems not only to have been a godly man but a citizen of much business capacity. He owned the mills at this point which after being successfully conducted were sold to the Miller Bros." (*History of Bergen & Passaic Counties, New Jersey*)

--Will of John Duryee: NJ #12682G. Signed Sept. 5, 1828; Probate Oct. 29, 1836:
In the Name of God Amen
ITEM: I will that all my just and lawful debts be paid as soon as convenient after my decease. I further will and direct that all my property be sold at public or private sale at the discretion of my executors within

one year after my decease excepting a coloured woman named DINAH which I give and bequeathe to my daughter ELIZABETH, excepting also a silver tea pot, sugar dish and milk pot which I give to my daughter ELIZABETH. I give and bequeathe to my beloved wife ELEANOR Fifty Dollars to be paid to her as soon after my decease as convenient. I further order and direct that after the discharge of my lawful debts the remainder of my estate be distributed to and among MY SIX CHILDREN in equal shares allowing to the children of my two daughters CATHARINE and JANE which are now deceased the same shares as would have fallen to their mothers if they were living to be divided among them in equal portions. And I do hereby constitute and appoint GEORGE J. Duryee and Jared F. Harrison executors of this my last will and testament hereby renouncing all former wills by me at any time heretofore made and declaring this only to be this my last will and testament this fifth day of September one thousand eight hundred and twenty eight.

Signed, sealed, published, pronounced and declared by the said John Duryee to be his last will and testament to presence of us who have hereunto subscribed our names as witnesses in the presence of the testator and in presence of each other. Harvey Harrison, Mary Harrison, Thomas Thompson.

Essex County... Harvey Harrison, one of the witnesses to the annexed writing purporting to be the last will and testament of John Duryee the testator therein deceased being duly sworn doth depose and say that he saw the testator sign and seal the annexed writing and heard him publish and declare the same as and for his last will and testament that at the time of the doing thereof the testator was of sound and disposing mind, memory and understanding as far as this deponent knows and as he verily believes, that Mary Harrison and Thomas Thompson, the two other subscribing witnesses thereto were present at the same time with this deponent and together with him subscribed their names thereto as witnesses in the presence of the testator and each other, and at the request of the testator and that said testator died more than ten days ago, to the best of this deponent's belief. Signed, Harvey Harrison
Sworn: October 29th, 1836: before me J. O. Drake, Surrogate

Jared F. Harrison, one of the executors in the annexed writing name being duly sworn doth depose and say that the said annexed writing contains the true last will and testament of John Duryee the testator therein named deceased as far as he knows and as he verioly believes, that he will as the executor therof will and truly perform the same first by paying the debts of said deceased and then the legacies therein specified as far as the goods, chattels and credits of said deceased will thereunto extend and the law charge him that he will make and exhibit into the

Surrogates office of the County of Essex a true and perfect Inventory of all and singular the said goods chattels and credits as far as the same have or shall come to his possession or knowledge or to the possession of any other person or persons to his use to his knowledge and that he will well and truly account when thereunto lawfully required. Signed: Jared F. Harrison

Sworn October 29, 1836 before me J. O. Drake, Surrogate

Probate of the foregoing will was duly issued as follows: I Jacob O. Drake, Surrogate of the County of Essex do certify the annexed to be a true copy of the last will and testament of <u>John Duryee,</u> late of the County of Essex deceased and that Jared F. Harrison, one of the executors therein named proved the same before me and is duly authorised to take upon

himself the administration of the estate of the testator agreeable to the said will. Witness my hand and seal of office the twenty ninth day of October in the year of our Lord one thousand eight hundred and thirty six. Signed: Jacob O. Drake, Surrogate."

--WILL OF JOOST DURYEE
Signed July 22, 1793 - Proved August 19, 1793

In the name of God. Amen. I Joost/George Duryee of Bushwick in Kings County and State of New York twenty second day of July in the Year of our Lord one thousand seven hundred and ninety three, and <u>in the Seventeenth year of Americas Independence</u> do make and Publish this my Last will and testament in manner following.

Imprimus it is my will and I do order that all my just debts and Funeral Charges be Paid as Soon as convenient after my Decease out of my Personal estate.

Item. I give and Bequeath unto my loveing wife the one Equal half of all my Buildings in the township of Bushwick during the time she shall remain my widow. Also as much of all my Furniture as She Shall Choose to keep, one horse and my Riding Chair, one Negro woman named Jude. Also Give unto my loveing wife Three Hundred Pounds Current money of the State aforesaid, to be paid out of my Personal Estate by my Executors as Soon as Convenient after my Decease.

Item. I give and Bequeath unto my Loveing Son Abraham all my Real estate in the township of New Utrecht in Kings County aforesaid, which he now is in Possession of to him his heirs and Assigns for Ever.

Item. I give and Bequeath unto my Loveing Sons Peter and George all my Real Estate in the township of Bushwick and Newtown also all my Real estate in the City of New York together with all the Farming Utensils to them their heirs and assigns for Ever. Jointly and Severally they the Said Peter and George Must Pay annually one third part of all the Neate proceeds of the Real Estate in Bushwick and Newtown to my widow during the time She Shall remain my widow and also must Furnish her with as much fire wood as She Shall want during the time She Shall Remain my widow Delivered at the House. Also that my two Sons Peter and George pay two Hundred pounds out of my Real Estate Bequeathed them to my Grandson George Van Pelt as soon as he Shall arrive to the age to Twenty one years. Also pay to my Daughter Catherine Willson one Hundred pounds one year after my decease to her or her heirs and Assigns. Also Pay to my Son Johannas(sic) four hundred pounds one year after my decease to him his heirs and assigns for Ever.

Item. it is my will and I do order that my Executors herein after named do Pay one Year after my Decease Two hundred Pounds in Such a Manner as they Shall think best for my Grand Son Peter Van Pelts Education, if Either of my Grand Sons Should die before they arrive to the age of twenty one years his Share being unpaid to be Equally divided to my Six Children, to them their heirs and assigns.

Item. the Remainder of all my Estate to be Equally Divided to my Six Children, Abraham, Peter, Johannas(sic), George, Elizabeth and Catherine Share and Share alike to them, their heirs and assigns for Ever.

Lastly. I do nominate, Constitute and appoint my Loveing wife Executrix and my four Loveing Sons Abraham, Peter, Johannas, and George, to be my Executors of this my Last will and Testament Declaring this to be my Last.

In witness whereof I the said Testator George Duryea have hereuntoSet my hand and Seal the Day and Year first above written.

(signed) Joost Duryee (seal)

MARRIAGES

--First(?) wife: Mary Lee, dau. of John Lee and possibly, Jannetje DeGroot; she was widow of Henry Brinkerhoff. In a 1774 New York petition, John Lee and Henry Brinckerhoff are listed side-by-side; John DeGroot is nearby. *(Valentine's Manual.* p.434. New York. 1850)

--Second wife, possibly: Mrs. Eleanor/Leah/Helen/Lanna Kierstead may have been the widow of John J. Kierstead (d. 1825) and daughter of John and Leah Riker, q.v., who are interred at the Old Sindle Farm, aka Van Ness Burial Ground. John Kierstead and John Riker each had considerable land at Singac.

--Will of John Kiersted: signed June 1, 1821; probate: March 15, 1826

"In the name of God. Amen. I John Kiersted of the Township of Acquackanonk in the County of Essex and State of New Jersey being of sound mind and understanding for which blessing I most devoutly thank my God do make and publish this my testament and last will in manner and form following that is to say

Item: my will is and I do order that all my just debts and funeral expenses be duly paid and satisfied as soon as conventiently can be after my decease.

2nd: I give and bequeath to my loving <u>wife, Lenah</u> if she survives me one bedstead, beds and bedding with all the furniture there unto belonging, and she may dispose of the same as she thinks proper and in addition to that I give her the use of so much of my household furniture as she may think proper to select during the time she remains my widow.

3rd: I give and bequeath to my son Cornelius one cow, the choice of my flock of cattel, two sheep and one hog and the colt called the Kilder, also one suit of decent Sunday clothes if he remains single till after my decease

4th: I give and devise to my son, John his heirs and assigns forever five acres of my Singack lot of land, to be taken of on the north end of said lot next to Caleb Bruens land

5th: I give and devise to my son, Aaron his heirs and assigns forever three acres and a quarter of my Singack land adjoining the lot I have devised to my son John.

6th: I give und devise to my son Abraham, his heirs and assigns three acres and a quarter of my Singack land adjoining the lot I have devised to my son Aaron

7th: I give and devise to my son Isaac his heirs and assigns forever all the remainder of my Singack lot of land adjoining the lot I have devised to my son Abraham

8th: I give and devise to my son Cornelius his heirs and assigns forever all the remainder of my Singack lot of land lying between the lot I have devised to my son Isaac and Passaic River containing about three acres and a quarter be the same more or less

9th: I give and devise to my sons Abraham and Cornelius the lot of land I bought of Isaac A. Van Giesen and commonly called the 'manner', that is I give and devise to my son Abraham his his heirs and assigns forever, all that part of said lot lying on the west side of the Ridge Road, and to my son Cornelius his heirs and assigns forever all that part of said lot of land lying on the east side of said Ridge Road

10th Item. It is my will that my <u>loving wife Lenah</u> if she survives me shall have the use of all the lands I have devised to my five sons, during the time she remains my widow, if she will accept of the same in lieu of her right of dower exclusive of the lease she have of my son Isaac.

11th: And whereas I have heretofore sold to my son Aaron a certain lot of land whereon he not lives, and whereas the said Aaron is still indebted to me on the purchase money in principal and interest at this time six hundred and ninety three dollars and twenty cents and I do order my executors hereafter named to collect from my son, Aaron all the ballance due me over and above the sum of six hundred dollars, as soon after my decease as conveniently can be, and after my decease I order my son, Aaron to pay to my loving wife <u>Lenah</u> during her widowhood twenty one dollars annually from the time of my decease. And if he pays the sum of twenty one dollars annually in half yearly payments if demanded by her during her widowhood or decease, which may first happen, than I discharge my son Aaron from the present of the said sum of six hundred , or any part thereof

12th: And whereas I have disposed of some part of my personal estate by Will, and if the remainder should be insufficient to pay my just debts and expenses then I do order my Executors hereafter named to sell so much wood of my Singack lot of wood land as will be sufficient to pay my just debts and expenses, and the wood if sold of must be sold along the line of Isaac Riker in equell with the whole length of said lot. And Lastly, I do hereby appoint <u>my loving wife, Lenah</u> Kiersted and my two sons Isaac Kiersted and Cornelius Kiersted Executors of this my testament and last will.

In witness whereof I have herewith set my hand and seal this first day of June in the year of our Lord one thousand eight hundred and twenty one. Signed Sealed Published and declared by the said John Kiersted to be his testament and last will in presents of us: *Garret Van Houten, Michael Fleming; John Zeluff"*

--<u>Will of John Riker</u>: signed June 1, 1808; probate July 3, 1809:(NJA:40:282). (New Jersey, Probate Records, Essex Wills 1803-1814, Vol. A; Image 114)

Item: my will is and I do hereby order that my beloved **(second)** wife CATHERINE be decently and well supported out of my estate and that my **FOUR** children hereafter named, do bear their equal proportions towards her maintainance, that is to say, I give here two good milch cows to be at her disposal, a Bed and Bedding, and such aritcles of household furniture …as may be necessary for her to keep house with, also her choice of one of the rooms in the house where I now live in, Fruit of all kinds growing on the Farm as she may want for her own use, one half of the garden, also six bushels of wheat, ten bushes of rye, fourteen bushels of Indiana corn, eight bushels of Buckwheat, pasture

and forddeer for two cows, fire wood for one fire, the grain to be furnished annually; also a pound of tea and fourteen pounds of sugar annually; the above article to be furnished to my said wife so long and no longer than she remains my
widow excepting the two cows which is her own property.
Item: my will is that all my just debts be paid out of my moveable property
Item: I give and bequeathe the use of my farm and buildings lying to the westward of the Turnpike road where it now run, to my son Isaac Riker during his natural life, including the land on the Bergen side to the westward of the Turnpike Road, after his decease my will is that John Riker, son of Isaac have the aforesaid land and buildings as his sole and exclusive property and at his own disposal, Provided nerverthless that my son Isaac shall have and I do hereby give him as his own property and at his own disposal two acres of said land adjoining the house and land hwere he now lives to run from the road to the River and provided that my Grandson John Riker shall pay to his two sisters Leah and Sally or their heirs the sum of seventy five dollars each whenever he sall become possessed of aforesaid property. I also give unto Isaac my son under the aforesaid restrictions and limitations the half of the lott in Singack known by the name of the Taylor lott. he is to have that part of the lott nearest the River.
Item-I give to my three daughters <u>Helena Kerstead</u>, Sally Zeluff and Lydia Van Riper the remainder of my farm lying to the eastward of the Turnpike duirng their natural lives to be divided equally among them according to the equity of the land after their decease my will is that John Kerstead, son of <u>Helena</u>, and John Zeluff, son of Sally Zeluff, my daughters and the heirs of my daughter Lydia if she shall have any heir, the said land as their sole property and at their own disposal provided neverthe less that if the said John Kerstead and John Zeluff shall or either of them shall die without heirs then the said Estate to be divided equally among the surviving Brothers and Sisters as the law directs.
Item. to my daughter Sally I give the use during her natural life of a certain lott of land on Long Hill adjoining land of Peter Zeluff to run as far as a certain stone fence being a division fence of said lott, after her decease to equally divided among her children, also her equal share with her sisters of my out lands at Singack not already mentioned under the aforesaid limitations and restrictions
Item. to my daughter <u>Helen Kerstead</u> I give the use of the remainder of the lot, on Long Hill with the exception of half an acre for a BURYING GROUND after her death to be equally divided among her Children, also her equal proportion of my out lands at Singack, given as above
Item: to my daughter Lydia, I give a certain lot in the great piece No. 4, containing about thirteen acres to be disposed off as she shall judge most

proper; also her equal share of the out lands at Singack as aforesaid, after her decease the said land at Singack to be divided among the aforesaid heirs.

My will is that my moveable property of whatever kind or description beequally divided among my son and three daughters aforementioned or their heirs. Provided nevertheless that Lydia, the daughter of Sally Zeluff be paid the sum of seventy five dollas as soon as she shall be of lawfull age out of the said moveable property.

And I do hereby contitute and appoint my Son Isaac Riker, <u>John Kerstead,</u> Peter Zeluff and Peter Van Riper, Executors to this my Last Will and Testament in testimony whereof I have hereunto set my hand and seal this twenty first day of June in the year of our Lond One thousand eight hundred and eight. Signed, sealed and declared by the Testator to be his last will and testament in presence of us. JOHN RIKER "LS" in drawn circle,Josiah Steel

- - - - -

1817-1822   Ava Neal, Rev.
                   A.B. Columbia College, 1810
                   Faculty. Rutgers College, 1813
                   Grad. New Brunswick Theo. Sem., 1816
                   b. abt 1793
                   d. May 24, 1840

--"Died on the 24th inst. the Rev. Ava Neal, in the 47th year of his age."
(*New York American.* May 26, 1840)

"Neal, <u>Ava</u>. Columbia College 1810; tutor in Ref. Ch. 1814; New Brunswick Seminary 1816; lic. by classis of New Brunswick; Pompton Plains and <u>Fairfield</u> 1817-22; Pompton Plains 1822-8; suspended in 1829; restored 1833; d. 1839"
(*Manual of the Ref. Ch. in American.* Corwin. 1922)

--"Neal, Ava. Columbia College 1810; term of ministry 23 years; d. 1839; age 58?; without charge 11 years"
(*Ccentennial of the Theological Seminary of the Ref. Church in America.* NY 1885)

"Rev. AVA NEAL. After being vacant about two years the church (Pompton) called the licentiate Ava Neal On the 9th of February 1817.

He was ordained and installed as pastor. In this call the church of Fairfield united with the Plains Church and received one third of his services and this arrangement continued down to 1823. Then the Fairfield Church feeling the need of more services released him and he was retained by the Plains alone until July 1828 through a pastorate of eleven years. During this time he received into the membership of the church seventy eight persons. He however became concerned in secular business and falling into irregular habits was in 1829 suspended from the ministry restored in 1833 and died in 1839 ." (*Proceedings of the New Jersey Historical Society.* pp.79-80. Vol. IV. *1918)*

- - - - -

1822   Abraham J. Swits, Rev.
        Grad. Union College, NY. 1817
        Grad. New Brunswick Theological Sem. 1820
        b. June 3,1794, Schenectady, New York
        son of General Jacob Swits and Margaret VanEps
        d. January 24, 1878, Schenectady, NY
        bur. Island Hill Cemetery, Buskirk, Rensselaer Co., New York
        m. May 1823, Hoosick, NY, Eveline Viele (1798-1873), dau. of Jacob L. Viele and Catrina Bratt
        bur. Island Hill Cemetery, Buskirk, NY

Served: Board of Superintendents at New Brunswick Theological Seminary.

--"Abram J. Swits: (1785-1878) 1821-1822 --Union '17; New Brunswick 1820--Missionary. in Classis. Supplied Amsterdam First. July 1857-July 1859 and Nov. 1862-Nov. 1863.(*History of the Montgomery Classis, R.C.A.* W. N. P. Dailey. NY 1916)

"During this interim (1863) the pulpit was mainly supplied by Revs. Abram J. Swits and Isaac G. Duryee of Schenectady. Mr. Swits on graduation from New Brunswick in 1820 had served as a Classical missionary in Montgomery for some time. For the last twenty-five years of his life he lived retired at Schenectady, and for about three years supplied the pulpit of the Port Jackson church (Aug., 1857-July, 1859, and Nov., 1862-Aug., 1863). Mr. Swits died in 1878 at Schenectady." .(*History of the Montgomery Classis, R.C.A.* W. N. P. Dailey. NY 1916)

--1825, July 26: son, John Livingston Swits b. Schenectady:
"1846 John Livingston Swits died suddenly at his home 25 North Ferry Street a few minutes before 7 o'clock Saturday morning April 13. Although Mr Swits had been ill for some time his death was unexpected Death was due to heart failure .....Mr Swits was born at the Viele homestead at Hoosick July 26, 1825. His father was Rev Abraham J Swits a former pastor of the Second Reformed church ..... Swits received his education in Schenectady Lyceum and entering the sophomore class Union College in 1843 He graduated in 1846 and began study of law in the office of & Potter He was admitted to bar in 1848. Mr Swits owing ill health never ..... Mr. Swits returned to Schenectady in 1874 settling at 25 Street where he has since. He organized and promoted local enterprises among which the Schenectady Free Hospital Dispensary. For twelve years was a member of the Board of Health. He was a member of Phi Beta Kappa Society, Sons American Revolution. the Society of New York and the Reformed Church. In 1874 Swits was married to Miss W Knapp of Jersey City. Mrs Swits died six months later 1878 he was married to Miss M Knapp a sister of his first wife who lived but two years the exception of his niece Mary M Swits who lived him Mr Swits is survived by near relatives The funeral services were held at his late Tuesday afternoon April 16 three o clock. The Rev C Hinds pastor of the State Presbyterian Church conducted services 1847." (printed as found) (*Union University Quarterly. Vol. IV, Iss. 1.* 1907 NY)

--1850 Census: 4Wd. Schenectady, Schenectady Co. NY: Abram J. "Suits" age 56, b. NY, clergy, Dutch Ref., real estate $29,000; Eveline, age 52, b. NY; Catherine Dutch, age 23, b. NY
--1860 Census: Schenectady, NY: Abram J. Swits, age 65, b. NY, clergyman Ref. Prot. Dutch; real estate $25,000; personal "$10,000; Eveline 'F', age 61 b. NY
--1870 Census: Schenectady, NY: Abram J. Swits, age 66, b. NY, retired Divine, real estate $10,000; personal $30,000; Eveline V., age 72; b. NY

--Legacies to: Hope College Theological Seminary; scholarships at Western Theological Seminary; 235 volumes to the Theological Seminary at Hope College. (*Reformed Church of America.* Records)

- - - - -

1823-1826 Herman Barkelow Stryker, Rev.
Grad: New Brunswick Theo. Sem. 1822
b. April 2, 1794, Port Richmond, Staten Island, NY, son of Rev. Peter Stryker and Sarah Barkelow
d. December 11, 1871, Huguenot, Staten Island, NY; bur. Monmouth Co., N.J.
m. February 26, 1818, Blandina Cadmus, dau. of Abraham Cadmus and Margaret Leslie

"Stryker, Herman B. son of Peter Stryker. b. at Port Richmond S.I., April 2, 1794. New Brunswick Seminary 1822 lic. Cl NB, Missionary to Athol, Caldwell, Johnsburgh and Warrensburgh, Warren Co NY 1822-3; Fairfield and missionary at Little Falls NJ 1823-6; Agent of Miss Soc 1826-7; Union Ch in Amsterdam 1827-33; also Miss at Johnstown in 1830; St Johnsville 1833-4; Glenville 2d 1834; 1837 without charge, 1837-61; Huguenots SI 1861-71; d Dec 11,1871. He was a pioneer in the temperance cause early identifying himself with the total abstinence movement and by his example and influence teaching this principle to his children and others. He was gentle affectionate lovely and generous in his disposition constant faithful and earnest in his work attending to all his duties with fidelity. He was a good theologian, a diligent student of history and a careful investigator of divine truth. He studied the Bible carefully and with prayer. He was especially fond of the prophesies. In his preaching he was terse, comprehensive, pointed, tender. His object was to comfort, edify, convince and convert. In this he was successful. In his early charges he had powerful revivals of religion. In one of them he preached nine successive weeks every evening in the week and three times on each Sabbath and large numbers were brought by him in the fold of Christ."(*Manual of the Reformed Church in America 1628-1902.* Edward T. Corwin. NY 1902)

--1826 April 8: his son: b. at Fairfield, NJ: (d. March 25, 1900: Peter Stryker, Rev. D.D.; President , General Synod, 1895)

--1850 Census: North Brunswick, Middlesex Co., NJ: H. B. Stryker, age 56 b. NY, minister of the Gospel; 'Blondena' age 50 b. NJ; A. C. age 26, b. NJ, bank teller; Sarah E., age 20 b. NY; Mary B., age 13, b. NY; 13 boarders: students

--1860 Census: 20 Wd. 2nd Dist. NYC: Herman B. Stryker, age 66, b. NY, minister Dutch Ref. Ch; Blandina, age 60 b. NJ; Mary, age 20, b. NY; Alexander C., age 35 b. NJ, minister Dutch Ref. Ch.; Elizabeth, age 25, b. NJ; Peter, age 33, b. NJ, minister Dutch Ref. Ch.; Caroline, age 26, b. NJ; Elizabeth, b. NJ; Henry, age 7, b. NJ; Herman, age 4, b. NY; Margaretta, age 2 b. NY; 2 domestics, b. NY

--1870 Census: Westfield, Richmond Co. (S.I.), NY: H. B. Stryker, age 76, b. NY, clergyman; Blandina, age 70 b. NY; Mary B., age 29 b. NY

- - - - -

1827 - 1829   James Glaen (sic) Ogilvie, Rev.
(1828-1832?)   listed as 'other minister' 1826
           by Ref. Church of America. (Presbyterian)
           b. August 26, 1792; bapt.Oct.14, 1792,
           First Presb. Church, NYC, son of Anthony
           Ogilvie and Elizabeth Cowdrey
           d. August 5, 1832
           bur. Fairfield Church Cemetery, q.v.
           m. Elizabeth W. Wilson (1794-1870)
           bur. Fairfield Church Cemetery, q.v.

Notes:
--See: James Glaen Ogilvie, Interment, Fairfield Ref. Church
--Served: Chaplain (Presbyterian) U. S. Navy (1825)

--"Ogilvie, James G. b. 1794. lic. 1826. Montville 1826-7; Missionary at Little Falls and Fairfield 1827-9; Fairfield 1828-32; d. August 5, from injuries received by being thrown from his horse." (*Manual of the Reformed Church in America.* Edward T. Corwin, D.D., NY, 1902)

--1796 Nov. 15: Will of Jonathan Cowdrey Sr. NY: "one third part to be equally divided between my grandsons James Ogilvie and Thomas Cowdrey Ogilvie, sons of my daughter Elizabeth Ogilvie to be paid to them when they arrive at lawful age"

--1818: "The Aurora Church was received into the Cayuga Presbytery on September 22, 1818, at a meeting held in Aurora; at a second meeting on the next day, Rev. James G. Ogilvie was ordained and installed the first pastor of the Presbyterian Church of Aurora." (*A Brief History of Aurora, NY.* Temple R. Hollcroft. NY. 1976)

--1819: "The Presbyterian church of Tomhannock was organized October 3 1819 under the style of the United Dutch and Presbyterian Society and among its earliest preachers were the Revs James G Ogilvie, Mark Tucker, Jonas Coe and Lebbeus Armstrong supplies. The house of worship was built about 1820 ..... (*Landmarks of Rensselaer County, NY.* Geo. B. Anderson. NY. 1897)

--1820: Published: by James G. Ogilvie: *The religious principles, and forms of government, of the following denominations : Friends, Hopkinsians, Episcopalians, Lutherans, Universalists, Baptists, Jews, Seceders, Methodists, Catholics, Presbyterians, United Brethren, Swedenborgians, Congregationalists, Dutch Reformed, collected from authentic sources*

--1822-23:"On Monday evening the 13th inst the Presbytery of New York installed the Rev James G Ogilvie as pastor of the 14th Presbyterian Church in the new chapel erected for their use in Provost street The Rev EW Baldwin preached the sermon from 2 Cor iv 7 The Rev Dr T M Adley delivered the charge to the minister and the Rev Samuel Nott the charge to the people This church has been gathered by its present pastor during the last summer and the chapel has been built since the 12th of September We most heartily bid the pastor and the church God speed and pray that they may be made a blessing."(*The Christian Herald and Seaman's Magazine, 1822-1823. NY. 1825*)

--1823: "The Fourteenth Church was organized January 10th, 1823. It erected a house of worship on the south side of Provost Street (now Franklin) near the foot of Varick Street. It was largely a private venture of the Rev. James Ogilvie, who had gathered the people together and personally assumed the financial responsibility for the building. In 1825, however, he became discouraged and sold the building to the Provost Street Baptist Church, and the Presbyterian congregation was dissolved." (*Brief Histories of the Churches Connected With the Presbytery of New York. Pre:1949.*)

--1824: Trial and Sentence of John Johnson, for the Murder of James Murray,: Connected with His Life and Confessions, and Explanations of the Various Reports Concerning Him, as Related by Himself to the Rev. Mr. Ogilvie, One of the Presbyterian Ministers of this City, who Regularly Attended Him in His Confinement, and to the Place of Execution." (*Joseph Desnoues.* NY. 1824)

--1827: "The following ministers belonging to the New York Presbytery reside in this city (1827) but have charge of no congregations The Rev Messieurs James G Ogilvie and ISC Frey and the Rev John M Mason DD STP of the second Presbytery of New York is likewise without charge " (*Description of the City of New York.* James Hardie, A.M., NY, 1827)

- - - - -

1833-1835   Henry Augustus Raymond, Rev.
A.B. Yale College, 1825
Grad. New Brunswick Theological Sem. 1828
b. July 10, 1804, Patterson, Putnam Co. NY, son of Clapp Raymond and Sarah Dunning
d. July 18, 1877, Cohoes, NY
m. #1, Sept. 1828, Susan Penniman Martin dau. of Squire Martin of New Brunswick
m. #2, July 1834, Catharine Maria Miller, of Little Falls, NJ, dau. of Isaac Slover Miller and Eleanor Voorhees; she d. aft. 1870, NY

--"Henry Augustus Raymond, the son of Clapp and Sarah (Dunning) Raymond, was born in Patterson, Putnam Co., NY on June 19, 1804. During his College courses the family resided in Poughkeepsie.

"On graduation he entered the Theological Seminary of the Reformed Church in America, at New Brunswick, N.J. where he took the full course in three years.

"In 1928 he was licensed to preach by the Classis of Poughkeepsie, and On January 7, 1829, he was ordained and installed as pastor of three small churches in Schoharie County. On September 11, 1828 he married Susan P., daughter of Squire Martin of New Brunswick who died July 15, 1829.

"In 1833 he took charge of the church in Fairfield, "Herkimer County" (sic.) and was married on July 10, 1834, to Catharine Maria Miller of Little Falls, New Jersey.

"In 1836 he began a long, prosperous and very successful ministry of nearly fourteen years in Niskayuna, Schenectady County which was succeeded by briefer settlements in other country parishes in Cayuga, Orange, Schoharie and Albany counties, until his retirement on account of growing infirmities in 1871. He then went to Schenectady to live while his youngest son was attending Union College. Later he went to live with his only surviving daughter in Cohoes where he died on July 18, 1877 at the age of 73.

"In each of his widespread and populous charges he was a most faithful and indefatigable pastor, abundant in ministerial labor, diligent and sympathetic in the care of his flock and seeing his work crowned with success.

"His children were four daughters and six sons. The youngest son (Andrew VanVranken Raymond, D.D.,L.L.D.) was graduated at Union College in 1871 and was subsequently President of that institution."
(*Biographical Notices of Graduates of Yale College*. Franklin B. Dexter. New Haven. 1913)

--1850 Census: Niskayuna, Schenectady Co., NJ: Henry Raymond, age 46, clergyman D.R.; Catharine, age 36; Susan 21; Ennis, son, age 14; Henry, age 11; Eleanor, age 10; Isaac, age 8; Aaron, age 6; Peter, age 3; Grace, age 1; all b. 'NY'

--1860 Census: Cobleskill, Schoharie Co., NY: <u>Henry A.</u> Raymond, age 56, Prot. Ref. Clergyman; C. M., age 46; Susan C., age 31; Ella A., age 21, music teacher; Isaac M., age 18; Aaron, age 16; Peter V., age 14; Andrew, age 6; Ada, age 3; all b. NY

--1870 Census: Watervliet, Albany Co. NY: <u>H. A.</u> Raymond, age 66, clergyman; C. M., age 55; Ella, age 28; Andrew, age 15; Adda, age 12; all b. NY

- - - - -

1836-1838 Asahel Bronson, Rev.
    b. December 28, 1793, New Milford, CT;
    son of Matthew Bronson and Mary Richmond
    d. December 25, 1882, French Creek, W.VA
    bur. French Creek Presbyterian Cemetery
    m. Feb. 1815, Poughkeepsie, NY, Mary
    Tompkins, dau. of Gilbert Tompkins and
    Maria Schryver.

--"Bronson, Asahel, b. 1794; ord. 1816; Wyantskill 1833-6; Fairfield 1836-8; Easton NY 1838-9; Amit 1840-42; Died. 1882" (*Manual of the Reformed Church in America.* Charles Corwin. 1922)

--In 1851, "Rev. John Teasdale writes The Baptist Recorder, that he had the pleasure, on the 1st instant, of baptizing Rev. <u>Asahel</u> Bronson, pastor of the Presbyterian Church at Stanhope, N.J. Mr. Bronson has for many years, been an influential minister of the denomination has has recently left." (*New York Times.* November 15, 1851)

--"In 1870 Rev <u>Asahel</u> Bronson DD then serving the church of Waynesburg became Stated Supply part of his time Dr Bronson continued to supply that church for some three years."
(History of the Presbytery of Redstone. Synod of Pennsylvania. Washington,PA. 1889)

--"Rev. Asahel Bronson DD. From Presb. Troy April 25, 1871, stated supply for Jefferson 1872; ss Mt. Vernon till 1880; preached one or two years in W. VA.; ret. April 1, 1881; died Dec. 25, 1882"*(History of the Presbytery of Redstone.* Synod of Pennsylvania. Washington,PA. 1889)

--1850 Census: Troy, Rensselaer Co. NY: 'Arabel Brownson' age '50' b. CT, 'O.S. Pres.' Clergyman; Mary, age 49 b. 'CT'; Mary, age 27; Matthew, age 24, 'O.S. Pres.' Clergyman; Clarissa, age 21; Gilbert, age 20, tailor; 'Darins', age 19, tailor; Cordelia, age 12; all ch. b. NY
--1860 Census: Sandy Hill PO, Kingston Twp., Washington Co., NY: Rev. A. Bronson, age 63 b. CT, Baptist clergyman; Mary, age 61 b. NY; Elias S., age 30 b. NY, physian; Cordelia, age 17 b. NY C.S. Teacher
--1870 Census: Waynesboro PO, Marion Twp., Greene Co., PA: Hannah Brooks, age 76 b. PA; Cordelia Brooks, age 30 b. VA; R. Flenniken, age 78 b. PA; A. Bronson, age 76, b. CT, minister
--1880 Census: Union, Barbour Co., WVA: Dr. E. S. Bronson, a ge 54, b. NY, physician; Nancy, age 42 b. WVA, wife; Dellett E., age 5 WVA; Asahel T. age 3 b. WVA; John S., age 1, b. WVA; Warric S. Smalridge, age 18, b. WVA, stepson; Asahel Bronson, age 86, b. CT, father, widower, minister; Clara J. Smith, age 45, sister, widow, b. NY

- - - - -

1838-1845   Joseph Wilson, Rev.
A.M., Rutgers College, 1837
b. abt. 1797, England;
d. May 1, 1878
m. "Mary Alice Hay Taylor,
b. Nov. 20, 1804, Philadelphia, dau. of
William Taylor, Jr. and Mary Alice Gazzam.
She d. at Fairfield, NJ." (Her parents were
b. at Cambridge, England.)
(*History of the Gazzam Family.* A. DeB. Mackenzie, 1894)

--Principal of Poughkeepsie Female Institute, 1836-38. Fairfield and Little Falls, 1838-45. Tarrytown, 1845-49. Fairfield, 1849-73. Published, "Selfishness and Its Remedy," Died, May 1, 1878.

"Among the pastors Rev Joseph Wilson occupies the most prominent place not because of the long duration of his office but more particularly because of his genial character learning and ability. He was fearless in the advocacy of what he esteemed the right and he possessed the aptitudes of leadership in a large degree. He invariably carried his auditors with him and secured the very general acceptance of his views He was a warm friend and a devoted pastor and has left an indelible impression upon this society." *(Hist of Essex and Hudson Counties.* p.850)

--1840 Census: Caldwell Twp. Essex Co., NJ: Joseph Wilson. 8 persons; adj. to John D. Speer and David VanNess pastor of the church at Preakness
--1844: "The connection between the Rev Joseph Wilson and the church at Little Falls has been dissolved Mr Wilson remaining pastor of the church at Fairfield "
--1850 Census: Caldwell Twp., Essex Co., NJ: Joseph Wilson, age 53, b. England, clergyman R. Dutch Church; Mary Ann, age 44 b. PA; Benjamin F. age 14 b. NY; Martha L. age 12 b. NY; Sarah G. age 6 b. NJ; Rebecca J. age 2 b. NY; 1 servant b. Ireland
--1860 Census: Caldwell Twp., Essex Co., NJ: Rev. J. Wilson, age 63, b. England, R.D. clergyman; Mary age 55 b. PA; Martha L. age 22 b. NY; Sarah G., age 16 b. NJ; Rebecca J. age 12 b. NY
--1870 Census: Caldwell Twp., Essex Co., NJ: Joseph Wilson, age 73 b. England, clergyman; Mary A., age 65, b. PA; Sarah G. age 24 b. NJ; Rebecca J., age 22 b. NY."

- - - - -

1845 - 1849   John J. Quick, Rev.
                   Grad. New Brunswick Seminary, 1839
                   b. September 7, 1810, Neshanic, NJ, son of James Quick and Mary Hageman

d. June 19, 1886, Reeder, Missaukee Co., MI
m. July 1839, Deborah Tunison(1805-1871)
dau. of Philip Tunison & Susanna Brown
bur. Traverse City Cem., Traverse City, MI

--"Quick, John J. N.B.S. 1839; lic. Classis of Philadelphia, 1839; Jackson, 1840-3, Fairfield, 1845-9, Wynantskill, 1849-54, Currytown, 1855-6, Mapletown and Currytown, 1856-61, Mapletown, 1861-2, without charge 1863-7, stated supply, Port Herkimer, 1867-8, without charge" (*Manual of the Reformed Church in America 1628-1878.*)

--"Rev Mr Quick was an amiable gentleman an earnest preacher and popular among his parishioners ." (*Hist. of Essex and Hudson Counties.* p.850)

--1850 Census: Greenbush, Rensselaer Co. NY: John Quick, age 40 b. NJ, pastor; Deborah, age '43' b. NJ; Susan, age 9 b. NY; Peter, age 6, b. NJ; Mary, age 1 month, b. NY
--1860 Census: Root, Montgomery Co., NY: John J. Quick, age 49 b. NJ, R.D. Clergyman; 'Taborah, age 47 b. NJ; Susan, age 18 b. NY; Peter, age 16, b. NJ; Mary, age 10, b. NY; Susan 'Timson' (Tunison), age 78 b. NJ
--1870 Census: Traverse City, Grand Traverse Co., MI: John Quick, age 60 b. NJ, farmer; Deborah, age 54 b. NJ; Susan, age 28 b. NY; Peter, age 26 b. NJ, teaching school; Mary, age 22, b. NY, teaching school

- - - - -

1849 - 1873 Joseph Wilson, Rev.
SEE ABOVE: (1838 - 1845)

- - - - -

1873-1877 Elbert Nevius Sebring, Rev.
Grad. Rutgers College, 1862
A.M. New Brunswick Theological Sem. 1865

b. September 22, 1836, Ovid, NY, son of
John C. Sebring and Elizabeth Covert
d. October 12, 1889, Leeds, Greene Co.,NY
m. Oct. 1865, Anna Tucker Beck (1834-1896)
dau. of Lewis Caleb Beck and Hannah Maria Smith

--"Elbert Nevius Sebring. W. Leyden NY. Born at Ovid NY September 22, 1836. AB (Rutgers 1862) Licensed by Classis of Geneva, 1865; Ghent, 2d, 1865-73; Fairfield, 1873-77; Prattsville, 1877-79. Middleburgh, 1879-84; Leeds and Athens, 2d, 1884-89. Died Oct. 22, 1889" (*Biographical Record, Theological Seminary New Brunswick 1784-1911.* pub. 1912)

--"The fifteenth pastor was Rev. Elbert N. Sebring, who was called from Middleburgh, New York. He was installed pastor of this Church in October, 1884. In 1885 the interior of the church was renovated and presents a beautiful appearance. Mr. Sebring continued pastor until October 12th, 1889, when the Master he so faithfully served called him to his Heavenly Home."(*Leeds Reformed Church Cookbook.* Leeds, NY. 1906)

--1850 Census: Ovid, Seneca Co. NY: Elizabeth Sebring, age 41; Arad, age 17, farmer; Elbert, age 14, John, 10; Elizabeth Minor, age 7; Henry Compton, age 26, laborer; Mary Kelly, age 15; all b. NY

--1860 Census: Ovid, Seneca Co. NY: Eliza Sebring, age 50; Arad, age 28, theology student; "Albert", age 23, theology student; John, age 19, theology student; Lewis Shertz, age 22, farm laborer; all b. New York

--1870 Census: Ghent, Columbia Co. NY: Elbert N. Sebring, age 33, b. NY clergyman; Anna, age 36; Lewis B., age 2; all b. NY

--1880 Census: Prattsville, Greene Co. NY: 'E. M. Sebriny" age 43 b. NY, clergyman; Anna B., age 44; Louis, age 12; all b. NY

- - - - -

1877   Mortimer Smith, Rev.* (i.d. data is presumed)
Apr.-Oct.   Union College, New York. 1865
                    Union Theological Sem. New York. 1866-67
                    Lane Theological Sem. Cincinnati. 1868
                    b. July 7, 1842, Chatham, Columbia Co., NY;
                    son of Joseph W. Smith and Ruth Benjamin
                    d. February 5, 1914, Madalin, Red Hook,
                    Dutchess Co., NY
                    m. Fannie M. .....b. abt.1848 d. aft. 1920

"Smith Mortimer. b Austerlitz NY July 7, 1842. Union College 1865; Union Theological Seminary 1867; Lane Theological Seminary 1868; ord. by Congr. Ch. Lebanon, OH, Miami Conf 1868: SS (stated supply) at the following places: Canfield OH 1870-1871; Wilton Ia 1872-1874; (1878, Missouri, without charge); Pierce City, Mo 1879-80; Byron Ill 1880-1882 Shopiere, Wis 1883-1885; Bloomington, Wis 1885-1887; also US Gov. Surveyor Sisiton Agency (Sisseton-Wahpeton Sioux) Dakota Terr. 1875-1876; Germantown NY 1887-1895; without charge, Disappears 1905" (*Manual of the Reformed Church in America.* NY, 1922)

"REV MORTIMER SMITH: My pastorate over those Churches was of about two years duration beginning about December 1885 and closing in October 1887. There were additions to the Churches but I do not remember now how many nor can I tell the number of funerals attended. Having recently closed my pastorate at Germantown my books are packed and so I have no access to the memoranda. During the brief pastorate we remember that the church edifice at Bloomington (Wisconsin) was very much rejuvenated and also an organ was purchased. We believe the Churches were out of debt and in a good harmonious and spiritual condition. Since leaving Bloomington I have been pastor of the Reformed Church of Germantown-on-the-Hudson, NY for nearly eight years until lately resigned." (*Fiftieth Anniversary of the First Congregational Church, Emerald Grove, Wisconsin.* Dec. 1896))

--"Smith, Mortimer: died Madalin (town of Red Hook), NY. Feb. 5, 1914" (*Union Theological Seminary in the City of New York. Alumni Catalogue 1836-1947.* NY 1948)

--1850 Census: Chatham, Columbia Co., NY: Joseph Smith, age 47, b. NY, farmer; Ruth, age 46; <u>Mortimer</u>, age 8; 4 other children; all b. New York

--1855 Census: Stephentown, Rensselaer Co. NY: Joseph W. Smith, age '46' manufacturer; Ruth, age '56' b. Columbia Co.; Frances, age '31'; Joseph W., age 16; <u>Mortimer</u>, age 12; Frelinghuysen, age 11; Cora E., age 4 (children all b. Columbia Co.)

--1860 Census: Chatham, Columbia Co., NY: Joseph W Smith, age 57, b. NY, wadding manufacturer $20,000 real estate; $20,000 personal; Ruth, age 56; <u>Mortimer</u> age 17; Frelinghuysen, age 16; all b. New York

--1862: Civil War Draft Registration: <u>Mortimer</u> Smith, age 20, single, b. NY, res. Chatham, NY, student Union College

--1870 Census: Canfield, Mahoning Co., OH: <u>Mortimer</u> Smith, age 28 b. NY, minister; <u>Fanny</u>, age 22, b. NY

--1880 Census: Sandoval, Marion Co. IL: <u>Mortimer</u> Smith, age 37, b. NY, parents NY, minister of the Gospel; <u>Fannie</u>, age 32, b. NY, father b. England, mother b. 'PA'; Stanley, age 1, b. IL

--1900 Census: Saugerties, Ulster Co., NY: <u>Mortimer</u> Smith, age 57 b. July 1842 NY, parents b. NY, capitalist; <u>Fannie</u>, age 51 b. Dec. 1848, NY, parents b. 'NY'

--1910 Census: Red Hook, Dutchess Co. NY Rev. <u>Mortimer</u> Smith, age 67, b. NY, preacher, own income; <u>Fannie M.</u>, age 62 b. NY

--1920 Schenectady City Directory: <u>Fannie M.</u> Smith, widow of <u>Mortimer</u>; res. Schenectady

- - - - -

1878 - 1880   Philetus Theodore Pockman, Rev. D.D.
                A.M.Rutgers College 1875 (same class as Louis John Lockwood, q.v.)
                Grad. New Brunswick Theol. Sem. 1878
                D.D. Rutgers College. 1894

b. February 26, 1853, East Greenbush,
Renssalaer Co., New York, son of John
Pockman and Almira Snook
d. November 1919; bur. Elmwood Cemetery
New Brunswick, New Jersey
m. 1881, Newark, Annie Latourette Boice
(1856-1927), dau. of George Bethune Boice
and Margaret Ann Zabriskie.

"--Philetus Theodore Pockman. Hasbrouck Heights NJ. Born at East Greenbush NY Feb 26 1853. Clergyman RCA. President Board of Education RCA 1908-12. President General Synod RCA 1911. NB Sem 1878. AM Rutgers 1878. DD Rutgers 1894 ." (*Catalogue of the Officers and Alumni of Rutgers College. 1766-1916.* Trenton. 1916)

--"Pockman Philetus Theodore b at East Greenbush NY Feb 26, 1853 RC 1875 NBS 1878 lic. Classis Rensselaer Fairfield NJ 1878-80. Greenville Jersey City 1881- 6. New Brunswick NJ 1887-1911. Pres Gen. Syn. 1911. Alden NY 1912 16 Hasbrouck Heights NJ 1916 19 d Nov 16 Pres Bd of Education 1908 12 Member Bd DM 1916 19 Pres Gn Svn 1911 DD RC 1894
"Dr Pockman was a genial man and most excellent pastor Wherever he labored he was a power for righteousness." (*Manual of the Reformed Church in America.* Charles Corwin. 1922)

"Philetus T Pockman Rutgers '75 pastor of the Dutch Reformed church at New Brunswick NJ recently visited Washington and in the name of (Beta Theta Pi) presented President Roosevelt with a badge of that fraternity " 1901

"Of the later pastors the Rev Mr Pockman whose stay was regretfully brief to his people occupies a prominent position as a minister able as a speaker affable as a companion and sincerely devoted to his high mission." *(Hist. of Essex and Hudson Counties,* p.850)

--1860 Census: East Greenbush, Rensselaer Co. NY: John N. Pockman, age 37, farmer; Almmira 37; Spencer B. 9; 'Philletus S' age 7; Lydia E., age 4; Ida G., age 1; all b. NY

--1870 Census: East Greenbush, Rensselaer Co. NY: Jno. Pockman, age 47, farmer; Almira age 47; Spencer B., age 19; Philetus 'F'., age 17; Lydia E., age 15; Jay D., age 7; Alvina A., age 3; all b. New York
--1880 Census: Caldwell Twp: P. T. Pockman, age 27 b. NY, boarder, minister; at res. of H. V. Doremus
--1900 Census: 2Wd. New Brunswick, Middlesex Co. NJ: Philetus T. 'Puckman' age 47, Feb. 1853, b. NY, minister; Annie L., age 44, Dec. 1856, b. NJ; Helen L. 16 NJ; Margaret Z., age 15 b. NY; Eleanor A., age 12 b. NJ; Theodore N.,age 10 b. NJ; Laura T., age 7 b. NJ; Georgianna B., age 5 b. NJ; George B. Boice, age 71, Feb, 1829, b. NY, father-in-law; Georgiana Boice, age 40, Nov. 1860, sister-in-law, b. Maine
--1910 Census: 2Wd. New Brunswick, Middlesex Co., NJ: P. Theodore 'Poehman', age 57 b. NY, m. 28 yrs. minister Reformed Church; Annie L.,a ge 53, b. NY, father b. NY, mother b. NJ; Margaret L., age 24, b. NJ; Eleanor A., age 21 b. NJ; Theodore N., age 19, b. NJ; Laura d., age 16 b. NJ; Georgeanna B., agge 14, b. NJ; George B. Boise, age 82, father-in-law, widower, b. NY, parents b. NJ; 1 servant

- - - - -

1881 - 1884　James Henry Owens, Rev., D.D.
　　　　　　　A.B. Rutgers College, 1878
　　　　　　　grad. New Brunswick Theol. Sem. 1881
　　　　　　　D.D. Lafayette. 1907
　　　　　　　b. January 4, 1857, Hyde Park, Dutchess Co. NY, son of Henry Owens
　　　　　　　d. 1942 Red Bank, NJ
　　　　　　　bur. Fernwood Cem., Jamesburg, NJ
　　　　　　　m. June 1880, Jamesburg, NJ, Letitia K. Van Nuis, (1854-1935), dau. of John L. Van Nuis (1812-1869) and Susan K. ..... (1821-1881)
　　　　　　　b. Fernwood Cem. Jamesburg, Middlesex Co., NJ

--"James Henry Owens. Paterson, NJ; Born at Hyde Park, NY January 4, 1857, son of Henry Owens. AB Rutgers 1878. Ordained by the Classis of Paramus 1881; Fairfield 1881-84; Bushnell IL 1884-1886; First Presbyterian, Perth Amboy, NJ 1886-94; Eastside Presbyterian, Paterson, NJ 1894..... D.D. (Lafayette, 1907)" *(Biographical Record. Theological Seminary. New Brunswick. 1784-1911.* 1912)

"Rev James H Owens his successor stands equally well approved. His people are thoroughly united and the church affairs are in a prosperous condition. " *(History of Essex and Hudson Counties,* p.850)

--1860 Census: Poughkeepsie, Dutchess Co., NY: Henry M. Owens, age 28, carpenter; Mary E., age 29; C. V. W., son, age 7; James H.,age 3; B. P. W. son, age 1; Susan Berbauer, age 14; all b. New York

--1860 Census: New Brunswick, NJ: Eliza Van Nuisse, age 68 b. NJ; John L., age 47 b. NJ, farmer; Susan, age 38, b.Ireland; Amanda E., age 7 b. NJ; Lettitia age 6 b. NJ; James L. age 4 b. NJ; Charles R., age 1, b. NJ

--1870 Census: Yonkers, Westchester Co. NY: H. M. Owens, age 43, b. NY, saloonkeeper; M. E. 40; Charles V.A. 17, drives exp. wagon; James H. 14, appr. to printer; Benjamin, age 13; George age 9; Emma J. age 8; Lewis age 5; Belle, age 6 months; all b. NY

--1870 Census: Kingston PO, South Brunswick, Middlesex Co NJ: Susan Van Nuis age 49 b. 'NJ'; Amanda E., age 17; Letitia age 16; James D. age 14; Charles R. age 10; Margaret W. age 8; all b. NJ

--1880 Census: Jamesburg, Middlesex Co., NJ: Susan 'Van Nins' age 59 b. Ireland, widow; 'Letisa R.' age 25, b. NJ, school teacher; James L., age 24, wid., works shirt factory; Charles R.,age 20, clerk in store; Mary L., age 18; Eugene L.,age 4 mos. (Jan.), grandson

--1900 Census: 4Wd. Paterson, Passsaic Co. NJ: James H. Owens, 42, b. Jan. 1858 NY, Presbyterian clergyman; Letitia R., age 44, b. Sept. 1856 NJ, 3 born 1 living; Helen R., dau., age 13, b. Dec. 1886, b. NJ; 1 servant

--1910 Census: Paterson, NJ: James H. Owens age 53, m.28 yrs. b. NY, parents NY, clergyman; Letitia K., age 54, b. NJ, father b. NJ, mother b. Ire.

--1920 Census: 3Wd. Macon, Bibb Co. GA: James H. Owens, age 63, b. NY, Presb. clergyman; 'Petitia K.' age 54; Amanda E. Van Nuis, age 67, sister-in-law

--1930 Census: Red Bank, Monmouth Co., NJ: James H. Owens, age 72 b. NY, no occup.; "Seletia" age 74, b. NJ, father NJ, mother Ireland

- - - - -

1884 - 1885   Herman Hinsdale Shook, Rev.
Pastor (and lawyer)
b. Feb. 28, 1846, Napanoch, Ulster Co. NY, son of Henry G. Shook and Olivia Maria Dexter
d. August 11, 1916, Oyster Bay, NY
m. July 1872, Manhattan, Annie Elisabeth Knight, dau. of Charles Knight and Jane Little

--"Shook, Herman H. b. Napanoch, NY, Feb. 28, 1846. lic. by N. Cl. L.I., Nov 12, 1883, ord. by N. Cl. L.I. Feb. 5, 1902 ; S.S. at Fairfield, Oct 1884 - Jan 1885, at West New Hempstead Ap-Sept 1885 at Greenwood Heights, May 1893 -Ap 1894, at Cold Spring, June 1895-July 1896, at Canajoharie, Oct-Dec 1897, supplying churches almost weekly at other times; pastor Locust Valley 1902-1905 A lawyer .d Aug. 11, 1916. Min Gen Syn 1917" (*Manual of the Reformed Church in America 1628-1922.* Charles E. Corwin. 1922)

--"HERMAN HINSDALE SHOOK. son of Henry G Shook and Olivia Maria Dexter his wife born February 28 1846 married July 25 1872 Annie E Knight Children 1983 i BERTHA KNIGHT born Apr 22 1873 married July 4 1896 Edgar S Knapp 1984 ii ELLA MAY born Dec 27 1880 died May 18 1891 1985 iii EDNA LOUISA born Dec 2 1884"

(*Hinsdale Genealogy*. H. C. Andrew, S. C. Hinsdale, A. L. Holman. Lombard, IL.1906)

--1850 Census: Wawarsing, Ulster Co. NY: Henry D. Shook, age 32, b. NY farmer; Mariah, age 30; "Beviese" son, age 7 b. NY; Herman, age 4, b. NY
--1860 Census: Brooklyn, Kings Co. NY: Henry "Shuck" age 46 b. NY; Olivia, age 45 b. CT; Revere, age 18 b. NY; Herman, age 14, b. NY
--1860 Census: 16 Wd. NYC: Chas. Knight, age 47 b. NY, cabinet mkr.; Jane, age 37 b. England; Chas. age 19 b. NY, upholstering; Annie age 17 b. NY; Saml. age 15 b. NY; Wm. age 13 b. NY
--1880 Census: Brooklyn Kings Co. NY: Herman Shook, age 34, b. NY, lawyer; Anna, age 34, b. NY, father NY, mother England; Bertha, age 7 dau. b. NY; Henry age 60, boarder, b. NY, parents b. Holland, commission merchant; Maria age 65 b. CT, parents b. C 'widow' "mother grand"
--1900 Census: 3Wd. Brooklyn, Kings Co. NY: Edgar S. Knapp age 27 b. Nov. 1872 NY, dealer; Bertha Knapp age 27 b. Apr. 1873 NY; Herman H. Shook, age 54, b. May 1846 NY, father-in-law, lawyer; Annie Shook, age 55, b. June 1846, mother-in-law; Edna Shook, age 16, b. Jan 1884 NY, sister-in-law; 1 servant
--1910 Oyster Bay, Nassau Co. NY: H. Herman Shook age 64 b. NY, father b. NY, mother b. CT, lawyer; E. Ann, age 64, b. NY, father b. NY, mother b. England

- - - - -

1885 - 1886   Benjamin Cory Miller, Rev.
               A.B., Rutgers College, 1872
               A.M.New Brunswick Theological Sem. 1875
               b. Jan. 22, 1850, Lima, Indiana son of
               Augustus Miller and Mary Dodge
               d. aft. 1925, North Hempstead, NY

m. March 1884, at Brooklyn, Mary Sutton, b. Dec. 1852; dau. of James Sutton and Esther ...

"BENJAMIN CORY MILLER. Central Islip, Long Island. Son of Augustus Miller, a carpenter, and Mary Dodge. Born January 22, 1850, near Lima, LaGrange County, Indiana. Lived in Indiana and Newark, N. J., till settled as pastor. Prepared for college at Newark High School. Licensed by Classis of Newark 1875. Ordained by Classis of Green 1875. Pastor of Reformed Churches : Roxbury, N. Y., 1875-1881 ; Gilboa, N. Y.. 1884-1885; Fairfield, N. J., 1885-1886; Franklin, N. J., 1886-1889; White House, N. J., 1890-1895. Pastor of Methodist-Episcopal Churches:New York East Conference; Good Ground, L. I., 1897; Stony Brook, 1898; Good Ground, 1899; Oceanside, 1900; Cannon and South Wilton, Conn., 1901 ; Cutchogue, L. I., 1902; East Norwich, 1903-1904; Port Chester, N. Y., King Street, 1905; Nichols, Conn., 1906; Clinton, 1907-1908; Middlebury, 1909-1910; East Meadow, L. I., 191 1 ; Westbury, 1912; Mattetuck and Jamesport, 1913 ; Banton and Woodville, Conn., 1914-1915; South Britain and Southbury, 1916; Central Islip and Hauppauge, L. I., 1917. Degrees: A.B. 1872, A.M. 1875, Rutgers. In Politics, Independent. Married March 26th, 1884, Brooklyn, N. Y., Mary Sutton, daughter of James and Esther Sutton. Children: Esther Hope, born January 20th, 1890; Ruth Theodora, born October 12th, 1893." (*Class of 1872. Rutgers College. p.8*)

--1850 Census: Newberry, LaGrange Co. IN: Benj. Hyer, age 32, cabinet maker; Almira Hyer, age 31; Hannah Hyer, age 9; Augustus Miller, age 26, carpenter; Mary Miller, age 21; Benjamin Miller, age 4 months (birthplaces not listed)
--1860 Census: Newark, Essex Co., NJ: Benj. C. Miller, age 54, Secy life ins. co.; Sarah,(nee Doremus?) age (50); Phebe J. Vansickle, (dau.)age 29; Peter D. Vansickel, age 30, patent roofer; Benj. Vansickel, age 2; Benj. C. Miller, Jr., (neph?) age 10; Hanah E. Miller, age 35; all b. "New Jersey"
--1870 Census:4Wd, Newark, Essex Co., NJ: Benj. C. Miller, age 60 b. NJ, Treas. (Mutual Life) Insurance Co.; Sarah, age 60 b. NJ; Benj. C. Miller, Jr., age 20, b. Indiana, student; also, P. D. and Phebe Van Sickle family.
--1900 Census: Hempstead, Nassau Co. NY: Benjamin C. Miller, b. Jan. 1850 Indiana, father NY, mother IN,

clergyman; Mary S., b. Dec. 1852 NY, parents b. England;
Esther H. b. Jan 1890 NJ; Ruth T. b. Oct. 1893 NJ
--1910 Census: Middlebury, New Haven Co., CT:
Benjammin C. Miller, age 60 b. IN, Methodist clergyman;
Mary S., age 57 b. NY; Esther H., age 19 b. NJ; Ruth L., age 16 b. NJ
--1920 Census: North Hempstead, NY: Ernest H. Anscomb, age 28 b. MA, statistician; Ruth T. Anscomb, b. NJ;
Benjamin C. Miller, age 69, father-in-law b. IN, father b. NJ, mother b. IN, no occup.; Mary S. Miller, age 65, mother-in-law b. NY, parents b. England

- - - - -

1886 - 1889   Louis* (Lewis) John Lockwood, Rev.
              A. M. Rutgers College 1875
              New Brunswick Theol. Seminary 1878
              b. Dec. 6, 1850, New Windsor, Orange Co., New York; son of David Conger Lockwood and Clarissa Jane Horton; nephew of the Rev. Lewis Conger Lockwood
              d. March 23 1902
              m. June 13, 1877, Mary A. Wyckoff, dau. of Rev. Cornelius Wyckoff and Ellen Voorhees Manley. She was born 1853; d. 1916
              bur. First Ref. Ch. Cem., New Brunswick

--"Lockwood, Louis John. b at New Windsor NY, Dec, 6 1850; Rutgers College 1875; New Brunswick Seminary, 1878; licensed Classis of N.Brunswick; Hurley, Jan 1879-80 ;Highlands NY Presb 1880-86; Fairfield NJ 1886-1889; without charge; d. March 23 1903". (*Min Gen Syn* 1903)

"An Insane Clergyman: The Rev. Lewis Lockwood, Pastor of the Reformed Church at Fairfield, is confined in the county asylum suffering with dementia. On Sunday night he tried to kill his wife and four children. Mrs. Lockwood fled to a neighbor's. Her husband set fire to the house and then jumped from a second-story window. He is 35 years of age."

--(*The New York Times*. January 23, 1889)

--1855 NY State Census: New Windsor, Orange Co. NY: David C. Lockwood, age 50 b. Orange Co., farmer; Clarissa age 46; Susan M., age 22; Sarah 19; Samuel 17; Catherine 15; Abby 13; Elias 11; Margaret age 8; Lewis, age 4; all b. Orange Co., NY

--1855 NY Census: Rochester, Ulster Co., NY: Revd. Cornelius Wykoff, age 45; Ellen, age 43; DeWitt B., age 13; Jane E., age 8; Ellen E., age 6; Mary Ann, age 2; all b. NY

--1860 Census: New Windsor, Orange Co. NY: David C. Lockwood, age 53, farmer; Clarry C., 49; Susan 28; Charles 26; Sarah 24; Catherine 22; Samuel 21; Abby 19; Elias 16; Margaret, age 12; 'Alonzo' (Lewis) age 9

--1870 Census: New Brunswick, Middlesex Co. NJ: Ellen F. Wykoff, age 58 b. NJ, $20,000 real estate $11,000 personal; Mary A., age 17, b. NY

--1880 Census: Hurley Twp., Ulster Co., NY: Louis J. Lockwood, age 28, b. NY, minister; Mary A., wife, age 27, b. NY; Jennie W., age 1, b. NY; Charles D., age 2 mos. b. NY; Ellen V. Wyckoff, age 68, mother-in-law, widow, b. NJ; 1 servant

--1900 Census: New Brunswick, Middlesex Co., NJ: Mary Lockwood, age 47 b. March 1853, NY, parents b. NJ, m. 23 yrs. 5 born 3 living; Jennie, age 21, v. June 1878 NJ, parents NY, ; Cornelius D., age 17, b. June 1882, b. NY, student; Edwin B., age 13, b. March 1887 b. NY; Geretta J. Bevier, cousin, age 46, b. July 1833, NY, father NY, mother NJ, kindergarten teacher

--1903 New Brunswick City Directory: Mrs. M. A. Lockwood, 112 Bayard St.

--1910 Census: New Brunswick, Middlesex Co., NJ: Mary A. Lockwood, age 54, widow, 5 born 2 living, b. NY, own income; Jeanette J., age 31, b. NJ; Edwin B., age 23, b. NY, clerk in music store;

--1913 New Brunswick City Directory: Edwin B. Lockwood; Jeanette Lockwood; Mary, widow of Lewis J. Lockwood; 112 Bayard St.

- - - - -

1890 - 1892   William Edward Bogardus, Rev.
Served:Civil War;Chaplin 19 NY Vol. Inf.
A.B. Rutgers College 1860
A.M. New Brunswick Theological Sem. 1863
b. June 30, 1834, Cohoes, Albany Co. NY, son of Rev. Cornelius Bogardus and Catharine E. Duryee
d. January 5, 1908, Brookdale, Essex Co., NJ
m. abt. 1872, Rebecca Meredith, b. 1847, Pughtown, PA, dau. of Dr. Stephen M. Meredith of Chester Co., PA

--"Bloomfield, NJ. Jan 5 --The Rev. William E. Bogardus, pastor of the Dutch Reformed Church in the Brookdale section for fifteen years, died at the parsonage in Bellevue Avenue this morning, after an illness of several weeks. He was born in Cohoes, N.Y., seventy-three years ago, and was a son of the late Rev. Cornelius Bogardus. In 1860 he entered the Theological Seminary at Rutgers College. Graduating in 1863, he accepted a call to the Middleburg, N.Y., Reformed Church. In later years he hald pastorates in Hawthorne, Cuddlebackville and Pleaasant Plains, NY: Saddle River, Oakland, and Fairfield, NJ. For a brief period he was a chaplain during the Civil War, with a Newburg, NY regiment. He was a direct descendant of Everardus Borgardus, who came to this country in the year 1622.

"Mr. Bogardus founded the Montclair Heights Reformed Church, and was the oldest member of the Newark classis. He is survived by a widow, who is a daughter of Dr. Stephen M. Meredith of Reading, Penn.

"The Brookdale Dutch Reformed Church was organized 105 years ago, Mr. Bogardus being the twelfth pastor." (*The New York Times.* January 6, 1908)

--"WILLIAM EDWARD BOGARDUS. AB 1860; AM 1863; Born Cohoes, NY June 30, 1834; Prepared at Franklin's Delaware Institute; Salutatorian at Rutgers 1858-1859; Editor of Rutgers College Quarterly

1862; Chaplain of 19th New York Volunteer Infantry 1863; Graduated from Theological Seminary of Rutgers College; Held following pastorates Hawthorne, Cuddebackville and Pleasant Plains NY; Saddle River, Oakland and Fairfield, NJ; Sermon on President Lincoln's Assasination; Contributor to the Press; Clergyman; brother of Francis McK Bogardus Epsilon 1857; Died Jan 8 1908. Last address Brookdale NJ" (*Delta Phi Catalogue 1827-1907*)

--1850 Census: Gilboa, Schoharie Co. NY: Cornelius Bogardus, age 65 clergyman; Catherine E., age 52; Ephraim B., age 19, student; William E., age 16, b. NY, student; Francis, age 14; Henrietta, age 7; all b. NY
--1870 Census: Newburgh, Orange Co. NY: Rebecca Meredith, age 22 b. PA, school teaching (adj. to John Bogardus, age 35, b. NY, school teaching)
--1880 Census: Washington Twp., Bergen Co. NJ: W. E. Bogardus, age 45, b. NY, minister Ref. Church; Rebecca, age 37 b. PA, parents b. PA
--1900 Census: Bloomfield, Essex Co. NJ: William Bogardus, age 66, b. June 1834 b. NY, parents b. NY, m.28 years, clergyman; Rebecca age 53 b. June 1847 PA, parents b. PA, 0 born 0 living
--1922: Arv. NY from Bermuda: Rebecca Bogardus, age 75, wid. b. 1847 Pughtown, PA; res. Skippack, PA.

- - - - -

1893 - 1895   John Woodruff Conklin, Rev.
A.M.Rutgers College 1874
Grad. New Brunswick Theo. Seminary 1876
b. December 30, 1851, Montville, NJ
son of Nathaniel Conklin and Elizabeth J. Woodruff
d. September 12, 1909, Newark, NJ
m. 1880, Elizabeth Jane Lindsley,b. 1852, Denville, NJ, dau. of Francis Lindsley and Elizabeth Sherman. She d. Sept. 22, 1937 Henderson Co., North Carolina

--"John Woodruff Conklin, Metuchen NJ. Born at Montville NJ, Dec 30 1851; Clergyman; RCA Missionary to India 1881-90; Field Secretary Board of Foreign Missions 1901-07; AM Rutgers 1874; NB Sem 1876; Died Sept 12 1909" (*Catalogue of Officers and Alumni of Rutgers College.* Trenton 1916)

--"John Woodruff Conklin, clergyman, was born in Montville, N. J., Dec. 30, 1851; son of Nathaniel and Elizabeth J. (Woodruff) Conklin; and grandson of Stephen and Catherine (Tailor) Conklin, and of Archibald and Catherine (Johnson) Woodruff. His first American ancestor, Ananias Conklin, emigrated from Nottingham, England, about 1636 and settled in Salem, Mass., where he was the first manufacturer of glass in America. He afterward removed to Easthampton, L. I., N.Y. John W. Conklin was prepared for college at the Newark (N. J.) academy and was graduated from Rutgers college in 1871. He entered the New Brunswick (N. J.) theological seminary of the Reformed church in America and was graduated in 1876. He engaged in preaching, 1876-80; was a missionary in the Arcot mission, India, 1881-90; acting secretary of the Board of foreign missions, 1890-92; and in 1895 he became a teacher in the Bible Normal college at Springfield, Mass. He was married in 1880 to Elizabeth Jane Lindsley. Rutgers college conferred upon him the degree of A.M. in course in 1874."(*Twentieth Century Biographical Dictionary of Notable Americans*, Johnson, Rossiter, editor)

--1860 Census: Pequannock, Morris Co. NJ: Nathaniel Conklin, age 37 b. Somerset Co., Ref. Dutch Clergyman; Elizabeth J., age 32, b. Newark; John W., age 8 b. Morris Co.; 4 other children
--1870 Census: Montville Twp., Morris Co., NJ: Nathaniel Conklin, age 47 b. NJ, minister of the Gospel; Elizabeth J., age 42; John W., age 18; 6 other children; all b. NJ
--1880 Census: Boonton, Morris Co. NJ: John W. Conklin, age 28 b. NJ minister of the Gospel, Ref. Dutch Church
--1900 Census: Springfield, Hampden Co. MA: John W. Conklin b. Dec. 1895 m.20 yr, b. NJ, clergyman; Elizabeth b. Dec. 1852 NJ; Elsie E., b. Feb. 1885, India; Archibald, b. Aug. 1886, India; Robert b. March 1891 NJ; Sherman b. June 1894 NJ

--1910 Census: Newark, Essex Co. NJ: Elizabeth J. Conklin, age 57,wid, sister-in-law,b. NJ, editor of magazine; Elizabeth W., age 25, b. India, school teacher; Archibald L., age 23, b. India, acct. at r.r. office; Robert H. L. age 19 b. NJ; Sherman L., age 16, b. NJ; at res. of Archibald W. Conklin.

- - - - -

1895 - 1896 George Hewson Peeke, Rev.
Grad. Rutgers College 1857
Grad. New Brunswick Theo. Seminary 1860
b. March 18, 1833, Rotterdam, Schenectady Co., NY, son of Christopher H. Peeke and Hester C. Mabie
d. Dec. 20, 1915, Sandusky, Ohio
m. 1860 Margaret Bloodgood Peck, b. Apr.1838 dau. of Garry Peck; she d. Nov. 1908; bur. Pomona, Tennesee

--"Peeke, Geo. H., (brother of Rev. A. P. Peeke,) R.C. 1857, N.B.S. 1860, lic. Cl. Schenectady; Miss, at South Bend, Ind., 1860-61, Glenville, 1st, 1861-63, Greenpoint, 1863-65, Jersey City, 1st, 1865-69, Davenport, 1869-72, Owasco, 1872-75 (Presbyt.)." (*Manual of the Ref. Ch. in America 1728-1902*)

--"His active ministry covered fifty-five years with prominent churches in Brooklyn, New York, Jersey City, New Jersey, Chicago, Illinois, Davenport, Iowa, Cleveland, Ohio, and Sandusky. He had great pulpit ability and more than average success as a pastor with a record covering a long pastorate, which few ministers have obtained."
(*A Standard History of Erie Co. OH.* Vol 1, p.464)

--"Margaret Bloodgood Peeke was the daughter of Mr. and Mrs. Garry Peck. She was born in Mechanicsville, New York on April 8, (1838). In 1860, Margaret married Rev. George H. Peeke, a Protestant minister. Rev. and Mrs. Peeke settled in Sandusky in 1883, where George served as the minister of the Congregational Church. Rev. Peeke later served a congregation in Cleveland as well. Rev. and Mrs. Peeke had six children, one of whom was well known Sandusky lawyer and local history author, Hewson L. Peeke. Hewson L. Peeke wrote in his book, A *Standard*

History of Erie County, about his mother, "She had a remarkably bright mind and wonderful conversational ability."
"Robert H. Stockman wrote in his book *The Baha'i Faith in America*, that while Margaret B. Peeke had been raised as a strong Protestant church member, her interests changed, and she became a Martinist. Martinism is a form of mystical Christianity. Margaret was the author of *Born of Flame, Numbers and Letters: or The Thirty-Two Paths of Wisdom*, and *Zenia the Vestal*."

--1850 Census: Rotterdam, Schenectady Co. NY:
Christopher Y. 'Leek', age 63 farmer; Hester, age 51; George, age 17, school teacher; 5 other children; all b. NY
--1850 Census: Richmond Twp., Tioga Co. PA; G. M. Peck, age 52 b. CT, farmer; M. B., age 51 b. CT; Margaret, age 13, b. NY
--1880 Census: Chicago, Cook Co. IL: George H. Peeke, age 47 b. NY, clergyman; Margaret B. age 42 b. NY, authoress; Hewson L., age 19 b. Ind.; Erastus C. B. age 15 b. NY; Grace A., age 11, b. NJ
--1900 Census: Perkins Twp., Erie Co. OH: George H. Peeke, b. Mar 1833. m. 40 yr b. NY minister; Margaret B. b. Apr. 1835, NY, father CT, mother NY, 6 born 2 living; Hewson S., son b. Apr. 1861, div. b. IN, parents b NY
--1910 Census: Perkins, Erie Co. OH: George H. Luke" age 77, widower, b. NY, own income; Hewson "Luke" age 49, divorced, b. Indiana, lawyer; 2 boarders(?)

- - - - -

1897 - 1902   Otto Leopold Frederick Mohn, Rev. D.D.
               Grad. Collegiate School, New York
               A.M. Rutgers College 1894
               Grad. New Brunswick Theo. Sem. 1897
               Rutgers College Letterman 1891- 1897
               b. February 1, 1874, NJ, Hoboken, NJ, son of Rev. Leopold Mohn,D.D. and Cornelia Huber
               d. aft. 1940

m. June 1896, Beverly, Burlington Co. NJ.
Rebecca Hovey Allen, b. Apr.6, 1875 dau. of
John Casdorp Allen and Jane Elizabeth Hovey

"OTTO LEOPOLD FREDRICK MOHN AB 1894 AM 1897 Born Hoboken NJ Feb 1 1874 Prepared at Collegiate School New York City Junior Orator Senior Orator 1897-1902 Pastor of The Reformed Church of Fairfield NJ 1902-1904 Pastor of The Greenville Reformed Church Jersey City NJ 1904-1907 Asst Pastor of The Marble Collegiate Church New York 1907 Pastor at Warsaw NY Ministry Warsaw Wyoming Co NY" (*Delta Phi Catalogue. 1827-1907*)

"Mohn, Otto L. F. (son of Leopold Mohn), b. Hoboken, N.J., Feb. 1, 1874; Rutgers C. 1894, N.B.S. 1897, lic. Cl. Bergen; Fairfield, 1897-1902, Greenville, Jersey City, 1902" (*Manual of the Reformed Church in America.* Corwin. 1902)

--1880 Census: Hoboken, Hudson Co. NJ: Leopold Mohn, age 46, b. Prussia, clergyman; Cornelia, age 43, b. NJ, parents b. Prussia; August age 13 b. NJ; Otto, age 6 b. NJ; Martha, age 2 b. NJ; Winifred, age 9 mos. b. NJ
--1900 Census: Caldwell Twp., Essex Co., NJ: Otto L. J. Mohn, b. Feb. 1873, m.3 yr b. NJ, parents b. Germany, minister; Rebecca H., b. June 1874 NJ, parents b. NJ; Elizabeth A., age 9 months b. Aug. 1899, b. NJ
--1920 Census: Dist 2, Richmond Co. Staten Island, NY: Otto L. Mohn, age 45 b. NJ, clergyman; Rebecca, age 44 b. NJ; Elizabeth, age 20 b. NJ; Rebecca, age 18 b. NJ; John Allen, age 15 b. NY; Halchen W., dau., age 12, b. NY
--1930 Census: Asbury Park, Monmouth Co. NJ: Otto L. F. Mohn, age 56, b. NJ, father b. Germany, mother b. NJ, pastor at church; Rebecca H. A., age 54, b. NJ, father b. PA, mother b. MA; John A., age 25, b. NY, parents NJ, telephone clerk

- - - - -

Interments
(Chronological Order)
Fairfield Reformed Church Cemetery

1829 June	Thomas Speer
1831 Dec.	Elizabeth Van Ness, wife of Isaac J. Van Wart
1832 Jan.	David, child of Thomas Van Ness
1832 March	John, son of John T. Speer
1832 August	James Glaen Ogilvie, Pastor (thrown from horse)
1832 August	Mariah Speer, wife of William Van Ness
1832 December	Sarah, dau. of Jacob S. Van Ness
1833 January	Christopher Sindle
1833 June	James, son of Thomas H. Stagg
1834 February	Sarah, wife of Josiah Francisco
1834 April	John R. Van Ness
1834 April	Sarah Mandeville
1834 November	William Van Ness
1835 March	Albert B., son of Samuel Dey
1835 June	Sarah, child of Peter Francisco
1835 August 8	Margaret, wife of Cornelius Dey
1835 August 25	Ralph Manderville
1835 August 24	Daniel Manderville
1835 December	William, child of Thomas Van Ness
1836 February	Polly Williams, wife of John Kiersted, Esq.
1836 July	Robart Van Ness
1836 July	Hester Francisco, wife of Henry H. Van Ness
1836 October	Mary Jacobus, wife of Francis C. Post
1836 December	Henry E. Van Ness
1837 May	Moses Dey
1837 November	Sophia, dau. of Thomas J. Kiersted

1838 February	Isaac Kent
1838 April	David Pier
1838 June	Thomas E., son of Ralph Jacobus
1838 August	Major Richard Speer
1839 February	Jemima, wife of J. Schoonmaker
1839 April	Stephen Cole (barn fire)
1840 March	Mary Ann, dau. of Isaac Riker
1840 April	Sarah Ellen, dau. of Thomas Van Ness
1840 May	James Theodore, son of Ogden Hall
1840 July	Catherine, dau. of Samuel Riker
1841 April	Elizabeth O., dau. of T. T. Speer
1841 June	Eleanor, child of Nicolas Bush
1841 December	Mary Catherine, dau. of Thomas H. Stagg
1841 December	Sarah, wife of Major Richard Speer
1842 November	Josiah Francisco
1842 December	Catherine, wife of Isaac Riker
1843 January	Isaac F., child of Francis Pier
1843, November	Elizabeth, child of Job Doremus
1844 January	Sarah Van Ness, wife of Henry H. Riker
1844 March	Abraham Blauvelt, son of Thomas H. Stagg
1844 March	Martha, wife of Henry Colyer
1844 April	Leah Ann, dau. of Thomas H. Stagg
1844 May	James A. Van Duyne
1844 August	Lucinda, wife of Peter Sandford
1844 October	Daniel Deeths
1844 October	Ann Dye, widow of Hassell Hopper
1844 November 11	Daniel D., son of Daniel Deeths
1844 November 15	Jacob Eugene, son of John A. Van Orden
1845 February	Phebe Ann, dau. of Thomas Van Ness
1845 February	Ellen, wife of David Van Ness
1845 June	Maria L., wife of Levi Carman
1845 August	Hester Dods, wife of David Pier
1845 September	Maria E., child of Nicholas Bush

1845 November	John Nelson, son of William Vanderhoof
1845 December	Eliza M., wife of John A. Van Orden
1846 October	Maria, wife of Thomas Speer
1846 November	George Wesson Carman
1847 April	Mary C., dau. of Cornelius Jacobus
1847 June	Sarah, wife of John J. Jacobus
1847 July	William A. Van Ness
1847 July	Jane Dey, wife of Simeon Doremus
1847 July	Mary, wife of James Peer
1847 September 12	George, child of Christopher Sindle
1847 September 17	Catherine, child of Christopher Sindle
1847 October 11	Peter, child of Francis Van Ness
1847 December	Aaron Van Ness
1848 January	John H. Mandeville
1848 April	Infant son of Cornelius H. Post
1848 July	Mary, dau. of John I. Quick
1848 July	Margaret Cadmus, wife of Henry T. Van Ness
1848 September	James Bentley, child of Francis Van Ness
1848 December	Ellen Ann, child of Henry Stanley
1849 June	Maria, wife of Andrew Francisco
1849 June	Isaac R., son of John Vreeland
1849 July	William Mead
1849 August	Amarintha, dau. of Ezra Colyer
1849 August 1	Ann Amelia, dau. of James Van Ness
1849 August 7	Catherine Van Houten, wife of James Van Ness
1849 August 13	Jean Welsh, wife of Hugh McCormick
1849 September	Sarah, wife of Ezra Colyer
1849 September	Samuel, child of Isaac J. Van Ness
1849 September 11	Thos. Henry, child of Francis Van Ness
1850 March	Sarah, wife of David Pier
1850 March	Almira A., dau. of Wm. Van Ness

1850 July	Susan Eliza Bone, wife of Daniel Deeths
1850 August	Emarintha, child of Henry Stanley
1850 September	Henry Colyer
1850 November	John J. Jacobus
1850 December	Emma L. child of Wm. B. Speer
1851 January 29	David H., child of Wm. Hamma
1851 February	John A. Kiersted, Esq.
1851 February	David Van Ness
1851 March	Mary, wife of Cornelius van Ness
1851 March	Elizabeth, wife of David Pier
1851 April	Francis C. Post
1851 August	John, son of William Hamma
1851 September	Julia Speer
1851 October	Emma M. Speer, dau. of Wm. Speer
1851 December	Oscar, child of Wm. B. Speer
1852 January	Newton Raymond, son of John T. Budd
1852 March	Henry Francisco
1852 April	Sarah Riker, wife of Benj. Canfield
1852 June	Esther Cook
1852 August	James E. How, great grandson of Esther Cook
1852 October	William, child of John Van Pelt
1852 October	Hugh McCormick
1853 January	Andrew Francisco
1853 February	Mary Jacobus, wife of Henry I. Mandeville
1853 May	John Riker
1853 May	Martha Louisa Van Duyne
1853 June	Sarah, wife of John I. Pier
1853 October	Emeline, child of William S. Jacobus
1853 December	Martyntje Witte, wife of Cs. Mastenbrock
1854 April	Caroline Cole
1854 April	John E. Van Ness
1854 April	Charles H., child of Isaac J. Van Ness

1854 May 21	John Zeliff (carriage accident)
1854 May 21	Jane Van Ness, wife of John Zeliff (carriage accident)
1854 June	Henry H. Riker
1854 July	Rachel J., child of Francis Pier
1854 August	Eliza Ann, wife of Peter Jacobus
1854 September	Aaron W. Budd
1855 January	Anna Lawrence
1855 January	Peter Francisco
1855 February	Ann Smith, wife of John Riker
1855 March	Aaron W. Kiersted
1855 April	Thomas R. Morrell
1855 April	Sarah, wife of Cornelius I. Van Ness
1855 June	Job, child of Peter D. Van Duyne
1855 July	Benjamin H. Bone
1855 July	Matilda Budd
1855 October	Margaret Bush, wife of Henry H. Van Ness
1855 October	Mary Jane, dau. of John I. Kent
1855 December	Margaret Doremus, wife of Garret Van Ness
1855 December	Caroline Smith, wife of Evert H. Van Ness
1856	Emma Maria, child of Nicholas Bush
1856 January 12	Ann Eliza Shurte, wife of Wm. C. Stratton
1856 January 23	Elizabeth, child of Wm. C. Stratton
1856 February	Emma, child of John Van Pelt
1856 June	William Van Ness
1856 November	William, son of Thos. H. Morrell
1856 September 8	Ann Isabelle, child of Wm. C. Stratton
1856 September 21	Caroline, child of Wm. C. Stratton
1856 December	Esther Cook, child of John H. Van Ness
1857 July	Josephine, dau. of Wm. Bush
1858 March	Agnes Bernard, child of John H. Van Ness

1858 April	Rachel Van Ness, wife of Job Doremus
1858 May	John A. Kussmaul
1858 June	Nelly Sandford
1858 July	Josiah, child of Peter Francisco
1859 January	Aaron Budd
1859 May	Infant son of Abraham Garabrant
1859 May	William B. Speer
1859 June	David Shurte
1860 January	Henry T. Van Ness
1860 Feburary	Webster T. Speer
1860 April	Lydia, wife of Benj. H. Bone
1860 May	James M., son of John Dulhagen
1860 May	John I. Pier
1861 January 25	Harriet, dau. of Jacob Jacobus
1861 February	Elizabeth, wife of Francis Pier
1861 April	Lucinda, wife of Zenas C. Speer
1861 June	Nancy Lockwood, wife of Barney Budd
1861 June	Francis Pier
1861 August 25	Seth, son of Peter D. Van Duyne
1861 August 23	Sarah Agnes, child of Isaac H. Riker
1861 October	Serna Luina, wife of Abrham L. Romaine
1861 December	Zillah, dau. of Henry Francisco
1862 January	Sarah Ann, dau. of David Pier
1862 February	Ephraim, child of Isaac H. Riker
1862 April	Wm. Webster, child of Henry Stanley
1862 April	Julia Mandeville
1862 May	Emily, dau. of Peter Bowman
1862 July	Peter Francisco
1862 July	Jotham Jacobus
1862 August	Evert H. van Ness
1863 March	Ira, child of Abraham Garabrant
1863 June	Earnest B., child of Henry Vail
1863 September	Rhoda Ann, child of Israel Budd
1863 October	Ezra Stiles Ely, deacon

1863 November	Mary Speer, wife of Joseph C. Baldwin
1864, January 18	Charles, child of John Van Pelt
1864, February 11	Everdear, child of John Van Pelt
1864 February 16	Nancy Van Ness
1864 February 21	Jane M. Courter, wife of Wm. B. Speer
1864 February 27	Frank, child of Henry Stanley
1864 March	Frank L. son of Richard T. Budd
1864 May	Joseph Condit Baldwin
1864 September	Thomas M. Speer
1864 September	John R. Van Ness, son of Cornelius I.
1864 September	David Boyd
1864 November	Thomas H. Stagg
1864 November	Caroline, wife of John T. Speer
1865 February	John T. Speer
1865 April	Samuel, child of Peter D. Van Duyne
1865 May	Benjamin Canfield
1865 June	William C., son of Peter Jacobus
1865 June	James C. Stagg
1865 August	Catherine E. Neafie, wife of George Van Ness
1865 August	Mary Ann Kiersted, wife of John Dulhagen
1865 September	Simeon Doremus
1865 October	Cornelius Dey
1865 December	Mary Eliza, child of Israel Budd
1866 January	Melva E., child of Henry Vail
1866 February	James F., son of Henry H. Van Houten
1866 March	Henry Clifford, child of Francis Van Ness
1866 June	Sophia D., wife of John Kussmaul
1866 October	Esther C., dau. of Nicolas Van Duyne
1867 February	Catherine, wife of Israel Budd
1867 April	William H. Zeliff
1867 June	Henry H. Van Ness
1867 August	Barney Budd

1867 December	Mary L Stagg
1868 April	Judson P., son of Bethuel Goodrich
1868 June	James O. Jacobus
1868 June	Mary A. Vanderhoof, wife of Peter Slingerland
1868 October	Rachel Dey, wife of Garrett Jacobus
1868 December	Henry Van Duyne
1868 December	James Bowman
1869 March 7	Malinda P., wife of Francis Van Ness
1869 March 18	Nettie A., dau. of Robert Van Ness
1869 April 16	Thos. Lester, child of Francis Van Ness
1869 May	Cornelius R. Jacobus
1869 September	John B. Vail
1869 September	Casiah Sindle, wife of Isaac Kent
1870 April	Peter Sanford/Sandford
1870 May	Cassie J., wife of Wilder Fairbanks
1870 May	Kate Mandeville
1870 July	Mary Elizabeth, wife of Thomas McCord
1870 October	Elizabeth W. Wilson, wife of James G. Ogilvie
1870 November 17	Carrie, child of Isaac J. Van Ness
1870 November 24	Rachel, wife of Cornelius Dey
1870 November 27	Maria, wife of Jacob Jacobus; wife of Henry Francisco
1870 November 28	Sarah E. Ryerson, wife of George Kent
1871 February	Cornelius I. Van Ness
1871 February	Jane Boyd
1871 February	Eliza Dods, wife of Peter F. Ryerson
1871 March	Louisa, dau. of Henry Francisco
1871 April	Anthony Ogilvie
1871 May	Isaac, son of Cornelius I. Van Ness
1871 October	Jennie Van Ness, wife of John W. Ackerman
1872 February	Peter Speer

1872 May	Peter D. Van Duyne
1872 May	George Sindle
1872 August	Obadiah Riker
1872 November	Tunis T. Speer
1873 January	Rebecca, wife of John J. Francisco
1873 March	Rachel Speer
1873 March 12	Marcus Francisco
1873 March 12	Infant child of Marcus Francisco
1873 April	John R. Van Ness
1873 May	Henry S. Doremus
1873 June	Harriet Sandford, wife of Peter Speer
1873 July	Annie R., infant of Zenas E. Jacobus
1873 August	Catherine Doremus, widow of Jas. A. Van Duyne
1873 September	Adeliah A., wife of Wm. Van Wert
1873 November	William I. Van Ness
1873 December	Welson, child of Benj. Van Ness
1874 July	Elizabeth R., wife of John L. Wilson
1874 October	John A., son of Ralph Jacobus
1874 October	Isaac Riker
1874 December	Mary, wife of Jacob Osborne
1875 February	Ralph Jacobus
1875 February	Robert L. Stagg
1875 February	Sarah Jacobus, wife of Isaac Van Ness
1875 March	Eliza Kiersted, wife of Cornelius A. Vanderhoof
1875 April	Mary E., child of Henry Stanley
1875 April	Mary L., dau. of Aaron E. Stagg
1875 May	Sarah Jane, wife of Abraham A. Garrabrant
1875 September	Phebe Ann Speer, wife of Henry I. Van Ness
1875 December	John Vreeland
1876 September	James M. Ashman
1877 March	John A. Romaine
1877 March	Josiah Speer
1877 July	Emma May Zeliff

1879 January	Maria M., wife of James M. Ashman
1879 January	Abraham Zeek
1879 April	Simon S. Van Ness
1879 April	Elizabeth Mandeville
1879 July	Martha, wife of Ralph A. Romaine
1879 September	George S., son of Peter J. Zeliff
1879 October	Mary Jane, wife of John Vreeland, Jr.
1879 November	Andrew, son of Andrew McCord
1879 November	Fannie S. Tuers, widow of Aaron Budd
1880 April	Sarah E. Van Ness, wife of Cornelius V. Bush
1880 April	John J. Francisco
1880 May	David Pier
1880 July	Sarah Ann, widow of John Vail
1880 August	Marthe Vincent, wife of Thomas Van Ness
1881 March	Lizzie, child of Benj. Van Van Ness
1881 April	Maria, wife of Henry R. Van Ness
1881 May	Milton Sindle
1881 November	Job Doremus
1881 November	Sarah E. Springsteen, wife of Geo. E. Speer
1882 April	Emeline Vanderhoof, wife of Thomas C. Jacobus
1882 June	Harriet Jacobus, wife of C. D. Van Ness
(1882 August)	Robert Van Ness
1882 December	George L. Shackleton
1882 December	Charlotte Pearce, wife of Wm. Bush
1883 March	Rachel Van Ness, wife of Wm. Mead
1883 April	John R. Dey
1884 February	Rachel Van Ness, wife of Nicholas Van Duyne
1884 February	Peter Jacobus
1884 February	Mary E. Riker, wife of Wilber E. Woodruff

1884 March	Matilda Hill, wife of Geo. C. Ryerson
1884 May	William S. Jacobus
1884 June	Mamie E., dau. of Wilder Fairbanks
1884 August	Nicholas Bush
1884 December	Fanny Van Houten, wife of Thomas H. Stagg
1885 January 10	Charles W., son of Peter S. Sindle
1885 January 27	Clyde C., child of Isaac Peer
1885 January 29	Henry Dey
1885 January 31	Charles V., child of Isaac Peer
1885 February	Joannah Francisco, wife of Richard Speer
1885 July	Catherine M. Eisenbrey, wife of J. W. Fairbanks
1885 July	Ida Bell, dau. of Milton Francisco
1885 September	Jesse Elmer, son of Isaac N. Kent
1885 November	Isaac J. Van Ness
1885 December	Francis J. Peer
1886 January	Isaac J. Van Ness
1886 February	Rachel Cole
1887 January	Thomas Van Ness
1887 December	Florence E. Husk
1888 January	Elizabeth Sigler, wife of Abraham Zeek
1888 January	Sarah Courter, wife of Henry Francisco
1888 December	John Kussmaul
1889 January	Margaret Jane, wife of Henry Van Duyne
1889 February	Peter S. Sindle
1889 June	Jemmima Miller, wife of Tunis T. Speer
1889 August	William Husk
1889 October	John Campbell
1889 November	Henry I. Van Ness
1890 July	Peter T. Speer
1890 August	Jane, wife of Simon S. Van Ness

1890 August	Israel Budd
1891 April	Susanna Y., wife of Peter A. Vanderhoof
1891 April	Jacob Osborne
1891 April	Mary E., wife of Peter J. Zeliff
1892 March	George C. Ryerson
1892 July	Isaac Canfield
1892 July	Lulu J. Ryer
1892 December	Ida Demarest, wife of F. C. Hennie
1893 February	Jane Paxton, wife of Isaac Riker
1893 May	Margaret A. Kiersted, wife of Robt. L. Stagg
1893 December	Dorcas Kierstead, wife of Peter D. Van Duyne
1894 January	Mary Ann Pearce, wife of Josiah Speer
(1894 April)	Susan Berry, wife of Henry Dey
(1894 June)	William Bush
1894 August	Hettie Stiles, wife of Thos. T. Speer
1898, January	Peter A. Vanderhoof
1899? November	Margaret V., wife of Wm. S. Jacobus
(1901 September)	Mary A. De Hart, wife of Isaac H. Riker
(1907 June)	George E. Speer
(1907 October)	Eleanor Smith, wife of Peter S. Sindle
(1908 November)	Thomas T. Speer
(no date)	Rachel A., child of Wm. Pier
(no date)	Richard, child of Wm. Pier
(no date)	Ella Aramintha, child of Josiah Speer
(no date)	Charles, infant child of Josiah Speer
(no date)	Infant, child of Wm. S. Jacobus
(no date)	foot stone P.A.V.N.
(no date)	'vault with a large blue stone cover no inscription
(no dates)	'many unmarked graves, and rough stones, without inscriptions'

Inscriptions
in page order as reported by
John Neafie, 1895
Fairfield Reformed Church Cemetery

Page 1
Cole, Stephen
Caroline, wife of John Bowman
John E. Van Ness
William A. Van Ness, son of John E.
Charles Van Ness, son of William E.
Maria Van Ness, wife of Wm. Van Ness
Maria, wife of Thomas Speer
Thomas Speer
Elizabeth O., dau of T. T. Speer
Jane Dey, wife of Simeon Doremus
Simeon Doremus
Henry S. Doremus
Job Doremus
Rachel Van Ness, wife of Job Doremus
Francis C. Post
Mary Jacobus, wife of Francis C. Post
Catherine E. Neafie, wife of George Van Ness
James Theodore, son of Ogden Hall

Page 2
Infant son of Cornelius H. Post
Thomas H. Stagg
Fannie Van Houten, wife of Thomas H. Stagg
Abraham Blauvelt, son of Thomas H. Stagg
Leah Ann, dau. of Thomas H. Stagg
Mary Catherine, dau. of Thomas H. Stagg
James, son of Thomas H. Stagg
John T. Speer,
Caroline, wife of John T. Speer
John, son of John T. Speer

Mariah, wife of William Van Ness
Thomas M. Speer
John J. Jacobus
Sarah, wife of John J. Jacobus
Martyntje Witte, Vrouw van Cs. Mastenbrock
Mary, dau. of John I. Quick

Page 3
Rev. James Glaen Ogilvie, pastor
Elizabeth W. Wilson, wife of above
Anthony Ogilvie
Henry H. Van Ness
Margaret Bush, wife of Henry H. Van Ness
Elizabeth, wife of Isaac J. Van Wart
Jemima, wife of J. Schoonmaker
Thomas R. Morrell
Henry Colyer
Martha, wife of Henry Colyer
Sarah, wife of Ezra Colyer
Amarintha, dau. of Ezra Colyer
Elizabeth, child of Job Doremus
Simeon, child of Job Doremus
Polly Williams, wife of John Kiersted, Esq.
John A. Kiersted, Esq.
Aaron W. Kiersted
Sophia, dau. of Thomas J. Kiersted

Page 4
John Zeliff
Jane Van Ness, wife of John Zeliff
William H. Zeliff
Emma May Zeliff
Mary Jacobus, wife of Henry I. Manderville
Ralph Manderville
David Manderville
Daniel Manderville
Sarah Manderville

John R. Van Ness
George, child of Christopher Sindle
Catherine, child of Christopher Sindle
Ellen Ann, child of Henry Stanley
Emerintha, child of Henry Stanley
Wm. Webster, child of Henry Stanley
Frank, child of Henry Stanley
Mary H., child of Henry Stanley
William, child of John Van Pelt
Emma L., child of John Van Pelt
Charles, child of John Van Pelt
Everdear, child of John Van Pelt
Infant son, of Abraham A. Garabrant
Ira, son of Abraham A. Garabrant

Page 5
Sarah Jane, wife of Abraham A. Garabrant
Ephraim, child of Isaac H. Riker
Sarah Agnes, child of Isaac H. Riker
William, son of Thos. H. Morrell
John Riker
Ann Smith, wife of John Riker
Henry H. Riker
Sarah Van Ness, wife of Henry H. Riker
Major Richard Speer
Sarah, wife of Major Richard Speer
William B. Speer
Jane M. Courter, wife of Wm. B. Speer
Oscar, child of Wm. B. Speer
Emma L., child of Wm. B. Speer
John Nelson, son of William Vanderhoof
Peter D. Van Duyne

Page 6
Dorcas Kierstead, wife of Peter D. Van Duyne
Samuel, child of Peter D. Van Duyne
Seth, child of Peter D. Van Duyne

Job, child of Peter D. Van Duyne
James A. Van Duyne
Catherine Doremus, widow of Jas. A. Van Duyne
Rachel, wife of Nicholas Van Duyne
Esther C., dau. of Nicolas Van Duyne
Martha Louisa Van Duyne
Anna Lawrence
Agnes Bernard, child of John H. Van Ness
Esther Cook, child of John H. Van Ness
Esther Cook
James E.(How) g.grandson of Esther Cook
Margaret Doremus, wife of Garret Van Ness
Henry T. Van Ness
Margaret Cadmus, wife of Henry T. Van Ness

Page 7
Aaron Van Ness
Nancy Van Ness
Andrew Francisco
Maria, wife of Andrew Francisco
John R. Dey
May Ann Kiersted, wife of John Dulhagen
James M., son of John Dulhagen
George Sindle
Nelly Sandford
Peter S. Sindle
Eleanor Smith, wife of Peter S. Sindle
Charles W., son of Peter S. Sindle
Thos. Lester, child of Francis Van Ness
Henry Clifford, child of Francis Van Ness
Malinda P., wife of Francis Van Ness
Henry I. Van Ness
Phebe Ann Speer, wife of Henry I. Van Ness
Adeliah A., wife of Wm. Van Wert

Page 8
James O. Jacobus

William C., son of Peter Jacobus
Judson P., son of Bethuel Goodrich
Thomas T. Speer
Hettie Stiles, wife of Thos. T. Speer
Henry Van Duyne
Margaret Jane, wife of Henry Van Duyne
James F., son of Henry H. Van Houten
Isaac Canfield
William S. Jacobus
Margaret V., wife of Wm. S. Jacobus
Emeline, child of Wm. S. Jacobus
Infant, child of Wm. S. Jacobus
Ezra Stiles Ely, Deacon
Benjamin Canfield
Sarah Riker, wife of Benj. Canfield
Isaac D. Van Ness
David Shurte
Ann Eliza, wife of Wm. C. Stratton

Page 9
Elizabeth, child of Wm. C. Stratton
Ann Isabelle, child of Wm. C. Stratton
Caroline, child of Wm. C. Stratton
George L. Shackleton
Benjamin H. Bone
Lydia, wife of B. H. Bone
Daniel Deeths
Susan Eliza, wife of Daniel Deeths
Daniel, son of daniel Deeths
Elizabeth R., wife of John L. Wilson
Catherine M., wife of J. W. Fairbanks
Cassic J., wife of Wilder Fairbanks
Mamie E., dau. of Wilder Fairbanks
Sarah E. van Ness, wife of Cornelius V. Bush
Abraham Zeek
Elizabeth Sigler, wife of Abraham Zeek
William Husk

Rachel Speer

Page 10
Andrew, son of Andrew McCord
Mary Elizabeth, wife of Thomas McCord
James M. Ashman
Maria M., wife of James M. Ashman
Emeline Vanderhoof, wife of Thomas C. Jacobus
Ralph Jacobus
Thomas E., son of Ralph Jacobus
John A., son of Ralph Jacobus
Weldon, child of Benj. H. Van Ness
Lizzie, child of Benj. H. Van Ness
John Campbell
Peter A. Vanderhoof
Susanna Y., wife of Peter A. Vanderhoof
Christopher T. Sindle
Milton Sindle
Simon S. Van Ness
Jane, wife of Simon S. Van Ness
John Kussmaul
Sophia D., wife of John Kussmaul

Page 11
John A. Kussmaul
Foot stone marked P.A.V.N.
Rachel Dey, wife of Garrett Jacobus
Peter Jacobus
Eliza Ann, wife of Peter Jacobus
Eliza Kiersted, wife of Cornelius A. Vanderhoof
Mary A. Vanderhoof, wife of Peter Slingerland
John R. Van Ness
Samuel Van Ness
Charles H. Van Ness, child of Isaac J. Van Ness
Carrie, child of Isaac J. Van Ness
Isaac J. Van Ness
Jennie Van Ness, wife of John W. Ackerman

George E. Speer
Sarah E. Springsteen, wife of George E. Speer
Jacob Osborne
Mary, wife of Jacob Osborne

Page 12
Isaac Riker
Jane Paxton, wife of Isaac Riker
Ida Demarest, wife of F. C. Hennie
Rachel Cole
Melva E., child of Henry Vail
Earnest B., child of Henry Vail
Vault w/ large stone cover, no inscription
Ann Dye, widow of Hassell Hopper
Cornelius R. Jacobus
Mary C., dau. of Cornelius Jacobus
John B. Vail
Sarah Ann, widow of John Vail
Israel Budd
Catherine, wife of Israel Budd
Rhoda Ann, child of Israel Budd
Mary Eliza, child of Israel Budd
Joannah, wife of Richard Speer
Robert L. Stagg
Margaret A. Kiersted, wife of Robt. L. Stagg

Page 13
Mary L., dau. of Aaron E. Stagg
James C. Stagg
Mary L. Stagg
Peter T. Speer
Julia Speer
Webster T. Speer
Tunis T. Speer
Jemima Miller, wife of Tunis T. Speer
Harriet Jacobus, wife of C. D. Van Ness
John A. Romaine

Rachel, wife of Cornelius Dey
Cornelius Dey
Margaret, wife of Cornelius Dey
Henry Dey
Susan Berry, wife of Henry Dey
Albert B., son of Samuel Dey
Maria, wife of Henry R. Van Ness
John J. Francisco
Rebecca, wife of John J. Francisco

Page 14
Zillah, dau. of Henry Francisco
Louisa, dau. of Henry Francisco
Ida Bell, dau. of Milton Francisco
Martha, wife of Ralph A. Romaine
Serena Luina, wife of Abraham L. Romaine
Lucinda, wife of Zenas C. Speer
Mary A. De Hart, wife of Isaac H. Riker
Mary E. Riker, wife of Wilbert E. Woodruff
Marcus Francisco
Infant, child of Marcus Francisco
Mary E., wife of Peter J. Zeliff
George S., son of Peter J. Zeliff
Nicholas Bush
William Bush
Charlotte Pearce, wife of Wm. Bush
Josephine, dau. of Wm. Bush
John Vreeland
Mary Jane, wife of John Vreeland, Jr.
Isaac R., son of John Vreeland

Page 15
Jesse Elmer, son of Isaac N. Kent
Sarah Jacobus, wife of Isaac Van Ness
John R., son of Cornelius I. Van Ness
Isaac, son of Cornelius I. Van Ness
Cornelius I. Van Ness

Sarah, wife of Cornelius I. Van Ness
Mary, wife of Cornelius Van Ness
William I. Van Ness
James Bowman
Emily, dau. of Peter Bowman
Francis J. Peer
Mary, wife of James Peer
Barney Budd
Nancy Lockwood, wife of Barney Budd
Newton Raymond, son of John T. Budd
Peter Francisco
John H. Mandeville
Elizabeth Mandeville
Julia Mandeville
Kate Mandeville
Jane Boyd

Page 16
David Boyd
Catherine, wife of Isaac Riker
Catherine, dau. of Samuel Riker
Mary Ann, dau. of Isaac Riker
Obadiah Riker
Maria L., wife of Levi Carman
George Wesson Carman
Eliza M., wife of John A. Van Orden
Jacob Eugene, son of John A. Van Orden
William Mead
Rachel Van Ness, wife of Wm. Mead
Emma Maria, child of Nicholas Bush
Maria, child of Nicholas Bush
Eleanor, child of Nicholas Bush
Sarah E. Ryerson, wife of George Kent
Sarah Ellen, child of Thomas Van Ness
Phebe Ann, child of Thomas Van Ness

Page 17
William, child of Thomas Van Ness
David, child of Thomas Van Ness
Thomas Van Ness
Martha M. Vincent, wife of Thomas Van Ness
David Van Ness
Ellen, wife of David Van Ness
Maria, wife of Jacob Jacobus; Henry Francisco
Christopher Sindle
Josiah Speer
Mary Ann Pearce, wife of Josiah Speer
Ella Aramintha, child of Josiah Speer
Charles, child of Josiah Speer
Eliza Dods, wife of Peter F. Ryerson
George C. Ryerson
Matilda Hill, wife of Geo. C. Ryerson
Lulu J. Ryerson
Florence E. Husk
Nettie M., dau. of Robert Van Ness
Robert Van Ness
J. C. Stagg

Page 18
Isaac Kent
Casiah Sindle, wife of Isaac Kent
Mary Jane, dau. of John I. Kent
Jotham Jacobus
Harriet, dau. of Jacob Jacobus
Frank L. son of Richard T. Budd
Moses Day
John I. Pier
Sarah, wife of John I. Pier
David Pier
Hester Dods, wife of David Pier
Elizabeth S., wife of David Pier
Sarah Ann, dau. of David Pier
David H., child of Wm. Hamma

John, child of Wm. Hamma
Catherine Van Houten, wife of James Van Ness
Ann Amelia, dau. of James Van Ness

Page 19
David Pier
Sarah, wife of David Pier
Robart Van Ness
William Van Ness
Peter Sanford
Lucinda, wife of Peter Sandford
Peter Speer
Harriet, wife of Peter Speer
Emma M. Speer, dau. of Wm. Speer
Mary Speer, wife, of Joseph C. Baldwin
Joseph Condit Baldwin
Peter, child of Francis Van Ness
James Bentley, child of Francis Van Ness
Thos. Henry, child of Francis Van Ness
Evert H. Van Ness
Caroline Smith, wife of Evert H. Van Ness
William Van Ness
Almira A., dau. of Wm. Van Ness
Henry E. Van Ness

Page 20
Hester Francisco, wife of Henry H. Van Ness
Annie R., infant of Zenas Jacobus
Sarah, dau. of Jacob S. Van Ness
Peter Francisco
Josiah, child of Peter Francisco
Sarah, child of Peter Francisco
Josiah Francisco
Sarah, wife of Josiah Francisco
Henry Francisco
Sarah Courter, wife of Henry Francisco
Aaron Budd

Fannie S. Tuers, widow of Aaron Budd
Aaron W. Budd
Matilda Budd
Isaac R., child of Francis Pier
Rachel J., child of Francis Pier

Page 21
Elizabeth, wife of Francis Pier
Clyde C., child of Isaac Pier
Charles V., child of Isaac Pier
Rachel A., child of Wm. Pier
Richard, child of Wm. Pier
Hugh McCormick
Jean Welsh, wife of Hugh McCormick
'Many unmarked graves and rough stones'

SOURCES

Anonymous. *Inscriptions from the Graveyard of the Dutch Reformed Church Fairfield.* Typescript. New Jersey Historical Society. 1904

Anonymous. *Register of First Reformed Church of Little Falls, N.J.,* typescript

Eberhart, Edith W. *The Doremus Family in America.* Gateway Press, Baltimore, 1990

Internet: *Google.com; Ancestry.com; Rootsweb.com; FamilySearch.org; Findagrave.com*

Federal Writers Project.*New Jersey, A Guide to Its Present and Past,* Viking, New York, 1939

Lockward, Lynn G. *A Puritan Heritage.* Caldwell NJ. 1955

Neafie, John. *Inscriptions on Tombstones in Fairfield, Essex Co., New Jersey.* Complete copy (typescript) by John Neafie. New York City. May, 1895 (Family History Library. Film 16511. Item 4. Microfilm 1939)

Nelson, William. *History of Bergen and Passaic Counties, New Jersey.* W. W. Clayton and William Nelson. Everts & Peck. Philadelphia. 1882

Nelson, William. *Documents Relating to the Colonial History of New Jersey. Marriage Records 1665-1800.* Press Printing, Paterson, NJ. 1900

New York Historical Society. Joseph Ditta, Reference Librarian. April 2014

Nichols, George King. *The Corby Family: Descendants of John Corby of Essex County, New Jersey.* New York Genealogical and Biographical Record. Vol. 131. No.1-4. NY. 2000

Onderdonk, Henry. *Revolutionary Incidents of Suffolk and Kings Counties with an account of the Battle of Long Island.* New York. 1849

Pierce, Glen. *Civil War Stories.* (150-page booklet on CD can be obtained from Hillside Cemetery Heritage, 107 Warren St., Clifton, N.J., 07013-1123.)

Proceedings of the New Jersey Historical Society. Vol. 6, p.227. Edison, NJ. 1921)

Rutgers University *Special Collections and University Archives.* Catherine Sauceda, librarian, New Brunswick, NJ. 2014

Shaw, William H. *History of Essex and Hudson Counties, N.J.* Philadelphia, PA. Everts & Peck. 1884

Stoutenburgh, Henry A. *A Documentary History of the Dutch Congregation of Oyster Bay,* New York. 1902

United States Federal Census Collection

Warner, P.R., *Descendants of Peter Willemse Roome.* D. H. Gildersleeve, New York, 1883

www.ingramcontent.com/pod-product-compliance
Lightning Source LLC
Chambersburg PA
CBHW050830230426
43667CB00012B/1944